D0856436

FROM
IDEA
TO
SUCCESS

FROM
IDEA
TO
SUCCESS

The Dartmouth Entrepreneurial Network's
GUIDE FOR START-UPS

GREGG E. FAIRBROTHERS
TESSA M. WINTER

New York   Chicago   San Francisco   Lisbon
London   Madrid   Mexico City   Milan   New Delhi
San Juan   Seoul   Singapore   Sydney   Toronto

The *McGraw·Hill* Companies

1 2 3 4 5 6 7 8 9 10   DOC / DOC   1 5 4 3 2 1

ISBN: 978-0-07-176079-9
MHID: 0-07-176079-2

e-ISBN: 978-0-07-176345-5
e-MHID: 0-07-176345-7

This publication is designed to provide accurate and authoritative information in regard to the subject matter covered. It is sold with the understanding that neither the author nor the publisher is engaged in rendering legal, accounting, securities trading, or other professional services. If legal advice or other expert assistance is required, the services of a competent professional person should be sought.

—From a Declaration of Principles Jointly Adopted by a Committee of the American Bar Association and a Committee of Publishers and Associations

McGraw-Hill books are available at special quantity discounts to use as premiums and sales promotions or for use in corporate training programs. To contact a representative, please e-mail us at bulksales@mcgraw-hill.com.

This book is printed on acid-free paper.

Contents

Introduction

The Entrepreneur Will Save Us?

Vision is the art of seeing things invisible.

—Jonathan Swift

Imagine a truly prosperous economy—prosperous because innovation thrives. Growth is sustainable and creates jobs for everyone who wants one: rewarding, fulfilling jobs for people all across the demographic spectrum. And that prosperity is widely shared. Imagine that opportunity is open to all people to make what they can of themselves. They can do well for themselves by creating value for everyone. People renew themselves over and over, all through their lifetimes. They do well *and* do good. Imagine that labor doesn't have to compete for jobs across borders, driving wages into the ground; it *complements* the innovation and creativity of new ventures, leveraging the amazing human capacity for creativity and building new things. It sounds so appealing. Would that we could see this today wherever we are. Sad to say, this is not exactly what we see. But that doesn't mean it isn't there.

Almost by definition, entrepreneurial value creation comes from someone being entrepreneurial. In good times, value creation adds fire to a thriving economy. In bad times, entrepreneurial value creation rekindles dimly glowing coals. Lately it seems there are more bad times than good. We see an economy with deep-rooted problems; no one is denying that. The economy has always had problems of one kind or another, yet everyone from average college grads looking for their first jobs to economists studying national economic trends seems more worried than ever, and they are all worried for one main reason: People cannot find the kind of work they want and need, at least not where they've always looked for it before. We need to create more good jobs.

There are really only three ways to create jobs: You can grow the companies you have, steal companies from somewhere else, or create new ones. As to growing and stealing, in the last three decades the developed world has been losing ground. Our existing firms are not growing much. According to the Bureau of Labor Statistics, from 2000 to 2009 the economy added essentially no new jobs.[1] Instead of stealing companies and jobs from elsewhere, we have been losing jobs to lower-cost labor

vii

markets overseas. In the last several decades millions of technology, manufacturing, and service jobs have moved to India, China, and elsewhere. Between 2000 and 2004, an estimated 2.7 million manufacturing positions, mostly in high-tech industries, were lost to foreign countries "aggressively pursuing technological leadership with their industrial policies, subsidies, and incentives."[2] In 2002, Forrester Research projected that by 2015, 3.3 million service jobs and $136 billion in wages will have moved offshore.[3] We will never turn back the economic clock and recapture those lost jobs. All we can do is create new ones. This means that if we are going to create new jobs, we are going to have to rely on growth through innovation, creating new companies and growing the ones we have with new ideas and new products.

Hence the new hope: *The entrepreneur will save us.* In a recent study by the Kauffman Foundation, Dane Stangler described the need for "a new discussion— one that not only promotes entrepreneurship, but specifically high-growth entrepreneurship . . . because top-performing companies are the most fruitful source of new jobs and offer the economy's best hope for recovery."[4] Mark Trumball wrote in the *Christian Science Monitor*, "The nation's entrepreneurial prowess may be the best hope to stem 9.7 percent unemployment."[5] Thomas Friedman in an op-ed for the *New York Times* stated, "If we want to bring down unemployment in a sustainable way, neither rescuing General Motors nor funding more road construction will do it. We need to create a big bushel of new companies—fast."[6] In 1987 David McClelland may have said it best: "There is no better way to provide a broad basis for rapid economic growth than to increase dramatically the number of entrepreneurs in a society. They represent a very small segment of the population, but their impact is crucial as they gather resources to produce goods and services, create jobs, and decrease dependency on government."[7]

Governments are also pushing entrepreneurship. They are even putting money behind it. Kathy Barks Hoffman of the Associated Press reported in February 2010, "Gov. Jennifer Granholm is counting on entrepreneurs to bring Michigan's struggling economy back from the brink. So much so that she plans to set aside $200,000 to teach budding entrepreneurs and help provide $43 million for small business loans."[8] Carl Schramm and Robert E. Litan wrote in the *Wilson Quarterly* in 2010:

> *[President Obama] embraced entrepreneurs near the beginning of his 2010 State of the Union address and has since outlined a series of steps to encourage "small business" to create new jobs: $33 billion in tax credits for hiring new workers and $30 billion in low-interest loans (from the Troubled Asset Relief Program) intended to spur community banks to lend to small business.[9]*

Entrepreneurship is big and getting bigger. Surveys show that between 4 million and 6 million Americans a year start 3 million to 4 million businesses for themselves, 20 to 25 percent by purchase and the rest from a standing start. Two-thirds start out home-based.[10,11] The U.S. Census Bureau reported that in 2006 there were 22 million sole proprietorships (excluding farms) filing tax returns.[12] This army of the self-employed operates over 70 percent of the nation's businesses. Many of these people want to learn how to be more effective with their businesses. They want to learn how to grow.

Here, so it would seem, lies the future of the American economy: in entrepreneurship, in creating companies, in creating value from nothing. So who are the entrepreneurs who create these new companies? What do they look like? Where do we find them?

For over 200 years economists and businesspeople have been trying to describe entrepreneurs and define who they are, but there is still not much of a consensus. *The Portable MBA in Entrepreneurship* says, "An entrepreneur is someone who perceives an opportunity and creates an organization to pursue it."[13] Entrepreneur.com says an entrepreneur is "someone who assumes the financial risk of the initiation, operation and management of a business."[14] Guy Kawasaki in *The Art of the Start* says, "The reality is that 'entrepreneur' is not a job title. It is the *state of mind* of people who want to alter the future."[15] By combining just these few definitions, we come up with a person who knows how to recognize opportunities, is comfortable assuming risk to execute on an opportunity, and is in a future-altering state of mind. These are entrepreneurs who want to create value and perhaps profit from doing that.

Note: There is another kind of entrepreneur. The historian Burton Folsom called them political entrepreneurs. Political entrepreneurs harness the power of the state to profit from special favors and restraints on competition.[16] Folsom offered the example of Robert Fulton, who obtained an exclusive 30-year concession from the state of New York for a steamship monopoly on the Hudson and profited handsomely from it until Cornelius Vanderbilt's technology innovations and lower costs—and a Supreme Court ruling in 1824—finally brought competition to the market. The result: more options and better service at a lower cost. Anyone doing business in many markets today knows the dysfunctions of crony capitalism.[17] This is not the entrepreneurship we are talking about. Our entrepreneurs create value through innovation, relentless execution, market competition, and sometimes just doing things better, faster, and cheaper. Imagine what kind of an economy we could have if more people did that!

I meet a lot of people with ideas and passion who ultimately decide against taking steps to make their ideas come to life. The most common reason? They think they just don't fit the description; they aren't entrepreneurs. Many people assume that the entrepreneur is a special kind of person, someone who can be readily recognized and categorized: Either you are an entrepreneur or you're not. In 2006, two-thirds of the over 200 entrepreneurs surveyed by Northeastern University's School of Technological Entrepreneurship believed that entrepreneurs are born, not made. Sixty-one percent cited their "innate drive" as the motivating factor for starting their own ventures, 21 percent their work experience, and

16 percent the success of entrepreneurial peers in their industry. Only 1 percent cited higher education as a means to becoming an entrepreneur even though many institutions are creating courses and programs and people are writing innumerable how-to books and articles to teach that very thing.[18] If entrepreneurs are born, not made, the focus should be on figuring out if you are one. But if this is not the case and entrepreneurs really can be made, if anyone can become entrepreneurial, the main question becomes: How do you help people become entrepreneurial?

In this book I want to reexamine some of these questions with you: Who are the entrepreneurs? and Where do we find them? Experience shows that there is no shortage of entrepreneurs. I think I know where to find them. In fact, the whole reason I am writing this book is that I think *you* can be one of those entrepreneurs, and I don't even know who you are! I believe that no matter what circumstance you find yourself in or what kind of an organization you are part of, you can become more entrepreneurial, you can create more value, and you can find more satisfaction in what you do each day. We all at one time or another have had ideas we think can create value and, however briefly, have been tempted to chase them. We have all found ourselves saying, "Wouldn't it be great if . . . ?" What's missing are three important things: how to decide if your idea is worthwhile, how to get started executing on it, and how to learn what it's going to take to make it happen.

That's what this book is about. I want to help you learn to fill in those gaps and figure out how to create value for yourself and other people (such as your customers). No question that appears in this book is purely rhetorical. I really do want you to think about these questions and work through the answers with me, and then I want you to go out and take your shot. It works, I promise.

But why should you listen to me? How could I possibly know what *you* need to do to move your idea forward? I think I can help mostly because I've been where you are many times before, both by myself and with hundreds of other people. I spent 23 years of my life working in the oil and gas industry all over the world, building companies and doing all sorts of other entrepreneurial things. Then, in the summer of 1999, I decided I'd had enough of that and wanted to do something new. Exactly what that was, I wasn't sure, so I moved with my family back to my alma mater, Dartmouth College, in the green hills of New Hampshire and spent a year turning over rocks and tire-kicking deals, looking around for an idea where I could do something socially valuable—pay my debt to society, if you will. Then, in the summer of 2000, a friend at Dartmouth College's Tuck School of Business and I started looking at all the people on campus. They had so many creative ideas and so much passion for creating value, but many of them had no clue how to make those ideas happen or even where to start. From the things I'd done in the past, one thing I did know: how they could make their ideas reality and, more important, how to help them figure that out for themselves.

Over the years, learning from watching others, from doing things myself, and from taking countless wrong turns, I have found that there is a method to this madness of beginning things, a systematic way to approach the entrepreneurial experience that almost anyone can apply. I began thinking about ways to put this method into the hands of people who could use it—to help people with ideas for companies, for nonprofits, for cool technologies turn those ideas into something real. I spent half a year going around the country looking at programs that teach entrepreneurship and help people build companies. I asked not only what those programs were doing and how well they worked but also what didn't work and what they would do if they could start again and base a program on what they'd learned.

This program became the Dartmouth Entrepreneurial Network, the DEN. We put the DEN in the provost's office at Dartmouth College to serve all of Dartmouth's schools as well as people among its 71,000 alumni around the world. Over the years we have worked seriously with over 300 start-ups, plus an uncounted number of students, faculty, staff, alumni, and friends of Dartmouth looking for advice, networking, or opportunities to learn. First and foremost the DEN set out to help people learn to be more entrepreneurial, starting with whatever knowledge or skills they had, whatever ideas they had, and wherever they were. I am the DEN's founding director and teach entrepreneurship courses each semester at the Tuck School. In addition, I am the founding chair of the Dartmouth Regional Technology Center (DRTC), a business incubator we built in 2006 in partnership with the state of New Hampshire and the U.S. Department of Commerce to develop technology-based companies with the potential for a significant social impact. I am on half a dozen boards, chair three, and can't keep a current list of the number for which I'm a formal (free) advisor. In the start-up world, there is no shortage of demand for help—just hardly any money to get it.

Beginning in January 2001, the DEN worked with people at Dartmouth College and the Tuck School of Business, helping them learn to be entrepreneurs and turn their ideas into reality. As of the date of this writing, the DEN has chapters in 12 cities around the country and is adding more each year. In those cities hundreds of alumni are working on their ideas, networking and connecting with each other and with us in Hanover. Most of these people are first-time entrepreneurs. Many started out knowing next to nothing about building a company, but each one, with a lot of questions and some guidance now and then, is working it out successfully.

Many of the university programs I visited around the country focused their energies on the opportunities they thought had the potential to be big financial successes. If you want to make a lot of money for your program or university, this seems the logical approach—focus only on the best ideas. But I wasn't convinced then and am even less convinced now that it's possible to pick the winners consistently, and many other universities have come to the same conclusion. We think it's a great idea to try to create successful companies that make lots of money for the founders and the college. Of course, it's nice when that happens, and we hope it does every time, but that's not our main goal. You see, at its core our program is about changing the people and helping them grow, not scoring big on licensing or only on a few hot start-up companies. It's about learning, and a college's one mission is learning. Companies can't learn; only people can do that. Companies are nothing without their people.

When people come to me to talk about their ideas, I try my best never to answer the question they're usually asking: *What do you think of my idea?* I don't think it's important what I think about their ideas. Most of the time, what do I know anyway? I'm only a geologist. I would much rather help them learn how to think about their ideas, how to make smart decisions, and, if they want to follow those ideas with passion, how to make those ideas come alive. I'm sort of the Will Rogers of entrepreneurship advisors: I've never met an idea I didn't like . . . so long as the other person is passionate about it. These are smart people. Most people are. I know that in time, with a little direction, networking support, and prodding, they will almost always figure out for themselves whether their idea is worth pursuing or not. Further, when they figure it out for themselves, they will have learned a way of thinking and acting that they can use over and over again. I love it when people come to me passionate about a really bad idea. Bad ideas are great learning kits. It's a shame to waste a good idea on a learning curve, and everybody has to learn sometime.

In the end, being entrepreneurial is about getting things done, because getting things done is how you create value. Ideas can't do that. In the early years of the nineteenth century Jean-Baptiste Say, a French economist, coined the term *entrepreneur*. He described an entrepreneur as someone who "shifts economic resources out of an area of lower productivity and into an area of higher productivity and yield."[19] Peter Drucker notes that Say does not describe a person, only his or her activities. At the DEN, we think entrepreneurs are defined not by who they are but by how they do what they do and, even more important, what they get done.

This book talks about *practice,* because in the end ideas are worth nothing. Only the execution of ideas creates value. True entrepreneurial behavior means seeking to do new things, create something from nothing, and solve problems. Some people have been doing this for a long time. They don't need a book like this to help them. For the rest, there's always a first time, a time when there's an opportunity or a compelling idea or vision but no idea how to begin. This book is for those people.

You might be one of those people. You probably aren't all that different from the people who come to the DEN's office at the Tuck School. You might have an idea or have identified a way to add value or do something innovative in your job, in the marketplace, or in your community. Maybe deep down you just want to have an impact, to have a sense that what you do really matters. Or perhaps you are one of the 22 million self-employed and want to grow your business; you see new opportunities or want to take on new challenges or build on new ideas. You want to learn to be more entrepreneurial. This book is written to talk to you, to help you learn to be a self-teacher and self-starter in becoming entrepreneurial. Like the DEN itself, the sole focus of this book is learning how to be entrepreneurial: how to come up with valuable ideas and then how to capture that value for yourself and your community.

In a way, entrepreneurial execution means doing at least a little of just about every aspect of business from strategy, to accounting, to production and management, to sales, business law, and finance. How are you going to learn all that?

I don't think learning has much to do with me or anyone else giving you a bunch of information, no matter how well presented or how useful and relevant. Theories, models, and lectures are all useful in their own right and everyone should know where to find them, but I think the focus ought to be elsewhere. I once asked one of our Dartmouth entrepreneurs, a longtime professor, researcher, and recognized expert in the psychology of learning, "What's the one most important thing I can know about teaching?" He replied, "There is only one important principle: The one who is doing the work is the one who is doing the learning." So I focus on *practice* and *experience* just as much as if not more than on theory and models procedures and information.

To get a better sense of what I mean by practice, think about something C. S. Lewis wrote in a short essay that appeared in the *Coventry Evening Telegraph* in 1945.[20] Lewis described what he saw as he stood in a dark toolshed on a sunny day. A sunbeam caused by a crack at the top of the door cut through the darkness, revealing tiny specks of dust suspended in the light. In the blackness of the toolshed, Lewis noted that the beam appeared as an object itself rather than just a source of illumination.

Lewis reflected that there were two ways he could think about that sunbeam. He could study its properties, measure it, calculate it. He could think about the diffraction patterns created by the dust particles, even analyze and examine how the senses work in allowing him to see the beam in the first place. This Lewis called "looking at" the beam of light. This is analytical, reductionist thinking.

But then Lewis moved so that the beam fell on his eyes. He looked through the crack in the door and saw the sun and the glorious day outside the toolshed. He called this "looking along" the beam. This is experiential thinking.

Descriptive analysis from the outside and experiencing something from the inside are fundamentally different ways of looking at things—looking at versus looking along. People like to look at hard questions. Researchers and academic thinkers do this; they look at a topic or thing, and this is important in gaining understanding and developing valuable concepts. They help us do the same thing through analyses, algorithms and heuristics, charts, theories, studies, and models. Their tools are reason and empirical observation, objective ways of thinking in which everyone can share and, for the most part, with which everyone can agree. For us, this is comfortable. We can do as little or as much as we'd like; partial answers are fine. Studying a thing from the outside doesn't demand too much from us. No decisions are required. There is no action as a result, and so there are no consequences. We can stop at any time along the way, go no farther, and be happy with the knowledge we've acquired.

Looking along, in contrast, is what we do when we experience something. More important, it happens when we experience something for a reason: looking along the beam to experience the beautiful day outside. Looking along is often more challenging than looking at. It means getting involved, venturing into the unknown with no certainty that you have what you need to make the journey and no guarantee that you will reach the destination. Getting halfway to the destination when you are looking along is no better than never having started. Once you get in, you're all in.

Both ways of thinking about things are important. It's easy to look at entrepreneurship, to study what makes entrepreneurs entrepreneurial or what makes them successful, and to provide frameworks, processes, and procedures by which you too can try to do it.

But just looking at cannot change a person; only looking along can do that. Having the knowledge you can get by looking at can help, but in the end you need both: the knowledge and the willingness to go out and apply it. If you believe you can become more entrepreneurial and do something meaningful, by all means learn all you can by looking at, but in the end you will need to get out and do it, look along, and learn by experience, try things, make mistakes, find successes.

An entrepreneurial mind-set is not a body of knowledge; it's a way of thinking and acting and executing. Being entrepreneurial involves being careful with what you think you know versus what you only suppose: the discipline of epistemology. Being in this mind-set means actually making decisions and not always knowing even after the fact if those decisions are right or wrong. It means always stopping to measure what matters and doing something meaningful with the information. Being entrepreneurial involves learning, especially being willing to make mistakes and learn from them. It means closing one's mind to the silly certainty that comes from hindsight. It's a way of relating to others, bringing people alongside or inside, building a team, driving a vision. Most important, being entrepreneurial means knowing that entrepreneurship and even being successful are not the goals of the endeavor. Rather, the goal is to *get something done*—to do something that is significant to you and to others, something that creates social value in some way and perhaps makes the world a better place than it was before.

This book is structured around both this content and learning theory. Research on learning proves that the two most important factors for information retention and application are a clearly defined context and the concrete experiences of the learner: actually using or applying the learned information. We learn best within a context and through experience. The chapters in this book are placed in three sections and incorporate this context-information-experience cycle:

1. "The Framework" sets the overall context to get you thinking about—and listening to—your own thoughts. It addresses and defines the most important things you need to understand, think about, and resolve in your mind

before getting started on an idea: things such as definitions, risk, and goals. "If you don't know where you're going, any road will take you there," and if you don't know why you are going there, you probably won't care enough to start. Life is all about expectations management. Entrepreneurs need to set and manage their expectations carefully and thoughtfully.

2. "Building Your Idea" presents the basic entrepreneurial tool kit: information that fits within the framework of the prior section. We want to help you understand each topic's key drivers, its specific needs and timing, what tools are available, and how and why you might use them. The entrepreneur always starts with a blank sheet of paper. Aspiring entrepreneurs often find this daunting, if not immobilizing. Moving from the blank piece of paper to a solid, growing start-up is one of the most exhilarating exercises in the world, but only if you know how to start. This section is about starting effectively, minimizing risk, and avoiding as many painful mistakes and problems as possible.

3. "Managing the Company." Most entrepreneurship books deal with getting started. A few talk about managing growth in start-up companies. None that I've seen adequately address the transition between the two. Other than the launch, the most dangerous time for a venture is the transition from a start-up to a going concern, the transition from exploration, sheer willpower, and creativity, through the inevitable course corrections, to an organization with defined processes, an efficient, profitable, and aggressively growing business. We don't try to address managing a growth company in this book, but we do discuss key managerial issues for the transition. If we don't take you all the way to a solid, growing company, when we finish, you at least ought to be able to see it from there.

All the chapters contain a framework for the topic and some reflections from entrepreneurs we have known. Each chapter closes with a short section of prompts: key questions to get you out and experiencing. No single book on the entrepreneurial experience can provide all the information a business founder and builder will need. This book does not try. At the back of the book is a resources section where we've listed additional resources we think are valuable for each of the chapter subjects.

I TO WE

One final point. This paragraph contains the last *I* to appear in the body of this book—because it's not about me. For one thing, as I consistently tell my future managers of America at Tuck, when you have an idea, it's always best if you communicate until others come up with it on their own; then it's their idea, and they will own it. For another, it may not take a village, but it always takes a team. The best leaders and managers are not bosses, they're encouragers. They are teachers and facilitators.

Most of all, they are *servants,* people who help other people be the best they can be and in fact push them to be more. The best leaders don't focus on themselves. They consciously try not to make it all about them. They don't just manage the project *or* the people; they help the people grow while they are getting the project done. Harry Truman was fond of saying, "It's amazing what you can accomplish if you don't care who gets the credit." So this book is written in the third person plural: *we.* There are three senses in which this is only fair.

First, whether they know it or not, a lot of good, really smart people from around Dartmouth, even from my Samson days, are writing this book for you, hundreds of them. What they did and what they learned constitute a massive library of experience and stories. Being able to experience and share with them along the way has been a great gift to me, and I'm hoping I can pass on at least part of that to you. It would be a crime to take credit for everything I learned from them and learned with them. We are all talking to you in this book.

Second, I could never write a book like this by myself. For one thing, it's not clear how good I am at writing. Even my coauthor says she doesn't understand my sentences. And beyond that, the "curse of knowledge" makes clear writing just about impossible for me. The curse of knowledge is the fact that once you know something well enough, it's impossible to know what it's like not to know it. At some point you lose the ability to talk to a person who doesn't have any of the background, any of the experiences or knowledge you have. It's a fascinating problem, well documented by research and literature.[21,22] Tessa Winter is a one-in-a-million former student who worked closely with me as she started two successful enterprises. She has experienced this process at Dartmouth, this method of learning to become entrepreneurial. She has experienced it in a way I never can, because she was on the receiving end while I was on the inflicting end. She has stood and walked in the shoes we want you to put on, and she knows how to talk to you in a way I no longer can. This book is our message to you. That's why we're writing it together.

Third and most important, this is not a book that will try to teach you anything. The course catalog at the Tuck School of Business currently says I teach four courses in entrepreneurship each year, plus one at the Medical School. I don't think I ever *teach* anything. Instead, the best I can do is *help people learn.* For every person, learning anything is a unique and special journey, one in which I, as an advisor, may come alongside for a while to support, to question, sometimes to badger, but always to encourage. Like them, you are the one who has to take the steps. If you are reading this book and want to learn to be more entrepreneurial, to try to make a success of some vision or idea, I can't teach you that. It's something we will have to do together. So most of all, the *we* in this book is *us:* you and all of us, all those people over the years at Samson and all our partners and competitors, at Dartmouth, at wherever; it's Tessa helping me turn poor writing into good writing, and it's me too. We will learn about this together, and then, if you want to really learn it, you will go out and try it!

The tragedy in life doesn't lie in not reaching your goal. The tragedy lies in having no goal to reach.

—Benjamin Mays

The entrepreneur is essentially a visualizer and actualizer. . . . He can visualize something, and when he visualizes it he sees exactly how to make it happen.

—Robert L. Schwartz

If you take too long in deciding what to do with your life, you'll find you've done it.

—George Bernard Shaw

You may be disappointed if you fail, but you are doomed if you don't try.

—Beverly Sills

NOTES

1. Bureau of Labor Statistics, "Labor Force Statistics from the Current Population Survey," http://data.bls.gov/PDQ/servlet/SurveyOutputServlet (accessed May 7, 2010).
2. Joseph Lieberman, Senate Office, "Offshore Outsourcing and America's Competitive Edge," May 11, 2004: 9.
3. Forrester Report, "3.3 Million U.S. Jobs to Go Offshore," November 11, 2002.
4. Stangler, Dane, "High-Growth Firms and the Future of the American Economy," *Kauffman Foundation Research Series: Firm Formation and Economic Growth* (March 2010): 2.
5. Trumball, Mark, "How America Can Create Jobs," *Christian Science Monitor*, February. 22, 2010.
6. Friedman, Thomas L., "Startups, Not Bailouts," *New York Times*, April 4, 2010: WK.9.
7. McClelland, David C., "Characteristics of Successful Entrepreneurs," *Journal of Creative Behavior* 26, no. 2 (1987): 219–233.
8. Hoffman, Kathy Barks, "Governor Pushes Entrepreneurship," *Associated Press Newswires*, February 4, 2010.
9. Schramm, Carl, and Robert E. Litan, "An Entrepreneurial Recovery," *Wilson Quarterly* 34, no. 2 (Spring 2010): 44–47.

10. Dennis, William J., "More Than You Think: An Inclusive Estimate of Business Entries," *Journal of Business Venturing* 12, no. 3 (May 1997): 175–196.

11. Dennis, William J., "Business Starts and Stops," *Wells Fargo-NFIB Education Foundation Series,* November 1999.

12. "Table 731: Nonfarm Sole Proprietorships—Selected Income and Deduction Items," U.S. Census Bureau, http://www.census.gov/compendia/statab/cats/business_enterprise/sole_proprietorships_partnerships_corporations.html (accessed September 2, 2010).

13. Bygrave, William D., and Andrew Zacharakis, eds., *The Portable MBA in Entrepreneurship* (Hoboken, NJ: Wiley, 2010): 3.

14. "Entrepreneur," in *Small Business Encyclopedia*, Entrepreneur.com (accessed June 3, 2010).

15. Kawasaki, Guy, *The Art of the Start* (New York: Penguin Group, 2004): xii.

16. Folsom, Burton, *Urban Capitalists* (Baltimore: Johns Hopkins University Press, 1981).

17. Folsom, Burton, *The Myth of the Robber Barons* (Herndon, VA: Young America's Foundation, 2010).

18. Taylor, Leslie, "Are Entrepreneurs Born or Made?" *Inc.*, October 24, 2006, http://www.inc.com/news/articles/200610/born.html (accessed September 21, 2010).

19. Quoted in Drucker, Peter, *Innovation and Entrepreneurship* (New York: Collins Business, 1993): 28.

20. Lewis, Clive Staples. "Meditations in a Toolshed," *Coventry Evening Telegraph,* July 17, 1945: 4.

21. Heath, Chip, and Dan Heath, "The Curse of Knowledge," *Harvard Business Review* 84, no. 12 (December 2006): 20–22.

22. Newton, L., "Overconfidence in the Communication of Intent: Heard and Unheard Melodies," unpublished doctoral dissertation, Stanford, CA: Stanford University, 1990: 33–46.

FROM
IDEA
TO
SUCCESS

Part One

The Framework

Chapter 1

Who Is the Entrepreneur?

Our so-called limitations, I believe,
Apply to faculties we don't apply.
We don't discover what we can't achieve
Until we make an effort not to try.

—Piet Hein[1]

In 2005 an AC Nielson survey found that 58 percent of Americans self-report they dream of starting a business and being their own boss.[2] Other writers report that the proportion is as high as two-thirds to three-quarters.[3] The number of Americans who are operating what might be called entrepreneurial businesses is estimated at 10 to 15 percent, and the number who actually start new businesses in a specific year is well under half a percent.[4] If so many people want to start and run their own businesses, why do so few actually do it? Is it because they think they know what it takes to be entrepreneurial and don't think they have it? In a 2009 survey, 82 percent of randomly selected respondents said they had at least once considered starting their own businesses but didn't do it; more said they believed there were critical things they didn't know than said they were worried about taking the risk.[5] Why this gap? What do they think they are missing? What do they think *entrepreneurial* means? What assumptions are they making?

Before people can decide anything, they must at least believe that they understand what they are deciding; they have to start with definitions of the words they are using to describe what they are considering. Even if they don't deliberately set out to define their terms carefully, they are working with implicit definitions. In fact, that is normally the case: People base decisions on words and concepts they have not taken the time to examine and understand. No wonder so much sloppy thinking and deciding (or not deciding) goes on.

If we want to know why people think they can't be entrepreneurial, let's start by defining some terms. To start, what is *entrepreneurial?* The confusion starts right away. Most people don't talk about *entrepreneurial;* they talk about entrepreneurs and entrepreneurship. Indeed, on the first day of class, when we ask our MBA students to define *entrepreneurial*, many respond that it is "starting a new company." That might be part of it, but no. Feeling clever, some will say *entrepreneurial* is a person who starts a new company. But if it is just someone who starts a new company, what about the repeatedly successful inventors who license innovations to others and never start their own companies? They are not entrepreneurial? How about someone like Thomas Watson of IBM or Ray Kroc of McDonald's who builds a great success on the smaller foundation of an existing company?[6] How about a person who starts a nonprofit or something big and new from inside an existing company?

Some students catch on to the idea and broaden the definition to describe *entrepreneurial* as a person driven to achieve, someone with a high tolerance for risk. Yes, this covers the objections, but it turns out that most studies of entrepreneurs don't support the notion that they are unusually driven to achieve.[7] Many years of research have turned up few substantial personality characteristics that predict who will be a successful entrepreneur.[8,9] As to being overly tolerant of risk, most entrepreneurs have a finely developed sense of risk and, when studied, don't turn out to have more tolerance for risk than managers in large organizations.[10] They don't embrace risk; they focus on quantifying and systematically eliminating risks.[11] Good entrepreneurs—the successful ones—identify what could go wrong and then take whatever steps they can to reduce the odds that this will happen, or they find another idea. Regardless, this is defining *entrepreneurial* as a person—a noun—or as an action—a verb. Look again at the part of speech: *Entrepreneurial* is an adjective.

Why is this important? Why does it matter if we are talking about a certain part of speech? The way we use words affects not only how others understand us but, perhaps more important, how we understand ourselves. Words frame our thinking, shape how we see opportunities, and expand or limit the way we see possibilities in the environment and in ourselves. Verbs and nouns, along with phrases such as "starting a new company" and "risk-tolerant person" are all or nothing. They reinforce the idea that you are or you aren't, you do or you don't. You're a have or a have-not. But working with the concept as an adjective frees you from binary either-or thinking because adjectives can work in degrees.

When you think about *entrepreneurial* as an adjective, you can come up with a list of synonyms. Here are some adjectives our classes often list when we ask them to describe a person who is entrepreneurial:

- Innovative and creative
- Self-motivated; takes initiative
- Flexible and adaptable
- Assertive
- Growth-oriented
- Opportunity-driven
- Active and dynamic

- Implementation- and efficiency-focused
- Productive in an unstructured environment
- Driven to create value
- People- and team-focused
- Decisive

Like any collection of adjectives, this set of characteristics can manifest in all kinds of combinations and degrees. Everyone has at least *some* of these characteristics. Instead of all or nothing, you can start to think about which entrepreneurial traits you possess and to what degree.

You see here a mind-set, a way of thinking and acting, an *orientation* rather than a person or a specific action. Howard Stevenson of Harvard Business School characterizes this mind-set as a "relentless pursuit of opportunity without regard to the resources controlled."[12] The entrepreneurial focus is on opportunity and results. It asks:

- Where is the opportunity?
- How do I capitalize on it?
- How quickly can I act?
- What resources do I need?
- How do I access those resources?
- How can I do more with less?
- Where do I want to be at the end?

An entrepreneurial person wants to pursue opportunities and results without worrying too much about process. Whatever process will turn the opportunity into reality is the right process.[13] Adjectives make it possible to execute, but they don't make it inevitable. When studied against measures of successful outcomes, only three characteristics seem to correlate much with success: proactivity, achievement orientation, and commitment to others.[14,15,16] Of course, studies that regress success measures have all kinds of methodological limitations, so don't take this to mean that all those characteristics aren't valuable in the entrepreneurial world. The studies are *looking at* entrepreneurial. You want to *look along* it.

In the end, ideas and innovation are nice, but it is execution that creates value. Stevenson declares, "There are innovative thinkers who never get anything done; it is necessary to move beyond the identification of opportunity to its pursuit."[17] In the entrepreneurial world, only results can create value and generate rewards.

It can seem daunting to go in one leap from a nearly clueless state of having an idea and not knowing where to start to running a successful business with all the skills and experience that entails. But remember what we said about all or nothing and adjectives. You don't need to go from one to the other overnight. It's a process. Imagine you are at the base of a tall cliff and all the mind-set and know-how of the successful entrepreneur are at the top. If you are at the base and success is at the top, no wonder it seems daunting. But what if there is a set of stairs leading up the cliff? On this staircase, each riser is one of the adjectives that add something; each step up makes you a little more entrepreneurial. Cultivating more of these characteristics and behaviors moves you up the steps so that you don't have to make the climb all at once, straight up. Looking at it this way, everyone starts out at least a little bit entrepreneurial. Almost anyone can climb a set of stairs, just as almost anyone can learn new habits and ways of thinking, one step at a time. You just need a little guidance on how to get started and what to look for.

Think about it another way. Normally, with adjectives you can plot two poles—tall and short, introverted and extroverted, hot and cold—and then describe a person or a situation as being somewhere in between. That's why we have words such as *more* and *most, less* and *least*—to modify adjectives. For *entrepreneurial*, the opposite pole is *administrative*—Stevenson calls this a "trustee" profile. He thinks about the trustee as

- Risk-averse
- Threatened by change or the unknown
- Security-inclined
- Process-driven
- Cautious, slow-moving, and structured
- Effective in predictable circumstances
- Control-motivated
- Resource-focused

The administrative mind-set focuses on *control:* having power over resources and process. It measures each presented opportunity against the available resources and accepted procedure, asking:

- What resources do I control?
- What structure determines our organization's relationship to its market?
- How can I minimize the impact of others on my ability to perform?
- What opportunity is appropriate?

The results are subsumed to process or procedure: If you do it the right way, it doesn't matter whether it works out. Procedure trumps results. In the administrative world, resource expansion generates rewards. The bigger your budget and staff, the greater your salary.[18]

At Cambridge University, Professor Barbara Sahakian and a team of cognitive neuroscientists study the differences between entrepreneurial and administrative mind-sets. In November 2008, they published the results of neurocognitive imaging studies that compared matched groups of entrepreneurs with managers who had no experience in venture creation: administrators.[19] In the experiment, Sahakian and her colleagues introduced their subjects to what they called "cold" processes—emotionally neutral tests—and then to risky, or "hot," process tests laden with emotional significance and involving the evaluation of reward and punishment. They found that entrepreneurs' brains were more active than managers' in the region responsible for making hot decisions, that they bet bigger and scored higher on tests for personality impulsiveness and cognitive-flexibility performance. The Cambridge research team concluded, "[E]ntrepreneurs and managers do equally well when asked to perform cold decision-making tasks, but differences emerge in the context of risky or emotional decisions. This functional impulsiveness of entrepreneurs combined with enhanced cognitive flexibility is a winning combination."[20]

Obviously, these Cambridge entrepreneurs and managers represent the end points of the spectrum. The vast majority of us fall somewhere in between, depending on our unique mix of entrepreneurial and administrative characteristics. If you think about plotting a large sample of people on this scale, entrepreneurial and administrative characteristics will be distributed normally (see Figure 1-1).

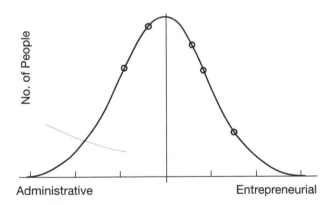

Figure I-I Scale for entrepreneurial and administrative characteristics.

If a population is sufficiently large and random, almost all the people, approximately 95 percent, will fall within two standard deviations—the little hash marks on the horizontal scale—of the mean or distribution center. That means most people will have some entrepreneurial characteristics and some administrative characteristics, whereas very few people (less than 0.5 percent) will be almost entirely one or the other. Odds are, if you have taken the initiative to pick up this book and read this far, you are fairly entrepreneurial but probably not Bill Gates.

Further, the Cambridge researchers wanted to know if the entrepreneurial and administrative traits we all possess are deterministic: Are we just born this way, or can we learn to think more in one mind-set or the other? That is, can people learn to be more entrepreneurial? It turns out the Cambridge researchers affirm that people certainly can become more entrepreneurial. Indeed, they state that specific courses on

> [R]isk-tolerance in both behavior and personality may also be desirable. ... We know that perception of risk is particularly sensitive to framing effects; therefore, training potential entrepreneurs to reframe their decisions may encourage greater entrepreneurial activity. One might argue that business skills can be acquired relatively easily from multiple sources. But if one is to boost entrepreneurial activity, and if risk tolerance and the ability to cope with ambiguity are barriers to achieving a cultural shift in society, then more focus is needed on understanding how risk and emotion are integrated into decision-making.[21]

Sahakian and her coresearchers argue for reframing risk, knowledge, and emotion in decision making to help people effectively work through and eventually thrive in uncertain, challenging conditions.[22]

Carol Dweck, a veteran social psychology researcher at Stanford University, studies human motivation and perseverance. She calls for a similar reframing, shifting our focus from innate talent or ability to effort and growth. Since the 1960s, she has repeatedly found that an "overemphasis on intellect or talent leaves people vulnerable to failure, fearful of challenges, and unwilling to remedy their shortcomings."[23] People cannot be comfortable in uncertain circumstances with this mind-set. Dweck went on to describe how a fixed view of intelligence or talent—believing that a person possesses a set or static amount of a specific trait—negatively affects motivation to action. When people with this fixed-trait theory fail, they generally assume that their failure results from a lack of intelligence or aptitude and are afraid to try again. They feel powerless to change the outcome. More to the point, they avoid challenges because those challenges might require effort outside their comfort zone and they might make mistakes, both of which make them appear less talented or gifted. Indeed, fixed-trait theorists often pass up the opportunity to correct their mistakes, presumably because they will not admit they made them in the first place.

Dweck also describes mastery-oriented individuals who "think intelligence is malleable and can be developed through education and hard work."[24] These people focus on learning and effort. If they fail at a particular exercise, they try harder the next time because they believe failure results from lack of effort—something they can control. This has a tremendous impact on motivation. People with a mastery-oriented mind-set seek out challenges because challenges offer learning opportunities.

So it turns out that believing entrepreneurial traits can be learned and developed actually helps a person grow in proficiency and effectiveness. We have to stop thinking that somehow people are born with a fixed set of skills, intelligence, aptitudes, whatever—that people are born entrepreneurs or they are not. Yes, one can argue that people are not all equal in their gifts and some will have an easier time than others, but this is not about that. This is about taking what you started with and developing it, growing it, making the most of it. Stevenson at Harvard, Sahakian and her Cambridge researchers, and Dweck and her colleagues at Stanford all believe that learning in the way we have described it is possible. Indeed, 20-plus years of experience in the business world and now 10-plus years at the Tuck School have proved this. People can pick up the entrepreneurial mind-set and skills and perhaps even help improve our economy and our future just as everyone seems to expect. You *can* move to the right on the entrepreneurial bell curve if you put your mind to it, and when you do, you can be as entrepreneurially effective as you make up your mind you are going to be (Figure 1-2).

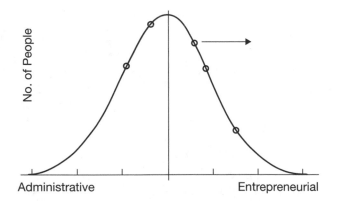

Figure 1-2 Becoming more entrepreneurial.

However, we can't *teach* you to get into the mastery mind-set, to thrive in uncertain conditions, to become more entrepreneurial. All we can do is point you in the right direction, give you the tools, and help you learn the skills. You are the one who has to go out and do it. In order to do this, to move to the right on the entrepreneurial scale, you need to know both yourself and who you want to be. You need to be able to set specific goals for yourself and incrementally develop the characteristics you want and need.

WHAT I KNOW NOW THAT I WISH I HAD KNOWN THEN

Nathan Sigworth, Gyrobike, PharmaSecure

While still an undergraduate engineering student, Nathan Sigworth coinvented a gyroscopic stabilizing front wheel for children's bicycles and cofounded Gyrobike (www.thegyrobike.com). He then went on to cofound PharmaSecure, Inc. (www.pharmasecure.com), which provides pharmaceutical packages with anticounterfeiting technologies in at-risk markets. He is currently CEO. As a repeat founder of successful technology companies, Nathan shares some lessons he has learned.

Starting

1. *Count the cost.* When three friends and I invented the Gyrobike, I gave up semester breaks to work in the machine shop, building and testing our project. When I started PharmaSecure with my college roommate, neither of us realized how complicated it would be and how much we would sacrifice to build this business, spending much of our twenties in foreign countries.
2. *Pick the friends you work with.* Working with trusted friends will help you make it through the hard times, but it will stress your friendship. No matter what, your friendship will be different. It may be stronger, or it may not make it at all.
3. *Kill ideas quickly.* Gyrobike came out of one week of brainstorming and nine weeks of intense testing. If it didn't stand up to our testing, we didn't want to waste our time on it. When the first kid learned to ride a bike in a few minutes on the Gyrobike, we decided to launch the business. A few years later I helped a friend start a telemedicine business with doctors in India and patients in the United States. The team defined success metrics for a pilot project and market research. When the metrics weren't reached, we shut the project down. As hard as this was, it let us get out of a complicated business before investing a lot of time and money.

Financing

1. *Become an investor yourself.* As I raised money for my own business, I invested some money in a friend's social enterprise. What I learned by being an investor showed me how to instill confidence in my own potential investors.

2. *Get on that plane.* Flying or driving to meet serious investors immediately is essential. (The same goes for meeting customers.) While raising money for PharmaSecure, I flew to Thailand to meet a potential investor. After we spent a week exploring jungles and mountains and talking about our similar values, he decided to invest in the company. I flew across the country to meet with another investor, who decided in 15 minutes to invest half a million dollars. I took many other meetings that didn't result in investment; all that matters is that some paid off.

3. *Raise more than you think you need.* When we finally got investor interest in PharmaSecure, we had much more than we had anticipated. Since it was the height of the 2009 financial crisis, we doubled our raise. Had we stuck with the original amount, a year later we probably would have failed.

Operating

1. *Learn to say no.* As an entrepreneur, you think you can conquer the world. PharmaSecure immediately gained interest in several different countries, but we didn't have the operational capability to deliver. Although this work was helpful in understanding markets, we should have focused on operations in one place first. Once we focused on India, we saw real sales traction.

2. *Execute well.* It is easy to get caught up in the goal of sales, but the operational capacity to deliver on your promises is essential. With our first customers we had delays in shipping. We lost deals to negotiation delays and poor operational preparation. Now we arrive at customer sites with everything needed for full implementation, and things go much more smoothly.

3. *Hire your "customer."* At PharmaSecure, we tried to sell and provide services to pharmaceutical companies without having someone experienced in that industry. We finally hired a plant manager from a major pharmaceutical manufacturer who has helped us better understand what our customers need and how to implement projects with them. I wish we had done this first.

4. *Take time off.* Take time off if you want your business to be successful and your life to be pleasant. Even though I was working and living in India, I committed the time and money to spend time with my friends and family in America regularly, which has given me the ability to be in India for a long time and live sustainably.

I'm still learning a lot, but these are a handful of things I wish I knew when I started; it would have made the last five years more like two.

So *who is the entrepreneur?* The answer is simple: anyone who is willing to be mastery-oriented, to learn, to face challenges and uncertainty, to start without knowing where the path may lead, to persevere, and to enjoy figuring it out along the way. Who can do that? Anyone who is motivated enough to want to do something meaningful. If you are like most of the people we've met in industry, academia, nonprofits, and government, no matter how excited you are or how burned out, deep down you want to have an impact, to have a sense that what you do really matters.

You can learn to be a self-teacher and a self-starter in becoming entrepreneurial. It starts with opening your imagination, shedding inhibitions and anxieties about yourself and your ability. If you are passionate about an idea, you can learn the rest or attract other people into your vision to help you turn it into something real. That's what this book is about: helping you learn, but learn by doing, not by studying. It's about giving you the framework, the context, the right questions, the places to start, and enough of a road map to help you build your entrepreneurial skills. You certainly don't have to start a company to put this into practice. With a little thought and preparation you can make things happen in whatever setting you choose, in whatever circumstances you find yourself.

So let's stop looking at this beam of light called entrepreneurial and start looking along it. If you want to learn how to swim, you have to get in the pool and try. No one ever learned to swim by sitting on the side of a pool and listening to someone else tell him or her how to do it. The rest of this book should provide you with enough knowledge and guidance to get started and then, we hope, motivate you to go out and do it.

QUESTIONS

- What do you hope to get out of this book? Do you have a plan to maximize your investment of time and effort?
- Do you think you are entrepreneurial? If not, or if you are not sure, do you want to be? Why? What might you do to make that happen?
- When you look around, do you see opportunities? Why do you think they are opportunities? Do you see a path to capturing the value in them?

NOTES

1. Hein, Piet, *Grooks II.* (Cambridge, MA: MIT Press, 1968): 33.
2. Bygrave, William D., and Andrew Zacharakis, *The Portable MBA* (Hoboken, NJ: Wiley, 2010): 5.
3. McArdle, Megan, "In Defense of Failure," *Time International* (South Pacific Edition), 175, issue 11, January 22, 2010: 35.

4. Fairlee, Robert W., *Kauffman Index of Entrepreneurial Activity 1996-2009* (Kansas City, MO.: Ewing Marion Kauffman Foundation, May 2010).
5. Alibaba.com QuickRead Report, May 2009, provided by company. Summary published online as "Three Out of Four Americans Believe New Entrepreneurs Are Key to Reviving Economy," June 2, 2009, http://news.alibaba.com/article/detail/alibaba/100111970–1-three-out-four-americans-believe.html.
6. Stevenson, Howard, *A Perspective on Entrepreneurship*, Harvard Business School, Case 9–384–131, April 13, 2006.
7. Ibid.: 2
8. Gartner, William B., "'Who Is an Entrepreneur?' Is the Wrong Question," *American Journal of Small Business* 12, issue 4 (Spring 1988): 11–32.
9. Low, Murray B., and Ian C. MacMillan, "Entrepreneurship: Past Research and Future Challenges," *Journal of Management* 14. no. 2 (1988): 139–161.
10. Brockhaus, Robert H., Sr., "Risk Taking Propensity of Entrepreneurs," *Academy of Management Journal* 23, issue 3 (September 1980): 509–520.
11. Ray, Dennis M., "The Role of Risk-Taking in Singapore," *Journal of Business Venturing* 9, issue 2 (March, 1994): 157–177.
12. Stevenson, Howard, and David E. Gumpert, "The Heart of Entrepreneurship," *Harvard Business Review* 63, no. 2 (March–April 1985): 85–94.
13. Ibid.
14. McClelland, David C., "Characteristics of Successful Entrepreneurs," *Journal of Creative Behavior* 26, no. 2 (1987): 219–233.
15. Covin, Jeffrey G., and Dennis P. Slevin, "Strategic Management of Small Firms in Hostile and Benign Environments," *Strategic Management Journal* 10, issue 1 (January–February 1989):75–87.
16. Zahra, Shaker A., "A Conceptual Model of Entrepreneurship as Firm Behavior: A Critique and Extension," *Entrepreneurship: Theory & Practice* 17, issue 4 (Summer 1993): 5–21.
17. Stevenson, 2006: 5.
18. Stevenson and Gumpert, 1985: 89–92.
19. Lawrence, Andrew, et al., "The Innovative Brain," *Nature* 456 (November 13, 2008): 168–169.
20. Ibid.: 169.
21. Ibid.
22. We discuss risk management and framing in Chapter 6.
23. Dweck, Carol, "The Secret to Raising Smart Kids," *Scientific American Mind* 18, no. 6 (December 2007–January 2008): 36–43.
24. Ibid.

Chapter 2

The Right Words to Say

Most controversies would soon be ended, if those engaged in them would first accurately define their terms, and then adhere to their definitions.

—Tryon Edwards

We use certain words every day. Those words have meanings and implications that affect the way we think about others and ourselves and about the present and the future. The way we define and use words can empower or undermine the way we think and act, especially the way we visualize what is possible or desirable. We must take care to understand what we really mean as we talk to others—and even to ourselves—about our ideas and plans. As Frank Luntz says in the subtitle of his book *Words That Work*, "It's not what you say, it's what people hear."

This is painfully true when talking to others, but it's even more so when we talk to ourselves. It's critical that we hear ourselves correctly. To do this and to make starting out a little smoother, let's take the time to get into the right mindset and set expectations for a few fundamental definitions.

WHAT IS BUSINESS?

Whether you are thinking about starting a for-profit commercial venture, starting a nonprofit social enterprise, or just doing something new and innovative within an existing organization, if you are thinking about executing an idea and making something happen, you are thinking about *business*. If you are not in business now and want an entry into this executor's world, it's wise to think a little about its nature. What is it like to be in this world? What are its defining characteristics? Is it like the world you are in now? The last question is particularly important to think about before going anywhere. If you don't, you might be in for culture shock. The rules of engagement in the public sector or academia, for example, are very different from those in the business world.

What exactly is business? There is no one definition, of course, but Walter Bennis and James O'Toole of Harvard Business School used an interesting phrase in a 2005 article about business school education, of all things. They defined business as "essentially a human activity in which judgments are made with messy, incomplete, and incoherent data."[1] In that short phrase they named

15

three hugely important concepts that are at the heart of what it means to function in business:

1. *Judgments.* Business is seldom rigidly deterministic. Yes, there are rules, models, analytics, procedures, and data that can help point you in the right direction, but in the end judgment always is needed. This is often the last thing people stop to think about.[2] The *Oxford English Dictionary* defines judgment as "the ability to form an opinion; discernment, discretion, wisdom, discretion, good sense; the action of mentally apprehending the relation between two objects of thought; prediction as an act of the mind." There are few serious decisions in business that don't require judgment far more than data and analytics. Judgment requires weighing options, considering the future, making intelligent guesses about probabilities, and, most of all, considering unintended consequences. For every identified consequence, there are also the things that didn't happen or that aren't obvious, and those things are often vitally important. Good judgment lets you see what is not seen.[3] Whether it's a dire unintended consequence or a great opportunity that is overlooked, judgment in business often is most valuable when you see what is not seen.

   People generally want things to be simple and formulaic: "If *x*, then do *y*." Business doesn't work this way, especially entrepreneurial business. There isn't always a process to follow. Gregg remembers from his Samson days the time a new hire from one of the top schools in the country, six months into her job, came into his office in tears. She said she couldn't function in Samson's environment. When asked why, she blurted out, "There's no procedure!" (Gregg couldn't help responding, "We don't have procedures here; we just have problems.")

2. *Messy, incomplete, and incoherent data.* Few decisions in life are ever black and white. Data is seldom conclusive. And data is not answers. In the world in which businesspeople live, data is often incomplete and never better than the questions used to generate it or the methods used to collect it. Framing the right questions is the most important step in getting meaningful answers. Defined, relevant, researched questions help you gather data that may lead to an answer. But even when the data are clear and conclusive—which isn't often—simple answers are rare. Sadly, most people seldom pause to ask, "What do we really mean by the terms we're using?" and "What is it we are really asking here?" As a result, they frame questions poorly and seek the wrong information. In the end, good decisions come from good judgment, and good judgment comes from experience. Asking the right questions and seeking relevant and meaningful data are the essential foundations of informed judgment.

3. *Activity*. All the best ideas, questions, data, and plans come to nothing without *activity*. Remember Howard Stevenson's words from Chapter 1: "There are innovative thinkers who never get anything done"?[4] In the end you have to do something. Only activity—execution, doing something— can create value. But how? Most people assume ready, aim, fire—think everything through, figure out a plan, perfect that plan, and then start. Although this may apply in sharpshooting, in building something from nothing you'll never have enough information to aim. You make the best progress when you ready, fire, and then aim. It's a matter of trial and error. This means getting out into your market, trying a new idea, iterating, and then trying again. It is sharpshooting by trial and error; you try a shot, see how close you got, adjust, and shoot again.

Nothing gets done if you sit around all day planning until you think you have it right; you'll find yourself stuck in ready-aim-aim-aim-aim.... The most meaningful information comes from activity and execution, seeing what works and what doesn't, not doing more research. The best entrepreneurs have a built-in impulse to action: They want to do things, and by doing things they figure out what is important along the way. Even if this is not your inclination, fake it at first. You'll see that it works. Actually it is often the most efficient way to innovate. After a while it may even grow on you.

WHAT IS INNOVATION?

There is a whole field of study and an extensive literature on innovation: what it is, how to do it, and why it's valuable. We can't do anything here but summarize some of the key points. First, Peter Drucker defined innovation as "an economic or social, rather than a technical term ... the means by which [entrepreneurs] exploit change as an opportunity for a different business or a different service."[5] Innovation fundamentally aims to create value—"new and different satisfactions"—rather than simply improve what already exists.[6] Although innovation can involve new technology or a new invention, it is a broader idea: doing something better to create value. This can mean new products, new services, new business models. Table 2-1 outlines some of the differences between industry and academia.

You don't have to be a high-tech scientist or engineer to be an innovator. Joseph Schumpeter (1883–1950), an influential economic theorist, described five different areas of entrepreneurial innovation: a new product or product quality, a new method of production or handling, opening a new market, conquest of a new raw material, and a new kind of organization.[7]

Table 2-1 Industry and Academia Compared

Industry	Academia
Short time frame	Long time frame
Applications orientation	Basic knowledge orientation
Proprietary interests	Open inquiry: publish or perish
Knowledge for profit's sake	Knowledge for its own sake
Lines of authority clearly established	Collegial culture; weak decision process and policy

Second, certain conditions and situations foster innovation better than others do. Periods of rapid change in science and technology, politics, or culture offer many opportunities as new markets develop and new needs arise. Today university and research laboratories produce a great deal of invention and advancement. Although this might seem like a natural place for innovation, complications quickly arise. The academic and business worlds have significant differences in culture that make the transition of an idea from the research lab to business execution on the street very difficult. Researchers and businesspeople often expect different things from the process. They define value differently, and they have contrary assumptions about how the world works. They use different nomenclature and vocabulary to talk about the same concepts, causing problems in communication and understanding. Also, academics and industry people don't work on the same timeline. People in the university often don't have the same sense of urgency about a project as people in the industry.

Third, innovation requires application. This means that although innovation often starts with the new knowledge coming out of university research labs, someone must use that knowledge to fill a social need before it can be called innovation. To make this transition from knowledge to innovation, someone must bridge the gap between the creators and the implementers. This means a deliberate sensitivity to the different cultural assumptions and behaviors on the other side. This might seem obvious, but it's one of the biggest stumbling blocks in turning knowledge into valuable innovation. At most universities, technology transfer offices live in this gap, as do commercialization and entrepreneurship offices such as the Dartmouth Entrepreneurial Network. Getting businesspeople and researchers to communicate and work together effectively is critical to innovation.

Because they hold a limited view of innovation or don't know where to look for it, many entrepreneurs miss the opportunity to create significant value and impact. By embracing Schumpeter and Drucker's expansive conception of innovation, you have a much better chance of finding the innovations that will take your idea to the next level.

WHAT IS EPISTEMOLOGY?

It's dangerous to think that you know something on the basis of facts when actually all you are doing is making an assumption that is based on little or nothing concrete. There is nothing more painful than having an investor call you out on something you have claimed to be true when you have nothing but your opinion to substantiate it. Entrepreneurs find themselves in this situation every day when they haven't thought through and substantiated what they believe they know. First-time entrepreneurs often discuss library research and talk about their impressions of the market or interest in a product. Or they may argue by analogy and compare their idea to a company that was successful with something similar: "We can replicate Facebook's viral promotion. . . ."

When an investor balks at something—say, your description of what the customer will pay—there is nothing more powerful than to reply with hard data: surveys, focus groups, testimonials, and, best of all, a purchase order or letter of intent to buy. At that point it becomes the investor's opinion against all those people and all that data, not against your assumptions or library research.[8] Substantiation is the difference between knowing and assuming.

Thus, how you think about what you know or believe is critically important, and figuring this out is the discipline of epistemology. Epistemology is what philosophers call the discipline of determining how we know what we know. You can never know something with 100 percent certainty; everything in life is a matter of probabilities. There will always be a chance you are right and a chance you are wrong. Therefore, you should maintain a healthy skepticism about what you think you know. Demand evidence. Relentlessly convince yourself of the important points. Ask questions continuously and get the answers; then ask more questions and get more answers.

Epistemology is valuable in everything you do, from your mundane everyday decisions to the most fundamental issues in your business and even in your life. However, most of the time we are terribly sloppy about the discipline of knowing *why* we think something is true or valid. We may think in any situation that the reason something is true is obvious to everyone, but this is rarely the case. In fact, often what we think we know is plain wrong. Psychology researcher Thomas Gilovich of Cornell has spent a lifetime studying exactly this issue. In his book *How We Know What Isn't So*, he identifies ways our minds work against us as we form conclusions about what we think we know[9]:

1. *Misunderstanding statistical regression to the mean.* If given enough time, usually a trend will return to a long-term statistical average. One outlier will tend to be offset by another; an upturn will balance out a downturn. For this reason it's dangerous to project growth curves too far into the

future. You can't sustain rapid growth forever. As Wall Street says: Trees don't grow to the sky. Inevitably curves will level or even reverse; outliers will return to the norm. Take care when projecting data that's too far from known averages.

2. *Failing to detect and correct for biases that result from incomplete or unrepresentative data.* What is necessary for science may be needless overkill for industry. Decisions in business often suffer from inadequate, unrepresentative, and biased data. The only antidote is to consider your information carefully: where you got it, how reliable it is, and how you think about it. A good first line of defense is to talk the data over with other team members or advisors before making a decision.

3. *Interpreting ambiguous and inconsistent data in light of preferences, pet theories, or a priori expectations.* It's easy to see what you want or expect to see, and since most data is messy, incomplete, and incoherent, you will always be at risk of erroneous beliefs rooted in wishful thinking and self-serving distortions of reality. The only effective defense is to be self-aware and maintain a stance of skepticism and inquiry. If it's important enough, refer to item 2 above: At least talk things over with others less attached to the situation—team members, directors, or advisors.

4. *Depending on distorted or secondhand information provided by other people or the media.* In business you can't do primary research on everything you need to know. You have to rely on publications, research, and the news. However, you can't take everything at face value. You need to avoid relying too much on this kind of information to make important decisions. If you are careful, you often can detect and filter biases. In contrast, distortion and shoddy, secondhand information are harder to spot.

5. *Thinking that others believe what we believe, that they are more like us than they really are.* This is critically important in market research. You have to listen to what customers are really telling you and not let your own beliefs filter their message. Further, within your team, it's dangerous to assume casually that others are more like you than they really are. This is a big problem in everyday work with your team, but it's potentially fatal in forming a team.[10]

6. *Failing to distinguish correlation from cause and effect.* The big problem with thinking that one thing causes another is that you stop looking for the real cause. People want to know that when they do something, they'll get the result they expect. Unfortunately, when they form mental rules for what causes any given what effect, they often rely on the fact that the two things appear to be correlated. Correlation means that two independent variables tend to move together; but they may not have anything to do with each other. For causation, one variable has to be both *necessary and sufficient* to

produce the other variable's action. Far too much bad science, bad politics, and bad business have come from failure to appreciate this fundamental principle.

The business journalist Niles Howard adds to this list of epistemology errors[11]:

- Giving information more weight than it deserves because it was easy to get.
- Confusing source reliability with predictive ability.
- Having too much confidence in memory; we remember events better than statistics.
- Attributing genius to winners and stupidity to losers.

Make sure you work with solid information. Nothing is more frustrating than discovering that things went wrong because you based your decisions on flawed and confounded information. Every entrepreneur must become a disciplined epistemologist.

WHOSE INTERESTS ARE YOU SERVING?

A large subset of the entrepreneurial world, even the world of entrepreneurial education, conflates venture capital–funded projects and entrepreneurship. It declares that only start-ups with paradigm-shifting innovations that are seeking high growth rates and dominating positions in billion-dollar markets are worthwhile. Those are great opportunities for entrepreneurs to pursue, but they are hardly the only ones that can be attractive for an entrepreneur. It's just that they are the only ones potentially worthwhile for venture capitalists. Regardless of what some might say, the fact that you aren't going for these things doesn't mean that you are not being entrepreneurial or that you won't find great success with your idea. Figure 2-1 compares venture capital and entrepreneurship.

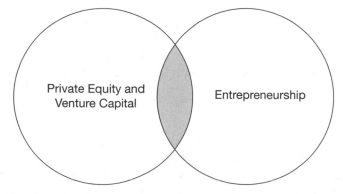

Figure 2-1 The relationship between venture capital and entrepreneurship.

Venture capitalists raise funds from outside parties and then invest that money professionally in early-stage companies. They make their return by selling those companies or taking them public within a certain period, at most 7 to 10 years. Their only goal is to distribute attractive returns to their investors. An entrepreneur's goal is to build his or her company into a stable going concern. Perhaps you will sell it for a great return in 7 to 10 years, but perhaps you won't. Or maybe the entrepreneur wants to pursue a nonprofit, which by definition can never be sold for a profit, or even a socially focused hybrid.[12] The point is that your goals and interests and those of venture capitalists are not necessarily the same. When they are—the shaded area in Figure 2-1 where the circles overlap—that's great and we hope you all make a lot of money. But if they aren't, you should maintain your focus on what you find important and not let investors unduly influence your thinking about goals, opportunities, or plans.

Our focus in this book is on you, not on the investor. We do discuss what's important to different kinds of investors since you'll probably need money to get started, and in that case it's really important what your investors think. However, never mistake their interests for your own. At best they coincide for a time. Sometimes they are hardly coincident at all, and when that happens, you are usually the one who loses.

WHERE DO I START?

The space above was intentionally left blank. That is all the entrepreneur starts with: nothing, a blank page. There may be a germ of an idea or an invention, but there is no plan, no money, and no team. People normally want to see where the path in front of them is heading. That is safe and comfortable. Entrepreneurs do not have that luxury. No one gives them a plan or a road map, only a blank piece of paper.

Where do you start? What should you do? Yes, entrepreneurs often have an idea or an invention, but as we will see in the coming chapters, there's not much value in ideas. Entrepreneurs add value through execution, doing things. But which things? For first-time entrepreneurs, knowing what to do next is daunting, but actually this is one of the best parts of starting something new! It's exciting and unknown. You can go anywhere. You start by putting things on that blank page.

Most people want some sort of specific plan or program preprinted on the page. Well, we can't help you there because we don't know your business, your resources, and your needs. Only you know about those things. So where does a plan come from? Fundamentally, people create plans and programs to answer questions. For example, if you are going on vacation, you ask: Where do I want to go? How will I get there? Where will I stay? What do I want to do? What can I pay for it? These questions help you narrow your options and ultimately create an action plan that fits your needs and resources.

With entrepreneurship, often people don't pause to frame their first questions in a meaningful and orderly way. They believe the questions are self-evident or assume the answers will become apparent over time. Few things work like this, especially in entrepreneurship. You need to be *intentional* about forming, defining, and asking smart questions. If you are, you'll have a much better chance of getting significant and valuable answers. Also, you can't expect to have your whole future mapped out in short order. You can try, but you will be wrong. Entrepreneurs find they always have to rework a plan at least once, usually many times. The launch is a process of discovery and adjustment. Life is easier if you get comfortable with that. Instead of defining the *first steps*, start by defining the *end goal*, then work backward to the right questions and some provisional ideas for a few first steps you can test. You'll have to sort out the rest as you go.

WHAT I KNOW NOW THAT I WISH I HAD KNOWN THEN

Keith White, IT security specialist

Keith White graduated from Dartmouth College in 1982, with a liberal arts degree in English language and literature; he got a job teaching school in inner-city New York. In 1995 he purchased a computer for $5,000 and left it on a rack at an Internet service provider (ISP), bringing Internet technology to city schools. His computing experience led to a position as director of media services and chair of a computer science department at a private school in Manhattan. From there, by way of involvement in operational risk management, Keith became vice president of operational risk management at Credit Suisse and was featured in a cover article on IT security threats in the September 2008 issue of Wall Street and Technology *magazine. Keith sees his whole life as a pursuit of opportunity through innovation and hard work. Here's what he says.*

Entrepreneurs generate value. But this is what entrepreneurs do every day: They create value out of nothing but their own ingenuity and hard work.

A liberal arts education can be a powerful foundation for an entrepreneur. It seems counterintuitive, but I feel my English degree was excellent preparation for work in technology. In college I learned two important things: Not all texts can be read in the same way, and if I didn't have a strategy for "reading" a certain text, I could develop one. In the same way, opportunity comes when we read the world around us in different ways. Sometimes a single change of view or perspective makes all the difference in seeing opportunities where others see only problems or nothing at all. Luck can be part of entrepreneurial success, but often it comes as part of seeing opportunity.

You need to conceptualize. Being able to see abstract relationships in any field not only accelerates the achievement of expertise but also leads to individual adaptability. A liberal arts education is excellent training because it prepares individuals to work with concepts and learn to digest information quickly, to confront the new, and to see meaning in it.

Stay current. Know what changes are occurring around you. Change brings opportunity, and small opportunities can grow. These days, changes are occurring within your home, within your local community, on a national level, even on a global scale every day.

None of this matters, however, unless your ideas are translated into action. Action on an idea that has an opportunity in its core is the indefinable ingredient that separates the alchemist puttering with lead from an entrepreneur who generates gold out of nothing.

In the end, enterprise is a balance of four verbs: generating value, investing, seeing opportunity, and translating an idea into a reality—G.I.S.T., Generate, Invest, See, and Translate. By these actions we know entrepreneurs, and by cultivating these behaviors in ourselves we may ourselves join this corps.

Trust your gut and take your own counsel. There are plenty of naysayers who are quick to tell others what they can or can't achieve. After you launch an enterprise, you have succeeded while the naysayer is still sitting in an armchair pronouncing about what can't be accomplished.

Entrepreneurship is more than a career. It's a vocation and a way of life.

From the time you first think about your idea and every time you think about it and all your planning, partition your mind and think as if you were three different people filling three different roles:

1. *Think like an investor.* How would an investor react to the thought that is going through your mind right now? If you knew those reactions, how would you address them to convince the investor or change your thoughts

so that they would be compelling to an investor? Note: Often entrepreneurs will say, "But I'm not planning to raise money from investors." It doesn't matter. Even if you are not planning to raise money, *you* are the most important investor in your company. You're investing your time even if you're not investing money, and time is infinitely more valuable than money. When the end comes, all the money in the world won't buy you more time. Thus, you should think as critically as any investor about your ideas every minute of every day.

2. *Think like your chief operating officer.* How will all these ideas be executed? What is going to be needed? When? Done by whom? Where will the money come from? How will you measure results? No idea turns into anything without relentless, effective execution down to every detail.

3. *Think like yourself in the future.* Imagine looking back from the end of the story. Can you imagine a narrative that leads from the ideas you are thinking about today to an ending that meets your personal goal? This is perhaps the most important thing, because in the press of day-to-day activity it is far too easy to drift off target bit by bit, so gradually that you never notice, until one day you see you are so far off course that you will never meet the goal that got you into this in the first place. Believe it or not, this happens all the time. More often than not entrepreneurs first realize they've achieved all kinds of things *except* their own goals at the end of the story: a sale, a merger, shutting down, or, worst of all, grinding it out day after day with no end in sight in a company totally different from the vision that started it. The best way not to end up there is to think about the goal every day.

Where do you start? What are the right questions to ask? That's what the rest of this book is about: using smart questions to fill in the blank page.

QUESTIONS

- How do you make decisions in a world where few things seem certain and you're usually drowning in data and starving for relevant information? Do you have a process, or do you just wing it? How well do you think your decisions work out?
- Do you have an idea? Do you know what to do next, or are you still looking at that blank piece of paper?

NOTES

1. Bennis, Warren G., and James O'Toole, "How Business Schools Lost Their Way," *Harvard Business Review* 83, no. 5 (May 2005): 96–104.
2. More on this in Chapter 18.

3. Bastiat, Frédéric, *Selected Essays on Political Economy*, S. Cain, trans.(Irvington-on-Hudson, NY: Foundation for Economic Education, Inc., 1995). Library of Economics and Liberty, http://www.econlib.org/library/Bastiat/basEss1.html (accessed June 3, 2010).
4. Stevenson, Howard, *A Perspective on Entrepreneurship*, Harvard Business School Case 9–384–131, April 13, 2006: 5.
5. Drucker, Peter, *Innovation and Entrepreneurship* (New York: Collins Business, 1993): 19, 33.
6. Ibid.: 34.
7. Schumpeter, Joseph, *The Theory of Economic Development: An Inquiry into Profits, Capital, Credit, Interest and the Business Cycle*, Trans. Redvers Opie (1911; republished by Harvard University Press, 1955): 66.
8. We discuss validating markets in detail in Chapter 4.
9. Gilovich, Thomas, *How We Know What Isn't So: The Fallibility of Human Reason in Everyday Life* (New York: Free Press, 1991).
10. More on the defenses against this problem in choosing cofounders in Chapter 8.
11. Howard, Niles, "Decisions, Decisions, Decisions," *Dun's Review* 117–118, no. 2 (May 1981): 98–101.
12. More on social entrepreneurship and alternative structures in Chapter 14.

Chapter 3

What's the Idea?

If you don't know where you're going, any road will take you there.

—Lewis Carroll, *Alice's Adventures in Wonderland*

You have an idea and think it's a *really* promising one. At one time or another, most people have an idea they are convinced will be a great success. That idea is often a product, but it can be a service, a charity, or even a new business model. Ideas can come from anywhere: from years of research and development, from a personal passion, or even from a flash of insight. Whatever the source, it's just an idea.

WHAT'S THE GOAL?

When most first-time entrepreneurs come to see us, they want to talk about their idea. Usually they want to hear opinions about it: "What do you think of it?" They may be looking for a specific kind of help. Maybe they want to talk about how they should start executing it. We always have the same response, because we haven't yet heard what is probably the most important thing. We ask them to put their idea aside for moment and talk about something else.

When you have an idea you want to pursue, the first thing you should think is not, *What do others think?* or, *What should I do now?*, but rather, *Why do I want to do this? What will success look like in the end?* It may seem a little counterintuitive at first to start at the end. It does to most first-time entrepreneurs. But if you know why you are doing something—really why, not just the superficial reasons—and have a good pencil sketch of success, you will have a much better chance of figuring out where to start, what you need to know, and what to do next along the way. It's vitally important that you think about the endgame at the beginning because you have a much greater chance of feeling you succeeded if you hit the goal that was really in your heart.

You would be surprised how many people set out with little or no understanding of their goal (or goals) and then are confused when they find themselves less and less happy as they progress and, worst of all, disappointed and disillusioned in the end, even a successful end, because it turns out it wasn't what they really were seeking. In short, "You can't get second things by putting them first. You can only get second things by putting first things first."[1] To get what you want, you need to know what you really want.

People picture success in an endeavor as a million different things. In politics and on Wall Street, "Success equals Results minus Expectations." In this formula, if you keep your expectations low enough, you'll succeed easily: Success is anything more than what others expected. That's why people in those sectors invest so much time and energy in expectations management. It's easy to succeed under this formula if you set your expectations for yourself low enough. We hope your expectations for your life and work are higher than this.

Some people equate the process itself with success. They may want to take their ideas and try to start something successful and think the experience itself will be a joy. A word of caution: If you think starting an enterprise will be all joy, you'll probably be disappointed. One of the most common refrains one hears from successful entrepreneurs is that *you can't imagine how hard it was.*

Other people say success is all about the money. Actually, there are plenty of easier ways to make good money. Very little entrepreneurial money comes easily—just ask a successful entrepreneur. Of course entrepreneurs like to make money as much as anybody else, but most are motivated more by making something worthwhile happen than by the reward of quick, easy money.[2,3]

Rosabeth M. Kantor, the Ernest L. Arbuckle Professor of Business Administration at Harvard Business School, says, "The middle of every successful project looks like a disaster." This invariably draws a laugh from experienced entrepreneurs, because they know it couldn't be more true. Nothing is easy, and you're never sure when it's safe to celebrate. Winston Churchill once said, "Success consists of going from failure to failure without a loss of enthusiasm." If you want to build your idea, this has to be your mind-set. Maybe it will be easy, but the odds are not in your favor.

Is it a lifestyle? We don't find many people going into entrepreneurship because they want to work long hours, stress their families, and have no life. Rather, for many entrepreneurs we know, success means somehow helping people, or making life better for someone. They want to add value. They want what they do to have meaning and significance.

But this is not about other people; it is about you. What's the real goal for you? Often when we start talking about aspirations with our first-time entrepreneurs, they think their goals are obvious, that is, until we ask them to describe their goals, to paint a clear picture. Then it quickly gets difficult to see how their idea fits into what they have just said they want from life and from the enterprise. Alternatively, the idea is sound, but there is a complete disconnect between their planned approach and their goals.

For example, we recently met two sisters, both parents of college-age children, who design jewelry. That is a pretty tough business: Competition is fierce, and margins are low. When the sisters started to sell product, they had some early success with customers, and so they started to think about quitting their day jobs to build the business full time. When they came to us, they asked all sorts of operational questions about next steps and how to go about this or that. But when we asked them, What's the end goal? they didn't have a clear answer. At first they talked about how a business making jewelry would be fun and more rewarding than what they were currently doing.

They didn't have a clear end goal in mind and weren't sure why it mattered. They thought something fun and more rewarding than what they were doing at the time was a good enough goal. Yet when we dug deeper, we discovered the real motivation: One sister needed to put four children through college at the same time, and the other, a divorcée, needed to build a stable income to support herself when her alimony ended soon. Knowing this, we did some simple arithmetic together to define the minimum scale of the business they would need to meet their goals. It was then that they realized the margins they could realize on their products were so small that they would need to build a huge business to achieve even their reasonably small financial goals.

They had been intending to build a business that would never get them what they needed financially. Knowing the real goals and incorporating them into strategy narrowed the sisters' options and focused them on the kind and scale of business they would have to build. Fortunately, in thinking about it this way, we thought about alternative approaches and focused on higher-priced, higher-margin products that incorporated an interesting technology and improved their margins by an order of magnitude. They shifted to a business that would leverage their design and passion for decorative accessories, meet their financial goals, and probably be more fun and less vulnerable to competition than the idea they started with.

This is a typical example, though of course not all have endings that are neat and happy. Talking to start-up people about their questions is a lot like therapy. Therapists and counselors say their clients usually present with a problem different from the real one at the root. Beginning with *What's the end goal?* seems to bring the real issues to the surface, and it ensures a connection between the individual's business and personal goals. This connection not only helps clarify problems in defining strategy, it excites and motivates entrepreneurs to move forward with a clear line of sight between what they are doing at any particular moment and the goal or goals that really matter to them.

Once you have defined the end goals clearly, you will be able to test various ideas and actions against a meaningful standard. Can you imagine a plausible scenario that starts with the issue at hand and leads to the desired goal? If you cannot, the idea, your imagination, or the goal needs work. Remember: "You can't get second things by putting them first. You can only get second things by putting first things first." If you have the end goal in mind, you have a much better chance of choosing some good first steps because you have a direction. Yes, no one can see so clearly into the future that every step in the process is obvious, but if you don't start off well, you'll be a lot longer getting where you want to go, if you get there at all. A clear vision of success and concrete first steps are the two most important things to have in mind as you get started. Everything in the middle will have to work itself out, and it can if you stay aligned with your ultimate goal.

One more introspection exercise: Think about what the whole entrepreneurial experience that lies ahead might be like. If you aren't sure you know, you probably don't. For a first-time entrepreneur, it's nearly impossible to know what it's like to build something tangible from nothing. Nearly every start-up entrepreneur we know at one time or another has said with great emotion: "You can't imagine how hard this is." That squares with our experience. Talk to entrepreneurs who have been through it—ask them about their successes *and* their failures—before you decide too quickly or casually that you're ready and know what you're getting into. We want you to walk into the business of being entrepreneurial with your eyes open.

IDEAS AND EXECUTION

You have an idea and want to do something with it. When people get an idea, they often feel like mountain climbers at the top of a mountain. They think: "This is going to be great; I'm going to make a lot of money. I better hurry before somebody else thinks of it." The reality is that when you have an idea, you are not on top of any mountain; you're at base camp, at the foot of the trail, and the mountain looms in the distance. Before you have an idea, you don't know you're even thinking about mountain climbing. When you get the idea, what you now have is merely a notion of where you might be going, a hazy view of the summit, far away and high above the plain. The hard work of climbing all lies ahead.

Think about this journey from idea to going concern another way. Growth normally plots like an exponential function. Let's plot your company's life on a chart, starting with where you are now with your idea and finishing where you hope to end up. Figure 3-1 shows where your idea is.

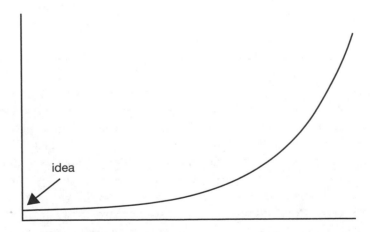

Figure 3-1 The growth of an idea.

Think about the scales for this graph of growth. The vertical axis is *value*, of course. Most people think of *valuation* as ultimate potential, the payout they eventually receive in dollars. This is right in one sense, but it's not the most helpful scale for start-ups. For them the most meaningful driver of valuation at launch is not ultimate dollar potential but *risk:* the chance it will ever succeed. Thinking about ideas and start-ups this way is tremendously important.

What it says is that every time you eliminate a risk that could kill your idea, your enterprise becomes more valuable. This is exactly how investors look at early-stage companies. The good news is that risk is a thing you can do something about: You can learn! The more you learn about your idea—your markets and customers, your technology, operations, finance, whatever—the more able you will be to eliminate risks, and as you learn, the value of your idea will grow (Figure 3-2).

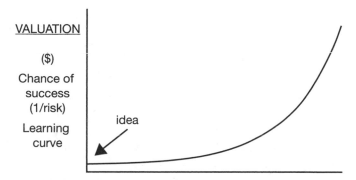

Figure 3-2 Valuation in start-ups is a function of chance of success.

What about the horizontal axis? When we ask this question, many people say the horizontal axis is time. But think about that for a moment. *Time* doesn't create *value* unless, of course, you're a bond investor. To create value in an enterprise you have to do something, actually lots of somethings: You have to *execute*. One of the few things we insist that our students take away from our entrepreneurship class is that ideas alone are worth next to nothing. All the value is in effective execution. Indeed, John D. Rockefeller often said, "The secret of success is to do the common things uncommonly well." It's not about the idea; it's about the execution. From the moment you decide to develop your idea, you've got to obsess over execution (Figure 3-3).

WHERE DO IDEAS COME FROM?

When people come to the Dartmouth Entrepreneurial Network (DEN) office, after we talk about their goals, they almost always launch into a detailed description of their ideas. We again tell them to put their ideas away, which can be bit

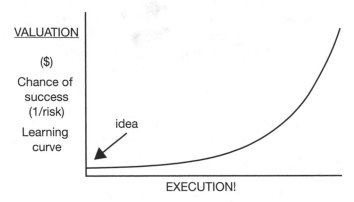

Figure 3-3 Execution creates value.

disorienting. Often they start to wonder if they are ever going to get to talk about their inventions. Instead we ask them, What need are you filling? What problem do you want to solve? The best ideas don't start with a product; they start with a need. We then ask our entrepreneurs to describe in as much vivid detail as possible the *person* who has the need or problem. More important, we ask them, Who will *pay* to have this problem go away? That person is their customer.

Interestingly, these two questions—What need are you filling? and Who is your customer?—often mystify our first-time inventor-entrepreneurs. They either think the answers are obvious or want us to answer the questions for them. Actually, these kinds of answers often don't turn out to be quite so obvious, and as far as answering the questions goes, the best anyone can do at arm's length is to suggest some good questions to start finding the answers that are really needed.

Most repeatedly successful entrepreneurs agree that the right thought process for coming up with a valuable idea is to start with a need. How painful or problematic is it? Painful or problematic enough that someone would pay to make it go away? This is the foundation of a successful idea. Some make the contrast between candy and painkillers. Candy is nice, but if you're hurting, painkillers are essential.

Equally important, can you describe in vivid detail who has this need or problem and who will pay to have this problem go away or this need be filled? This person is the customer. Who is the customer? is one of the most important questions a start-up entrepreneur will ever answer. The customer is the person who pays you to fill a need or make a problem go away. It's not always obvious who the customer is.

Consider this: You use Google every day, but you probably aren't Google's customer. Instead, you are a beneficiary, a user, of Google. Only the people who *pay* Google to place AdWords or purchase another Google product are Google's customers. Even nonprofits define customers this way: They are the people, programs, and institutions that give money to a nonprofit. As early as possible, it's vitally important that you be able to talk about the need you are filling and the customer who is willing to pay you to fill it. Only when you know the need and can describe the customer can you meaningfully define the *solution*, that is, the product or service you will offer. With this combination in hand—the need, the customer, and the solution—you are ready to go out to the street and see if you are right.

WHAT IS YOUR MARKET?

Arguably the most important question for the entrepreneur is: Will customers really buy my product in sufficient numbers for a high enough price that I can cover all my costs and make a good profit? Or, as investors often say, will the dogs eat the dog food? To answer this question, you must know your market. There are two types of markets—the total market and the addressable market—and investors watch for people who confuse the two. The *total market* is the total revenue generated in any single sector of the economy. Enterprise software or automobiles would be an example of a total market. These are big numbers. Market share as a percentage of these markets is a nice big number, but it's essentially meaningless. Nonetheless, many inexperienced entrepreneurs use these kinds of numbers. You need to stay focused on your *addressable market:* the sum of all purchases customers make as if every one of those purchases in the market was your product. Admittedly, this number is often harder to figure out than the total market, but it's the only one that is meaningful. With markets, bigger can seem more appealing, but sometimes dominating a niche market is a better strategy than scrapping with a plethora of big established players in a large market.

Further, high-growth markets are extremely valuable. Gaining traction and building sales growth in fast-growing markets is much easier than fighting established competitors for market share in a slowly growing or stagnant market. In a high-growth market you can grow your company even with a mediocre increase or no increase in your market share, whereas in a slowly growing or stagnant market everything is about competition, and competition is a great killer of profits.

WHAT IS YOUR VALUE PROPOSITION?

Alongside need, customer, and market, the other question investors usually ask is, What is your value proposition? In a way, this is a catchall term that has a dozen meanings. Some people mean the unique value you provide your customers. Others think about combinations of product, price, service, access, benefits, experience, and any number of other characteristics. Still others think about the plan for making profit from the company's activities. Although these are all important factors, when an investor or anyone else asks about your value proposition, he or she generally is looking for a high-level description focused on how your idea leads to value. Your value proposition is the embodiment of three simple formulas:

Customer Need + Solution = Product
Number of Customers × What They Will Pay = Addressable Market
Product + Addressable Market = Value Proposition

If you can describe all this clearly, you are ready to get on with executing. Remember that successful entrepreneurs do the following:

- Create a vision.
- Communicate the vision to others.
- Recruit and motivate a talented team.
- Execute the vision: integrate, lead, raise money, sell customers, do a little of everything, and leave when it's time.

WHAT I KNOW NOW THAT I WISH I HAD KNOWN THEN

Gail F. Goodman, Constant Contact

Gail Goodman is the chair, president, and chief executive officer of the e-mail marketing solutions company Constant Contact. The company was founded in 1995 as Roving Software, and Gail assumed its leadership in April 1999. In the summer of 2001 she was writing the shutdown plan with not enough money in the bank for the next payroll when she persuaded her venture investors to keep the company going. The company went public in the fall of 2007 and is now an industry leader with over 200,000 customers, growing 35 percent annually. Gail was named American Business Awards 2009 Executive of the Year and Ernst & Young's 2008 New England Regional Entrepreneur of the Year.

Gail talks about things she learned along the way that she wishes someone had told her when she was starting out.

1. Really know who your customer is. Don't go out with a product; let your customers tell you what they need and help you shape the product.
2. Although the economics of your business doesn't need to work when you start, it has to work eventually. Figure it out as you go, but be patient. If you fine-tune your profitability too soon, you probably will never scale. Lifetime revenue is what counts. Recurring revenue is the best model. You don't have to keep selling to get that revenue every year.

3. Focus, alignment, and collaboration are the keys to team success at Constant Contact. We have absolute alignment on the executive team as to points 1 and 2 above. The leader can't be involved in everything, so people have to be able to act on their own. Debate and discussion are okay so long as people commit in the end. People don't own ideas if they don't shape them. Entrepreneurship is a team sport.

WHERE DO YOU START?

Once you've roughed out a valuable idea and have a good sense of its market's size and growth rate, the first step is *not* to go out and start making the product. Rather, you should first spend the time, effort, and money needed to *validate your market*. This means getting solid evidence that your potential customers value what you are offering and will pay you well to get it. This is the time to get a sense that the dogs might actually eat the dog food. Chapter 4 looks closely at the idea of market validation. It's something you should start doing early and never stop doing. Validating your market is just the beginning of executing on your idea. Crafting your idea in terms of a need makes you focus on a customer. This customer focus helps you define your value proposition, which in turn sets you up to validate your idea and understand its worth.

After this, if you decide to build your own venture rather than sell or license your idea to others, it's time to execute, to get things done. Chances are, you'll have to execute the majority of the time with resources you don't control. To do this effectively, you'll need to do the following:

- Take the initiative
- Frame the appropriate questions and actions
- Execute effectively
- Take risks intelligently
- Pay close attention to detail
- Learn how to learn

And you thought it was going to be quick and easy!

QUESTIONS

- If you have an idea, can you write it down in a few sentences?
- Can you now write down some reasons why someone should think your idea is valuable? How valuable do you think it needs to be for you to want to pursue it?
- What should you do next with what you have written down?

NOTES

1. Lewis, C. S., "First Things and Second Things," in *God in the Dock* (Grand Rapids, MI: Eerdmans, 1970): 278–281.
2. Benz, Matthias, "Entrepreneurship as a Non-Profit-Seeking Activity," *International Entrepreneurship and Management Journal* 5, no.1 (March 2009): 23–44.
3. Amit, Raphael, Kenneth R. MacCrimmon, Charlene Zietsma, and John M. Oesc, "Does Money Matter? Wealth Attainment as the Motive for Initiating Growth-Oriented Technology Ventures," *Journal of Business Venturing* 16, no. 2 (2001): 119–143.

Chapter 4

Thinking about
the Market

The only way to know how customers see your business is to look at it through their eyes.

—Daniel R. Scroggin[1]

Solid third-party evidence of an attractive market of customers who will buy a product is one of the most valuable things a start-up can have in hand. The process of gathering this evidence is called *market validation.*

WHY DOES MARKET VALIDATION MATTER?

Knowledge really is power when it comes to market validation. The more information you have, the stronger your story is and the more value you offer potential investors and customers. It seems at times that everything in a start-up is essential—even potentially fatal if ignored—but few things are as critical as validating your market, proving to yourself that the dogs really will eat the dog food. Confirming your customer base early and often saves time and money and protects the whole enterprise from costly restarts and failure. If customers don't want to buy your product, don't you want to know that before you sink money and effort into building a company and making a product? It seems self-evident, but you'd be surprised how often companies do little market validation or neglect it altogether.

If you're going to fail for lack of a market, you want to *fail fast.* You shouldn't want to invest any more time and effort than necessary to discover any fatal flaws in the market's appetite for your idea.[2] It's actually simple: Think about questions likely to reveal potential market problems and ask them. In market validation you obtain solid third-party data to answer the ultimate question: Will customers really buy my product in sufficient numbers for a price high enough that I can cover all my costs and make a good profit? Start the moment you first have your idea or, better yet, when you first sense a customer need and have ideas about solutions. Gather as much data and information as possible to build a good evidence-based understanding of your idea's potential value and your customers' demographics: where to find them, how to talk to them, and how many will buy your product. A caveat: Unfortunately, nothing guarantees that your research will hold up when you go to market. There are lots of examples of solid research that later bombed. Nevertheless, thorough market validation, early and often, immeasurably improves your odds of success. At the least, a "no" answer from a market validation study is pretty reliable. It's the "yes" answers that can't always be counted on. Besides, you never know: Your customers might give you a better idea for how you can fill their needs and collect their money.

In addition to learning whether customers will embrace your idea, when you validate the market, you need to understand how you can differentiate your idea from the competition. Failing to differentiate a product leaves you in *commodity hell,* "the place where executives find themselves when they cannot convince customers that their widgets or services are better than those of their ever-burgeoning competitors."[3] The best way to avoid commodity hell is to differentiate between value and simple utility. *Utility* is a product's usefulness; *value* is what customers think the product is worth to them. Wheat flour has utility; it's a commodity. When someone turns it into organic whole-grain bread, it has added value for a health-conscious customer who will pay a premium for that value. Utility has become differentiated value. When a company markets specialty and "premium" flours to serious home bakers, it has turned a commodity into a value-added, differentiated product. It's important to understand what motivates and interests your customers and then work to apply that knowledge to product creation, promotion, and pricing.

Associated with differentiation is the idea of barriers to entry, both the ones you face and those you want to create to keep your competition out. In market validation research you want to understand both kinds of barriers intimately. We'll discuss competition and barriers to entry in Chapter 11. This chapter is about establishing an attractive, validated market in a way that can reduce your idea's inherent risk drastically and make you attractive to investors and others.

WHAT IS MARKET VALIDATION?

Market validation refers to methods and practices that can help you confirm your customers' interest in and willingness to buy your product. This includes doing basic market and competitor research, identifying promising market segments, understanding customer needs, defining and refining the product, actively engaging target customers for reactions and feedback, and perhaps getting a provisional commitment to buy. In going through this process of validating your market, you eventually will figure out the most effective way to talk about and position your idea. When you encourage your potential customers to think and talk creatively with you, you'll often find that they come up with ideas fundamentally different from, and maybe better than, what you had in mind.

WHEN SHOULD YOU START?

You can't start knowing your future customers or getting inside your potential market too early. Inventing or innovating before thinking about a market is like creating a solution and then looking for a problem. Sometimes you can guess a good solution by connecting a need you haven't researched to a product or service that fills it, but this usually happens when you already have a sound sense of the customer universe. Often when people innovate this way they are their own target customers.

Carefully studying a market or problem also can stir up ideas that define a solution that the market is already signaling it is interested in buying. In contrast, inventing something cool and then looking for an interested market is seldom successful. But however you arrive at an idea, you should always study the market and the customer before seriously investing in product development or, worse, launch. It seems self-evident that making something without knowing people will buy it is not a good idea, but you would be surprised how often it happens. The earlier you start, the better. You can even start looking at the market before you develop the idea; just never stop.

WHO SHOULD YOU ASK?

Market validation amounts to little more than shooting in the dark unless you carefully define your target market. You should understand the size of the market, be able to describe it simply, and be able to tell people how big it is in dollars. You should know its demographics and who may be serving it (potential competitors). You should understand growth and other trends. Even if you think you know your market, carefully review primary sources, many of which you can access in any good library. Be familiar with business press coverage. A number of industry reports are publicly available in libraries or online, and university libraries sometimes can give you access to proprietary analyst and industry survey reports such as IDC and Gartner and Forrester. If you know people at a business school, ask them for help. They often have access to a treasure trove of expensive and difficult-to-find licensed reports and studies.

Studying competitors is essential. Although competitors may be a threat, they are also a source of information about the market. Studying your competitors in detail gets you started on differentiation and barriers to entry. For the purposes of preparing your market validation research, knowing the competition gives you a wealth of information about your customers' purchase habits and what they want. When you interview potential customers, have a thorough knowledge of the competing products—both what's out there now and what's coming in the future—because more than likely your customers will. They will expect you to explain why your product is better. When you are entering a market to go against competitors, remember that your proposition to customers can't just be good; it has to be better.

Beyond primary research and getting to know the competition, different circumstances call for different approaches. Think about your circumstances before you start your research, because they will affect both how you frame your questions and who you want to answer them. For example, consider the difference between entering an existing market with a new product and entering a new market with an existing product. In an existing market you have to differentiate your product to capture demand that is being served by others, whereas entering a new market means you have to create new demand for a product they can see in another market. Or are you taking a new product to a new market? In these circumstances, you may have to educate your potential customers not only about your product but about their need for any product like it—a doubly risky challenge.

In his book *Crossing the Chasm*, Geoffrey Moore lays out a useful framework for thinking about market validation, product launch, and growing a customer base. Moore thought about a framework of innovation diffusion developed by sociologist Everett Rogers, in which Rogers observed that new innovation is adopted in a market along a predictable progression of different segments, beginning with *innovators* and *early adopters*—those most inclined to try new and different things—going through what he calls *early* and *late majorities,* and finally including the *laggards*.[4] In this framework, the groups have different adoption patterns and choose to purchase a product for different reasons. The innovators and early adopters are few in number and love innovation for its own sake. They are generally comfortable with technology, enjoy learning new things, and for the most part are tolerant of the higher costs that come with newly introduced innovations. In contrast, those in the early majority, particularly business buyers, look for products that improve their return on investment; they are looking for innovations that will help them save or make money. This early majority is influenced by the early adopters, but its needs and decision processes are different. Few innovations can prosper only in a market of innovators and early adopters. The big numbers are all in the early and late majorities. To penetrate those segments you have to make the leap from one set of buyer needs to another. What worked on one side of the chasm probably won't work on the other; in fact, it may be counterproductive. This is Moore's chasm, and crossing it is the big hurdle on the way to sustainability and profit. The ultimate market validation question you are seeking to answer is: How will you cross the chasm (see Figure 4-1)?[5,6]

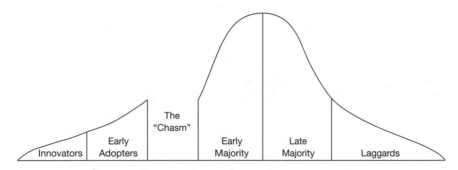

Figure 4-1 Moore's market chasm.

Source: Geoffrey Moore, *Crossing the Chasm: Marketing and Selling High-Tech Products to Mainstream Customers* (New York: HarperCollins, 1991; revised 1999 and 2002): 17.

You may not start at the beginning of this curve with the innovators and early adopters. For instance, if you are introducing a new variation of an existing product, obviously you should start your validation in the large majority markets that will count when you launch. Of course, carving market share out of an established market with entrenched competitors brings its own set of challenges, and in this case your validation will focus there.

In a sense, crossing the chasm focuses on time; you think about what happens when. But you can look at validation another way: How is the market segmented? Which segments might be most promising for you? There's always a trade-off between reaching for a broad market and entering a narrower, more defined market segment. In broad markets the main draw is market size: the sheer number of potential customers. In a segmentation-focused strategy, the coherence of the segment allows you to hone your appeal and competitive advantage more tightly, but you need a much larger market share.

You should consider carefully how to segment your market, how you might best position yourself for entry, and how you would defend a profitable market share. The more defined the customer base and the better you know your segment, the more likely your product or service will get traction. In 1990 Hewlett-Packard management charged a division manager, Michael Clarkin, with introducing the light-emitting diode (LED) into new markets. The LED market promised to be big but diverse. Different markets were likely to find different value propositions and approaches appealing. Clarkin's group broke the lighting market into segments, looking carefully at the value chain to define the parts that would be most likely to adopt this revolutionary product.

WHAT I KNOW NOW THAT I WISH I KNEW THEN

Michael Clarkin, SYKES

Michael Clarkin leads the marketing activities of SYKES, a global leader in out-sourced customer contact management solutions. In addition, Michael is the founder and president of Trilogy Consulting, which develops customer-driven strategies for companies in information technology (IT) system integration, enterprise software and medical devices, semiconductors, network security, and wireless and optical communications. Over 10 years at Hewlett-Packard, Michael held marketing and business management leadership positions in California, Germany, Hong Kong, and Malaysia. We asked him to recall a market validation project at Hewlett-Packard he often uses in our Tuck classes and to share the lessons learned.

In 1990, Hewlett-Packard charged me and a team of marketing managers with introducing the LED into new markets. After years of simple uses such as digital clocks and colored lights behind keypad buttons, LEDs had made a breakthrough in brightness and were suddenly as bright as the common incandescent bulb. So we set out to identify the best markets where we could go head to head with a technology people had found satisfactory for over a hundred years. The automotive market was an early choice because of the LED's advantages in reliability, faster turn-on time, and design flexibility.

Incandescent bulbs in cars were highly unreliable and burned out often. Warranty costs on defective taillight bulbs could be 10 to 20 times the cost of the bulb. The appeal of an indestructible LED seemed obvious.

Our LED lightbulbs got bright more quickly than incandescents. The advantage was only a fraction of a second, but that extra fraction of a second could make a big difference to safety. In a driving simulator at the Detroit Auto Show we proved that a fraction of a second might give a following driver an extra 10 to 15 feet of braking distance.

And by chance we learned that some vehicle designers saw in our little round dots of light an awesome design tool to create new shapes and styles:

"art lighting on a car." We were still skeptical; as a group they had no buying power or budget of their own, and they were often deeply buried and highly protected in the car companies.

Fast forward 20 years and you know how this all played out. After much time and fruitless effort, we learned dealers make money on warranty repairs, so they found no appeal in cutting warranty claims for burned out lights, and manufacturers are sensitive to what their dealers want. There are still no regulations requiring these safer lights on cars. But nearly every cool, sleek, or elegant car taillight today is made of those LED dots—the lighting paintbrush of the car industry.

We learned some lessons the hard way with this exercise:

- As engineers, we focused on applications that made sense to us. Only when we talked to customers (dealers) did we learn how different their priorities were from ours. Don't assume customers think like you do.

- Our ambition to get our lights into every last new car through government regulation blinded us. We spent months trying to influence lawmakers and consumer advocate groups to support our safety proposition. If we had done our research, we'd have found that it took over 15 years for armies of dedicated advocates to get seat belts required in every car. Car companies resist new safety devices as long as they can.

- We learned to do our homework earlier on how decisions are made inside corporate customers. Although designers didn't have any budget, it turned out they had immense influence in car companies. When they found a way to make their designs more unique and cool, the industry had to change fast to remain competitive.

- New and improved doesn't automatically mean enthusiastic adoption. Substituting for a satisfactory and entrenched hundred-year-old technology can be really hard. It takes a strong reason for a buyer to throw away ingrained habits.

- You can think and analyze things to your heart's content, but there is no substitute for talking to customers.

Inexperienced market validators often make a fundamental error in selecting interviewees. When your idea targets consumers—as contrasted with industry buyers whose job it is to purchase for their companies and who know their market intimately—it is easy to interview people whose responses are irrelevant or downright misleading. Be sure the consumers you interview are really potential buyers.

Most people are willing to answer a market validation question, but if they are not the people who will buy the product, their opinions are not worth much. In our class, we often ask who would like to own a Mercedes-Benz SL65 AMG Roadster, 604 horsepower (Figure 4-2), that goes from zero to 60 miles per hour in 4.2 seconds. Of course most hands go up. Then we ask how many of them are in the market to buy *any* car in the next year or two. Only a few hands go up. Finally, we ask how many will have $198,750 to spend on a car in the next year or two. Seldom does a hand go up, and usually it belongs to a smart aleck. This is the difference between *feedback* and *validation*. To get validation, you need to be talking to people who are qualified *buyers* for your product.

Figure 4-2 Validation or feedback?   © Courtesy of Daimier AG

This also applies if you plan to sell a product or service to a business customer rather than an individual consumer. You need to interview qualified potential buyers, but with an added complication. Here you usually have to contend with corporate decision-making processes, not just an individual. To interpret properly what you hear, you will need to know how the company makes buying decisions. Often decisions go through a chain of several people, many of whom have the power to veto but not the power to approve. For example, a company may have a gatekeeper who screens out salespeople. There will be people who influence the decision—an employee who uses the product, an IT manager who focuses on technical factors, an economic benefits watchdog—and perhaps other managers who advise but can't approve. Then there will be the actual decision maker. Often the influencers provide the most creative ideas for enhancing a product and can give you important validation. But be careful: It may not be obvious to you at the time, but influencers cannot confirm whether their organization actually will buy. Although often you won't be able to access a decision maker directly, try every way possible to get a sense of how the entire decision-making chain will react to your product. Access to interviewees often is simply the art of the possible and you will take what you can get, but it always pays to know how the real purchasing decision will be made.

WHAT QUESTIONS SHOULD YOU ASK?

Once you have identified your targets, you should think carefully about what you really want to know. Probably this is not just a start-to-finish exercise but an iterative process of trial and error. In determining your questions, you should also take into account the likelihood that your targets can give you meaningful answers. Building prototypes to show to customers can be good, but be careful about how much you invest before you validate. In validation, especially if you have a sample product in hand, the temptation to cross the line from asking to selling is almost irresistible. At this point, you shouldn't be selling. You are looking for honest answers that predict future behavior and for criticisms and input to develop the product further. Mostly, you want to provide your potential customers with every chance to think creatively about features and improvements. You'd be surprised how often they'll think of something you didn't.

A product is not a unity. You should think of it as a collection of different features and elements, any combination of which can make for a compelling and competitive offering. All kinds of things make up the appeal and value of a product or service, and any one or combination can be a compelling advantage (Table 4-1).

Beyond the product itself, your business model can create value. Think about Amazon or Dell. You too may end up delivering a known product in a new way. Sometimes explaining a business model to a potential customer is tougher than

Table 4-1 Elements of a Value Proposition

Product Elements	Service	Price	Access	Experience
Features	Access to service	Financing	Channels	Expectations
Aesthetics	Replacement	Comparative	Web presence	Consistency
Performance	Quality	Perception	Transportability	Follow-up/support
Ease of use	Customer care	Relation to need	Cost	Function, utility
Availability and access	Warranty	Switching cost	Delivery	Emotion
Quality	Maintenance contract	Margin	Regulation	Fun
Durability, reparability	Cost of service	Total cost of ownership	Limited access	Social proof
Safety	Automated	Residual value	Location	
Flexibility	Customer relationship	Visible	Easy to find	
Selection	As a product development tactic	Consistent	Convenience	
Useful life	Self-help	Reasonable	Timeliness	
Guarantee policy	Ordering	Stable		
Follow-on products	Delivery	Comparable		
Emotional connection	Returns			
Brand	Use and repairs			

introducing a new product because a new model is often more difficult to visualize. In such an instance, validating the idea is doubly important.

With your test bed and your product's most important and salable elements defined, you are ready to draft some questions to try out in your interviews. Remember, these interviews are not about facts; they're about reactions. You are as interested in the emotion behind a statement as in the statement itself. Don't ask only yes or no questions. Ask open-ended questions and follow-up questions. Try to get inside the customers' thinking and tease out their emotional reactions. Remember, an important goal is to learn about the customers' needs and problems, not just their reactions to your product. You hope for an outright declaration of their intent to buy, which you may or may not get, but you should always be able to draw out new and creative ideas to improve your product. Thus, there is a balance of directed questions and open-ended conversation.

Background Questions

- What are your titles/positions/responsibilities in the company?
- What do you most worry about? What keeps you awake at night?
- Can you describe the microenvironment you think my product might address?
- Can you describe the factors in your environment that might affect your adoption and purchasing decisions?
- Can you tell me about the economic and budget issues that affect purchasing and pricing? (Does the potential customer or company have the money?)
- Can you tell me about the purchase decision processes? (Who else should I talk to?)

Other Questions You May Want to Ask

- Do I correctly understand your need? Do you see this need persisting into the future? Do you feel my product will meet the need?
- What alternatives do you see to my product?
- What benefits do you see in the product? What features or capabilities are appealing? Not appealing? What's missing?
- How can I best reach others like you? Where do you go for information on products and solutions? Press? Trade journals? Media? Trade shows and conventions? Direct sales?
- What do you think about the price? (How does the customer react?) Is this product a nice-to-have or a must-have? Do you want it? Why and how badly?

(*Note*: The price you want is the price the customer is willing to pay. Pricing is not cost-plus! Customers may be willing to pay a lot more than simple cost plus some average profit.)

Questions to Ask Yourself and Topics to Consider After Hearing from Your Customers

- What trade-offs do you see? (Do you sense a willingness to use? To buy?) Are particular purchase terms or structures appealing or potentially determinative?
- Do you detect any opportunities to get advantage from unique capabilities or assets that you have? Do you see any competitive differentiators? What kind of support might you need? Would it make a difference in the purchase decision?
- Do you see opportunities for expansion of the product or other up-selling?
- Pay special attention to preferences that might work against you, objections, or criticisms.

HOW DO YOU GET THE INFORMATION?

Here are several ways to get the information you need:

1. *Surveys,* although the least definitive gathering method, often provide your first glimpse of the market. Sometimes you can engage specialized consultants to help you maximize the yield of useful information with the most efficient survey sample set. Otherwise, you can use one or more of the many basic survey resources available: SurveyMonkey, eSurveysPro, and Zoomerang, for example. Surveys are especially useful in the early stages to help you define your target market and your questions. Just don't view your online survey results as definitive validation. These results are notoriously misleading, usually in the direction of overoptimism. Telephone surveys are better but still provide only superficial information.
2. *Focus groups* can yield a lot of rich information, especially if you need creative insights into product improvement. Although this information-gathering tool is powerful, you have to watch out for groupthink and participants who aren't qualified buyers.
3. *Demos and product tours* can get you into your customers' homes or places of business. They are best used early in the process for validating basic concepts or late in the process when you are using validation interviews as an opening to try to make a sale.
4. *Interviews* are the richest source of validation. Ideally, you'll conduct the interview in the customers' place of business so that you can absorb all

sorts of environmental cues and insights in addition to what they actually tell you. The more time you can get, the better, but of course longer interviews will be more difficult to obtain. Use your network for access and favors. You can also cold-call, advertise, and use e-mail lists to find potential interviewees. Naturally, your acceptance rate will be lower, but these impersonal contact methods can help you get a broader sense of the market.

It's wise to start your interviewing with a few less important targets so that you can refine your approach and questions. You'll get better at validation as you go. Think carefully about your interview method and style. Always remember that you have one mouth and two ears. Use them in that ratio. You want to know what they have to say; be careful not to fall into the trap of push polling people for their opinions. Market validation is interviewing, not selling. Further, it's not just about what your interviewees tell you, it's also about what you see. Look everywhere the customer will let you: into processes, problems, and people. Also, let them ask you some questions. It's a really good sign if they want to know the price, so don't jump to that so quickly that you don't give them a chance to ask on their own. The goal is always to get an indication that they are interested in buying. Go into every interview hoping you come home with a purchase order, a conditional purchase letter, or a letter of interest from the decision maker. You won't get all that many, but these types of written indications of intent to buy are major assets in raising money.

You also want to take with you to the interview as many team members as you can. Taking an engineer or scientist involved in product design and development is always advantageous. Not only will your scientists or engineers help establish rapport with the customer's technical people, having your technicians in the room to hear validation and criticism firsthand helps with buy-in to your findings later. If your technical people are not there, you will often find when you get back to the office that they will resist the customers' criticism and pepper you with lots of defensive questions: "Didn't you ask them ... ?"

Another problem to which you should always be sensitive is what we call the Aaron Kaplan problem. Dr. Aaron Kaplan is a friend of ours, a successful interventional cardiologist and medical device entrepreneur who talks about this challenge in market validation when he speaks to our class. Aaron says, "When I show people a picture of my daughters, they usually say something like, 'Aaron, those are the two most beautiful girls in the world!'" Aaron says he loves his daughters more than anything in the world and thinks they really are the most beautiful girls in the world. But he's their father, and he knows deep down that it doesn't matter what his daughters look like. They could look like frogs and people would still tell him his daughters are the most beautiful girls in the world. People won't tell you your kid—or your latest idea—is ugly. This is the challenge of getting people to tell you honestly what they think about your idea, especially people who know you well. The most valuable feedback in the world is honest feedback even if it tells you that your idea or product is ugly. Unfortunately, this is often the hardest kind of feedback to get. You have to work at making people comfortable enough to tell you the truth.

Although gathering the information is important, it's only the first step in market validation. The next step involves what you do with the information. As soon as you can after an interview, discuss the outcomes as a team. Reduce your findings to actions that help you adjust your approach for future interviews and integrate key findings into your product and story. Keep track of solid validation data. It's worth a lot when it comes time to raise money.

WHO CAN HELP YOU?

Probably you have little or no money when you are first vetting your idea and considering whether to pursue it. Validation has to be done, but unless you're willing to spend your own money or your precious seed dollars, you'll be doing it yourself. Fortunately, you can learn market validation passably well by doing it. Practice makes perfect. If you have the money and the inclination, market research consulting firms can help you. Consultants generally charge $100 to $300 an hour. Some will help prepare you to do the bulk of the work yourself if you ask. You'll get the highest yield per dollar if they work with you to form the questions, train you to do the interviewing yourself, and then help you interpret the results. There are agencies that can do larger projects, but the cost can run into the tens of thousands of dollars or more. Whether on your own or with an army of professionals, market validation done well can make all the difference. Many consumers are familiar with the Jetboil, a creation of Dwight Aspinwall and Perry Dowst. Their careful market validation was literally the foundation on which they launched a successful company.

When you have done your market validation homework, you're ready to define what it takes to turn your idea into value and, if it's a for-profit, dollars. It may be that you like your idea, you want to execute it yourself, and grow a successful enterprise. Or it may be that you aren't sure you're the right person to take it forward, especially if it's an invention that would be more valuable in the hands of an existing company. In this case, you may want to consider marketing your idea as a license. The nature of the idea or the product sometimes makes this decision obvious. Other times the pros and cons will be more balanced. In Chapter 5 we'll examine the two alternatives, what each involves, and the advantages and disadvantages of each.

WHAT I KNOW NOW THAT I WISH I HAD KNOWN THEN

Dwight Aspinwall, Jetboil and Human Capital Institute

Dwight Aspinwall is a cofounder and director of Jetboil, Inc., the market-leading manufacturer of portable hot drink and food appliances. Jetboil products are sold at outdoor retailers throughout the United States and in over 30 other countries. Before Jetboil, Dwight cofounded Intermap, Inc., a publisher of business mapping software, and subsequently joined Vicinity, a provider of Web-based maps and driving directions. He currently works for the Human Capital Institute in Wilder, Vermont.

It took nine months for my partner Perry Dowst and I to build our first Jetboil prototype. I remember holding it with pride. It was about the diameter of a can of tennis balls and a little shorter. It was, I thought, perfect. After celebratory hugs I said to Perry: "When can we start to make them?"

"First we have to test it," he said.

At Gillette, my partner had practiced the mantra of "test early, test often." New product ideas are shown to users at every phase of a product's life cycle. The testing reveals the product features that people like and dislike. Early corrective action saves time and money by avoiding lengthy blind forays.

On a peak foliage weekend soon afterward, Perry and I hiked a little ways down one of the White Mountains' most popular trails. We brought our prototype, a competitor's stove, a folding table, and a clipboard full of questionnaires. As hikers passed, we asked them to stop and have a look at our invention. In the span of a few hours we spoke with 30 groups and learned two things: (1) The idea was a hit, and (2) we had to make it bigger.

Over the course of the ensuing months, we built two more major designs based on feedback from user testing. We also presented the designs to buyers at Eastern Mountain Sports (EMS), our first customer, and incorporated their feedback.

Due to innovative design and thorough testing, EMS wrote Jetboil their largest stove order ever—almost a year in advance of production. With this order in hand, we were able to secure $1 million in start-up funding for the company.

QUESTIONS

- Can write a paragraph or two listing all the important things you know about your customer?
- Who might give you a prospective purchase order or nonbinding letter of interest to buy before you build the product?
- How will you know when you have enough information to proceed with confidence?

NOTES

1. Daniel R. Scroggin, president and CEO of TGI Friday's, Inc., quoted in LeBoeuf, Michael, *How to Win Customers and Keep Them for Life* (New York: Berkley Books, 1988): 65.
2. Hall, Doug, "Fail Fast, Fail Cheap," *Bloomberg Businessweek*, June–July 2007.
3. Buchholz, Todd G., "Drowning in Red Ink," *Wall Street Journal*, May 30, 2007: D8.
4. Moore, Geoffrey, *Crossing the Chasm: Marketing and Selling High-Tech Products to Mainstream Customers* (New York: HarperCollins, 2002): 9–25.
5. Rogers, Everett M. "Categorizing the Practices of Agricultural Innovations and Other Adopter Categories," *Rural Sociology* 23:4 (1958).
6. Rogers, Everett M., *Diffusion of Innovations* (New York: The Free Press, 1962): 148–191.

Chapter 5

Intellectual Property and Licensing

The Congress shall have power ... to promote the progress of science and useful arts, by securing for limited times to authors and inventors the exclusive right to their respective writings and discoveries. ...

Constitution of the United States of America, Article 1, Section 8

Next came the Patent laws. These began in England in 1624; and, in this country, with the adoption of our constitution. Before then, any man might instantly use what another had invented; so that the inventor had no special advantage from his own invention. The patent system changed this; secured to the inventor, for a limited time, the exclusive use of his invention; and thereby added the fuel of interest to the fire of genius, in the discovery and production of new and useful things.

—Abraham Lincoln, "Second Lecture on Discoveries and Inventions"[1]

Ideas and their expression are valuable assets, but only if you protect your ownership of them. In this chapter we examine how ideas and their expression can be turned into property with tangible value. We will summarize the different kinds of *intellectual property* and review the process of conceptualizing your property and protecting it. The future value of your ideas and your company probably will depend on how wisely and effectively you do this. Thus, you should know the basics and understand how to work with professionals to get the best possible results.

WHAT IS INTELLECTUAL PROPERTY?

The World Intellectual Property Organization (WIPO), a specialized agency of the United Nations, defines intellectual property as follows:

> *Intellectual property (IP) refers to creations of the mind: inventions, literary and artistic works, and symbols, names, images, and designs used in commerce.*
>
> *IP is divided into two categories: Industrial property, which includes inventions (patents), trademarks, industrial designs, and geographic indications of source; and Copyright, which includes literary and artistic works such*

as novels, poems and plays, films, musical works, artistic works such as draw-
ings, paintings, photographs and sculptures, and architectural designs. Rights
related to copyright include those of performing artists in their performances,
producers of phonograms in their recordings, and those of broadcasters in their
radio and television programs.[2]

WHY IS INTELLECTUAL
PROPERTY VALUABLE?

One way to protect an invention or idea that you think has value so that others
can't copy it and compete with you is to keep it secret. This can work in theory,
but often someone can reverse engineer your innovation and copy it anyway.
Similarly, without copyright protection, anyone can copy something you've written and try to sell it. Many ideas by their nature must be shared to have value, but
sharing raises the problem of securing the value to the creator. Thus, to foster an
environment of innovation to benefit society, well before the U.S. Constitution
was written, the courts of Old World kings granted monopoly grants on patents
and other intellectual property to inventors as an incentive to create and commer-
cialize new inventions. For you the macroeconomic theory of intellectual property
rights may be less interesting than the ways in which their protection can be valuable to you, and they can be very valuable indeed.

   In an information-intensive economy in which knowledge and innovation
increasingly drive value creation, intangible forms of value such as intellectual
property are ever-greater contributors to enterprise value:

> *In 1982, physical assets such as plants, factories, and equipment constituted*
> *62% of manufacturing companies' market value. Today they represent less*
> *than 30% of their market value. … Revenues from the licensing of patent*
> *rights have skyrocketed in the last ten years, increasing from $15 billion in*
> *1990 to more than $110 billion today.[3]*

   For example, IBM's aggressive intellectual property effort increased its annual
patent-licensing royalties from $30 million in 1990 to nearly $1 billion in 2000.
To match that net revenue stream, IBM would have to sell roughly $20 billion
worth of additional products each year, an amount equal to one-fourth its worldwide sales.[4]

   Innovators have three forms of legal protection—patents, copyrights, and
trademarks—available to them. A patent applies to a specific product, method, or
design. A copyright protects the expression of an idea in a fixed medium, such as
a written work, a drawing, or a musical score. A trademark protects a name, phrase,
or symbol that you might use to identify yourself, your company, or one or more

of your products. All these legal protections provide you with a right to control and monetize your ideas and to keep others from taking your ideas and competing with you. Accordingly, they can be a foundation of value creation, but only if you take steps to document and secure your rights.

Competition is a great killer of profits. Aggressive protection of your intellectual property rights is one of the best barriers to competition. Intellectual property (IP) not only is important to your own operating profits, it is a key focus for investors and eventually for anyone considering the purchase of your technology or your company. It can even create for you an option to license[5] your patents or copyrights to others for development, manufacturing, and sales.

Intellectual property management also involves taking steps to ensure that you avoid violating others' IP rights intentionally or otherwise. Infringement damages can be punishing. For example, when the courts found that Eastman Kodak had infringed on Polaroid's patents for instant cameras in 1990, they ordered Kodak to pay $925 million in damages and shut down its $1.5 billion manufacturing plant, leading to the laying off of 700 workers. Kodak also had to buy back the 16 million instant cameras it had sold, at a cost of $500 million.[6] In 2006, BlackBerry maker Research in Motion (RIM) paid $612.5 million to NTP, Inc., a Virginia-based patent holding company whose main asset is a portfolio of 50 U.S. patents, to settle NTP's claims that RIM was using its patents in its BlackBerry products without a license or payments to NTP.

The field of IP law and litigation is massive, complex, specialized, and subspecialized. It's not a field for amateurs, and unless you are an experienced patent lawyer, you are almost certainly an amateur. This is one place where you will have to turn to specialists for almost all creation and prosecution of your IP assets. Still, you hold ultimate responsibility for managing your company's IP matters: assets and liability avoidance alike. That's why we think you should have a basic understanding of when to think about IP strategy and how to manage your professional help. For one thing, you must start the thought processes and devise the strategies, because only you know what ideas are in your head and where you are trying to go with them.

Further, you have to make the decision to call in the experts when you think you need them, and to know when you need them, you have to know how they can be valuable to you. Thus, in the end you must be responsible for your strategy and your decisions. You must decide direction: what you need to get done and how to do it. You should never let outside experts do this part for you. Although their guidance and execution will be instrumental all along the way, as you work with them effectively and make good decisions, you will need your own grounding in the basics of IP: the different forms, their value, and how to secure that value. This chapter discusses some of those key factors and gives you some direction on where to go for more resources.

PATENTS

Patents confer on their holders the exclusive, government-granted right to prevent anyone else in the country from making, using, selling, or offering to sell the patented product or process in that country. Each country has its own patent laws and its own processes for filing and securing patents. Patents do not grant a blanket right to make, use, or sell a product and its component parts; you are always subject to any prior patents. A patent is also an *exclusive right*, not an entitlement; that means that you, not the government, must enforce your ownership and exclusivity. If you discover that others are infringing on your patents, you must file a complaint and engage the courts yourself to prosecute the violation, and that can get expensive quickly. In other words, a patent is nothing more than a license to sue infringers.

Although patents and portfolios of patents can be important barriers to competition, they are seldom sufficient to keep determined competitors from finding ways to design around your patents. Aggressive competitors can even build their own portfolios of patents around the edges of your patents as a way to impair your ability to sell in the marketplace. In short, a patent is a tool, not a cure-all for competition and imitation. It's wise to combine a good IP strategy with aggressive execution and continued innovation to get ahead of competitors and stay ahead.

With some exceptions, the exclusive rights granted by patents issued after June 8, 1995, last for 20 years from the application filing, 14 years from patent issuance for design filings. By law, inventors own the patents on their inventions, but they can assign their patents to others. Only the inventor or inventors or their assignees can apply for a patent. In most countries, the first party to file a patent is deemed to be the inventor, but as of this writing, the United States still recognizes the first to invent as the inventor, not the first to file, although this may be changed in pending legislation. Thus, the courts often must decide who really was first with a claimed invention. A famous aside: For years, Elisha Gray contested the original Alexander Graham Bell telephone patent—one of the most prominent and valuable patents of all time—and there is substantial evidence to suggest Gray indeed invented first.[7] Accordingly, it's critical to maintain incontrovertible documentation of invention at all times. A bound inventor's notebook with detailed notes, diagrams, and material pages signed and dated by credible witnesses is the gold standard. If you are in any doubt about what constitutes adequate documentation, consult your IP attorney. You should also take a look at good print sources such as Fred Grissom and David Pressman's *The Inventor's Notebook*.[8]

Grounds for Patenting

To be able to patent an idea, you not only need to have a concept, you must *reduce it to practice*. In interpreting patent law, the courts consider a concept the "formation in the mind of the inventor, of a definite and permanent idea of the complete and operative invention, as it is hereafter to be applied in practice."[9] Reduction to practice is the *embodiment* of the concept of an invention. The embodiment of an invention can be any of the following:

- *Actual reduction to practice:* "Requires that the claimed invention work for its intended purpose."[10]
- *Constructive reduction to practice:* "Occurs upon the filing of a patent application on the claimed invention."[11]
- *"Simultaneous conception and reduction to practice":* "In some instances, such as the discovery of genes or chemicals, an inventor is unable to establish a conception until he has reduced the invention to practice through a successful experiment."[12]

Patents can be granted on processes, methods, and materials that are "novel, useful, and non-obvious." These are technical terms that describe three tests an idea must pass in order to be patentable:

- *Novelty.* Your claimed invention must not exist anywhere else in the world in a patent; it cannot appear in public knowledge, be described in presentations or in a printed publication, or have been in public use or for sale more than one year before the first patent application date.
- *Usefulness.* Your invention must have current, significant, and beneficial use as a process, machine, manufacture, or composition of matter, or as an improvement to one of these. You can find the technical definitions of these terms at the U.S. Patent and Trademark Office (USPTO) Web site (www.uspto.gov).
- *Nonobviousness.* Your invention must not be obvious to a person having ordinary skill in the pertinent art as it existed when the invention was made.

Failure to meet any of these three tests is grounds for denial of an application. In addition, you must be able to provide a written *enabling description* of the invention in the application. This means that you must be able to reduce your invention to writing—no performances or demonstrations—and describe it so that anyone reasonably practiced in the art is capable of building or doing what you are describing.[13]

If the idea meets the three patentability tests, it must fit into one of the categories of inventions defined by the patent code as eligible for patenting:

Utility Patents

- A machine or device
- An article of manufacture
- A process or method for producing a useful, concrete, and tangible result

- A composition of matter
- An improvement of an invention that fits into one of these categories

Design Patents

- The industrial design or ornamental appearance of an object

Plant Patents

- An invention or discovery involving asexual reproduction of distinct and new varieties of plants

The law sets limits on inventors' ability to file patent applications:

> *A person shall be entitled to a patent unless—*
> *(a) the invention was known or used by others in this country, or patented or described in a printed publication in this or a foreign country, before the invention thereof by the applicant for patent, or*
> *(b) the invention was patented or described in a printed publication in this or a foreign country or in public use or on sale in this country, more than one year prior to the date of the application for patent in the United States....*[14]

Any of the stated conditions that prohibit a patent filing or cause it to be denied is known as a *statutory bar*.

Naturally occurring phenomena such as photosynthesis, abstract ideas such as algorithms not applied to a useful purpose, and laws of nature such as $E = mc^2$ and $F = ma$ are not patentable. Although software code can be copyright protected, it is not directly patentable. However, on the basis of the case *State Street Bank & Trust v. Signature Financial Group* (1998), the underlying business method or algorithms embodied in software can be patented so long as you can describe the idea in writing and depict it in a process depiction such as a flowchart. Patents have been granted and upheld for mutual fund administration and application programs, process or machine controls, internal or operations programs that direct the handling of data in a computer's operations, and, most famously, Amazon's "One-Click."[15] Subsequently, *In re Bilski* (U.S. Court of Appeals for the Federal Circuit, 2008) created additional confusion over the tests to be applied to determine whether an abstract idea is eligible for patent protection, requiring that a method patent claim must be either tied to a device or transform matter in order to be patentable. On appeal in *Bilski v. Kappos* (decided June 28, 2010), the U.S. Supreme Court ruled that this was one test but not the only one, leaving unresolved the question of how easily one can patent the ideas and algorithms behind many software and Internet products.

The most common failing of a patent under a statutory bar is that prior art is found to have existed at the time of invention. *Prior art* can be any information in the entire body of human knowledge, including publications, presentations, an earlier patent, prior use, or sale of the invention. If your invention has already been described or if it would be deemed obvious on the basis of prior art, you won't be able to obtain a patent. It's often a good use of attorney dollars to have your IP attorney run a thorough prior art search early in the process. No matter how good you are at searching, your attorneys generally will turn up at least a handful of prior patents and other literature that challenge your claim of originality. You and your attorney then will think about how to draft claims that are novel in light of prior art. Many inventors who declare that they have searched everywhere and found "nothing like" their own invention express dismay when handed a patent or publication almost identical to their own drafts. One of our Dartmouth inventors swore that such a late-discovered patent plagiarized his own description—it was almost word for word in several places—but for the fact the patent was issued a year before he started working on his project.

Perhaps more pertinent, prior public disclosure by the inventor or inventors (i.e., you) is also prior art. *Public disclosure* means *any* disclosure of information—a publication, an oral presentation such as a poster session at a conference or in the classroom, or even a conversation—that happens before the patent application that may be considered an enabling description and therefore a public disclosure. In some cases public disclosure of an invention can even be its use, market testing, exhibition, or sale or an offer for sale containing the contents of a claim or the invention products. In some circumstances, you can get a public use exception for experimental purposes or beta testing, but not if you have received any payment. Consult with your experts early before you test the limits on public disclosure. As you will see in the next paragraph, it's far better to think about this before making the disclosure.

In the United States a statutory bar applies to all public disclosures made *more than one year* before the date of a first domestic or international patent application filing. Thus, you have a one-year grace period between the date of a public disclosure and your first filing. If you don't file in that year, you lose the ability to patent. In contrast, the patent law in almost all other countries with important markets sets a statutory bar on public disclosure with no grace period. Patent rights in many foreign countries with sizable markets are often important to investors and eventual acquirers, and so you need to pay careful attention to the public disclosure issue. It's far too common for inexperienced or careless inventors to make public disclosures in reliance on the American one-year grace period and later regret having extinguished their chances to seek patents in important markets such as Europe and Japan.

Of course you need to be able to talk to people, especially potential investors, about your invention. If you want to talk about your invention before making any patent filings, a simple way to avoid the issue is to make enabling disclosures to others only after they have signed a nondisclosure agreement[16] binding them to protect the confidentiality of what you tell them. To be effective, nondisclosure agreements must be legal agreements with defined statutory elements. They must do the following:

- Include a promise by the receiver of information to
  - Avoid unauthorized use or disclosure—use only as intended.
  - Limit use and disclosure to parties identified in the agreement or obtain written permission to disclose.
  - Exercise appropriate care in preventing the same [unauthorized use of disclosure] by others.
- Describe what information is protected. It's a good practice to create a schedule or exhibit listing the shared information.
- Mark all documents "confidential" and number and label them.
- Include a statement preserving your ownership of intellectual property rights, current and future.
- Include a reasonable term and expiration.
- Avoid ambiguity (e.g., verbal representations).

Some first-time entrepreneurs are so paranoid about discussing their inventions or ideas that they won't say anything to anyone who doesn't sign a nondisclosure agreement. Nothing labels you as inexperienced so quickly. Investors seldom, if ever, sign nondisclosure agreements to hear about an opportunity, especially for the first time. Most people will react the same way. Indeed, any investor will tell you that you must learn how to talk about your ideas without impairing your IP rights or putting yourself at risk of theft. Striking this balance is something everyone must sort out for himself or herself. To be sure you are protected on disclosure with respect to the statutory bar, at some point you might consider filing a provisional patent application with the USPTO. It's less complete but less expensive than a nonprovisional application. We discuss provisional patents and other deferral strategies later in this chapter.

What's Needed to Patent

A patent filing has three basic parts: drawings showing an embodiment, a written description, and claims. Patents generally take this form:

- Title
- Cross-reference to related applications

- Field of the invention
- Background
- Summary of the invention
- Brief description of the drawings
- Detailed description
- Claims
- Abstract
- Drawings

You can find the U.S. filing process at http://www.uspto.gov/patents/process/index.jsp. Note that seeking patent protection requires full public disclosure of the work in detail and therefore precludes maintaining any trade secret protection in the same work. You will have to pay filing fees, which differ depending on the size of your company. Also, if someone other than the inventors plans to own the patent, you will have to go through assignment procedures and filings.

Filing and prosecuting a patent is complicated, lengthy, and time-consuming. Drafting descriptions and claims is a highly specialized process. Sometimes, to save money, inventors will draft most of the claims with some guidance from their attorneys and a final review by the attorneys at the end. This can work, but you should never file all by yourself. Remember, a patent's value lies not in the grant by the USPTO but in its ability to stand up in court. When you sue for infringement, invariably the defense will challenge the validity of your patent, and so you want everything in your patent to be able to withstand whatever challenges creative lawyers mount against it.

Invention and Ownership

A patent filing must name at least one inventor, and it's critically important that you name all the inventors. Courts can invalidate a patent for failure to name a coinventor or for naming as an inventor someone who did not contribute to the invention. In addition to your carefully documented inventor's notebook, you should create a written recital of the relevant facts of invention: who, what, when, diagrams, data, and so on. This not only establishes the date and priority of invention but supports claims of ownership of an invention.

In industry, employees usually agree at hiring to assign work-related inventions to the employer, sometimes *all* of the inventions they create while employed with the company whether work-related or not, and so in those cases ownership claims are usually clear. In university settings, ownership policies can be more nuanced. Here the circumstances of invention can become crucial in determining whether the university will make a claim to an assignment. For individuals working together there is no substitute for written ownership agreements.

Absent other agreements with different provisions, by law each inventor individually and jointly owns all the rights conferred by the patent. Patents confer two basic rights: a *right to practice*—to make, use, or sell the invention—and a *right to exclude* others from doing that. When there are two or more inventors, each *individually* holds the right to practice and the other inventor or inventors have no authority to prohibit this practice. This means that the inventors could all go their own way and each make and sell the product in competition with each other or license to different companies to do the same thing. The inventors also have the right to exclude others beyond the inventing group from practicing. The right to exclude is the more valuable of the patent rights. Generally, companies want that limited monopoly, not just the right to make and sell. However, when there are two or more inventors, only by *acting together* can they confer a single right to exclude and anticipate the extra value that brings.

Therefore, the earlier in the process that inventors enter into some kind of cooperation agreement, the better. Often the easiest way to accomplish this is to incorporate and have the inventors create a company by incorporating and assign their patent rights in exchange for shares. Starting a company creates a clear legal structure for sharing the value, making decisions, and monetizing patents, but it needs to be done carefully and with consideration of the tax effects. In the alternative, a simple cooperation and joint IP management agreement can suffice. Universities or corporations that co-own patents routinely enter into these agreements with each other, designating one party to manage the patent, license it on behalf of everyone else, and handle the administration of the license revenues and operations afterward. As with any agreement that involves money, the parties should discuss their interests up front and make sure to create a structure appropriate to the needs and resources of the parties. You will often need professional help for the final drafting. When possible, establish agreements early, when the risks are high and the apparent value is still speculative. People somehow tend to be more reasonable and agreeable when a lot of money is not already at stake.

Deferral Strategies: Provisional Patents

The USPTO offers the option of filing a *provisional patent* as a quick, low-cost way for inventors to secure patent-pending status and public disclosure protections without starting the full time-consuming and expensive process of filing a nonprovisional patent. This streamlined and inexpensive option allows you to label your invention patent-pending, talk about it, and test it in the marketplace before deciding if you want to invest in a nonprovisional patent.[17] A provisional application contains the following:

Description

- Enabling/complying written description
- Complying drawings, if necessary

Claims

- Not required

Filing Fee

- Approximately $110 for small entities

Cover Sheet

- States that application is provisional
- All inventors' names
- Inventors' residences
- Title of the invention
- Name and registration of attorney or agent and docket number
- Correspondence addresses
- Any U.S. government agency that has a property interest

You can convert a nonprovisional application into a provisional one within one year of filing. In some cases the ability to convert to the nonprovisional patent can defer further costs until you can gather more information. This is helpful if you discover a reason not to pursue the present provisional application. Further, the USPTO holds a provisional application on file but does not read it as part of the subsequent nonprovisional filing examination. However, the provisional application can be an important document in court.

Once you file a provisional application, you have 12 months to convert the filing to a nonprovisional patent application with all the normal timelines and deadlines. As long as you convert within 12 months, the *priority date*—the date of first filing—remains the date you filed the provisional application, thus protecting any public disclosures you made. Keep in mind that you cannot extend a provisional filing. If you fail to file a nonprovisional application before the end of 12 months, you lose your priority date and any protection against public disclosure. If you made a disclosure and let your provisional application lapse, you lose the option to file internationally and the U.S. one-year grace period dates retroactively from the time of your first disclosure made without protection of a separate confidentiality agreement.

There is an additional potential disadvantage to a provisional patent. The contents of the provisional filing must reasonably resemble the final description and claims in the nonprovisional filing. In an infringement case, if the court decides the final description does not resemble the provisional closely enough, it may disallow the provisional filing, leaving you without patent-pending protection between the date of any public disclosures and the filing date of your first nonprovisional filing. If more than a year has lapsed in that instance, the court probably also will disallow your patent on the grounds of public disclosure.

Patents in Other Countries

U.S. protections do not apply abroad. Although each country has its own patent laws, there are some treaties that partly aggregate patent filing and prosecution. For example, a single filing at the European Patent Office provides protection throughout the European Union, though this protection is not one universal patent but rather independent national patents enforceable by each national court according to its own national legislation and procedures. Outside of this option, if you want a right to exclude in any specific country, you will have to file directly with that country or group of countries. Under the Paris Convention for the Protection of Industrial Property, 173 member countries recognize a priority date of first filing in any member country and defer their individual national patent application requirements for up to one year.

Filing a first application in one country or under the Patent Cooperation Treaty (PCT) buys you time to make decisions on filings in other countries. Some inventors like to start the process with a PCT filing—the *international* phase—which you can file with the International Bureau of the World Intellectual Property Organization (WIPO) or with the patent office of any PCT member country. The PCT will publish your application 18 months from the file date. Starting with a PCT filing allows you to work with a unified filing process and delay the more costly and complete national or regional filings, giving you more time to decide how much investment in patenting your invention might be worth. Filing a PCT also triggers a prior art search by the International Searching Authority (ISA), from which an applicant can request a written opinion on the patentability of the invention; this sometimes is important in deciding how much to invest in patenting. A PCT filing is not a patent; only countries can grant patent protection within their borders. You eventually will have to file a *national* phase—nonprovisional patent applications with all the countries in which you want protection—in accordance with national rules and in the national language. Thirty months after the earliest priority date under a PCT or national filing, the international phase ends and the individual rules and deadlines of the separate countries govern all future proceedings. Translation and filing costs mount quickly with each additional nation. In the end, international patent strategies often depend on balancing how much you can afford with how much you think you need the protection.

Patent Strategies

Although the technical execution of the patent is primarily your IP specialists' job, you are always responsible for your IP strategy. The way you make your patent claims is an important and complicated question. Broad claims provide maximum leverage in the marketplace, but they are hard to sustain as the USPTO examines your application or, even worse, if your patent is challenged in court later. Narrow claims are stronger but leave more room for other people to work around the edges. Usually the best strategy is to assemble a portfolio of claims, a combination of broad and narrow.

A second key consideration as you prosecute your application is how to handle confidentiality. Unless your idea can be copied or reverse engineered easily, until you make your idea public, you always have the option to revert to trade secrets rather than filing a patent. Unlike patents, which have a limited life, trade secrets never expire; they can only be reverse engineered or stolen, and in the case of theft, if you take the required precautions, you can have recourse in court; this is discussed below. It is strategically important to decide *when* your ideas will become public. In most countries and under the PCT, publication occurs 18 months after filing. In the United States, you can keep even your filing confidential until patent issuance if you pledge not to file in other countries that demand publication after 18 months.

Making your patent details public can expose you to damaging scrutiny from competitors. Sometimes well-heeled competitors carefully analyze patent filings for ways to "engineer around" a patent exclusion or to invent around the edges of your patent and file patents of their own. This practice, known as *bracketing*, may later prevent you from making and selling your invention because you find you need to use technology that they have patented by using your own filing as a guide. Some companies defend against bracketing and engineering around by product clustering, filing not just one patent but a family or portfolio of patents on different aspects of an invention. Inventors often file separate patents for individual components so that if a particular patent or claim has a flaw, they don't lose all their protection in one infringement proceeding. It is important to pay attention to publication dates and set a strategy that incorporates the pros of protection with the cons of publication. Remember that in patent filing research, you can do to your competitors all the things they can do to you.

Third, the key issue in patent enforcement is infringement. From the moment you first become patent pending, you should think about how you will monitor the industry environment and protect your rights. Preventing others' infringement as early as possible is not always the best strategy. Sometimes letting a competitor rack up violations and damages gets you more leverage if and when you file a claim. Make sure you talk to your lawyers and other IP professionals early and often.

Further, you should think about creating a vigilant internal monitoring system to guard against infringement of others' patents by your company. Few things can be as distracting and potentially financially damaging as going to court for allegedly infringing on another's patents.

Finally, sometimes inventors determine that an invention is not worth patenting but still wish to have freedom to operate in using or selling something involving that invention in the future. There is always the worry that someone else will file a patent on the same or a similar invention, and the inventors could find themselves unable to use their own invention. To prevent such a possibility, often inventors deliberately publish their inventions to add them to the prior art, blocking future patenting by others who attempt to incorporate their ideas. Called *defensive publishing*, this practice essentially involves publishing enabling descriptions or disclosures in such a way that time, date, and content are incontrovertibly documented and publicly available to prior art searches. Scientific or trade journals are one option. With the Internet, useful sites such as the Prior Art Database at IP.com accomplish the same thing.

COPYRIGHTS

Under federal law, a copyright grants its holder the exclusive right to prevent others from reproducing and distributing the protected works. The holder alone may reproduce the work, prepare derivative works, distribute copies or recordings of the copyrighted work, and perform or display the copyrighted work publicly. The law provides for recourse and monetary damages for violation of these rights.

A copyright does not protect ideas. Instead, it applies to the reduction of an idea or concept to a tangible medium. To have copyright protection, a piece must be the author's original work and contain some minimal level of creativity. Words, short phrases, and slogans are not eligible for copyright, although they may be eligible for trademark. Similarly, you cannot copyright ideas, procedures, processes, systems, methods of operation, concepts, principles, or discoveries, although you may be able to patent them. Authors have copyrights over original works of authorship, including the following:

- Literary and certain other intellectual works, both published and unpublished
- Dramatic and musical works, including pantomimes and choreographic works
- Derivative works
- Musical recordings
- Artistic works

- Web pages
- Video and computer games
- Software code
- Pictorial, graphic, and sculptural works
- Motion pictures and other audiovisual works
- Sound recordings
- Advertisements and commercials
- Instruction manuals
- Presentations and talks
- Data tables, labels, diagrams, and drawings
- Databases if originality and creativity are involved
- Business plans
- Architectural drawing and renderings

Accordingly, copyrights are important to people in media businesses such as print, film, music, entertainment, theater, and the Internet. Writers, artists, composers, performers, photographers, designers, and architects rely on copyright protection for their livelihoods. Under the U.S. Constitution, the author of a work owns the copyright. However, the so-called *work-for-hire* rule grants employers copyright to works their employees create within the scope of their employment so long as both parties agree in writing that such works will be owned by the employer. Independent contractors also can work under work-for-hire arrangements; however, absent a contract clause so stating, the individual authors own the copyright.

Copyrights remain effective during the life of the creating individual plus 70 years. Work-for-hire copyrights last 95 years from the date of publication or 120 years from the date of creation, whichever comes first. You do not have to register works to own the copyright; copyrights exist upon reduction to a tangible medium. To improve your chances of enforcement and financial recovery for damages, you should mark all materials "Copyright" or © with your name, the year of publication, and "All rights reserved." If you want to sue for infringement, you must have registered with the Register of Copyrights.[18] If you want to rely on statutory damages rather than proving actual damage, pay attention to filing deadlines.

TRADEMARKS

The identity of your company and all the associations that go along with it are an essential component of branding strategy. These can be among your most valuable assets. No one would dispute the value of symbols and logos such as the red and white Coca-Cola logo, McDonald's golden arches, and the Nike swoosh. The law provides companies with a measure of protection against competitors attempting to confuse identities in the minds of consumers through the use of similar symbols or signals of identity. These are trademarks and service marks.

A *trademark* is an exclusive right granted to an owner to use a name, logo, or unique design in connection with its goods as an indication of the source of those goods. When certain criteria are met, any identification used to distinguish goods or services from those of competitors can be trademarked:

- A word, phrase, or name
- A slogan
- A design, shape, or symbol
- A picture
- A device
- A product or packaging shape
- A sound or musical phrase
- A color
- A smell

Service marks reserve the same protections to entities that provide services rather than goods. Collective marks are used by cooperatives, associations, or other collective groups (e.g., Rotary International, World Council of Churches). Certification marks are used by persons other than their owners to certify a particular quality (e.g., ISO 9000, Underwriters Laboratories).

A trademark is limited to the class of goods or services with which the owner is associated. Marks must be distinctive in regard to the source of goods or services. *Fanciful* marks (such as Coca-Cola®) are accepted as distinctive. A *descriptive* mark may require that you show that consumers recognize it as distinctive.

Trademarks can be registered with the federal government at the U.S. Patent and Trademark Office, but they also exist under common law. In the United States, you use the ™ symbol to assert your common law trademark rights under the Lanham Act. The first individual or company to adopt a common law trademark owns the right and can protect it. Claiming common law ™ protection doesn't cost you anything in attorney or filing fees, but it limits your exclusive use to the geographic location of the trademark's commercial use. The first to adopt a common law trademark owns the right and can protect it. Since registration often follows when a product bearing a common law mark proves successful, you're wise to invest in a trademark search before creating your mark. Careful consideration of distinctiveness is wise at the beginning lest you find your later trademark registration fails on the grounds of infringement or absence of distinctiveness.

You federally register a trademark with the USPTO, which examines the mark for distinctiveness. If the USPTO finds your mark distinctive, you can adopt the ® symbol in place of the ™ symbol. The USPTO gives actual trademark ownership to the first to file in reference to actual use or intent to use. Once registered, the mark's owner can stop anyone in the United States from future use for the initial registration term of 10 years. A mark does not expire as long as it remains in use and does not become generic. "Escalator," "yo-yo," "aspirin," and "cornflakes" once were trademarks but lost their protection when they became widely used and their owners did not take steps to preserve their rights.[19] The initial term of federal trademark registration is 10 years, and you can renew indefinitely for 10-year terms as long as the mark remains in use. When a mark is no longer used for a period of over two years, the registration is terminated.

As with other IP, you need to respect trademarks owned by others. Infringement on another's mark can lead to all sorts of hassles or worse. Many big companies have people assigned to identify potential infringements and act to end them and/or seek compensation.[20] Take care to avoid names and logos that are similar to those of others; this includes plays on words or names such as Victor's Secret (Victoria's Secret) and South Butt (North Face). These are real examples that led to problems for small companies that thought they were being clever.[21]

TRADE SECRETS

Every business has nonpublic information it uses for business purposes and wants to keep confidential from outside parties, especially competitors. Any such nonpublic information can be a *trade secret*. Information commonly treated as proprietary and secret includes the following:

- Ideas and inventions
- Business practices or strategies
- Business, marketing, sales, or manufacturing plans
- Internal processes, formulations, and communications
- Financial information and contractual terms
- Lists and contacts
- Proprietary software

Formally defined, a trade secret is

(1) any information, including any formula, pattern, compilation, program, device, method, technique, or process, that (2) provides a business with a competitive advantage from not being generally known by a company's current or potential competitors or readily discoverable by them through legitimate means, and (3) is the subject of reasonable efforts to maintain its secrecy.[22]

There is no registration, formal process, or time limit for the protection of trade secrets. State trade secret laws provide protection and recourse against improper acquisition and dissemination of secrets provided that you have taken certain customary steps to protect your information. However, these laws protect only against unlawful dissemination, and you must take legal action against the person or persons responsible for wrongly acquiring or disseminating your information.

Under the right conditions, you can look to the courts to protect your interests. You may be able to obtain a court order preventing disclosure or use and even collect monetary damages or, in some cases, punitive damages. Criminal charges are rare. Of course, taking the matter to court is time-consuming and expensive, and it is often difficult to prevail; also, the parties you are pursuing need to have enough assets at risk to make it worth pursuing monetary and punitive damages. Thus, preventing theft of secrets is far preferable to relying on the courts after the fact.

If secret information becomes publicly available by legitimate means, you lose any recourse under the law. The courts do not protect carelessly made disclosures or mistakes. Accordingly, as early as possible, you should create mechanisms and practices restricting access to the information you want to protect. Have nondisclosure/confidentiality language in some kind of document that binds everyone in your company. Most commonly these are employment agreements, independent contractor agreements, board agreements, or confidentiality/nondisclosure agreements.

Further, you should mark all confidential information and restrict access even inside the company. In a court proceeding, the reasonableness of your efforts to protect valuable secrets is an important factor in the success of claims for injunctive relief or damages. Once you have significant value in trade secrets, you should consult with your attorney about developing a trade secret protection program. The program should indicate which information is secret, track employee and other nondisclosure agreements, and define practices for handling the secret information. Defined practices include the following:

- Restrict access to those with a need to know.
- Label documents "confidential," "proprietary," "restricted," or "secret."
- Create secure procedures to securely store marked materials on-site and track their use. Implement "clean-desk" policies governing confidential materials.
- Practice good computing and database security practices: passwords, encryption, and copy/read-only protections. Secure communication lines. Keep personal and business work separate on business computers and networks.

- Institute logbooks for visitors and employees using sensitive materials.
- Securely destroy unnecessary materials.
- Protect access to labs and prototypes.
- Take extra precautions when holding internal conversations in public settings or in the presence of visitors.

Former employees are the most common problem with respect to trade secret abuse. To protect against this, many companies require confidentiality provisions and attempt to restrict employees' ability to work for industry competitors for a period of time after their employment ends with noncompete language in contracts. This area of employment law is complicated. The courts must balance the interests of the company with the fundamental right of an employee to earn a living in the best available setting. Courts will invalidate an agreement they deem unreasonably restrictive. In making such a determination they look to the time limits on the restriction, the geographic scope, and the nature or definition of "employment." If you need to use noncompete language, consult a lawyer with good background in human resources law because an unreasonable agreement won't do you any good.

LICENSE OR MAKE IT?

Once established, any form of intellectual property (IP) has the potential to become valuable and make money. Unfortunately, realizing this potential is far from inevitable. IP by itself certainly won't realize anything meaningful. Whether the idea's embodiment is now a patent or a copyright, someone has to do something—actually many things—to create, manufacture, and eventually sell the product. That someone might be you, either by choice or because you have no reasonable alternative, or it might be another company because you have transferred access rights to that company via a license or a joint agreement.

Many inventors don't think about starting companies when they create a new technology. They would rather continue their research in peace, and so they seek a license for their ideas. Licensing, in essence, is renting your intellectual property to someone else so that that person can use it legally while it's still under patent. A license is a contractual grant that usually confers on the licensee the right to develop, make, use, and sell the subject IP. License provisions usually include the following:

- Definitions of the markets or *fields of use* in which the licensee holds the patent's right to exclude
- Royalty payment, equity grants, or some share of the revenue generated by the product or products containing the IP

- Often an advance, a minimum, a royalty, or another cash payment to reimburse for things such as patent costs or cash advances before first sales
- Provisions for allocating value among multiple patents in a single product
- Sharing of proceeds on sale or sublicensing
- *Milestone payments* to the licensor upon achievement of predetermined objectives such as successful testing, passing regulatory hurdles, and first sales
- Commitments to proceed diligently in developing and marketing the IP or relinquish it back to the licensor
- Definition of who will prosecute patent filings and pursue infringement claims
- Confidentiality and reporting

To maintain more control over future development and the potential financial rewards, some inventors keep their patent rights and build up a company to bring their technology to market themselves. In many cases, though not all, both licensing and building a company are possible. Thus, the first fork in the road that you probably will encounter in thinking about developing an idea is whether you will do it yourself by starting your own enterprise or license it to someone else. There are pros and cons to each approach.

Advantages of Licensing

- If the IP is developed and marketed successfully, the licensors receive a revenue share.
- Licensee does all the work, bears the costs, and takes all the risk.
- Licensee generally has the in-house resources and expertise to develop, manufacture, and sell the product.
- Licensor's IP may be only a component of a final product, and so there is no realistic alternative to doing it alone. Licensor is dependent on licensee to integrate the IP into a product, make it, and sell it.
- Licensors can focus on what they do best in their job, in their lab, or at home.

Disadvantages of Licensing

- Licensor loses control over prosecution and development of the IP.
- Revenue share is small. Royalties vary depending on sector and product but generally run 2 to 6 percent. Sometimes licenses grant equity in the licensee, especially when it is a small company or the IP is foundational. Equity can be a much better deal; the licensor benefits from the company's total future value growth, not just revenue related to its own IP.

- Licensing carries the risk of nondevelopment or being "prioritized out." Not infrequently, companies license a patent to get it off the street so that it doesn't compete with their own established products. Further, in bigger companies especially, internal competition for investment dollars and priority often means that ideas "not invented here" get shelved.
- It's hard to get a company to give you a good licensing agreement. Most patents expire worthless.

Advantages of Building Your Own Company

- When you start your own company, you begin with total control over development and your team lineup. Control is one of the key drivers to value.
- You have 100 percent of the equity to share with a team and recruit investors.
- You set the priorities; there is no risk of being sidelined.

Disadvantages of Building Your Own Company

- You have to secure the team and funding.
- You have to learn the business or find the right knowledgeable people and recruit them.
- You have no infrastructure and no established market.
- You must put an incredible amount of time and effort into the company, often without a guarantee that it will amount to anything.

Both licensing and starting your own company are difficult. There's no right answer for every invention or piece of IP. The fact is, the more you develop your idea before you take it to market, the more valuable it becomes and the less you face the risk that it will all come to nothing. A licensee is more likely to pick up a working prototype, and with better terms, than just an idea. A *product* entering the marketplace is far more attractive than a prototype, because you've reduced not only the technology risk but the manufacturing and sales risks as well. If you are actually proving significant sales, you've almost moved beyond licensing your IP and into the realm of selling a revenue stream and a company. Thus, if you really want to maximize your chance of a financial success from your IP, the early stages of licensing and starting a company begin to look a lot alike: The farther you can take development and remove risks, the more value there is and the higher the chances of success are. It's all part of the calculus of execution and risk both from your perspective and that of outside investors and potential licensors or acquirers; this is the subject of Chapter 6.

WHAT I KNOW NOW THAT I WISH I HAD KNOWN THEN

Bob Mighell, Tilting Motor Works and World Medical Equipment

Bob Mighell is the CEO of his own medical equipment company, World Medical Equipment in Seattle, Washington (www.worldmedicalequip.com). An engineer and avid motorcyclist, six years ago he invented a safer, more stable motorcycle with two wheels in the front and a rear power wheel, all of which lean into corners. He founded his own company, Tilting Motor Works (www.tiltingmotor works.com), to pursue his idea. His biggest decision was whether to license the technology or manufacture and sell a product himself. Bob describes his decision.

In 2009 the USPTO granted me a patent for my "Tilting Wheeled Vehicle." To monetize the invention I had to decide whether to produce the bikes myself or try to license the patent to a major motorcycle manufacturer. At Honda I foundered on a "not invented here" mentality; BMW had no interest because they were working on something similar. Two friends who licensed technology to different major manufacturers were bitter about the outcomes, which ranged from early abandonment to losing money in a joint venture.

In the end I concluded that my best path to market will be to build and sell front-end conversion kits, not complete motorcycles. This will greatly lower my cost of entering the market and testing biker interest in the product. In the future I may revisit the licensing question, working from a stronger market and negotiating position.

Some important lessons I think I've learned from this experience:

1. Hard as it is to get a patent (only about 40 percent of applications were granted in 2009), it's infinitely harder to monetize one. Only about 5 percent of granted patents are commercialized, and only a fraction of those are successful.
2. Licensing seems easy, but it's not. Between not invented here, lack of interest in unproven inventions, and risks of poor treatment, licenses are no panacea.
3. When you try to license a patent, even with a working prototype, you're talking to R&D people, who often see you as competing with their own projects. When you prove the market and are selling product, often you are talking to business development people, whose job is to acquire successful products and businesses.

4. The jump from idea to working prototype is huge. The jump from working prototype to production-ready is even bigger. Each step takes longer than you would like and is more expensive than you plan.
5. You used to be able to fund your company when you had a working prototype. Now investors want to see sales.
6. There is no substitute for true passion for your idea. People will want to get involved and help you for nothing just to be part of something on the cutting edge.
7. Persistence is a virtue. The road is long, arduous, and not for the weak.

QUESTIONS

- Do you think you have any of the forms of intellectual property in your business? Which ones? (Remember to be creative; it's not just about patents.)
- Have you kept an inventor's notebook of inventions and good documentation of the circumstances of invention?
- Do you think your idea is patentable? If so, test it against the patentability criteria. Do a thorough search of prior art that would preclude meeting the novelty test.
- Can you write down a sketch of a plan to protect your property and estimate what it will cost you? (Remember to include time and opportunity cost.)[23]

NOTES

1. Lincoln, Abraham, "Lecture on 'Discoveries, Inventions and Improvements,'" February 22, 1860, in *V Complete Works of Abraham Lincoln,* John G. Nicolay and John Hay, editors (New York: Francis D. Tandy Company, 1894): 113; reproduced in Gerhart, Eugene C. *Quote It Completely—World Reference Guide to More Than 5,500 Memorable Quotations from Law and Literature.* (Buffalo, NY: W.S. Hein, 1998): 802.
2. World Intellectual Property Web site, http://www.wipo.int/about-ip/en/ (accessed September 4, 2010).
3. Rivette, Kevin G., and David Kline, "Discovering New Value in Intellectual Property," *Harvard Business Review* 78, issue 1 (January–February 2000): 58–59.
4. Ibid.: 55–56.
5. Licensing can enable you to monetize an invention without having to do all the work of developing, making, and selling it yourself. We address licensing later in this chapter.

6. Rivette and Klein, 2000: 65.

7. Shulman, Seth, *The Telephone Gambit: Chasing Alexander Graham Bell's Secret* (New York: Norton 2008).

8. Grissom, Fred, and David Pressman, *The Inventor's Notebook* (Berkeley, CA: Nolo, 2008).

9. *Hybritech Inc. v. Monoclonal Antibodies, Inc.*, 802 F.2d 1367, 1376 (Fed. Cir. 1986) [quoting 1 Robinson On Patents 532 (1890)].

10. *Brunswick Corp. v. U.S.*, 34 Fed. Cl. 532, 584 (1995).

11. Ibid.

12. F.Supp. 740, 742 (S.D.Cal., 1994) [citing *Amgen, Inc. v. Chugai Pharmaceutical Co., Ltd.*, 927 F.2d 1200, 1206 (Fed. Cir. 1991)].

13. The U.S. Patent Act, 35 U.S.C. §112, reads: "The specification shall contain a written description of the invention, and of the manner and process of making and using it, in such full, clear, concise, and exact terms as to enable any person skilled in the art to which it pertains, or with which it is most nearly connected, to make and use the same, and shall set forth the best mode contemplated by the inventor of carrying out his invention."

14. 35 U.S.C. §102, "Conditions for patentability; novelty and loss of right to patent," (a) and (b).

15. In 1999, Amazon successfully sued Barnes & Noble, claiming infringement on its One-Click purchasing application.

16. Nondisclosure agreements are discussed in more detail in Chapter 13.

17. For more information, see www.uspto.gov/web/offices/pac/provapp.htm.

18. You can find the Register of Copyrights at http://www.copyright.gov/.

19. Bagley, Constance E., and Craig E. Dauchy, *The Entrepreneur's Guide to Business Law* (Mason, OH: Thomson/South-Western/West, 2003): 531.

20. Maltby, Emily, "Name Choices Spark Lawsuits," *Wall Street Journal*, June 24, 2010: B13.

21. Ibid.

22. Bagley and Dauchy, 2003: 489.

23. Opportunity cost is the cost of other things you could be doing with that time and money. The question is whether they are better spent on the other things or on the IP.

Chapter 6

Risk

Whenever the ratio of what is known to what needs to be known approaches zero, we tend to invent 'knowledge' and assume we understand more than we actually do. We seem unable to acknowledge that we simply don't know.

—David L. Rosenhan, "On Being Sane in Insane Places"[1]

Are you worried about risk? You should be. A new idea is not much more than a bundle of risks. Almost nothing is proven; virtually everything can go wrong. If you decide to start an enterprise from your idea, you may be exchanging a secure situation and a steady income for a leap into the unknown. Perhaps you do not have a secure alternative and figure your idea is your best opportunity. There are almost always alternatives to starting a company. Very few people have nothing at risk. Risk is everywhere. How should you think about risk?

WHAT ABOUT RISK?

What is risk? *Webster's Collegiate Dictionary* provides the classical definition: "hazard; peril; exposure to loss or injury." Other definitions focus less on peril, injury, or damage and more on risk as hazard. Still others define risk as a more value-neutral term that is essentially synonymous with uncertainty—the existence of more than one possibility when a certain outcome is not known.

Sometimes people talk about risk in quantitative terms, treating it as a noun, a measure of uncertainty, a set of probabilities assigned to different possible outcomes. The science of estimating probabilities and expected values can be very valuable, but failure to understand the full dimensions of risk and hazard can have dire consequences. Economists generally refer to *uncertainty* when they discuss future outcomes that are not known with confidence and *risk* when they discuss uncertainties in which some of the possible outcomes are undesirable. Although you can measure and express both risk and uncertainty as probabilities, your assessment will be accurate only if you have enough information. Unfortunately, this is seldom the case. Some people look at risks not only as present problems to be addressed but also as future issues to be avoided, mitigated, or even exploited to one's advantage. Seeing into the future is an exercise in risk analysis and risk management, but who can see clearly into the future?

Risk is also a verb meaning to expose to a chance of loss, hazard, or danger. The difference between noun and verb is an important one, a distinction between risks we *face* and risks as we *take* them. Some risks just are and can't be avoided, but others we choose to take, expecting rewards if we win. When you decide to embark on something entrepreneurial, you essentially choose a context infused with risk. Most choices in the entrepreneurial environment involve a calculus between taking a chance to attain something good and the counterbalancing chance that some things will happen that are not so good. The idea, of course, is to take the risks when the risk-reward ratio looks favorable and avoid them when it does not.

It sounds easy. All you need to know are the probabilities and the rewards. It's one thing to predict the outcome of a coin toss or a roll of dice. Although you don't know the outcome of any particular trial, you do know the odds, and, given enough independent trials, reality approximates the odds. Of course, most real-life situations are not so obvious or simple. When you face a decision involving complex risks, many times you can't know the odds. Sometimes you'll know some of the factors that can affect the odds and be able to use them to help you reach a marginally informed decision. At other times the best you can do is guess at the good outcomes and ask: What's the worst that can happen? If the worst isn't too bad and the upsides are good, you may go for it. "Entrepreneurs will most likely take the risk of failure if the losses are constrained on the downside and the potential rewards are high on the upside."[2] Still, wouldn't it be nice if there were a better way?

There is no perfect way, but you'll be better off if you appreciate the important difference between *perceived* risk and *actual* risk. Thinking about risk is seldom just a cold calculus; it triggers all kinds of emotions, and this makes it hard to untangle the reality of risks from our perceptions. We need to remind ourselves constantly that emotional perceptions are not reality, even though they can create reality. If your emotional reaction to risk is out of proportion to the reality in either direction—too anxious or too cavalier—you cannot make good decisions. The core of risk management and mitigation is understanding the future realistically, making the most grounded and realistic assessment of possible future outcomes, and making the best guesses about the probabilities of those outcomes. This is a matter of investigating, reflecting on, and in the end deciding what you really know versus what you are only imagining or guessing—again, epistemology. Or as Frank Knight, an important twentieth-century economist and risk theorist, said:

> It is our imperfect knowledge of the future, a consequence of change, not change as such, which is crucial for our understanding of the problem. ... It is difficult to think of a business "hazard" with regard to which it is in any degree possible to calculate in advance the proportion of the distribution among the different possible outcomes.[3]

Said perhaps a little more simply, you can't calculate the risks, but you have to proceed anyway. Taking risk is not an all-or-nothing decision in life and business, but it is ubiquitous and universal. We all constantly face and take risks, often without realizing it. Little in life is guaranteed, and so dealing with future uncertainty is one of the core functions inherent in creating and running any enterprise.

As you embark on building a business, you must consider all kinds of risks, even though you won't be able to assess many of them realistically. Nevertheless, it pays to keep them in mind. In their book *Technology Ventures*, Richard Dorf and Thomas Beyers provide a comprehensive table with five families of risk factors that start-ups face.[4] Although this list certainly isn't complete, it makes a good point. You'll have no shortage of risks:

Market Uncertainties

- Customer
- Market size and growth
- Channels
- Competitors

Organization and Management Uncertainties

- Capabilities
- Financial strength
- Talent
- Learning skills
- Strategies

Product and Processes Uncertainties

- Cost
- Technology
- Materials
- Suppliers
- Design

Regulation and Legal Uncertainties

- Government regulation
- Federal and state laws and local ordinances
- Standards and industry rules

Financial Uncertainties

- Cost and availability of capital
- Expected return on investment

It has been said that managers accept risks in part because they don't expect that they will have to bear their consequences. The same thing can't be said for entrepreneurs; risk goes with the territory. The entrepreneur takes risks every day and faces the very real possibility that the desired outcomes won't arrive. Unfortunately, the only preparation for dealing effectively with risk many entrepreneurs ever get—if they get any at all—comes from working as a manager or under one, and managers don't face risks the way entrepreneurs do. Risk implies winners and losers; it has personal and professional consequences. However, people don't often think through those consequences, ignoring or underappreciating them until it's too late. As an entrepreneur, it is imperative that you work diligently to recognize, manage, and eliminate risks as early and often as possible. Think clearly and constructively about risk—how to recognize, analyze, and live with it—and how to make it work for you. This is the single most effective way to add value to your idea and your start-up company.

WHAT DO YOU DO ABOUT RISK?

People generally react to risk in one of two ways: They are cavalier—Alfred E. Neuman's "What, me worry?"—or they are terrified—a deer in the headlights. Both are wrong. In a way, risk is your friend. Many people make good money quantifying risks. Just ask any insurance actuary or casino operator. Entrepreneurs make money quantifying risks too. Almost by definition, each risk you eliminate or reduce increases your venture's inherent value. You are the person starting an enterprise with little or nothing but an idea. The main value you bring to the effort is that your work will eliminate risks one by one, and that's what creates value in a company. The only appropriate reaction to risk—the entrepreneurial reaction—is to work systematically to eliminate the risks you can and quantify the ones you can't.

This means that when it comes to risk, there is no substitute for *knowledge*. Only by gaining knowledge can you reduce uncertainty. Knowledge allows you to know which risks are worth taking and which are not, how to take them, and how to position yourself to benefit from uncertain outcomes. Thus, the first step in dealing effectively with risk is to learn to gain that knowledge. The more you learn, the more you will know the right steps to take and what you can do to give your idea more substance and resilience, which after all are the things that will make it more valuable. But you need to learn not only knowledge that's already out there—information you need to find—but also knowledge that doesn't yet exist, such as customer preferences; that is information you must discover or create. This is one of the most important things you as the founder-entrepreneur must obsess about every day: What do I need to discover? What do I need to learn, and how do I learn it?

Learning is not a mystery, an autonomic process, or a lucky accident. You can be systematic about learning what you need to know, and this means essentially learning how to learn. Once you know that, you can figure out what's important much more efficiently and effectively and then work on achieving those things. How do you learn? A kindergarten poster put it succinctly: "Learning is 5 percent hearing, 10 percent seeing, and 85 percent doing."

A full 5 percent of what you learn on any topic you learn by hearing, listening to someone talk about it, or reading about it. All kinds of *heard* information comes from books, lectures, classes, and advisors; these are all great resources. The only trouble is that there is so much good information out there that you can't possibly access it all, much less internalize it; this is especially troubling because this information is only 5 percent of your learning. The main challenge becomes defining what's relevant. Sifting information effectively comes with experience, and you aren't going to get that by reading a book. Even if you could read and remember all the information out there, in terms of building your business and reducing risk, it's still just 5 percent of what you need.

A full 10 percent of what you learn, you learn by *seeing*. If you watch someone else do something, you internalize that action on many levels. In his book *Blink*, Malcolm Gladwell writes, "We learn by example and by direct experience because there are real limits to the adequacy of verbal interaction."[5] Psychologists call this *imitative* or *social learning*, noting that it is "a group of learning mechanisms in which observation of other individuals facilitates or enables the acquisition of a novel behavior"[6] and "the learning of an act by seeing it done."[7] It is almost automatic—hardwired learning. Numerous psychological studies of both humans and primates document the instinctive acquisition of innovative behavior by simply seeing others acting out those behaviors.[8,9,10,11] This effect is so pronounced that it spontaneously occurs even between species; chimpanzees, for example, imitate novel behavior they observe in humans.[12,13] If one of the best ways to reduce risk in your venture is to become a more effective entrepreneur and leader, you will learn the most about that through imitative learning. Observe people who do this effectively and successfully, who do it really well. The more you are around them, observing them closely over long periods, the more you'll find you can't help absorbing their behaviors and ways of thinking. If you can, recruit team members who have behaviors or skills you want to learn or even go to work for someone you admire and want to be like. Spend as much time with those people as you can. You'll be amazed at how much you absorb without sensing that it's happening. This is the 10 percent.

Then there's *learning by doing*—the 85 percent. Aristotle said, "What we have to learn to do, we learn by doing." Most of what successful entrepreneurs learn about their ideas and almost all of what they learn about executing, they learn by doing. This is the ready-fire-aim strategy again. Saras D. Sarasvathy, at the University of Virginia's Darden School of Business, studies learning by doing, a process she calls *effectual reasoning*. She explains the process as executing first and continuously, learning what works, and then building a plan and a strategy:

> *Unlike causal reasoning, which comes to life through careful planning and subsequent execution, effectual reasoning lives and breathes execution. Plans are made and unmade, cast and recast through action and interaction with others on a daily basis. Yet at any given moment there is always a meaningful picture that keeps the team together, a compelling story that brings in more stakeholders and a continuing journey that maps out uncharted territories. Through their actions, the effectual entrepreneurs' set of means, and consequently, the set of possible effects changes and gets reconfigured.*[14]

In this way, an entrepreneur learns about the potential opportunity. This is the market validation discussed in Chapter 4. It's the competitive research involved in a prior art search that was examined in Chapter 5. It's the effective positioning against the competition that will be covered in Chapter 11. It's building prototypes, creating proofs of concept, refining design—it's trial and error. For the first-time entrepreneur, this effectual reasoning, this ready-fire-aim strategy is the way to learn how to be an effective entrepreneur. Good information is 5 percent; watching others work is 10 percent. However, 85 percent is getting started, doing what you can, and correcting as you go along. Things like this book, others' advice, and what you see successful people doing may help you get started, but that's all they can do. Most entrepreneurs have this testimony. You just can't teach people how to swim while they stand by the side of the pool and practice with you. They have to get in the pool. G. Christian Jernstedt, the Dartmouth professor who studies learning, put it this way: "The one who's doing the work is the one who is doing the learning."

ON MISTAKES

One of the biggest reasons this is true is that mistakes are a terrific teacher. Peter Brabeck, Nestle's CEO, said, "The biggest problem with a successful company is that you don't learn from success. Learning from failure is so much easier." Indeed, in 2001 an Accenture study reported that

> [Seventy-one percent] *of executives say that aversion to risk and failure is stopping people in their organizations from acting entrepreneurially. GE doesn't promote senior executives unless they have a significant failure to their name, in the belief that if a person has never failed, he or she has not been sufficiently innovative or aggressive.*[15]

While Gregg was at Samson, managing geologists drilling for oil and gas, there were years when the dry hole percentage was so low that he had to tell them they were not drilling enough dry holes. Of course, he didn't intend for the geologists to drill where they knew they would miss. The point was that they were not taking enough risk. Without taking risk, you'll never reap the great rewards. Risky investments almost always command higher rates of return. A smart entrepreneur removes risks and reaps the rewards for having taken on a risky opportunity. George Bernard Shaw said, "A life spent making mistakes is not only more honorable, but more useful than a life spent doing nothing."

First-time entrepreneurs—and many others besides—often make the mistake of treating their ideas like babies. Babies are endearing. Babies are helpless. They are utterly dependent. Someday they will grow up to be clever, strong, and resilient, but when they are babies, they need to be loved and nurtured, protected from all the bad and nasty things that can hurt them. This is the way many entrepreneurs think about their ideas. They protect their ideas when they are just born. They feed and nurture them and protect them from harm until they are ready. They try to build as much substance into their ideas as possible and wait as long as they can to take on the hard risks, things such as, Will customers really pay for their products or services? Will the prototypes really work the way they need to?

The fact is, ideas are not babies. It makes no sense to coddle an idea. From the first day your number one objective is to find out as quickly and cheaply as possible if your idea has a fatal flaw. Basically, it's like saying you should not coddle your baby; you should take it by the ankles and knock its head on the desk. No one does that to babies to prove what won't kill them. But with ideas the goal is to eliminate the risks that will kill an idea. Remember the point in Chapter 3: The value in early-stage companies is almost entirely a product of the future upside potential discounted by the chance that it will fail—the risk.

Continuously ask yourself, What might I find out about this enterprise that would make me want to stop? There is no glory in sinking money into an idea that eventually is going to die because of a failing you could have found earlier. Smart entrepreneurs spend a lot of time thinking about their ideas' risks. Then they figure out how to test those risks, starting with the ones that are cheapest and most likely to be fatal, because if those cheap, highly probable risks are going to kill the deal, they want to know it early. This is the so-called *fail-fast* or *derisking* strategy: Do everything you can to take on the hard risks and put your idea through its paces. In terms of risking both capital and time, it's by far the most efficient approach to entrepreneurship. Every time you eliminate a risk that could kill your idea, your enterprise becomes a little more valuable; there's that much less of a chance it will fail. Remember: Effective execution to eliminate risks *early* creates the value in a start-up. Your ideas are not your babies; make them prove themselves early and cheaply, before you raise a lot of money from others and find the fatal problems with their money or, even worse, a lot of your own.

WHAT I KNOW NOW THAT I WISH I HAD KNOWN THEN

Dwight Keysor, Tales Mixed Drinks

While a student at the Tuck School, Dwight Keysor founded Tales Mixed Drinks to make and sell premium premixed bottled cocktails. He felt he could avoid the high costs of promotion and marketing with a local guerrilla marketing campaign. It was a seemingly simple concept, and he wondered why it hadn't been done. He thought about paying to formulate some samples and testing with customers, but fortunately, he first dug deep into the nuances of alcohol sales and distribution. It turned out that excise taxes on spirits in the United States are high, and two layers of third-party markups to distributors and retailers don't leave room for profit at the price consumers are willing to pay. In the end, he moved on to other ideas. Dwight says he learned a few valuable lessons from Tales.

1. Speak with as many industry experts as possible. Get perspective from parties experienced in your industry. You'd be amazed at how much people will share.
2. Thoroughly evaluate your value chain. Spirits companies lose most of their profit through incentives paid to distributors and retailers, not through expensive consumer marketing campaigns. Through digging deeper into my value chain, I learned grassroots marketing would never make up margin lost to higher cost of goods sold.
3. Question the need for every dollar you spend. Many third parties you think you will need to do validation work will want to be paid. Each time, ask yourself, Is this absolutely necessary? Can it be done without spending money? The formulation company I worked with wanted thousands of dollars for a detailed cost analysis. I already had a rough estimate of what my cost of production would be; there were other potentially fatal risks that seemed more important. I did a market study that was free and learned what consumers were willing to pay. Even if I reduced costs by 15 percent, the margins were too thin. I found the important answer that killed the deal and didn't spend thousands of dollars that wouldn't have made a difference to the final decision.
4. Separate your mind from your heart. The thrill associated with a great idea can be addicting, particularly when you're constantly reinforced by

those around you. Friends, family, and maybe total strangers will encourage you to move forward because they're excited about your idea, but that doesn't mean it's a good idea. It may be difficult to walk away from an idea after you've invested a lot of time and energy, but it will be worse explaining to investors that you lost all their money.

QUESTIONS

- What does risk mean to you?
- How well do you handle uncertainty? Can you make decisions under uncertainty? How do you do that? Do you do it in a timely way? How do you define timely?
- Do you feel you have to know how things will work out before you make decisions?

NOTES

1. Rosenhan, D. L. (January 19, 1973). "On Being Sane in Insane Places." *Science* 179 (4070): 257..
2. Dorf, Richard C., and Thomas H. Byers, *Technology Ventures* (Boston: McGraw-Hill, 2005): 125.
3. Knight, F., 1921: III.VII.1, III.VII.25.
4. Dorf and Beyers, 2005: 128.
5. Gladwell, Malcolm, *Blink* (New York: Little, Brown, 2005): 71.
6. Call, J., "Levels of Imitation and Cognitive Mechanisms in Orangutans," in Parker, S. T., R. W. Mitchell, and H. N. Miles, editors, *The Mentalities of Gorillas and Orangutans: Comparative Perspectives* (Cambridge, UK: Cambridge University Press, 1999): 317.
7. Voelkl, B., and L. Huber, "Imitation as Faithful Copying of a Novel Technique in Marmoset Monkeys," *PLoS One* 7, e611 (July 2007): 1–5.
8. Stoinsky, T. S., J. L. Wrate, N. Ure, and A. Whiten, "Imitative Learning by Captive Western Lowland Gorillas in a Simulated Food-Processing Task," *Journal of Comparative Psychology*, 115, no. 3 (2001): 272–281.
9. Voelkl, B., and L. Huber, "True Imitation in Marmosets," *Animal Behaviour* 60 (2000): 95–202.
10. Whiten, A., V. Horner, C. A. Litchfield, and S. Marshall-Pescini, "How Do Apes Ape?" *Learning and Behavior* 32, (2004): 36–52.
11. Zentall, T. R., "Imitation: Definitions, Evidence, and Mechanisms," *Animal Cognition* 9 (2006): 335–353.

12. Hayes, K. J., and C. Hayes, "Imitation in a Home-Raised Chimpanzee," *Journal of Comparative and Physiological Psychology* 45 (1952): 450–459.

13. Whiten, A., D. M. Custance, J. C. Gomez, P. Teixidor, and K. A. Bard, "Imitative Learning of Artificial Fruit Processing in Children (Homo sapiens) and Chimpanzees (Pan troglodytes)," *Journal of Comparative Psychology* 110 (1996): 3–14.

14. Sarasvathy, Saras D., "What Makes Entrepreneurs Entrepreneurial?" *Darden Case Collection* ENT–0065 (2004): 3.

15. Accenture Consulting, "Liberating the Entrepreneurial Spirit," 2001.

Part Two

Building Your Idea

Chapter 7

Building a
Business Plan

*In preparing for battle, I have always found that plans are useless, but
planning is indispensable.*

—Dwight D. Eisenhower

If one plan won't do, then another must.

—John Augustus Roebling[2]

Any business plan is about communication. Externally, the business plan serves as
a company's statement to potential strategic investors, major customers, and significant vendors or suppliers. *Everyone* asks to see your plan. This alone is reason
enough to develop the best possible plan early and keep developing it as you gain
more information and grow your company. However, although people want to see
your plan, they probably won't read it. This is particularly true for potential
investors, perhaps the most important intended audience for the plan. At most
they'll flip through it.

WHY CREATE A BUSINESS PLAN?

In his 2009 doctoral thesis at the University of Maryland, Azi Gera concluded that
venture investors do not rely on the contents of a start-up's business plan to make
their investment decisions. Instead, he found, investors seldom do more than read
the summary and perhaps skim the plan.[3] Brent Bowers of the *New York Times*
added:

> *Jeff Fagnan, general partner of Atlas Venture in Waltham, Mass., which pro-
> vides seed money for young businesses, said he agreed with the [Gera's] study's
> main premise. "I've never given funding to an entrepreneur who had a busi-
> ness plan with him when he walked into my office," Mr. Fagnan said.
> "Never. Most of the information you find there, five-year financial forecasts
> and so on, is not relevant."*
>
> *He says he looks for "market validation," hard evidence that the entre-
> preneur has actually sold his product or at least lined up enthusiastic poten-
> tial customers. Mr. Fagnan says that, rather than reading a report, he wants
> to hear the evidence in PowerPoint slides, whiteboard presentations or
> "somebody just talking."[4]*

To an investor, far more important than a detailed plan are things such as the impression the team makes, who referred the opportunity to the investor, the market and its validation, the presentation, and even the basic business proposition. However, although investors may not scrutinize your plan, they will skim it for the key points, and they may give some sections—those addressing key areas—a close read if they're interested. Plans are a qualifier, something that many people expect to see even if they don't do anything with them. There are other reasons building a good business plan is an important step in starting up, but generally one of them is not to close a financing. Other people besides investors—such as potential employees, future customers and suppliers, and strategic partners—will pay more attention to your plan and may read it in detail. These people are trying to get a sense of your company's substance before they deal with you.

In the end, *you* are the most important audience for your plan—you and your team. Internally, drafting and redrafting a business plan, especially for a start-up, creates clarity of vision, forces you to think things through comprehensively, and stimulates you to imagine a variety of risks and outcomes. It structures ongoing communication within your team, directs your focus to the most important goals, and builds consensus around a course of action. The exercise of creating a plan helps you identify gaps in your preparation and differences of opinion that have to be reconciled before the venture can move forward. You almost always learn something about yourself and your company when you write or modify the business plan. Most important, putting a plan down on paper early creates an accountability structure for you and your team, setting operational benchmarks and timelines for execution. Down the road, showing how you have met those benchmarks on time will be a valuable tool for impressing investors and other outside parties.

In this chapter we'll help you think through the elements of a business plan. We won't give you a recipe or a fill-in-the-blanks worksheet but a framework of things you should think about as you start. No pilot takes off from a runway without carefully going through the preflight checklist. You shouldn't either. There is no single template for planning, not even our framework. There are, though, key questions investors and others look to answer when they think about your business, and so we will look at planning as an exercise in answering questions. But remember, this is only a framework. In this chapter we don't cover everything you should consider. You'll need to read the rest of the book for that. This chapter just gives you some structure and guidance for putting it all together. Keep in mind that thinking through these things and building a good plan is not a one-time exercise. As you launch and build, you learn new things each day that will change the way you think about the future, and eventually those changes should make their way into your plan. Sometimes those changes will be small; other times they'll be fundamental course corrections that make the difference between failure and success.[5]

THE PITCH

Business plans and all their component parts are communication tools. Your ability to get things done is only as good as your ability to communicate your business to others: what you are doing and why it matters. Communication starts with a short *pitch* summarizing the most important points of the business. The pitch is not about telling a whole story and making a sale. The pitch has only one crucial objective: to get the listener interested enough to say, "Tell me more."

There are two kinds of pitches: the elevator pitch and the pitch sheet. The *elevator pitch* is a short verbal presentation that should leave the listener excited and wanting to know more. The *pitch sheet* is short, a one- or two-page summary—almost a brochure—that hits the high points, is heavy on layout and graphics, and tells your story in a compelling way. When people say, "Tell me about your idea," they're looking for the elevator pitch. When they say, "Send me your summary," they're looking for your pitch sheet, not a plain-text abstract or the executive summary from your business plan. With the pitch, you're always selling, not providing information. In Chapter 17 we discuss the communication practices that go into creating a successful first pitch and a compelling summary.

THE PLAN AND PRESENTATION

Sooner or later, you'll have to present your business opportunity and plan of action to someone—most likely a potential investor—and so you want to create a plan in a conventional form. But if you go out and look for templates or guidance to help you write the first plan, you'll probably drown in all the resources.[6] Fortunately, there is a consensus on what people expect to see. Investors and others interested enough to hear about your business have two things on their minds: greed and fear. They want to get excited about the potential to make money, and they want you to quiet their fear of risk. From the moment you start talking or they start reading, they'll have dozens of questions. A good plan and presentation answer the obvious questions before they're asked. Our template business plan is just a collection of these questions grouped by the subject areas that matter most to investors and others. If you write a plan and presentation answering these questions, you'll cover what people care about.

Plans typically come in two forms: a written plan and a PowerPoint presentation. Increasingly, people just read through the PowerPoint version. In plans and presentations, brevity is a virtue. Details never sell a deal. The articulation of your plan should be simple, significant, and short. A good plan and presentation focus on the key points and substantiate them. For the presentation, Guy Kawasaki in

The Art of the Start provides a great guideline he calls the 10–20–30 Rule: 10 slides, 20 minutes, 30-point font.[7] That's it. The written piece should be 10 to 20 pages max. Include all the other background and detail in appendixes, which can be as long as you like. People seldom read appendixes, but they can be valuable for reference or to show how thoroughly you have done your homework. One of our DEN companies was in a highly competitive space with a solidly differentiated product. In their 12-page plan they had less than a page on the competition, but in the appendix they included a thorough 16-page survey of the competition with a significant amount of both public and proprietary detail. As competitive as the space was, when investors saw the appendix, no one doubted that the company had done its homework and had a competitive advantage. Still, that level of detail has no place in the plan itself. Keep the plan simple, short, and significant. You should include a concise one- to two-page summary—an abstract of the plan—at the beginning of the written plan.

For the actual form of the business plan and presentation—the formatting, writing style, and so forth—we normally just have students look through our collection of good plans and presentations, choose one or two they like, and then imitate them.[8] Here we'll focus on the content. This is our template—basically a 10-slide presentation covering all the basic questions. Your plan sections can mirror this template as well.

Slide 0: Who Are You?

- What is your company name?
- Who are the founders?
- What do you do?
- Why is that important? Why do customers love it? How is what you do valuable?

Slide number zero? Yes, we're cheating on 10. The point is that every page and slide is valuable real estate. Information overload kills understanding and buy-in. Don't overfill your space with dense text and too many words but use every square inch and every minute of presentation time wisely and for maximum impact. We are serious about the 10–20–30 Rule. Use all your space to convey *meaningful* information. Even the section headings or, for the written plan, the descriptive table of contents should convey information. You want to use the opening slide to introduce yourself, your company, and your team. You also need to be able to explain what you do and why it is important and valuable in two sentences or less.

The title page is also the place to display your contact information prominently. Normally the CEO or founder is the contact. Believe it or not, people often forget to display their contact information. What could be worse than finding out people were really interested in your deal but gave up because they couldn't figure out how to contact you?

A quick note about confidentiality. This is a tricky issue. The information in your plan will probably end up in the hands of people you didn't intend to have it. Still, you have to disclose enough to give your listeners a fair understanding of your company. Also, Regulation D—Rules Governing the Limited Offer and Sale of Securities without Registration under the Securities Act of 1933—requires that if you want to raise money from private investors, you must, among other things, be diligent about controlling the distribution of plans and presentations. To cover both points, you should mark your plan copyright with your name and the year,[9] which puts recipients on notice of copy restrictions. We also encourage people to add a note at the bottom such as the following:

Proprietary and confidential. Do not copy or distribute to others without prior permission of [Company Name].

There is nothing binding or enforceable about this notice, but it sends the signal that you are expecting the readers to respect the confidentiality of what you are telling them and trusting them to honor your request. Number the plans you share and keep a register of names and dates.

Slide 1: What's the Need?

- What need are you filling or problem are you solving?
- How is this need relevant to your listeners and readers?

The best idea is a need that finds a solution, not a solution in search of a need. If your readers and listeners recognize the validity of your need, you have a solid shot at capturing interest and buy-in. Your need should be specific with a clear and relevant solution. Investors want plans for aspirin to cure a headache, not candy that tastes good. Further, to be relevant you need to present the need so that your listeners identify with the mind-set of the customer. You want to convince your listener that your solution is a cost-effective means of filling that need. It's much easier to win an audience if they internalize the need and picture themselves buying your product. Some of the best words you can hear are "Yes, I would buy that."

Slide 2: What's the Market?

- Who is your customer?
- How well do you know that customer?
- What is the size of the market?
- What are the key facts about the industry? Trends and growth rates?
- How have you validated your market and customer demand?
- What makes you confident the dogs will eat the dog food?

Ideally, this slide and section demonstrate the market's size and growth rate. You should be able to describe your customer profile accurately, including its key characteristics and demographics. You'll also want to present the high points of your validation work clearly[10]—everything that convinces you that customers are really going to buy.

Slide 3: What's the Product?

- What is the solution to the need?
- How will you make money?
- What will people pay for this product or service?

What your product does is important; how it does it may or may not be. You need to strike a balance between technical detail and relevance. *Technical* is not important, but *credible* is. Some listeners will want more detail to substantiate your product claims, especially if the product involves new or innovative technology. You can always add more technical detail. If they're interested, they'll ask for it. The key is to show you have something solid that works. Most important, you need to answer the question "How will you make money on the product?" Of course, profit is more than just pricing, but substantiating market demand at your price is incredibly powerful information. Remember the product elements from Chapter 4:

- *Product.* What needs does it meet? What benefits does it provide?
- *Service.* How will it be supported?
- *Price.* It's not cost-plus. Optimal pricing balances willingness to pay with volume of demand. Pricing is an art.

- *Access.* How do customers get it?
- *Experience.* How does it feel to use it?

Slide 4: What's the Operating Plan?

- What are your goals and how will you achieve them?
  - Proof of principle?
  - Development and validation?
  - Production?
  - Marketing/promotion/distribution?
- How will you *sell*—not market—the product?

Some entrepreneurs like to think they are really clever if they use a new business model to deliver a new product, as if a new and original business model could help them outwit the competition. Of course, any competitive angle must be defensible to be worthwhile, and this often is overlooked in the thrill of creativity. But there's a bigger problem here. You're taking two major risks at once: a new product and a new operating model. Risk is expensive. If you are taking a new product into the market, you have plenty of risk in terms of product development and market acceptance. Why would you want to increase your chances of failure by trying an unproven business model? The experienced entrepreneur tries wherever possible to take either a product-market risk *or* a business model risk, not both at once.

The operating plan is simply what you are going to do to get all the necessary work done, in what order, and on what timeline. Somewhere you will want to spec out carefully everything needed for each of these steps—resources, people, funding—but this kind of detail doesn't belong in the plan. You can put it in an appendix if you like, but the important thing is to have done it and be prepared to show it if asked.

Do you know the difference between marketing and sales? It's sad how few business plans seem to. They almost always have an extensive marketing section with all the elements—product, pricing, promotion, place—but few ever mention the *sales* plan. Selling happens when someone persuades a customer to *buy* the product and then closes the sale. Promotion can help generate interest, but salespeople make sales. Only sales create revenue. Your operating plan should explain how you will build out a sales effort and eventually a sales team. Also, your sales projections should always be grounded in realistic assumptions about your sales effort: costs, time, staffing, and projected yield per unit effort.[11]

Slide 5: What Are You Doing about the Competition?

- Who is the competition, present and future?
- What are your barriers to competition? (Intellectual Property?)
- How will you defend profits and market share?
- How are you different?

Competition is one of the burning questions that always come up quickly when you talk to investors and others about your plan. You want to answer this question before they ask it. Never say: "No one is doing this." Even if you think it's true, never say it. There is no faster way to be dismissed as inexperienced and naive. We have yet to see an opportunity that has *no* competition. Even the status quo and inertia are competitors. More often than not someone else is already doing what you are planning or has independently thought about the same idea and is right behind you. Even if you don't have those competitors, you will have people who will deliberately follow and imitate you—so-called *fast followers*. Bottom line: You'll always have competition, even if it's just the customer's thrift. We further discuss your competition in Chapter 11 and provide you with a features table example, which we suggest you use in the competition section.

Competition is not just a problem. It's also a great source of information and ideas. Study your competition relentlessly from the very start and never quit.

Slide 6: Who Is on the Team?

- Who will put this plan into action?
- Why are these people qualified?
- What is their track record?

As you will see in Chapter 8, the team is the single most important factor to investors. Be honest. No team has everything it needs. Show the holes in your team and explain how you plan to address them. Investors are not impressed with the terrific experienced person you will hire once you get funding. They want to see your team now. Beyond your execution team, your boards of advisors and directors can provide credibility, experience, and contacts. Next, think about your service providers: attorneys, accountants, and so on. Do they add credibility? Prominent, respected investors, if you have them, make great reference team members. The people story is so important that we'll spend the next three chapters discussing it.

Slide 7: What Are the Financial Projections?

- What are your assumptions?
- What are your projections for sales and costs?
- What happens to the cash?
- How are you set up to deal with your cash needs?

Think of financial projections as a narrative: You're telling your potential investors a story. You are imagining what will happen in the future as you carry out your plan based on as much detail and support as you have in hand. Let's hope you've done your homework and your numbers are more than just guesses out of thin air.

Your assumptions in the financial projections are far more important than your bottom line. Everyone expects the financial forecasts that make up your pro forma to work. Pro formas always work. Think about it: Who would project that a company will lose money and go broke? The more important questions are: What are the assumptions in the pro forma? Are these assumptions factually supported? How do they turn into good forecasts? Bottom-up forecasts are best. Build a sales forecast that's not just some percentage of the market and a growth rate. Build one that is based on the number of potential prospects, the number of sales calls and their hit rate, and the sales close rate per unit time. Remember Slide 4: It's not about how you market but about how you sell. You should show how thoroughly you've thought about that here.

Avoid putting too much detail into your financial projections. You don't need to show every cost line and every quarter in the summary financials. Make it simple to follow in a font large enough to read. You can put the detail in appendixes. Most people are more interested in the assumptions and their basis anyway.

It's always tempting to say: "These are really conservative numbers." You can say it, and it may indeed be true, but it will rarely make any difference to investors. Most people say it. The fact is, no matter what you use for numbers, investors invariably will halve the revenue, double the costs, and double the timeline projections. Just forecast your best guess with solid support for your assumptions and let nature take its course. An effective approach to the conservatism-optimism issue is to bracket your base case with two sensitivity cases: a downside case that shows the worst that can happen without failure and an upside case that captures how it might look if things go better than expected. This anchors the range of outcomes for your audience and highlights which factors in the plan really affect performance and risks.

Some people feel they should somehow estimate the company's value. Until you have a stable operating and growth history, attempting valuation is not a good use of time or electrons. Sometimes investors will ask a start-up to calculate for them the value of the enterprise. If asked, don't do it. It doesn't mean anything. One successful repeat entrepreneur we know actually packed up and left a meeting with a prospective investor when the investor persistently asked him to value his company on the basis of his prerevenue pro forma. He said: "Anyone who wants a valuation based on these kinds of guesses is not the right partner for us. Clearly you don't understand start-ups."

In your pro forma, show an income and expense (I&E) projection that sums to a cash flow projection and cash balance at the bottom. Financial earnings are not a focus in early-stage companies. It's all about cash. The general format for a pro forma I&E looks something like this:

Pro Forma I&E Format

Sales volume
Pricing

REVENUE
Sales revenue
− Any discounts, other offsets to revenue
+ Net sales
+ Other revenue
= **Total revenue**
− Cost of goods sold
= **Operating margin or "gross profit"**

OPERATING EXPENSES
Sales and marketing
+ Research and development
+ General and administrative expenses
= **Total operating expenses**

NET INCOME

NONOPERATING INCOME (EXPENSE)
Interest income (interest expense)

INCOME BEFORE INCOME TAXES

INCOME TAX PROVISION

NET INCOME/LOSS

Cash balance, beginning of period
Operating cash flow, in period
Financing
Cash balance, at end of period

Remember, start-ups fail only when one thing happens: They run out of cash. Show how you expect the cash to behave. Having solid and evidence-based assumptions rather than precise numbers is the primary goal of the pro forma. Most of the important numbers are just guesses anyway. Some people will ask for balance sheets too. Usually what people want to know is what your current finances look like—cash, receivables, payables, debt—and sometimes the ownership structure. Unless you already have revenue, balance sheets are basically meaningless. Ownership structure is better communicated in a cap table, but this can contain sensitive information and should be left for the serious stages of a discussion.

Slide 8: How does the investor make money?

- What makes your deal more valuable in the future?
- How might it end?
- What are the upsides and/or exits?

You are seeking investment; private equity investors are looking for a *return* on their investment. They don't just want to get their money back. They don't even want their money back with dividends. They want a multiple of the capital they've invested.[12] If your investors are limited partnerships, as most venture capital investors are, they have to deliver a return on their partners' investment within a defined timeline. This means that if you take angel or venture capital investment, your investors will expect your company to turn into cash over a realistic time horizon. A realistic timeline is in the eye of the beholder, but in venture capital, this is generally no more than four to eight years.[13] However, though investors do want that quick return, many say they won't invest in a founder who isn't building for the long term. They don't want someone who is in it for a quick sale, but they also don't want to fight with a founder over liquidity. Nobody said life isn't complicated. Normally, the most salable companies are the ones that grow dynamically under solid management, and so to some extent both views are right. You need to show that you understand both the short-term and long-term views.

When you're writing your plan and presenting your start-up, be aware of your audience's future expectations. You can speak to both short- and long-term interests by talking about what your company might be worth if successful. This is not a valuation so much as a description of how ownership interests might turn into cash. Think about who might be interested in your company. Most liquidity events occur by acquisition or merger, not by going public in an initial public offering. You also should think about your company's logical strategic acquirers. Not everyone sells to Google, Microsoft, or the current acquirers of the month in your space. In talking about potential future value and liquidity, recent sales of comparable companies are powerful, something like: "If we perform as projected, in _____ years, we will look like Company _____, which sold last year to Company _____ for _____ million dollars." A list of several comparable sales is even better. It shows an active market.

Slide 9: What money do you need, and how will you spend it?

- What do you need?
- How will you use the money?
- What are your milestones?
- What will you have to show for it when you're done?

You need to define how much money you are looking to raise, assuming that you need to raise money. This shouldn't be just the total number but should include a well-thought-out breakdown describing how you will use the funding. For prototyping and proof of concept? For regulatory hurdles? To hire salespeople?

Early-stage money is incredibly expensive. You don't want to raise more than you need, but you also don't want to raise so little that you can't get to cash self-sufficiency or raise more money on later, better terms. Big salaries for the team are a nonstarter. Your goal here is to create a work program that, when completed, materially increases your company's valuation and fits within the amount of money raised. No one wants to fund a bridge to nowhere. Think about the money you might need in later rounds, if any, and explain how you will be positioned to raise it.

Slide 10: What Is the Timeline?

- What have you done to date? What momentum have you created?
- What risks have you eliminated?
- What are the next steps?
- What is the timeline? What will you get done and when?

Unlike an operating plan, which looks at the global, long-term future and includes lots of generalities, next steps are concrete and are tied to a clear timeline. The goal is to communicate that you have an impulse to action, are prioritizing important action, and know the steps that can lead to an increase in your company's value.

You'll probably want to close your presentations with a summary slide of key takeaway points. For the written plan, you should include the summary at the beginning rather than at the end.

WHAT I KNOW NOW THAT I WISH I HAD KNOWN THEN

Tom Brady, Plastic Technologies

Dr. Tom Brady is founder, president, and CEO of Plastic Technologies, Inc. (PTI), and oversees the operations of six other PTI companies engaged in specialty manufacturing, advanced product development, and technology licensing. Founded in 1985, PTI and its companies employ 200 people worldwide, and PTI is recognized internationally for its expertise in plastic packaging technology. Every day you use products invented and developed by PTI. Dr. Brady sits on the Ohio Governor's Third Frontier Advisory Board and was founding chair of the Northwest Ohio Regional Technology Alliance (RTA), an alliance of northwestern Ohio businesses, public-private partnerships, and educational institutions with the mission of "diversifying our economy into the technology sector." Tom is now interim dean for the Judith Herb College of Education at the University of Toledo. Tom says he learned many lessons the hard way, including the following:

- Life does not always go as you plan it. Be flexible and opportunistic.
- Make financial management a priority.
- Leadership is about making others successful. Hire people smarter than you and be loyal to them.

- Knowing your business is more important than running your business.
- Never apologize for doing the right thing. Don't compromise on integrity—ever. Good reputations are hard to build and easy to lose.
- Listening is more important than being really smart.
- Owners make really good employees.
- It takes a champion to make something new happen.
- It is okay to fail.
- It is better to do the right thing than to do things the right way.
- Be the best in the world.
- "Build it and they will come" does not apply to starting a business. It's what the customers think that counts.
- Laugh a lot and have fun!

Your plan and presentation are never done. Your first plan is mostly hope, and hope is not a plan. As you learn more, get more feedback, and gain knowledge of the market, your plan should evolve and grow. But you should check your outcomes periodically against the earlier guesses in your plan. You can learn a lot by looking back over the various projections and assumptions you made and seeing what really happened. Often what you missed turns out to be more instructive than what you got right. Of course, in the end it's about execution, but good planning drives good execution.

QUESTIONS

- Do you think you need a business plan for your idea? (*Hint:* The answer isn't automatically yes.) Why? If yes, does it need to be now?
- Who are the main audiences for which you are writing the plan?
- Can you make an inventory of what you know and what you don't? And for what you don't know, can you make a list of which items you can fill in with additional work? Can you define what that work is?
- How will you ensure that everyone on the team proactively participates and buys in?

NOTES

1. Nixon, Richard, *Six Crises*, "Khrushchev" (Garden City, NY: Doubleday, 1962): 235.

2. John Augustus Roebling, 1806–1869; German-born architect famous for his wire rope suspension bridge designs, including the design of the Brooklyn Bridge.
3. Gera, Azi, "Do Investor Capabilities Influence the Interpretation of Entrepreneur Signals? Theory and Testing in the Private Equity Setting," Kirsch, David A., and Brent Goldfarb, advisors. Digital Repository at the University of Maryland, University of Maryland, (College Park, http://www.lib.umd.edu/drum/handle/1903/9617).
4. Bowers, Brent, "Investors Pay Business Plans Little Heed, Study Finds," *New York Times,* May 13, 2009.
5. See Chapter 20, "Correcting Your Course."
6. The day we wrote this text, we searched the term *business plan* and Google returned 775 million hits.
7. Kawaski, Guy, *The Art of the Start* (New York: Portfolio, 2004): 49.
8. If you want access to our library, go to www.greggfairbrothers.com.
9. See Chapter 5, "Intellectual Property, and Licensing."
10. See Chapter 4 for details on market validation.
11. For more on sales, see Chapter 16, "On Sales and Selling."
12. For more on financing, see Chapter 12, "Financing."
13. For more on liquidity events and investors, see Chapter 22, "Liquidity Events."

Chapter 8

The Founding Team

If I could solve all the problems myself, I would.

—Thomas Edison

It is people who turn an idea into something tangible. They get a product to the customer; they drive investment. Any time investors are asked about the most important factor in their decision to invest in one opportunity instead of another, the answer is always the same: the people, the team. Nothing else comes close. Indeed, in controlled experiments, investors make totally different decisions about opportunities if they have only seen the team present versus only read the business plan.[1]

WHY DO YOU NEED A TEAM?

What do we mean by a team? The word's origins lie in the idea of yoking animals together to do work. Today one might say a team is a group organized to work together. From an entrepreneurial perspective this definition is too broad. It lumps together two different ways to organize and work as a team, only one of which works in an entrepreneurial environment. Success in an entrepreneurial environment depends on dynamic, interdependent interaction between individuals or subgroups. In teams in bigger companies, people tend to work pretty much alone, coming together in meetings to report and coordinate. Perhaps these loose collections of specializing people are teams, but this kind of team doesn't work well in an entrepreneurial setting. Studies of entrepreneurial teams show that their members can't afford long periods of time apart. You need to cooperate and communicate continuously and intensely to be able to respond to rapidly changing conditions; you need to have the ability to integrate new information and opportunities in real time. In this type of team one member's actions directly affect everyone.

Investors often see start-ups in four parts: the technology or product, the market, a full management and operational team, and the investment. They want the founder to present them with the first three; once they have those three, they add the investment. One venture investor friend likes to describe investment opportunities in surfing terms. The surfer represents the founder's team, the wave is the market demand, and the surfboard is the product or technology. Obviously, investors like to see a competent and experienced surfer on a great surfboard commanding the power of a big wave. Unfortunately, life is seldom so generous. You could imagine a surfer on a wave, but without a board. He or she has a team and knows what the market wants but doesn't yet have a good way to fill that need.

This is not ideal but certainly fixable; a good team eventually will find the right product to serve the market demand.

Alternatively, you could imagine a surfer on a board but no wave. The founder presents the investors with his or her team and the product but can't establish demand in an attractive market. How appealing is that?

Or imagine looking at a board and a wave but no surfer: a product and a market demand but no team. Unless you have the people who can make the product into something tangible and put it in the hands of eager customers, little else matters. Or imagine a board and no wave at all—just a product, no market or team. It sounds silly, but you would be surprised how many would-be entrepreneurs and inventors present that picture to investors. When our friend is asked if he had to choose only one of the three—the surfer, the board, or the wave—which would he take, without hesitation he says the surfer. At the least the surfer can swim to shore and find another board and wave. Even if products or markets bomb, good teams usually figure it out.

Therefore, regardless of your interest in outside investment, if you want to build a successful company, your first priority should be to get a good team of people behind you. Substantial business research shows that when the social interaction of start-up teams works well, early-stage entrepreneurial teams consistently outperform individuals acting alone in a variety of settings and tasks.[2,3] In one study 83 percent of all the successful high-growth technology start-ups in the San Francisco peninsula were founded by teams, not single individuals; including all firms—failed and unsuccessful as well as successful—60 percent were founded by teams.[4] Teams dominate not only in the sample of successful launches but in their impact on performance afterward.[5] Investors look to the capabilities of an entire team, not just a leader, and pay careful attention to the way the team members interact.[6] Basically, a reasonably functioning team will catch the mistakes and correct the deficiencies of its individual members while retaining most or all of their good choices and positive traits.

Further, creating a company requires a wide variety of information, a rich Rolodex of contacts, and many different skill sets. Unless you are the one in a million who has everything your start-up company will ever need, you probably won't be able to build much of a company on your own. Building a team will diversify the talent, round out the business and industry experience, enlarge your network and contact access, and increase the sheer number, not to mention the quality, of ideas and possibilities you can explore. Beyond the tangibles, having a team around you helps psychologically. Team members can empathize with and support one another through the difficult times that inevitably arise during the launch. An entrepreneur from a Silicon Valley start-up said, "When you wake up in the middle of the night and begin to wonder if you were crazy to have started a company, it helps to know that others are with you."[7] You can't get that on your own.

A full team has many components: founders, early employees, contract labor and consultants, professional service providers, investors and lenders, and directors and advisors. In this chapter we'll cover the founding team: who the members are and how to create one. In Chapter 9 we turn to directors and advisors, and in Chapter 10 we cover building a team of employees.

WHO IS A FOUNDER?

Founder is a label with some amount of prestige. It carries connotations of creativity and innovation, determination, native intelligence, and a sense of fearlessness. Founders create something from nothing. Many entrepreneurship and start-up resources talk about founders, but most seem to assume that everyone knows what a founder is. In practice, it's not so obvious. Strictly speaking, in business, the founders are the people who establish the company; that is, they take on the risk and reward of creating something from nothing. As we discussed in Chapter 3, an idea by itself is not a company, but companies start with an idea. Some companies start out as one person's idea and stay that way. More commonly, one or two people have an idea but then pull in a group to help turn that idea into substance. The people who make that happen are the founders. They split the original ownership in some way and then work to bring in the resources they need to build an enterprise. Everyone who comes in after this initial ownership division is an employee. Everyone who is not a founder works for, partners with, sells to, buys from, or invests in the founder or founders.

From the very beginning you should ask: Do we have what we need to found this company, or should we find more cofounders? To answer this question you must look in the mirror and honestly assess who you are, the pieces you have, and the pieces you lack. If you've already started something like a company or regularly go out and do things you have never done before, you probably have a good idea of who you are and what you need. But if you don't, you should spend some time in introspection. What are your strengths and weaknesses? Ask some people who know you well in case your mirror is a little rose-colored. Here are some questions to ponder:

- Do you have the technical knowledge to put your product together or build your service?
- Do you have a business development background?
- What do you know about operations?
- Do you know how to sell?
- Do you know how to manage investors or anything about finance?
- What is your background in recruiting and managing people?

Unless you already have a company and investment that gives you cash for hiring people, filling these holes with employees is not usually an option. Some may work for equity only, but that's not usually the case. We understand that bringing someone else into your deal as a cofounder may not seem like an attractive option at first. If you bring them in, you have to give them part of the company and then work with them. Work styles may not mesh; personalities, goals, ways of thinking, and many other things may cause conflict. But not bringing in cofounders is even more costly. Learning curves are expensive; everything you don't know and need to learn is a cost to your company, including the cost of mistakes. There is no perfect answer, but in a start-up when you have to do everything all at once, learning it all is hard and time-consuming.

Once you know yourself, your strengths, and the gaps you need to fill, you have the beginnings of a team shopping list. Probably you will want one or more people—cofounders—to complement what you bring and help you get going. Of course, there's only so much room in a founding team, and so you want to consider carefully who you choose. Make sure that you know exactly what needs you expect them to fill and that you believe they will in fact fill those needs. You want to take care not to be casual about making your choices and later discover you have a less than optimal core group. Sharing ideas is fine; committing yourselves too early to becoming a company often isn't.

HOW DO YOU FIND THE FOUNDERS YOU WANT?

You may have a founding team already. By accident or by design, you may have built one as you created the idea. But if have not done that, you are in for a challenge. Building a great team with little more than an idea is no layup. Building a good founding team is hard work and is fraught with risk. There is no guarantee of success. Unless you have landed a fat investment and have lots of money to spend, you have limited tools to work with. There is always a tension in putting together a founding team. You have to try for the best people, the most experienced and talented, but at the same time realize that the incentives you have to offer are thin. If you are looking for cofounders, almost by definition, mostly what you have are a good idea and the opportunity to sacrifice a good-paying job somewhere for little more than blood and toil, tears and sweat, with the chance for a big win at the end and, one hopes, a lot of fun and excitement along the way. Not the most appealing package to everyone, especially experienced entrepreneurs and managers who have lots of options. But for some people, this is exactly what they crave. If you find some and they look solid, they are the right ones for you.

But if you aren't finding those perfect people, you might have to take Teddy Roosevelt's advice: "Do what you can with what you have, where you are." This could mean founding a company with someone you know well, a good friend or coworker. Knowing your cofounder or cofounders well eliminates one set of risks, but prior history and relationships bring their own baggage. Also, following this advice could mean founding a company with people whom you've never met but who have the right backgrounds and experience. You might not have your judgment clouded by a prior relationship, but unfamiliarity leaves you open to all the risks of compatibility, capability, and trustworthiness. There's no easy answer.

What should you be looking for? You want people who are passionate about your vision, can articulate it clearly, and are self-motivated to work hard and execute effectively. You don't want to be pushing a rope with your cofounders. Founders shape the company culture, its philosophy, and the processes that will go on inside it. They should be people who will set the right tone for your company or organization. Your cofounders should be good communicators, tenacious and creative, self-starters with lots of initiative and energy. Good entrepreneurs are opportunity-driven and flexible. You want people who work well with others, have a mature understanding of risk and how to deal with it, and are driven to learn and achieve. It helps if they have some special aptitudes, relevant experience, and extensive contact networks. Credibility counts with investors and customers. Experience and great networks are some of the most valuable assets you can find but are often hard to attract. Most important, you want people whom you want to be around.

What do you absolutely want to avoid? There are some obvious ones: founders with outsized egos, those who need to be in control, and people who require inordinate amounts of your time to do their job well.[8] It's often difficult to recognize these types of people at the outset, but they can make it almost impossible for you to do your job, and we know that's hard enough as it is. This is another reason you should date before you marry. You must get to know your potential cofounders well, in a variety of settings, before signing any sort of binding contract so that you can spot problems early.

Further, people with too much industry experience can create issues in a founding team. Founders are often tempted to recruit someone with an extended career in a large company. Although this can bring valuable exposure and industry experience, it also can bring the kind of big company background that is incompatible with the small company environment. Navigating structure and process is a key skill in a big company. Success and even survival depend on political acumen. Big companies' managers are often highly specialized and work under conditions that hinder integrative, creative thinking, trying new things, and taking on risk. These types of managers are used to having people and resources available to help them solve problems and do their jobs, not to mention the fact that overhead costs are much higher in bigger companies, in which overhead dollars often are expended to the point of wastefulness to get things done and solve problems. Of course, none of these things—money, people, narrow specialization, process, and structure—exist in a start-up. Investors sometimes say that big company managers suffer from the "white glove problem"—the assumption that someone else will do it regardless of what "it" is—and for good reason. Someone often does. If you are considering bringing in a person from a larger company, be sure you know what you are getting into and that he or she does too.

In the end, you probably won't find everything you want in one place. Remember Teddy Roosevelt's advice—"the perfect is the enemy of the good." With that in mind, where do you start looking? Your own and your contacts' networks are the logical place to start. For leads and introductions to good people, experience is unanimous: Beyond recruiting your own circle of relationships, the single most reliable and successful source is referrals from people you know well. Help-wanted ads are the worst. You'll probably surprise yourself with who you know and who your contacts know. Paint a good word picture of the person or people you want and then spread the word frequently and widely. Persuading good people to help found your company is one of the most important sales you will ever make. Success with the founding team is important; give it the attention it deserves.

You need to know your cofounders well before they become your cofounders. That means either you already have a relationship established or you take serious time to build one before you commit. Negative surprises can kill a team. Always check references thoroughly regardless of how people came to you or how they appear in the initial meetings. If a person is someone with whom you have a pre-existing connection, think carefully about your relationship. Are you mixing a business relationship with a social one? There is a grain of truth in the old wisdom: "Never do business with friends or family." Launching a company isn't like having drinks once in a while or even spending all your leisure time together. Don't assume that because you are friends and get along well, you will make good business partners. We've seen any number of social relationships put under stress because friends have gone into business together. Therefore, tread carefully. But to be fair, we've seen the reverse happen too: Friendships reach a whole new level through a shared business, and people with little or no relationship become great friends through the circumstances of a launch.

HOW DO YOU PUT A FOUNDING TEAM TOGETHER?

There is no hurry to lock people into your team. Inexperienced founders often rush too quickly into becoming partners and formalizing a growing relationship. One day they have informal discussions, and all of a sudden, the very next day, they are incorporating and issuing shares. This is not wise. Starting a company is every bit as serious a commitment as getting married and every bit as hard to unwind if things don't go well. This is why we feel one of the more important pieces of advice a founding team can hear is to date before you marry. It's important to take the time to get to know your potential partners well before you establish a binding legal relationship.

Unfortunately, just as in many marriages, when most teams come together to launch an enterprise, they haven't discussed important issues that will affect their future together. Just as the point of departure for you in Chapter 3 was to think first about your goals, the same thing is true for prototeams, except it's far more complicated because now everyone's goals not only have to be articulated and understood but have to be blended in a way that accommodates all the individual aspirations. Far too often this never happens; founders aren't even clear about their own goals, much less careful about sharing them, and end up starting companies for the wrong reasons.[9]

With marriage, there are plenty of counseling resources to help young couples talk these important issues through to agreement. Who decides? Who is responsible? Who gains? Who learns?[10] With entrepreneurship, if there were such a thing as a business launch therapist for founding teams (and we hope there isn't; founders need to save their money for more important things!), the sessions might look something like the following sections.

What Will You Each Contribute to the Team?

For some reason, cofounders often neglect to ask this question. They assume that everyone is contributing the same things or that they will work it out as time goes along. Neither is a good strategy. You want issues like this out in the open for a number of reasons. First, this answers the same set of questions that (we hope) you spent so much time thinking about for yourself: your assessment of what personal assets you bring to the team and the assets you need. Second, what people contribute to the company's launch should determine how they split current and future ownership of the company's shares. At time zero, pro rata might seem fair, but invariably over time, one or more parties usually end up making a disproportionate contribution and second thoughts start to creep in. Some of this hindsighting is inevitable as circumstances change, but we've noticed that if you look closely enough, imbalances are often evident at the beginning. As a discussion starter, here's a partial list of possible ways founders can make contributions. We have no doubt that if you get creative—and we think you should—you'll think of more.

1. *Money*. It's rare that a company can start up without spending any money at all. At the very least, there are some legal and miscellaneous expenses. Sometimes you need cash for early prototyping, travel, and equipment. The

team can all chip in pro rata, but for two reasons it's not wise to assume that this is the best way to do it. For one thing, you may not split the ownership shares pro rata based on your assessment of your other relative contributions. For another, the team members may not all be in the same financial situation, and some may be unable to contribute their allotted share.[11]

2. *Effort.* Who's going to do all the work? In a start-up, you seldom have much, if any, money to pay people to do things. One or more of the cofounders must do the work, many times without pay other than equity shares. This reality opens two dimensions to consider. First, there's the past work that has been done up to the time of incorporation, and second, there's future work: everything that still needs to be done. For example, inventors normally do much of their work defining the idea or building the prototype before incorporation, but the business development people and salespeople can't do much until after the idea is finalized and the company has been established.

   Although people often assume they understand the nuances of contributing effort, if there is ever a case in which assumptions can get people into big trouble later, this is it. People seem to have a natural tendency to underestimate the efforts of others and overestimate their own. Honest discussion early and often is not a cure, but it will help you avoid real problems in later recognizing effort fairly.

3. *Third-party work in kind.* Clearly, third parties are not part of your founding team, but sometimes service providers such as corporate and IP lawyers, accountants, marketing consultants, and Web designers will contribute some early effort to a start-up without being paid at the time, especially if a relationship or family connection is involved. Often, these service providers do this because they hope for a corporate account later or will take shares in the company instead of cash. You should make certain you understand which, if any, start-up fees and services the third-party providers assume will be paid in equity and realize that cash fees are being waived, not deferred.

4. *Time.* Any manager will tell you that time is not effort. Unfortunately, people can and often do devote a great deal of time to something but apply very little effort and so accomplish next to nothing. Still, the reverse is at least partly true: You have to commit time to apply effort and get results. One of the key early decisions in founding a company is how much time each of the founders is going to contribute. At first, some of the founders may not be able to quit their day jobs and work full time in the company. Others, for whatever reason, may be able to. Therefore, to avoid future conflict you need to not only discuss but clearly define this and agree up front who is putting what amount of time into the company and when.

5. *Assets.* Often one or more founders make contributions in kind to the company: things such as equipment, use of space, materials for prototypes, supplies, and sometimes vehicles or real estate.

6. *Intellectual property.* As we saw in Chapter 5,[12] intellectual property—patents, copyrights, sometimes trademarks or trade secrets—is tangible property that can have significant commercial value. Of course at start-up most intellectual property carries only *potential* value because you must create and sell the embodiment of that IP to capture its value. Almost always, inventors need to assign or sell their IP to the company for an equity share. Sometimes founders underappreciate the tangible value in IP that inventors are contributing to the company and fail to respect the fact that after making the assignment the inventors have turned over their baby to the company. For inventors this can represent years or even a life's work. They are looking to the team to turn the IP's potential value into actual value. Some inventors have a hard time parting with their IP and want to license it to the start-up instead of assigning it. Investors take a dim view of this relationship, and many will not fund a start-up that doesn't own the founders' IP outright. In short, the issues surrounding IP and ownership are highly complex and need to be considered carefully and talked about openly in splitting up the equity.

7. *Networks and relationships.* Many entrepreneurs will tell you that business success depends largely on two things: timing and relationships. Although you will work out timing together, some of your founders will bring significantly greater networks to the table than others. It is almost impossible to value this kind of contribution with any precision, but you should never underestimate the value of access. If you are the one bringing your Rolodex into the company, you should be sure the other founders recognize its value. If you are one of those other founders, you should be sure you actually have access to those good networks.[13]

8. *Start-up/small company experience.*[14] All things being equal, having someone on your founding team with successful start-up or small company experience is an asset. Not only is experience valuable to investors, it shortcuts a great deal of learning and making mistakes. Many founding teams find it difficult to assign tangible value to this type of asset, but they should be prepared to compensate experience in order to acquire it. Some ideas to keep in mind when you assess the worth of experience: its market value—that is, what other companies offer a person with that experience profile—and the total time, effort, and money saved as a result of the experience.

9. *Reputation and credibility.* Reputation and street credibility are intangible assets whose worth is difficult to measure, but they add a great deal of value in everything from dealing with investors and getting access to customers and partners to recruiting people into your firm.

We hope you are beginning to see that all these resources—and there are many more—are important to the company but are qualitatively very different. Splitting a company's equity is inherently a unit conversion problem. You must take all the different contributions and reduce them to one common metric: the equity share. To avoid big problems later, you need to be sure you list them all and thoroughly discuss their relative values. If people are not insulted at time zero when you ignore their contribution, they almost surely will be later.

How Should We Split the Pie?

Investors emphatically take the position that company ownership should be distributed widely and fairly among early-stage team members.[15] It's virtually a given that the founding team will all be significant owners in the company and its future success. For first-time founders and often repeat founders too, one of the biggest questions is: How should we split up the pie? This is a difficult subject with lots of emotion and expectation in it. To make matters worse, it's entirely subjective. There is no simple formula or mechanical process and no right answer. Nonetheless, it's fundamentally important to do the best you can to get this right the first time. It's expensive and difficult to fix it later, and nothing guarantees that it can be fixed at all.

To start, many business writers and entrepreneurs talk about the pie as if it were a single entity. If you are talking about ownership in the company, it's true that there is only one whole; you only ever get 100 percent to split up. But ownership can be split into a number of different forms. These forms—common stock issues, option pools, and sometimes warrants—carry varying claims on the value of the company. They aren't all equal ways of thinking about ownership.

On the surface, counting heads and dividing that number into 100 percent may seem fair, but it probably isn't. Pro rata is appropriate only if by some odd coincidence everyone brings exactly equal contributions to the table. There's no precision to splitting up the ownership, so in one sense, of course, it's a negotiation. But you are a team, and so everyone needs to be satisfied with the outcome. In thinking and talking through this process, there are three main areas to consider.

First, as we discussed, founders bring all kinds of resources and assets to the business: past, present, and future. Valuing those resources and assets is an important part of determining initial ownership division.

The second point to consider in splitting up the pie is founder motivation. Your equity allocation should help motivate your founders to give their full effort to launching and building the company. One good way to incentivize staying committed and contributing is *vesting*: earning your ownership over time rather than all at once, a subject we discuss below and again in Chapter 13.

Third, you should contemplate the possibility of changes in your circumstances, such as the addition of new team members or investment, when you structure the equity division.

How Should We Value Contributions?

To value the individual founders' relative contributions as one splits the pie, we often encourage our students and founders to use the list of assets from the previous section as a checklist. You should think about the relative contribution of those assets to the company's future value. For example, take a hypothetical software company interested in creating new desktop computer-aided design (CAD) software for architects. The company has three founders: a software programmer, an architect with significant CAD experience but little software background, and a former CEO of a CAD company with a strong sales background. They took the list of assets in the previous section and assigned each asset a percentage of the total equity without worrying about how much of each asset each of them might be contributing. To arrive at this percentage breakdown they spent a long time discussing how the contribution of those assets would increase the company's value. They might have looked at the assets as they are presented in Table 8-1.

Table 8-1 Breakdown of Assets

Asset Class Contributed	% of Value Contribution to the Company
Money (investment by founders)	15.0
Effort	
Past work done by founders	5.0
Work to be done in future by founders	40.0
Work in kind by vendors	5.0
Time commitment	10.0
Tangible assets contributed	5.0
Intellectual property assigned	10.0
Networks and relationships	5.0
Reputation and credibility	5.0
Share of company to each	**100.0**

Then they started thinking about how much each founder might contribute to each of those asset categories:

- *Money.* They believe they need $100,000. The architect will put in $25,000, and the CEO $75,000.

- *Effort (past)*. To date the architect and programmer have put in a lot of time building specs for the software; the CEO has not done much yet.
- *Effort (future)*. The architect and CEO have full-time jobs and will keep them until there is a beta product, at which point they will leave their jobs and go full time with the company. The programmer is going to work full time to code the beta software. Once the beta is done and they launch, all of them will work for equity until they raise a venture round or decide to pay themselves out of their cash flow and grow more slowly.
- *Work in kind by vendors*. Some outside programmers are going help with the coding for equity.
- *Time commitment*. Until the launch, the programmer will work full time for equity until there is money to pay him. The architect and CEO will work as they can in off hours.
- *Tangibles*. The programmer will contribute the computers and programming software the company needs to get up and running, and the CEO will contribute a furnished office and connectivity during the start-up period.
- *IP assigned*. The architect has two patents on new CAD algorithms for engineering analysis. The programmer has a copyright on a working software module around which he will build the new product.
- *Networks*. The architect and the CEO have great networks in the industry.
- *Reputation*. The CEO's last company was very successful, and he has a great reputation with investors.

Having done this assessment, the group estimates the value of each person's contribution as a percentage of the total for that asset class. They create something that looks like Table 8-2.

There is nothing scientific or precise about this process; it's important to remember that. This is only a framework to address the most important points and help you think about relative values as you try to decide on a fair allocation of founding equity. Here's the process again: Break down asset contributions into discrete, definable categories and assign relative percentages to each category. Then consider who is bringing what to the company in each asset class at a more concrete and granular level. Beyond helping you split up the pie, discussing and agreeing on this helps you create expectations about effort and accountability for yourself and the other founders. Finally, assign those contributions to categories and allocate percentage points to each unique input.

Note that in this example each founder's equity percentage ended up close to the default pro rata one-third. However, if they had started with pro rata, they might not have thought through contribution value and arrived at a solution that seemed fair to everyone. For example, without such a prior granular discussion, it's

Table 8-2 Estimate of the Value of Each Person's Contribution as a Percentage of Total for Each Asset Class

Asset Class Contributed	% of Value Contribution to the Company	%Share of the Value Class Contributed by Each Person				Comments
		Programmer	Architect	Former CEO	To Outsiders	
Money (investment by founders)	15.0		25.0	75.0		The architect will put in $25,000 and the CEO, $75,000
Effort						
Past work done by founders	5.0	50.0	50.0			The architect and programmer have put in a lot of time on spec'ing a project. The CEO has not done much.
Work to be done in future by founders	40.0	33.3	33.3	33.3		They will all work full-time for equity once there is a beta product.
Work in kind by vendors	5.0				100.0	Some outside programmers are going to do part of the work.
Time commitment	10.0	90.0	5.0	5.0		The programmer will work full-time for equity until there is money to be paid. The architect and CEO will work as they can in off hours.
Tangible assets contributed	5.0	50.0		50.0		The programmer is contributing computers and software. The CEO is providing furnished office space and connectivity.
Intellectual property assigned	10.0	25.0	75.0			The architect has two patents on new CAD algorithms for engineering analysis. The programmer has copyright on a working software module they will build the new product around.
Networks and relationships	5.0		50.0	50.0		The architect and the CEO have great networks in the industry.
Reputation and credibility	5.0			100.0		The CEO's last company was very successful, and he has a great reputation with investors.
Share of company to each	**100.0**	**29.8**	**30.1**	**35.1**	**5.0**	

likely that the discussion over money might have come later. In that case the CEO and the architect would have received an even larger share of the company, since they might have insisted on being treated as investors as well as founders. Or the programmer might have considered the equity division unfair, as he will work full time on the company at the beginning, funding all his own living costs, whereas the other two have only committed hours on the side while still collecting paychecks from their jobs. In every instance, the founders can look to the table and see where their contributions are recognized and, perhaps more important, see what is expected of them in the future.

What Are Everyone's Expectations?

Whether or not you get as rigorous as a prorated spreadsheet of contributions, it's critically important to spend some serious time and conversation getting to know your fellow founders. Having solid relationships in the founding team enables you to guide and manage everyone's expectations, an asset essential to the successful launch. Expectations management is foundational to dating before you marry. You want everyone to be on the same page with what you want to happen and when in a number of different areas:

1. *Roles and professional growth.* You need to think about and discuss the roles each founder expects to fill both now and in the future. Some people expect the opportunity to grow into management and executive leadership roles as the company grows. Others are happy to remain in technical or functional roles. After talking it through, you may find that some founders' expectations for growth and responsibility can't be met or that those remaining in functional roles eventually will become subordinate to other, later additions. Founders need to be aware of these possibilities.

    Further, some founders look forward to becoming a structured, growing concern whereas others thrive in the freewheeling, high-pressure environment of the start-up world and are reluctant to let it go. Without serious discussion, this can become a major point of friction and disappointment, even disruption in the company.

2. *Titles.* Some people care more about titles than others. In many start-ups, executive titles don't mean much because normally the founders don't have the experience that goes with those titles and there aren't many, if any, subordinates in the company. But because titles do assign a relative pecking order, they can be important to some founders and serve as a source of hidden friction or hard feelings. This may be an extreme example, but one start-up we know listed its four undergraduate founders as follows:

    a. Founder and chief executive officer

    b. Cofounder and chief operating officer

c. Cofounder and chief technical officer

d. Cofounder and president of marketing

   Needless to say, there was an e-mail from the last founder to the other three: "How come you three guys get to be chiefs and I gotta be a president?"

   Think about how the founders will feel about their titles and then balance that against how those titles will look from the outside. Outsiders tend not to take titles in start-ups too seriously, but grandiose titles can make you look naive and inexperienced.

3. *Compensation.* You need to talk with the founding team in the beginning about anticipated salaries. You should know and be able to manage what they expect for the start-up period, when there is often little or no money to pay anyone; later on in the launch, when money is available but very limited; and eventually in the event that the company does really well. It's not safe to assume, as many founders do, that your team is realistic in the same way you are about compensation in the present and future. You should seek advice from experienced people such as your directors and advisors and then talk with the team early and often to get everyone on the same page.

4. *Working environment.* Personal satisfaction with the start-up experience depends a great deal on corporate culture and the working environment. You can't take it for granted that your founders will all like the same type of working environment: One may like structure and order, and another may prefer a chaotic, creative environment. You don't need everyone to work the same way, but you and the team do need to know and understand key differences so that everyone can be successful.

5. *Important decisions.* Launching a start-up requires making decisions. It's imperative that you structure the decision making early or there will be problems with process later. Some decisions will be strategically important, whereas others will be mundane operating decisions. You and your team need to decide which types of decisions belong in each category. Then you need to discuss how you will make those decisions. Important and strategic decisions require serious accommodation of founders' opinions, if only because they are major holders in the company. However, you can't require unanimity on all decisions. Consensus is hard enough, and you will need to define what you mean by consensus on important decisions. By a vote? The vote is by head count or equity interests? Normally, shareholders vote by equity ownership and boards vote by head count. We encourage our companies to require a "supermajority" vote for things such as taking on a major investment or debt, big strategic deals or partnerships, and major divestments. You need to define what you mean by a supermajority. In politics, 60–40 is a landslide, but in a founding circle, owners may be looking for more protection. Your directors, advisors, and attorneys can

offer lots of good advice on decision-making strategies, but in the end it's about philosophy.

6. *Control.* Watch control terms very carefully. In most business situations, control is probably the single best predictor of who comes out ahead. In a company, control can be shared with many parties or centralized in one person or a small group. Never share control evenly, especially if there are only two of you. Experience consistently shows that this creates a high probability of trouble later.[16] There has to be a means of making decisions, especially when there is not agreement. In the early days of a start-up, you should discuss how much control the founding team has and how much it will delegate to the board of directors. Limited liability companies (LLCs) don't have a board requirement, but for corporations the responsibilities and obligations of a board are partly set by law. The type of control that founders want to exercise over their venture should inform their corporate structure choices as well as the way they draft bylaws and choose the board members. As a corporation matures, the board of directors will assume more control over the company to look out for the interests of all the shareholders. The mechanism for eventually turning control over to the board needs to be discussed early so that there's no ambiguity. Eventually, the board will exercise considerable control. We were involved in a company a few years ago in which the board eventually had to force the founding CEO to resign and make way for a more competent leader even though the CEO still owned over 50 percent of the company.

7. *Guidance and sources of information.* Founders should think seriously about and discuss where they will look for important information, guidance, and advice. Although most guidance and advice come from founders' preexisting relationships and past experience, not all sources of advice are equal or even desirable. Founders may not agree on the value and credibility of sources of advice. They should discuss this extensively and agree on sources of input that they particularly respect and wish to utilize. If some sources cause concerns or fail to engender trust and confidence, you should discuss this openly.

8. *Growth rate, scale, and funding strategies.* Growth goals create pressure and stress. Expectations for growth help determine how a company launches and operates and especially how it handles investment decisions. When founders bootstrap their company, they generally avoid major investment and "live off the land," but this often requires that their companies grow slowly and survive tough times in the early days. If a bootstrap is successful, the company remains relatively autonomous and the founders retain a large share of its equity. In contrast, taking private equity investments can reduce the financial stresses of launch and increase initial growth rates, but

it also decreases founder autonomy and control.[17] Sometimes it even means the founders end up out of their own company.

Growth also brings all kinds of internal stresses. The flat, unstructured environment that made the start-up nimble and adaptable can become unmanageable chaos if processes and policies are not put in place as the company grows. Founders often have very different thoughts about this transition from an entrepreneurial to a managerial environment, and hard feelings can result from misplaced or disappointed expectations. Smart founders think about and discuss this transition in advance.

9. *Exit strategies.* Some very successful entrepreneurs and investors we know declare great impatience with founders who start a company in order to sell it. They say that only people who are interested in building and maintaining a thriving going concern can establish a great company. In contrast, most angels and private equity partnerships are investing to get a financial return, and this means turning their interests into cash within a reasonable time frame by either selling the company or taking it public.[18] Founders can have very different expectations about the company's ultimate fate. The founding team needs to discuss and resolve these differences before incorporation to avoid disappointment or damaging disagreements later.

10. *Future stock pool.* You and your team must realize that you will need to share company ownership with the people who come in after you. Whereas at the founding you divide 100 percent of the stock among yourselves, you will need to issue additional shares and options for others, especially for future employees, very soon. To do this, founders commonly reserve a "pool" of shares to be issued in the future, commonly 15 to 20 percent, although it can go to 30 or 35 percent. You should start thinking about this early, especially if you are considering outside investment. You should create such a pool yourself rather than waiting for investors to do it, because when you do it, you will have more control over structure and percentages. Remember that although your equity percentage will decrease as the company grows, the real worth of your share will increase as the company's value grows.

What Will the Future Look Like?

It's tough to make predictions, especially about the future.

—Yogi Berra

The middle of every successful project looks like a disaster.

—Rosabeth Moss Cantor, Ernest L. Arbuckle Professor at the
Harvard Business School

Some start-ups lead charmed and endowed lives right from the start and sail to a marvelous exit. Many more scrap it out, starve in the desert, and barely make it across. Some never get to the finish line. Although some ventures begin with more promise than others, it's nearly impossible to foresee life after founding. All you can say—and we hear this time and again from successful entrepreneurs—is that it will be immeasurably harder than any first-time entrepreneur could imagine.

You should think about three things at founding in regard to this uncertainty. First, will anyone stop contributing to success or even hinder it but be impossible to remove? Entrepreneurs call these "barnacles": people who fasten on to the hull of the ship, can't be removed easily, and slow you down. Of course, no one starts out expecting to end up this way, but the sad fact is that it happens. You can protect the company from barnacles by having everyone vest his or her equity ownership over time rather than buying it or getting it assigned to him or her all at once. Under a vesting arrangement, a predetermined portion of the equity ownership is earned in each period of time so long as the person is still employed or in some other defined relationship with the company. For example, a cofounder may expect to earn 30 percent of the company over a period of three years, earning 2.5 percentage points at the end of each of the next 12 quarters. Normally, vesting is accomplished through a stock-purchase agreement containing a vesting clause which provides that on termination of the relationship with the company, the employee automatically assigns back to the company any unvested shares. You can tie vesting to any condition you can think up, such as achievement of certain milestones or work product, but this is usually impractical. It is exceedingly difficult to come up with ironclad definitions of success, and in the end most people agree that vesting should be tied to a continuing relationship that is governed by a relationship (or employment) contract or is at the discretion of the board.

Second, founders can face the opposite risk: indentured servitude. At some point in the future, a founder may wish to leave the company for whatever reason but feel compelled to stay involved long past the time when it is rewarding or enjoyable or risk facing significant losses of interest. This risk can be part of the initial arrangement but also can be a result of major dilution by the remaining owners after leaving the company. There is some legal recourse for dilution but not if the penalty is part of original arrangement that was agreed upon at founding. To avoid unhappy founders and lawsuits, you and your cofounders should discuss these possible future scenarios to get everyone on the same page.

Third, people needs change over time. Few people have the range of skills and aptitudes necessary to succeed in the unstructured, flexible environment of a fledgling firm and the strategic leadership and operational management temperament suited to a larger established firm. In some sample sets of successful start-up companies, as many as half the founding teams are not intact after five years.[19] In fact, it has been found that the breakup rate among founding teams is higher than the divorce rate among people getting married.[20] Some founders love the start-up world and, as their companies grow beyond it, recycle themselves back to the founding stage, leaving later growth and wealth preservation to others. Others don't want to do this. Either way, you and your attorneys should structure flexible ownership and founder-employee agreements to treat people well, reward their contributions fairly, and let them go when needs change. This flexibility protects both your people and the company from the repercussions of difficult transitions.

How Do We Put This All Together?

What do you do after all this talk and kumbaya, assuming you make it that far and are still all ready to go? Good intentions are fine, but of all the information in this chapter, the most important thing to remember and take to heart is this: Never make vague promises such as "You will receive XX percent equity in the company" and never stop at verbal promises. We strongly recommend that you and your founding team confirm all these major points, spell them out in great detail, and then write them down.

But before you do that, a note about writing things down: Unless you have a license to practice law, we advise against creating anything that later could be construed as binding, especially by mistake. Believe it or not, in most states courts can enforce as binding any document or even verbal understanding that uses words such as *agree* and *agreement*.[21] You should never put yourself in the position of making an agreement until you actually agree and are ready to document it—*correctly*—with an attorney. Never rely on handshakes and verbal understandings. People's memories are malleable, and unfortunately, money has a way of making this worse. Be careful. Mistakes here can be very expensive.

Once you and your cofounders have all approved a nonbinding list of these points, you are ready to go to the lawyers. Give your list to the lawyer to use as a guide and framework. This will help you get what you want written into the bylaws and key agreements while keeping legal fees down. In Chapter 13 we take you from here through incorporating, creating all the necessary documents and agreements, and hiring and effectively managing your attorneys. Although it's good to defer incorporation long enough to do all the dating and get things defined, you should incorporate before creating material assets, signing agreements such as independent contractor agreements or leases, hiring employees, and raising money.

WHAT I KNOW NOW THAT I WISH I HAD KNOWN THEN

Jeff Crowe, Norwest Venture Partners

Jeff Crowe has been a general partner at Norwest Venture Partners since 2004, focusing on investments in software, Internet, and consumer arenas. Before Norwest, Jeff served as president, COO, and board member of DoveBid, Inc., a privately held business auction firm that expanded during his tenure via internal growth and acquisition from $10 million to $120 million in revenue and 400 employees. From 1990 to 1999 Jeff was cofounder, president, CEO, and board member of Edify Corporation, a venture-backed enterprise software company focused on voice and Internet e-commerce platforms and applications. Jeff was responsible for all strategic and operational activities as the company went from start-up in 1990 to $80 million in revenue and 400 employees. Edify went public in 1996 and was sold to S1 Corporation in 1999.

As I look back on my venture investments, including both successful and not so successful companies, I see one overriding factor in all of them that heavily influences the outcome: the founding CEO.

In my high-performing companies, the founding CEOs have had some or all of the following characteristics:

- A powerful vision for the company and a passion for making that vision come to life
- An exceptional skill in communicating their vision and passion in a way that inspires others to listen to them, follow them, and buy from them
- Great entrepreneurial instincts and fundamental business judgment
- The ability to attract top talent—in many cases, people who are better than they are—and to retain and motivate that talent
- Intimate knowledge of the customers and markets they aim to serve
- Remarkable energy and work ethic
- A penchant for speed of execution, combined with flexibility
- An optimistic nature combined with an ability to withstand disappointment and come back fighting

It is rare for a founding CEO to have every one of these characteristics, but the successful founders have most of them. At the end of the day, they are both strong leaders and sharp businesspeople.

Ironically, even in my less than stellar investments, the founding CEOs have had several of these qualities that are ingredients of success. However, in each case it has turned out that these CEOs lacked a couple of characteristics that ultimately proved to be critical. The missing qualities usually involved some combination of misreading customers and markets, mediocre hiring, inability to quickly change direction, and inconsistent business judgment. The misses almost never resulted from these CEOs having insufficient energy, work ethic, optimism, or persistence.

Given my experiences as a venture investor and having been a founding CEO myself, I think that it is important for founding CEOs to continually do an honest self-assessment, a real gut check, at each stage of the company's growth. How do you stack up against the CEO determinants of success? Your personal scorecard is a likely indicator of how your company will fare.

WHAT I KNOW NOW THAT I WISH I HAD KNOWN THEN

Tim Healy, CEO and Chairman of the Board, and David Brewster, President, EnerNOC, Inc.

Founded in 2001 by Tim Healy and David Brewster while they were students at Dartmouth's Tuck School of Business, EnerNOC has grown exponentially to become a leading national provider of energy management for utilities, commercial, institutional, and industrial customers. The company conducted a successful initial public offering in 2007 and in 2010 generated profits on nearly $300 million in annual revenue.

Prior to EnerNOC, Tim worked in the Energy Technology Laboratory for Northern Power Systems, Inc., Merrill Lynch, International Fuel Cells (now UTC Fuel Cells), and Commonwealth Capital Ventures, an early stage technology venture capital firm. Shortly after graduating from Dartmouth, he cofounded Student Advantage, which went public in 1999.

Prior to EnerNOC, David worked at Beacon Power Corporation. David also evaluated emerging energy technologies for Winslow Management Company, an environmentally-focused investment management firm, and developed corporate strategies for SolarBank, a global capital fund for the financing of solar energy systems.

Starting with just themselves, and then a skeleton staff in Boston, they built a stellar company of over 500 employees, and still continue to grow. They offer these lessons-learned on building a solid foundation for that kind of success:

The right foundation from the start is critical. If you find you have any below-average leaders, shed them at once. Otherwise, the longer they are part of the team, the more rapidly they will multiply the number of average and below-average people in the organization. Start-ups cannot afford that.

Interviewing with excellence matters. Don't hurry. Take your time to find the ideal, highly motivated person. The right people will become passionate about your business. They won't let a deliberate process stand in the way of joining you, even if it means enduring a lengthy process. At EnerNOC we have candidates interview with as many people at our firm as we can—including the people they will manage. Good managers should want to know their players—let manager candidates meet as many as possible and make sure everyone's input is considered and valued. A baseball manager or football coach who gains immediate respect of his team by meeting with them before the season starts will understand them as persons, not just players, developing the rapport to coach them to their highest levels when the games matter.

Continuity is key. An offensive line in football is just five people who usually hold the key to whether plays can be successful or total busts. The best offensive lines generally have members with an intimate understanding of one another that only comes from years of playing together. The ability to work together, to understand where everyone will be during the play, to interpret unspoken signals, to assist the right man at the right time instinctively—lines with the longest continuity do this effortlessly, unconsciously, and consistently over time.

In the same way, founders and, later, leadership teams with continuity have learned how their teammates think, and how best to work together to solve challenges as they arise. They understand one another, interpret unspoken signals in meetings, work in concert to win opportunities as they materialize in real time. They understand the competition's tendencies and react together to meet them. Continuity ensures that an ability to work effectively as a team forms and improves over time. This is a unique competitive advantage. Many great teams can point to longevity of playing or working together as an element of their success.

Once you and your cofounders commit and form the company, this solid foundation of relationship and culture that you have laid together will pay continuing dividends in helping you work effectively as a team. Any relationship worth having requires hard work. Remember to support and affirm each other and never take each other for granted. This might sound touchy-feely, but it's important. Further, teams need good leadership to function properly. In a start-up, leadership often shifts between team members, depending on the context, so each team member will both lead and follow at various points along the way. The best leaders see their function as helping others do what needs to be done. They serve the people around them and ensure that everyone has what's needed to do things well. They facilitate, exhort, and serve their team, coming alongside to help individual members perform at the highest level. But leaders can be effective only if others are willing to follow them. Building a good ethic of followership in which team members affirm the leader and pull together to get things done is necessary to the success of the venture.

QUESTIONS

- If you are going to put together a team, can each of you each write an open letter to the other members describing your goals for the enterprise, your reasons for joining, and what you think success means to you?
- Have you talked candidly with each other about how you will work together, make decisions, resolve conflicts, and bring in new members?
- Have you dated before you start incorporating and splitting up ownership?

NOTES

1. Pentland, Alex, *Honest Signals* (Cambridge, MA: MIT Press, 2008): vii–ix.
2. Lechler, Thomas, "Social Interaction: A Determinant of Entrepreneurial Team Venture Success," *Small Business Economics* 16 (2001): 263–278.
3. Hackman, J. R., "Why Teams Don't Work," Chapter 12 in *Theory and Research in Small Groups*, R. Scott Tyndale, ed. (New York: Plenum Press, 1998): 245–267.
4. Cooper, Arnold C., and Albert V. Bruno, "Success among High-Technology Firms," *Business Horizons* 20 (April 1977):16–22.
5. Timmons, Jeffry A., "Careful Self-Analysis and Team Assessment Can Aid Entrepreneurs," *Harvard Business Review* 57, no. 6 (1979): 198–206.
6. Kamm, Judith B., et al., "Entrepreneurial Teams in New Venture Creation: A Research Agenda," *Entrepreneurship Theory and Practice* 14, no. 4 (1990): 7–17.

7. Cooper and Bruno, 1977: 21.

8. Robbins, William, *Seed-Stage Venture Investing* (Boston: Aspatore, 2006): 56–57.

9. Timmons, 1979: 199.

10. Hackman, 1998: 261.

11. A side note about money in the founding team: There are two ways to put money into your start-up: as a loan or as start-up capital. If you lend the money to your company, you can take that money out at any point in the future as a loan repayment without paying tax. In contrast, if you put the money into the company as start-up capital, it becomes part of your basis, and if you want that money out at some point in the future before selling the company, you will have to take it out as a dividend or compensation and in either case pay income tax on it.

12. Chapter 5 discusses these issues in greater detail and provides additional resources.

13. See Chapter 9 for more information on networks and relationships.

14. We address industry experience later in this chapter.

15. Mamis, Robert A., "Golden Handcuffs (Using Stock Options to Hold Key Employees)," *Inc.* 5 (1983): 59–64.

16. Thurston, Philip H., "When Partners Fall Out," *Harvard Business Review* 64, no. 6 (1986): 24–29.

17. In Chapter 12 we cover investment issues in greater detail. Particularly, we discuss some of the advantages and disadvantages that private equity investors bring to companies.

18. Taking a company public is a rare occurrence. See Chapter 22.

19. Cooper and Bruno, 1977: 18.

20. Timmons, 1979: 202.

21. We discuss binding documents and agreements in greater detail in Chapter 13.

Chapter 9

Building Boards

A word to the wise ain't necessary, it's the stupid ones who need the advice.

—Bill Cosby

Early-stage companies generally gather a board of directors and at least one board of advisors. Directors and advisors should be one of the most trusted and useful sources of guidance, experience, and information for a founding team, Experienced, technologically knowledgeable, highly regarded entrepreneurs lend legitimacy to a start-up and help bring investment into the company. The choice of both directors and advisors is critically important and has a lasting effect on an enterprise's future. The two boards have very different responsibilities and compositions. By statute, the board of directors has a structure and certain legal responsibilities to govern and maintain the financial health of the company. Advisors aren't necessarily part of a formal board and have no particular official duties. In this chapter we will look at advisors and directors in some detail, focusing on why you need them, what they do, how to choose them wisely, and how to use them effectively.

THE BOARD OF DIRECTORS

Why do you need a board of directors? For starters, if you've decided to incorporate as a corporation, the law requires that you have a board of directors. If you've decided to incorporate as a limited liability corporation (LLC),[1] the law doesn't require you to have a board, but start-up LLCs often build one anyway. The first board of directors typically contains a combination of people who work at the company—typically one or more founders during the start-up period—and outside individuals who have no operating role in the company. Also, investor groups, if the company has any, often take one or two seats. In accordance with corporate bylaws, shareholders elect the board of directors to fulfill a number of duties. The law specifically stipulates some of these duties, and custom and usage support others.

THE ROLES AND RESPONSIBILITIES OF THE BOARD

The list following shows how the board members represent and protect the interests of all the shareholders:

Legal Duties and Liabilities of Directors

- *Duty of loyalty.* The directors must act only in the corporation's and share-holders' best interest. They must never use their positions to put their own interests ahead of those of the shareholders.
- *Duty of care and oversight.* The directors must make a reasonable effort, using customary business judgment, to promote the success of the corpo-ration and make informed decisions. They also should oversee the corpo-ration's financial activities and confirm that processes and procedures are in place to ensure that financial activities and reporting are appropriate and compliant as well as prevent illegal activity.

Formal Responsibilities

- Approve and amend the bylaws.
- Select and appoint officers.
- Review and approve significant financial transactions and declare dividends.
- Review and approve financial statements and audits.
- Oversee the affairs of the corporation.

Informal Contributions

- *Guidance.* Supplement the team's knowledge and expertise; provide coun-seling and advice.
- *Signaling.* Lend credibility and legitimacy.
- *Relationships.* Provide contacts and networking for business development, people, and funding.

WHAT DO YOU LOOK FOR IN A DIRECTOR?

You have to build your board of directors; no one else is going to do it for you. It's not easy, but what follows should help you work through the process. Think about who you want, recruit them deliberately, and, as your enterprise slowly gains sub-stance, climb the quality ladder.

There is no hurry to build a big board. It's far easier to add directors than to shed them. The more your company grows and proves itself, the higher you can reach in recruiting members. Also, small boards are easier to work with and man-age, though small boards make it harder to get a quorum for some meetings if the members are busy people. You can't have binding votes without a quorum.

Once you've incorporated, a good rule of thumb is to start with five board members and eventually increase that number to seven or even nine. We think it's a good idea to have your five directors in place before you raise outside capital. This way you've had a chance to put your stamp on the board composition before you bring in investors, who usually want a seat and will influence many aspects of the company, including future board additions. Bringing in external parties early may be uncomfortable at first, but it's advantageous for outside directors to outnumber those who hold operating roles in the company.

You want to bring a great many things into your company through the board, but if two directors are from the founder group, you have only a small number of seats to work with. The more assets you can find in any single person, the better. If you don't have everything you need on the board, you will have gaps in your resource base. Because you don't want to be without, you'll have to fill those gaps elsewhere. As you look for potential board members, frequently remind yourself of everything you need so that you don't waste a seat.

But what do you need? Here by no means a complete list and you cannot expect every candidate to have all of them, but you'll want to think carefully about at least these few characteristics and try to get as many as you can in the collection of your members:

- Previous entrepreneurial experience building a successful company
- General business, particularly management and strategic, experience
- Technical/industry expertise
- Reputation and a network of valuable relationships
- An intimate understanding of the customers and market
- An accounting/financial background for oversight and planning
- Gender, background, and cultural diversity to reduce chances of mistakes from groupthink
- Wisdom and zeal for learning new things
- A service provider or strategic partner for perspective and access to resources

Beyond the technical assets board members can bring to the table, character and personality matter immensely. Look for people with whom you and the rest of your team work well, but perhaps even more important, remember that the board will serve in many circles as the face of your company. Recruit directors who will be a positive personification. A small company must manage its message and public image relentlessly in every sphere, but many founders overlook the board as a key resource for doing this. Although you can't control what your directors say or do, you certainly have control over the choice of members. The people on the board should be insightful, reflective, and observant. You should be able to speak openly with your directors in both good circumstances and bad, certain that they will respect your confidentiality and offer good advice. You must be able to rely on them and know they will stand with your company and keep its best interests at heart.

We also suggest that you seek directors who have a well-developed sense of integrity and care deeply for other people. Although the success of your venture may not depend on the board members' sense of justice or morality—some successful companies choose a very different profile—when your directors exhibit integrity and care for others, they probably will treat you the same way. Remember, you will turn control of the company over to the board when you incorporate. You need to be able to answer the question: Will this person do the right thing for the company and for the other people involved, even if it's hard? This is not just a hypothetical question. In Chapter 8 we mentioned an incident in which Gregg served on a board that realized it had to fire the founding CEO, who still owned over 50 percent of the company. It was not an easy decision to make, but in the end everyone, including the CEO, agreed it was the right thing to do.

A director will spend somewhere between four and eight workdays a year on board activities, inclusive of preparation, meetings, and between-meetings communications. Unfortunately, anyone who fits the right technical and character profile probably won't have a lot of extra time. On the basis of what you know, how available do you think they will be? You should be vigilant about respecting their time and not wasting it so that you can access their time when you really need it.

Your board needs will change as the company develops. When the company is fighting for its life and trying to establish a beachhead, the most valuable directors have access to resources, have experience in strategy development, and know how to consolidate the vision and build an execution plan. As the company takes root, a good board will help it navigate the transition from a start-up to a sustainable, growing company. In more mature stages, you need a board with systems management and higher-level finance experience to keep the company on a positive trajectory. It's always advantageous to include people who have taken a company across one or more of these transitions. Finally, although this may seem counterintuitive, having directors who have made mistakes and learned from them is exceptionally valuable at all stages of a company's life. These people are particularly well equipped to help you avoid repeating their mistakes or, one hopes, making too many of your own.

HOW DO YOU PUT A BOARD TOGETHER?

Identifying desirable candidates is the first task in assembling the board. This may seem obvious, but you would be surprised how many start-ups just grab some people they know and cobble a board together so they can get on with what they think are more important things. If ever there was a time to be diligent and do things thoroughly and deliberately, this is it. At the founding stage, everyone—founders, other directors, employees, anyone you know and trust—should help you look.

Cast your net as wide as is possible and practical. Your own networks and relationships can be good sources of directors, but those people shouldn't be the only ones you consider. It's exceedingly rare to find the most qualified people with the full range of backgrounds and experiences you need within your circle of friends and acquaintances. Seek out honest and insightful input on your candidates. This probably seems self-evident, but in reality honest assessments of people can be hard to find. Unless you prod, people tend to avoid giving fully candid and balanced opinions of a candidate's strengths *and* weaknesses. Also, professional investors, even if they are not your own investors, can be an excellent source of information. It's their job to assess people and know who they can rely on, and so they often have extensive networks and can give informed advice. Just as with cofounders, you should always date before you marry. Get to know potential board members in a variety of settings. Work with them as advisors or even bring them into board meetings as observers and participants in nonconfidential matters. If you handle this well, people you never decide to solicit for a board seat still will represent valuable relationships.

As you identify promising candidates, if you are reaching high enough, you'll probably be selling more than buying. Selling often means telling a candidate why he should come to you, in contrast to buying, which is letting a candidate tell you why she would be good for your company. When you are an early-stage start-up, if you find yourself more in a buyer's shoes than a seller's while recruiting directors, you're probably not aiming high enough. When you are trying to find the best candidates, you have to balance selling hard with being judicious and cautious about your choices.

Manage the candidates' expectations of both your demands on their time and their compensation at the outset. For the most part, start-up directors are not motivated mainly by money or the prestige of being on a blue-ribbon board. Most directors know that one of the biggest challenges facing a start-up is having enough cash, even when it's venture-funded, and so they don't expect more than token cash compensation above expenses, if anything at all. Instead, they often like the challenge and stimulation of being in the start-up sector, meeting new people, or staying involved in a field they love. Indeed, one of the most common motivations we hear directors articulate is a sincere desire to give back. Often they will say something like, "Someone helped me get started when I really needed it, and I feel I should do the same."

All the same, you shouldn't expect your directors to serve for free. Most commonly, start-ups offer outside directors a 0.1 percent to 1.0 percent equity share as common shares under a stock-purchase agreement or options at the current valuation, with both vesting over some period between three and five years. You do not normally offer founders, internal management, or investors additional compensation for board participation.

HOW SHOULD A BOARD WORK?

Founders often fail to appreciate how the board should relate to the people in the company. As a rule, the board has only one employee: the CEO. Of course, board members should be acquainted with the company's operations and personnel and a good CEO will welcome a degree of familiarity, but in normal circumstances there shouldn't be regular contact between company personnel and the board. The board should open lines of communication with personnel only if the company is in serious trouble and/or top management is potentially part of the problem. Then interaction between employees and the board can serve as a principal means of getting on top of a deteriorating situation. Difficult circumstances such as these are the perfect illustration of the value of outside directors with lots of maturity and previous experience. In any other circumstances, the board's relationship is primarily with the CEO and to a lesser extent the chief financial officer (CFO).

Most bylaws provide for the election of a chair to lead the board. The actual role of the chair and what leading the board really means vary significantly across companies and boards. Officially, the chair is responsible for setting the agenda and chairing the board meetings, but in practice, many CEOs set agendas and run the meetings even if they don't hold the title of chair. In many instances, the CEO is also the chair of the board, merging the top executive and board governance functions in one person. If the CEO is not the chair, the company can have either an executive or a nonexecutive chair. An executive chair normally holds an official position in the company and in addition to managing the board works closely with the CEO, is intimately involved in high-level strategy and new initiatives, and serves as a public face for the company. A nonexecutive chair maintains the relationship between board and CEO and is often involved in coaching and development. The chair, if only for his or her ability to shape the board's agenda and preside over the meeting, is influential within the company. For that reason alone, you should consider your choice of a chair carefully.

A good board fosters engagement, debate, and collegiality. Members ought to be free to ask provocative questions even to the point of playing devil's advocate, probe deeply, and not jump too quickly to a conclusion or uniform agreement. Don't be afraid of a little healthy discussion. One CEO-chair of a tremendously successful entrepreneurial company often said with a touch of pride that he liked a board with a diversity of opinions but wished someone would agree with him once in a while. Even with that diversity of opinions, the board almost always reached consensus and always committed to decisions. The important thing in any company is that once a decision is reached, everyone commits fully to it.

A number of things that should happen in the board environment:

- *Governance.* The board is primarily responsible for maintaining and updating the company's structure and making all of its major decisions. From time to time, the directors should review the structural elements of the company, such as bylaws and major policies, particularly those related to legal and regulatory compliance. The board also must ensure that the company has adequate operational and financial controls.

- *Reports.* The CEO will report to the board regularly on company performance, financial status, and key activities and achievements. A good board will not just receive information but ask probing questions, look for holes and opportunities, and press to be sure that attention to detail and accuracy is part of everything the company does. In reviewing reports, the board should add value, not just internalize information. No board members like to show up to hear a collection of reports and information they could have read in advance or done without.

- *Accountability.* The board should review and approve financial reports and audits. It also should require regular reports to ensure compliance with applicable law and regulations.

- *Strategy and discussion.* The board should take time to consider, suggest, and discuss future plans and important matters of strategy. You, as the founder(s), gathered these board members for their experience and advice, and so you should give them the freedom to raise issues of their own and deliberate as needed.

- *Decisions.* The board should not feel it needs to vote unanimously to make a decision. Some boards, particularly inexperienced ones, may worry that dissent will undermine commitment to action. But it's healthy to allow strongly felt dissension to have a voice provided that the entire board fully commits to and acts on the final decision. In the end all that's essential is that a board, like any team, commit fully to a decision once it's made and do everything to carry it out. Andy Grove, CEO of Intel, made this the core of Intel's operating philosophy: free discussion, clear decisions, and full commitment.

You might not need to touch on each of these topics every time you meet as a board, particularly if you meet frequently, but each topic should be addressed regularly and as needed.

A common question that arises is how to handle length of term or tenure for members on a board. Generally, board members leave a board in one of three ways: Their term ends, they resign, or they die. It's not easy to get a member to move on if he or she doesn't want to, but sooner or later you almost surely will be in a situation in which a board member may have to go. Since you may not be able to force a resignation and don't want to have to kill the unwanted member, it's a good idea to establish terms for members and stagger them, generally three to four years. This gives you the flexibility to end the relationship gracefully with a member who isn't working out and bring in new ideas and new blood from time to time. But you should think about balance between refreshing with new people and building the deep trust and intimate understanding of each other than can come only from long terms of service. More than one CEO has found that in a tight moment or under a severe time constraint, that kind of trust and understanding made all the difference in successfully handling a big decision or urgent crisis.

Here's a list of some good board meeting practices to think about in advance of the first meeting so that you appear prepared regardless of how inexperienced you may be:

- *Frequency.* The frequency of board meetings depends on the stage of the company. You usually want to shoot for 8 to 12 times a year for early-stage companies and 4 to 6 times a year for more developed companies.
- *Materials.* Always route materials in advance. If you are preparing the agenda, you should send a preliminary copy at least to the board chair two to three weeks in advance of the meeting to seek input on how to frame the proposed agenda items and any additions the members think should be put before the board. Once you resolve the points, prepare a clear agenda, including supporting documentation, and route it to the board long enough in advance of the meeting to allow review and consideration. Remember, the night before is not long enough in advance.
- *Preparation.* Raise critical or potentially contentious issues with each board member before, not during, board meetings.
- *Communication.* Keep the board members informed. Talk to them frequently and informally.
- *Deliver bad news promptly.* Directors are like bankers; they hate surprises. Give everyone time to think about bad news, maybe even making calls and doing some homework, before meeting to deal with a problem. When you present problems, be proactive in suggesting potential solutions or key factors to consider. Always remember that framing the right questions is the most critical step in getting good answers.
- *Observers.* The board often will invite key employees and/or nondirector founders to attend board meetings as observers. If the board has to discuss sensitive issues, it should go into executive session, which is closed to everyone but directors.
- *Conflicts of interest.* When a director identifies a situation in which the company's and his or her own interests might conflict, that director should immediately raise this and recuse himself or herself from participating in proceedings involving the issue. This should be reflected clearly in the minutes as a protection for both parties.
- *Confidentiality.* What is said in a board meeting should always stay there. Confidentiality is expected as an integral part of the duty of loyalty.
- *Subcommittees.* When you get big enough, subcommittees generally handle certain practice areas, such as compensation and audit.

ADVISORS AND ADVISORY BOARDS

Sadly, the days of a couple of old and trusted advisors are gone. The quickly changing business environment requires start-ups to seek out the best advisors earlier and involve them more thoroughly than was done in the past. Indeed, technology- or science-based companies commonly have two advisory boards, one focused on technical issues and the other focused on business execution. You use advisors most effectively if you anticipate both positive and negative events and engage them before those events affect your organization.

Here is a list of what advisors do for a start-up:

- Increase your credibility with investors, customers, and corporate partners.
- Provide you with accountability, experience, important advice, and technical input.
- Offer networking to resources, experts, money, and so forth.
- Act as a sounding board for scientific or technical matters.
- Provide access to upper echelons in academia, corporate organizations, granting agencies, professional societies, and the like.
- Encourage favorable publicity, publish, or speak about the company.

There is inherently less at stake when you choose advisors than when you select directors. In contrast to boards of directors, individual advisory relationships and boards of advisors are not governed by law and provide only nonbinding advice. Advisors have none of the organizational or fiduciary responsibilities and liabilities that go with being a director. They may not even have the time commitment or structured relationship. Although some companies convene their advisory boards regularly and work with a formal agenda, others just sign up advisors and work with them individually as needed. Generally, the more developed a company, the more structure and process in interacting with advisors.

Where can you look to recruit good advisors? As with anything else involving finding someone or something, use your network. There are many sources, among them:

- Prominent industry players
- Investors and lenders
- Professionals: attorneys and accountants
- Vendors
- Customers
- Consultants
- SCORE, regional economic development staff members

Sometimes if you are pursuing particularly busy and highly credentialed people, they can't commit the time or accept the liability inherent in the director role but might allow you to add their names to the advisory board so that you can benefit from their advice and reputation. Indeed, when a start-up signs a person as an advisor, that person more or less grants that venture permission to use his or her name in its public materials. Early on, sometimes simply signing a prominent business or technical person as an advisor can increase a start-up's apparent value because outsiders assume that if a person of that stature is willing to be associated with the start-up, there must be something worthwhile about it.

People may give you advice once in a while without expecting anything back, but if you want to sign them as advisors and use their names, they'll often expect something in return. You should put together a short written advisor agreement providing them with modest compensation in the form of vesting stock or options. This document also provides a diplomatic way to bind an advisor to confidentiality.

Before you sign people as advisors, be sure you understand their expectations and what they want out of a relationship with you and your company. With strangers, it's a good idea to be a little skeptical about their credentials and advice until you get to know them. It's always wise to spend time with people before you engage them in your venture. However, since you aren't really doing much marrying with advisors, you probably can get away with less dating. Even so, healthy and well-developed relationships are much more productive and amenable.

Here are some simple practices that will help you get the most out of your advising relationships and leave your advisors feeling their engagement was worthwhile:

- *Expectations management.* What do the advisors want out of the relationship? Keep their answers in mind as you work with them. That way you'll be sure to make them feel their time with you was well spent. All people have objectives they want to meet, whether they disclose them or not. The more you know them, the more you can make them feel that working with you is a rewarding experience. Likewise, if there are unrealistic expectations, this is the mechanism to reveal them and fix things before they get off track.

- *Organization.* Set a context. Ask questions. Be concise. Advisors aren't inside your head; they can only work with what you tell them. Before meeting with your advisors, take some time to reflect on the real issues and figure out what is bothering you. Remember the importance of framing the right questions.

- *Due diligence.* In this case, it means digging deeper, asking the same question more than once. Listen carefully for hints that might lead to valuable insights or information. Advisors often know a lot more than they realize about an issue or question.

- *Agreement.* If you talk to more than one advisor, you'll get differing, if not contradictory, advice. Remember that it's only advice. In the end, you have to make the calls.
- *Understanding.* Think and reflect aloud with your advisors. Show them you understand what they are saying. Act on their good advice; advisors appreciate that.
- *Appreciation.* Always thank them for their time and advice. They aren't helping you for the money. A nice bottle of wine or some flowers go a long way.

WHAT I KNOW NOW THAT I WISH I HAD KNOWN THEN

Phil Ferneau, Borealis Ventures

Phil Ferneau is managing director and cofounder of Borealis Ventures in Hanover, New Hampshire. In addition, he teaches at the Tuck School of Business, is a fellow of the Dartmouth Entrepreneurial Network, and serves on the board of the Dartmouth Regional Technology Center. Phil has led Borealis's investments in Adimab, Medical Metrx Solutions (acquired by AIG Altaris Health Partners), and GlycoFi (acquired by Merck & Co.). He currently is a director for the Borealis portfolio companies Avedro, Bar Harbor Biotechnology, Direct Vet Marketing, FetchDog, and Pooled Clinical Data Partners.

As a partner at Borealis Ventures, I've observed the board dynamics of our portfolio companies, including eight investments I've personally led since we founded Borealis. As a faculty member at Dartmouth's Tuck School of Business, I've also helped many entrepreneurs wrestle with board composition and operational issues. I've seen how dysfunctional boards can distract CEOs, lead companies astray, and fail to catch early warning signs in time to avoid a crisis. I've also seen how effective a board can be when the CEO and directors understand their roles and operate as a true team. Here are three observations:

Most CEOs Expect Too Little from Their Boards

Too many CEOs view their boards more as an obligation than as a resource. They distribute perfunctory reports just before board meetings (or, worse, only afterward) and waste precious time reporting past financials and opera-tions. As a result, those boards can't contribute an informed, independent per-spective and end up little more than a rubber stamp. By contrast, a proactive CEO encourages an informed and engaged board, sends out useful materials well in advance, frames appropriate issues for debate, and encourages active engagement beyond formal meetings. These best-practices CEOs expect more from their boards, and they usually get it.

Smarts Alone Don't Make Great Directors

Shortfalls come in all varieties. Sometimes a director doesn't have relevant experience to contribute. A longtime big company executive may not under-stand the start-up world. A director can have too much relevant experience and have a hard time letting go of it. Some persist in viewing today's chal-lenges through yesterday's lenses or forget they are coaches now, not players. Some venture investor directors are inconsistent, whipsawing the company as they flip-flop on strategic issues based on dynamics within their own investment partnerships. Directors can be spread too thin—particularly investors serving on too many boards—to the point where they can't stay on top of what's happening with the company.

The Best Boards Work as a Team

Working as a team doesn't always come naturally, especially when an investor director has joined the board after a difficult fund-raising negotiation or when a founder director has been steered out of the CEO role. But directors need to put differences behind them and work together to advance the busi-ness. They should identify and nurture complementary strengths. Embracing differences and fomenting debate are the first defenses against groupthink. Effective boards consciously challenge assumptions but then pull together to forge consensus and crystallize their guidance to the CEO. The best teams interact regularly outside formal board meetings. If you want a tightly knit team, start with a smaller board and judiciously add directors over time; the more directors on a board, the more difficult it can be for them to work smoothly together.

QUESTIONS

- Can you write down the key assets you want to secure in your board seats: reputation, investment, experience, and so on?
- What role do you want to play on the board of directors?
- What do your advisors think about your strategy for the board of directors?

NOTE

1. For more information on corporations and LLCs, see Chapter 13.

Chapter 10

Employees and Other People Resources

The employer generally gets the employees he deserves.

—Sir Walter Raleigh[1]

Founders may give birth to a company, but rarely can they scale it to any significant size by their efforts alone. Almost directly after the actual launch, if not before, you will need to start bringing in additional people to make things happen in a timely fashion. For most companies the cost of people looms as one of the largest—second only to the cost of goods sold—and in many companies it is the biggest. Remembering that people drive success, you will find that building out your team beyond the founders is one of the most important things you can do for the company's future. In this chapter we will discuss how to decide about what you need, where to find those people, and how to interview and hire them. Whole books have been written on this subject. With only a chapter, the best we can do is provide a framework, define the key questions, and suggest resources to fill the gaps.

PEOPLE RESOURCES?

You can't hide a mediocre player in a start-up. In the cash-limited start-up environment, each person adds significant cost, and so everyone has to contribute. In thinking about adding people, never take on costs you don't need, especially recurring fixed costs. Remember: companies fail when they run out of cash. Although raising a lot of money is an obvious solution, it's seldom a realistic option. Further, this may seem counterintuitive, but many investors believe that a company launching with as little money as possible actually has a higher chance of succeeding than one with cash to burn. The cash-limited company has to be careful about who it hires and what they will be doing. It can't assume money will solve its problems, and so it has to learn to do a lot with a little. Therefore, the first question to ask any time you consider hiring is, "Do we really *need* to incur this cost?" Of course, don't be so careful that you hinder growth. It's tempting to try to do too much with a little only to find that little actually gets done. Like everything in business, hiring is a judgment call based on messy, incomplete, and incoherent information. You can't wait around for perfect clarity or direction. In the end, only action makes a difference. Bring in outside help but only when you absolutely need it, not when you just want it.

The employer-employee relationship is governed by a host of laws and regulations that will influence your operations management and generate future obligations for the company. In short, hiring someone as an employee means taking on serious long-term obligations. It also means making a commitment to a full person when often there may not be a full person's worth of work to do in that function in an average week. Also, there are many support functions in a small company that don't need to be performed in-house at all: bookkeeping, legal, auditing, payroll, and benefits administration, for example.

Fortunately, you don't have to give up your flexibility and assume the risks and burdens of full-time employees to get the people-based resources you need. For work that should be done in-house, you can retain someone as a consultant or independent contractor to maintain flexibility and limit long-term commitments.

Independent contractor arrangements are bounded rather than open-ended. Usually the company determines the hours needed. There are no benefits to administer. The terms of the contract rather than the legal regulations that come with an employment relationship govern the company-contractor relationship. This increases your flexibility dramatically because you can negotiate the terms to meet your needs. When you create the contract, you should always include a provision giving you the option to terminate the contract at any time with a reasonable period of notice. This maintains your flexibility in the future so that you can react to changes in circumstances or people needs. Finally, a contracting arrangement can be a good way to bring someone into the company eventually as an employee. It's the ultimate date before you marry. The arrangement allows you to get to know and work closely with a person before you commit to anything long-term. Table 10-1 shows different independent contracting arrangements:

Table 10-1 Independent Contracting Arrangements

Type of Arrangement	Participants
Per diem/hour vendors for special services	Attorneys
	Tax specialists
	Technical consultants
	Market researchers
Regularly recurring engagements	Bookkeepers, controllers
	Human resources administrators
	Maintenance and janitorial staff
	Public relations personnel
	IT systems administrators
	Telemarketers

Table 10-1 Independent Contracting Arrangements (*Continued*)

Type of Arrangement	Participants
Outside service firms	Janitorial staff
	Payroll/benefits administrators
	Call/support center staff
	Fulfillment (e.g., inventory, packaging, shipping) staff
	Installation/service/repair staff
	Contract research lab staff
	Training staffs
Specialized consultants for bounded projects	IT projects and coding products personnel
	Design staff
	Engineering/technical/science staff
	Regulatory consultants
	Lobbyists
	Strategy, management, technical consultants
	Training personnel
	Fund-raising personnel and executive recruiters

The downside to an independent contractor relationship is that since contractors don't have a stake in the company, they may not think as passionately as an employee would about its long-term future. They may do only what's necessary to get the specific job done or, worse, fill their hours without necessarily looking to improve the quality or process. Also, if you've contracted with someone for part-time work only, you might not be able to have that person when you need him or her; the contractor might be out working for someone else.

Under whatever arrangement you are thinking of hiring someone, you need to pay close attention to the relevant laws and regulations. There are significant and somewhat complicated employment and tax law distinctions between an employee and an independent contractor. Misunderstanding this distinction or misapplying the independent contractor label can result in serious consequences down the road. There are a number of tests to determine whether you are avoiding obligations and liabilities by incorrectly—i.e., *illegally*—treating people as independent contractors when the law would deem them employees. The full expanse of this issue is beyond the scope of this book, but there are plenty of resources available to help you keep your employee arrangements within the law. To start, check out the IRS Web site (www.irs.gov) and Bagley and Dauchy's *The Entrepreneur's Guide to Business Law.*[2]

WHEN DO YOU NEED PEOPLE?

Remember what we said in Chapter 8: Your people needs change over time. Some people can change and adapt as a company evolves. Some can learn to fill new functions and make the transition from creativity and a broad spectrum of responsibilities to more specialized roles or higher-level management. Others can't. Tim Lewis, an advisor to a Dartmouth company, uses Tuckman's four phases of group development to describe the evolution that companies and people experience: forming, storming, performing, and norming.[3] When a company is just starting to come together in the chaos and uncertainty of the launch, it's *forming*. In this environment, you need a freewheeling creative person who has endless energy and needs little structure or process to get things done. As the company moves into serious product creation, enters the consumer space, and begins generating revenue, it's *storming* the market. Here you need a fanatical salesperson and production leader to help you build the product, sell the customer, and grab the largest possible market share. Next, as the company carves out its market and hits its stride as a recognized and growing company, it's *performing*. In this context, you need consistent operations managers who will help you grow well, meet customers' needs, and exceed their expectations. Eventually, if the company grows big and complex enough to need process and procedure to function, it has to start *norming*. As the focus of this book is primarily on forming and storming, we emphasize people who are right for those first two developmental stages.

In short, each stage of company development requires a different sort of person. Your people needs will change over time. Some people can remake themselves to remain important contributors across all these phases, but make no mistake, it is a remaking. It may or may not be a tragedy that people needs change this much as you grow, but it is the reality. This means that sometimes people from the previous stages can become liabilities to future growth. Therefore, when you talk to potential employees, you should always try to understand their potential to develop and grow with the company or their comfort with the notion that they may want to move on if the company grows past a certain size. Some candidates may be experienced and wise enough to understand how companies evolve and be comfortable with the phases they love or don't love. Many probably will not. Either way, you want employment relationships that are successful over time for both the company and the person. You should discuss the terms of a successful relationship with potential employees the first time you meet them. You don't want to waste your time or theirs on something that won't fit now or won't last long as you grow.

You also want to keep those successful employment relationships as long as possible. We can't emphasize enough that in building a team, wise founders should always think about both the present and the future. This means finding not only the best possible people for today's needs but also those who have the potential to remain good contributors in the future as things change. Perhaps most important, building for the present and the future means managing expectations and commitments to plan for—and accommodate—the inevitable transitions in people and positions as those changes come. To do this effectively, you must communicate to your cofounders and employees a clear picture of the present and future needs, explaining the structures of compensation and contracts that will make transitions within and out of the company as positive as possible for everyone.

WHAT DO YOU LOOK FOR?

Just like the founders, the first people you hire will help shape every aspect of the company from performance expectations and its chance of success to the interpersonal dynamics of the office, the company culture, and the image you present to the outside world.

It's hard to find something you aren't looking for. Although this may not apply to everything in life, it certainly pertains to looking for employees, especially employees for an early-stage company. Before you begin thinking about the first round of interviewees, spend some time creating a clear picture of the role you want to fill and the person you want to fill it. Then make sure everyone involved in the search sees the same picture. To get this clear picture, you need to think about three different dimensions of the position:

1. *What are the needs the position fills?* Think about the gaps in your resource base.
2. *Does the actual position you are describing fill those needs?* You've got to tie your description of the position clearly to your needs.
3. *What kind of person would best fill those needs?* This is not about filling a position; it's about filling a need. Think about the person who will best be able to do well what needs to be done.

We recommend creating two written documents to help you answer these questions and go through the process of hiring good employees:

- *An external document.* This is a general position description that will help you communicate what you need to others. Keep in mind that you will most likely share this description with everyone involved in the search process, perhaps even with the candidates. It should contain the position title, the purpose, its accountabilities and responsibilities, the reporting structure, and the required and desired background and experience.
- *An internal document.* This should be two lists: a detailed list of characteristics and qualifications defining the ideal individual and a list of the lower limits of what you will consider. Creating a document like this stimulates

innovative thinking about the different kinds of people who might be good for the position and the places where you might find those people. The first list describes the ideal characteristics, background, and experience a *perfect* candidate would possess. The second list notes the minimum traits and experience a candidate must have to be considered for the position. Of course, you'll probably never find the ideal person, but the lists will enable you to see what's there and what's missing in each candidate as well as help you compare and decide between candidates. This is a private document; you won't show it to many, if any, outsiders, and you'll certainly never show it to candidates. Smart candidates can be good at telling you what they think you want to hear.

What traits will you want to see in a candidate? A good list is provided in Table 10-2, which is based on the discussion of entrepreneurial and administrative traits in Chapter 1.

Table 10-2 Entrepreneurial and Administrative Traits Compared

Entrepreneurial Traits	Administrative Traits
Innovative and creative	Risk averse
Self-motivated; takes initiative	Threatened by change or the unknown
Flexible and adaptable	Security inclined
Assertive	Process driven
Growth oriented	Cautious, slow moving, and structured
Opportunity driven	Effective in predictable circumstances
Active and dynamic	Control motivated
Implementation and efficiency focused	Resource focused
Productive in an unstructured environment	
Driven to create value	
People and team focused	
Decisive	

As you've probably guessed, we're interested in the entrepreneurial traits for early employees. They work, and the administrative traits don't do well in an early-stage environment. But beyond these basic entrepreneurial traits, you'll want to consider a number of other highly valuable characteristics, actions, and reactions for your list:

1. *The basics.* Almost certainly you want your first employees to
   a. Be intelligent and enthusiastic
   b. Love hard work and have fun doing it

  c. Possess distinctive skill sets and/or demonstrate technical competence
  d. Have experience and a history of accomplishment
2. *Culture fit.* You want new employees to be a good culture fit. You want them to understand, appreciate, and buy into your corporate culture as well as demonstrate the ability to work well in a team.
3. *Goal-oriented.* We have always found that overtly goal-oriented people do best in a start-up environment. Normally, the specific nature of their personal goals doesn't much matter so long as they aren't antithetical to successful job performance. What matters is that they show a pattern of clearly defining goals for themselves and mapping out plans to accomplish them. If they naturally create this pattern for themselves instead of having to be told what to do all the time, they probably will do it for you too.
4. *Impact.* Entrepreneurial personalities generally are motivated much more by a desire to achieve things than by the need to accumulate power or status or be part of a group and enjoy being social. Indeed, you can hear few more positive things in an interview than "I'm frustrated where I am. I want what I do to have more impact."
5. *High-energy.* Although a high-energy person can also be high-maintenance, having hyperenthusiastic, creative people in a launch team, people who make the right things happen, pays dividends time and again. You might say this type of employee has an impulse to action.
6. *Flexibility.* Inflexibility can kill a small team, especially if it is mixed with high energy, and the two often go together. Rigidity is dangerous because it not only impairs a start-up's ability to incorporate new information and change direction rapidly but also causes serious interpersonal problems. If you find high energy combined with flexibility, you have the makings of a superstar.
7. *Communication and cooperation.* Good communication and interpersonal skills are essential in a start-up. It's especially important that the technical specialists and the business generalists be able to communicate well with one another. One of the most important principles in team dynamics is that cooperation and communication can cure almost all ills.
8. *The unknown.* You want to know that your future employees can handle stress and change well. They'll get plenty of it in a start-up. Indeed, people who thrive on challenges and the unknown are a great asset to an early-stage venture. But remember that if you grow big enough to create structure and process, they'll probably become dissatisfied and want to leave. This is another reason to put mechanisms in place to ease transitions from one developmental stage to the next.
9. *Success.* Look for a history of accomplishment. If a candidate excelled in a past position or assignment, it's likely that he or she will do it again for you. In most settings, people will achieve at the level they set for themselves, and so you want a track record of aiming high and hitting the target.

10. *Goals.* It's wise to know and understand a potential employee's career and life aspirations. Goals tell you a lot about who a person is and who he or she wants to be. Look for these things to fit with your vision of the company's future.

11. *Work history.* Look carefully at the companies for which your candidate has worked. Many founders think they want employees with big company backgrounds because they'll bring experience with them. Yes, these candidates normally bring technical discipline, specialization, and process. Although these are all valuable, in the start-up and small company environment you'll need integrative innovative thinking, flexibility, and a willingness to do whatever needs to be done. Sometimes candidates from big companies don't have these types of work habits. They are used to structure and think in terms of process and politics. What you want is someone who already has transitioned into a small company and been successful there.

12. *Motivation.* Make sure you understand why a candidate wants to work for your company. You'll probably see two types of people (excluding people terminated for cause). The first group has left their big company semi-involuntarily, through a buyout package, or because of dissatisfaction with their pace of advancement. They think they want something new, exciting, and challenging but don't understand how different the start-up world is from the one they left. The second group abandons the big company in good standing because they are dissatisfied and frustrated with the structure and politics. They want to do more, faster without all the bureaucracy. This is your target group; they are telling you they want to have impact.

We find that successful candidates normally have good grades from a good school (a filter for intelligence and effective work habits), have two to five years of experience at a big well-run company, and are dissatisfied. They are ready to move faster, to do more. If they have more big company experience, candidates often struggle with the transition to a fast-moving entrepreneurial environment, with making lots of decisions quickly even when all the facts aren't known, with being versatile enough to handle lots of different things at once, and with being willing to roll up their sleeves and do things they used to have underlings to do for them. If they have less experience, they may lack technical excellence, discipline and focus, knowledge of the importance of getting the details right, and an appreciation for orderly process.

It's said that *A* people hire *A* people and *B* people hire *C* people. The truth is that whether or not you're an *A* person, you want to hire *A* people. Most successful CEOs will tell you that dangerous employees avoid hiring anyone better than themselves for fear of being passed over. As a founder, nothing should be more exciting than hiring someone better than you! This means your company is growing beyond its founders. Hiring above yourself is a prerequisite to success no matter how high an *A* you are.

Finding the right person is a difficult process. Be patient. Clearly define the position, the gap you need to fill, and the person you would love to see fill it. Hiring the wrong person is expensive and draining. But remember that in the end you have to do something. The perfect can become the enemy of the good.

WHERE DO YOU FIND YOUR PEOPLE?

Great teams are made from great people. You want to find the best people of course, but you need to maintain a realistic picture of the odds you will consistently be able to do this throughout the process of hiring. Most traits follow a normal distribution in a population. This means that a few people have a high degree of any particular trait, a few more have almost none of it, and the great majority have some amount in between (Figure 10-1). Translation: The odds of hiring a superstar are not good. For one thing, superstars are very rare, and for another, though you may have a compelling idea, you are still a start-up with no money and little more than blood, toil, tears, and sweat to offer. It's exceedingly painful to find the perfect person and discover that you are unable to interest him or her in your opportunity. Your job as you hire is to cheat the odds. Do everything possible to make your opportunity attractive and compelling and then sell it to the right people.

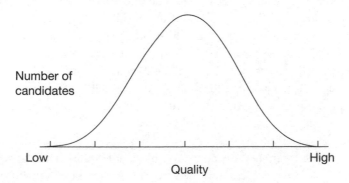

Figure 10-1 The quality of candidates is normally distributed such that great people are rare.

The sources you use to find and attract good people can help you cheat the odds and get the word out that you have a great opportunity for the right person. Start with your personal connections. Work through your networks and referrals from people you know. Though hardly the largest candidate pool, this is almost always the best source for good people because your contacts have already done a good deal of filtering and selling. Since most of your connections probably know you and your venture well, they're already proactively promoting your opportunity and screening people for fit. Of course, you still need to be careful about people helping out friends and those who don't know what you're doing, but referrals generally reduce hiring risk and produce promising candidates.

Everyone you know can give referrals: people already in the company, directors and advisors, service providers, customers, investors, family and friends, and even neighbors and vendors. An alma mater's career development office can be a great source if you develop a relationship there. Even trade associations and clubs can be a source, although they often lack the personal knowledge that makes referrals so valuable. Another source, often overlooked, frequently produces the highest hiring success of all: people who come to you. A friend of ours, the late Bob Koski, founding CEO of Sun Hydraulics, a very successful engineering and manufacturing company, consistently found that his best early hires were the ones who came and pressed him for a job. Bob said that every person he hired from this source turned out great, whereas personal referrals worked out about 50 percent of the time.

Advertising and job postings are one of the most common ways to draw candidates. You should never miss a chance to think creatively about where to publish. Go beyond the usual suspects: Craigslist, Monster.com, and so on. Hunters don't just wander around anywhere in the bush looking for game; they go where the game is. Think about where your desired candidates are looking—trade journals, specialty Web sites—and be visible there. The most successful posting is a clear and concise description of the company and the position. These descriptions should both make the position exciting and help potential applicants self-screen. The external description we mentioned early is a great place to start, but you'll often want to reduce it to a compelling sound bite. If you can't describe the whole job in a few sentences or bullets, it's probably too complicated to advertise. Job postings can be useful for technical and functional positions, but for more complicated, higher-level openings, they are generally ineffective.

You also can outsource recruitment to professional search consultants. The type of the open position—functional, technical, or high-level management—and the amount of money you can afford for fees will dictate the consultants you want to consider. For functional and technical positions, you can find firms that charge a reasonable fixed rate by the hour or work on a contingency basis. As you get into higher-level positions, search firms usually work on a retainer and require a percentage of the final pay package, which can get expensive fast. But when your network can't bring you the candidates you need, this may be the only realistic option, especially for highly specialized technical and upper-level management positions. Use your networks to inform your choice of firm as work quality varies significantly. You want to know what you're getting.

HOW DO YOU HIRE THE CANDIDATES YOU WANT?

Especially when advertising, steel yourself for the added step of disciplined screening. Applications usually come in more volume than you anticipate. Once your opening is public, you will quickly see how valuable prescreened referrals from your friends are. You can't interview everybody. It's important to have a good regimen for screening applications so that you interview only promising candidates. The résumé is the first level of filter. People think résumés are really important and feel the need to tell their whole career story. Actually, résumés don't give you much of the information you need to decide about hiring a candidate. Their primary value is to you help you screen down to a short list of promising candidates. In résumés, look for the following:

- Matches to your basic screening criteria and job description
- Indicators of promising future performance: relevant accomplishments, experiences
- Education and work history; progression of increasing responsibility
- Basic personal attributes: organization, grammar, mistakes
- Obvious negative screening markers
- Key gaps, particularly timeline gaps

With this screen, you can usually separate résumés into three piles: the obvious rejects, the candidates you definitely want to interview, and those about which you are unsure. If the definitely interview stack is large enough, sometimes you won't even have to look in the unsure pile. The next step is often a phone interview to determine if you want to bring in a candidate for an in-person interview.

The in-person interview should be an intense, complex exercise for you, the company, and the candidate. In a good interview, a number of things happen concurrently:

- You and the candidate get to know each other. Your job is to find out about all 12 things in the list earlier in this chapter. The candidate should be looking to know more about you and the company. A word of warning: Exercise caution if candidates sell so hard that they don't try to find out about you or the company. Always ask them if they have any questions, preferably at the beginning of the interview, before they have a chance to read you for what they think you want to hear. The questions they ask often give you insight and information you'd miss if you just grilled them. Some candidates will have done a lot of research, will pull it out, and will ask from a prepared list. Some will not expect the question but extemporaneously come up with something insightful from what they've observed or learned from past research. Think what you'd learn if a candidate just looked at you blankly and didn't have any questions. That happens more often than you would guess.

- Be realistic: Candidates are coming to the interview to sell themselves. Who would want a candidate who didn't? It's natural that they will feed you carefully shaped and filtered information. Therefore, you need to look beyond face value in their answers and try to probe beneath the pat story. Getting beyond a simple question-and-answer discussion and into a free-flowing conversation helps tremendously.

- Not only are candidates selling you on themselves in the interview, often you have to sell them on your opportunity too. The best candidates almost always have other options, and if you want them, you have to make the case that you are the best option. That will not happen by itself. Although it's hard to both scrutinize the candidate and sell your opportunity, it's not impossible. Telling a candidate all the great things about your company and the opportunity doesn't automatically mean you are saying to the candidate that he or she is right for the job. Then again, there are times when you have to quit being noncommittal and shift to overt selling. One of the most important questions to run through your mind constantly from the first encounter with any candidate is, Am I buying at this moment or selling? Like everything else, hiring is judgment call in a world of messy, incomplete, and incoherent information.

You and your team should think about how to structure the screening and interview process. Do you want to interview multiple rounds? An extended process can yield important information, but it also can drag everything out, and the more attractive candidates probably have other options. You want more than one person to interview a candidate in more than one setting. Gregg often asked a handful of future coworkers to take a candidate to lunch and be completely open about the company, their positions, and how they felt about things, both positive and negative. This was healthy for the candidate, and the coworkers were often amazingly perceptive in reading the candidate.

When you sit down for the actual formal interview, here are some questions that can yield important insights into a candidate:

- *What are your long-term goals?* At first, candidates normally say something about their career and professional goals, generally a stock answer that tells you nothing and reflects little thought. But if you press beyond career and ask about life goals, you can learn you a lot.

- *What are your short-term goals?* Same situation. Press to their personal goals. Candidates with a pattern of personal goal setting and thoughtful planning generally prove to be effective performers.

- *What are your extracurricular activities?* Activities or hobbies outside the office? Family time? An exercise regimen? How disciplined? Community service or church?
- *What do you read?* This is normally an unexpected question, and so it can yield some important insights. You want to know if the candidate is disciplined enough to keep up with relevant technical and business issues. Further, what a candidate reads for pleasure and enrichment tells you volumes about him or her as a person. Footnote: Gregg never ceased to be surprised by how often he would find candidates not telling the truth about a book they claimed to have read when he had read that book; sometimes this can reveal things about a candidate that no other questions do.

Will you plan second interviews or multiple rounds? How will you and your management team make the hiring decisions? Which members of your team will participate, and on what timeline? If you want to impress candidates with your company's energy and decisiveness, think about checking their references in advance, deciding everything in-house that day, and sending them home with an offer.

Finally, always check references on any candidate you don't personally know well, even if referred by someone you trust. It says on the back of the one-dollar bill, "In God we trust," and Jean Shepherd's corollary adds, "All others pay cash."[4] That reference you trust might be telling you the truth or might be doing the candidate a favor. The best references are people who know or have worked with the candidate and are *not* listed on the job application. You can't always find these references or get them to talk to you, but when you can, the information is doubly valuable. Even the most promising candidates can have hidden surprises. Gregg recalls one referral candidate who was so promising that the hiring committee wanted to send him home with an offer. On a whim Gregg told the staff to check references anyway. The first reference listed on the application was surprised by the call: "Don't you know his history? He was convicted of throwing acid in a judge's face." The story checked out. Always call references.

HOW DO YOU OFFER?

Making a candidate an offer is a complicated business. You have to pay attention to customary practices, market conditions, and all the complexities of employment law and regulations. In addition, making an offer requires you to structure the salary and compensation package, and negotiate and close with prospective employees. You probably don't know all the ins and outs of all this, and you probably shouldn't. You'll need help to get it right, this is something you want to get right the first time. Otherwise you might find yourself locked into, employment terms you don't want later on. Some of the best help can come from your directors and, to some extent, your advisors if you thought ahead and chose some with relevant experience. Also, with structuring and closing, good human resources (HR) consultants and employment attorneys are helpful until you have resources in-house. Cutting corners on professional help in this area can be tempting, but it can be costly in the long run. Here are the main elements in structuring an offer:

- *Salary.* It's highly unlikely that you, your directors, or any of your advisors know the market well enough to define prevailing salary ranges. For almost any salaried position, you can look for market information on survey Web sites such as www.salary.com and www.radford.com. In setting salaries, there are two important things to keep in mind:
  - The salary is only part of a total compensation package. The entire package includes benefits, signing and/or recurring bonuses (if any), commissions, profit sharing, and incentive compensation plans such as stock options. Taken together, these elements constitute your company's total cost and the employee's total value. Many salary surveys try to include information on all these elements, but it's almost impossible to compare incentives such as stock options. In the ideal case, both you and the employee fully value the entire package and agree that it's competitive, fair, and comparable to the market.
  - Salary levels generally correlate with the size of a company: The older and larger the company, the higher the salary. Theoretically, larger ownership shares in small, early-stage companies make up for this cash gap. Candidates and employees have varying perceptions of what these can be worth, but taking risk into account, only the lucky ones do really well with ownership shares versus cash. This is yet another reason it's hard to attract top management talent to start-ups.
- *Bonuses.* There are two different kinds of bonuses used to attract and reward employees:
  - A signing bonus can incentivize employees to sign with you or help ease compensation cuts they might take to join your venture. You also might have to provide a moving/relocation bonus to cover employee transition costs.
  - Since fixed, guaranteed salaries seldom motivate performance, some companies use a variable bonus tied to outcomes to reward accomplishment. Sometimes this works, but frequently these recurring bonuses become just another form of expected annuity, detached from performance. In an early-stage company, the more you can tie compensation to growth in the company's value, the more you will align everyone's incentives.

- *Benefits packages.* For benefits such as vacation time, sick time, and health plans, you should norm to companies of your size in your industry. Affiliation and trade groups often have useful group buying plans for standard benefits. For any nonstandard benefits, you probably should engage an HR consultant to help you. The cost of benefits is significant and often is overlooked or underbudgeted by inexperienced entrepreneurs, especially when they are doing their first financial forecasts in their planning. Mike Gonnerman, the author of *Ask Mike,*[5] advises:

  The employer's share of FICA and Medicare alone now costs an employer 7.65% of payroll, plus unemployment, workman's comp, and other payroll-related charges. Some of these costs have cutoff points (for instance, you'll pay FICA only on the first $106,800 of an employee's earnings, but Medicare is unlimited). Then there's health insurance, perhaps a dental plan, disability, retirement fund matching, and other benefits that you'll probably have to offer to attract quality employees. Health insurance—a big cost that's bound to keep growing—also varies widely depending on the plan, employee contribution, family coverage, etc. And when you need to hire temps or extra people to cover key employees who are on vacation or away for extended training, that's another real out-of-pocket cost that should be included in your calculations. For most companies, the benefits percentage is also much higher for lower-paid employees. If you spend $600 a month for insurance for an employee who earns $24,000 a year, for example, that's a hefty 30% of the employee's payroll just for basic health coverage.

- *Retirement plans.* Start-ups and early-stage companies tend to defer retirement benefits until they grow to at least a dozen or two dozen employees. Below that, plans can be more trouble, distraction, and cost than they're worth. If you feel you need a plan, consultants or outsource organizations can help.
- *Severance packages.* State laws vary on minimum severance requirements for full-time employees as well as the amount you have to pay. This can be one of the more difficult negotiations with prospective employees, especially higher-level managers. It's not unusual for a leadership-level candidate to ask for a year's salary as a lump-sum severance payment. This is unappealing for two reasons:
  - A severance package increases the cost of transition, adding the price of firing to the cost of hiring a replacement.
  - When a candidate insists on a big severance package or argues about the definition of termination for cause, he or she can begin to look riskier than you thought. You can reasonably assume that the more a prospective employee pushes for a large package, the more likely it is that he or she someday will need it.

Avoid big severance packages whenever possible. That said, it's only fair to agree to a reasonable number of weeks to compensate a candidate for taking a chance on you. You should make severance pay conditional on signing a termination agreement. This agreement can contain important confidentiality provisions, releases from possible future claims, and even reasonable noncompetition provisions. (Note: If you plan as a rule to provide only statutory severance, the more frequently you give beyond this, the more likely a court may be later to award someone more severance on the grounds that this was your common practice.)

- *Stock options.* Stock incentive plans, usually in the form of options, are one of the main compensation elements founders use to attract people to early-stage companies. It's easy to err by giving too much too early or by giving so little that you fail to attract the best people, so take care with this and use an experienced attorney. Mistakes with options can be hard to fix later. Plans don't need to be complicated, but they do need to be appropriate and effective. Unfortunately, you won't find any good survey resources for stock options. There are some general equity percentage standards for the various employee levels, though, and your directors and advisors can advise you from their operating experience. Grant equity incentives judiciously. Although employees may undervalue stock incentives relative to cash now, options can be expensive in the long run. Finally, pay attention to the tax issues. They can be terribly costly if you aren't careful.

Until you are big enough to have resources in-house, use good employment attorneys and HR consultants for drafting template agreements, closing, and managing HR administration. Develop a system of good hiring practices and record keeping. Do it early and follow it. If you do, you'll always have good data on employees, compensation, vesting schedules, and so on. Further, investors do a lot of due diligence in employee records to check that things are appropriate and in order. You don't want them to find unresolved problems or gaps in your records.

As we may have said too many times already, remember that your people needs will change over time. We're being repetitive, because as much as most founders seem to understand it, they consistently ignore it, and ignoring it inevitably leads to problems. The kind and caliber of people you can attract at the start of a venture are usually different from what you can attract later on. As you grow, people with more experience and stature will join your organization and some of your pioneers may leave. Your compensation system should be structured to accommodate those changes. It needs to reward good work and discourage wasted time while allowing people to join and leave without undue disruption to the corporate structure. This means a flexible, fair, and transparent system with good vesting policies and clear employee agreements.

Finally, in all this, remember what counts most. Compensation is a cost-benefit issue. Cost is critical to an early-stage company, especially cash cost, but so is performance. Although you shouldn't have to bribe people to be productive, especially in a cash-poor start-up, you should pay people fairly. Fairness, like beauty, is mostly in the eye of the beholder, but fortunately, unlike beauty, the market provides a guide. You should be glad if your employees earn well above the market if they help make the company a success. If your compensation structures are sound, that's just what will happen.

Most of all, remember that it's usually not just about the money. At heart, most people want to do something that's intrinsically valuable and meaningful. Survey after survey on job satisfaction has shown that although employers think employees rank pay and job security highest, employees actually rank those things far lower. Instead, employees say that meaning, significance, working environment, and, above all, being appreciated most significantly shape their motivation and happiness at work. Some of the most valuable things you can do are share credit for successes, compliment and publicly recognize good work, and just say thank you.

HOW DO YOU SIGN THEM UP?

If you are efficient and prepared, you and your attorney will work ahead of time to have ready a boilerplate package of employment documents.[6] Fortunately, these documents are fairly standard and shouldn't take a lot of legal time and money to create. Also, most of them can be cloned and reused as needed without having to go back to the attorney. Just make sure as you create those initial documents that the attorney gives you a good education on the basics, a primer on the important employment law that applies to advertising, interviewing, closing, managing, and terminating. You probably should keep a good checklist for reference as you recruit and sign employees. Pilots never take off in an airplane without clearing their checklist. Neither should you.

Further, use written agreements only to clarify and resolve vague issues, memorialize verbal intentions, and protect against changes in people and conditions. Written agreements are not a guarantee against disputes or a substitute for consensus, good intentions, or continued alignment of interests and benefits. Written agreements are not magic; they cannot force a person to like you, perform at the level you need, or even honor the agreement. In the end, a written agreement is only a license to sue, and you don't want to have to sue (or defend against a suit) to protect your interests.

WHAT SHOULD YOU WATCH OUT FOR?

Employment law, regulations, tort law, and taxation are hugely complex issues, and they all apply to you the moment you start the process of hiring your first employee. Your attorneys, HR consultants, and tax experts will help you do things right and keep out of trouble, but your own understanding of important areas is your first line of defense. You cannot assign to outside service providers the responsibility to act prudently and know the issues. Know which areas can affect you:

- *Employees versus independent contractors.* Employees' rights and benefits are heavily regulated and protected. Independent contractors are exempt from many requirements, especially those related to benefits and overtime. Tax and state authorities scrutinize classification of workers as independent contractors, so be knowledgeable about the criteria and how to meet them. There is more on this in Chapter 13.
- *Legislation and legal liabilities.* There are substantial workplace protections in the federal Civil Rights Acts of 1964 and 1991—antidiscrimination, sexual harassment, age discrimination—the Americans with Disabilities Act, and the Family and Medical Leave Act. See Chapter 13.
- *Fair labor standards.* The federal Fair Labor Standards Act governs minimum wages, overtime pay, and the use of child labor.
- *Worker's compensation.* State statutes require companies to insure income loss and medical expenses from work-related injuries.
- *Occupational health and safety.* The federal Occupational Health and Safety Act and related state statutes require that a place of employment be free from recognized hazards and designate agencies to inspect and enforce compliance.
- *Recruiting and hiring practices.* Case law and legislation deeply affect advertising for employees; interviewing and offering, particularly as to antidiscrimination; invasion of privacy; and immigration law.
- *Workplace privacy.* Surveillance of employees, especially their Internet and e-mail behavior, is regulated. Gathering, use, and custody of health information are strictly restricted by law.
- *Terminations and discharges.* There is extensive case law and regulation around termination practices and severance policies. Employment completely at will is largely a thing of the past. Procedures for termination can make the difference between lingering problems and clean separations.

NOW WHAT?

Not to belabor the obvious, but once you hire people, you have to manage them. Although repeat start-up founders and first-time entrepreneurs with previous management experience will have little trouble with this transition, first-timers often underestimate its demands. People management is different from entrepreneurial pioneering. You now have to get other people to do things instead of doing them yourself (Figure 10-2). This means thinking much more about making decisions and planning, organizing, controlling, and measuring performance. If you can do this successfully and make this transition, you have gone through one of the most important and difficult personal conversions a founder ever has to make, and make no mistake—many never do.

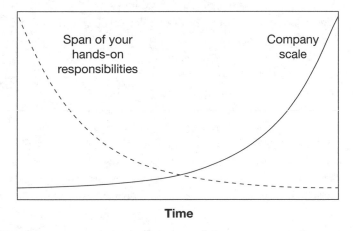

Time

Figure 10-2 As the company grows, the founding CEO may shift from hands-on activity to managing the work of others.

WHAT I KNOW NOW THAT I WISH I HAD KNOWN THEN

Peg Blout, Mascoma Corporation

Since 1997 Peg Blout has led human resource and administrative functions in demanding, high-growth, rapidly changing organizations. She is currently the senior director of human resources for Mascoma Corporation, a leading venture-backed cellulosic ethanol technology company. Previously she held senior human resources roles at the drug development company Momenta Pharmaceuticals, growing the company from 5 employees to over 200 through three rounds of venture capital funding, an initial public offering, and a new drug application. At Momenta, Peg led all areas of human resources, including strategy, recruiting, employment law and labor relations, policies and procedures, employee development, and tactical HR support. Before Momenta she filled similar roles at Sage Hill Venture Capital Partners and Lexicon, Inc. a consulting company that grew from 22 to 70 employees before being acquired in 1999. Peg offers these reflections on hiring people:

- Often hiring managers are clear about what technical skills are required. But it is just as important, if not more so, to focus also on character and behavior. The behaviors of an employee can literally make or break a company. The HR leader should always plays a key role in identifying what qualities are needed in a candidate in terms of both character and behavior. Before you hire someone, you need to be able to articulate answers to these questions:
  - What is the culture of the organization?
  - Is work ethic important?
  - What about integrity?
  - Will the new hires be working independently or on a team?
  - How important is flexibility?
  - How well will they fit the existing culture?
- Remember, recruiting has two views: how the organization sees a candidate and how the candidates see the organization. When hiring, be sure candidates see accurately what the company is and wants to be.
- Hire to complement strengths already present in the organization.
- Don't wait too long to build a robust and efficient system for recruiting. Identify who in the organization should be involved and engage them early and often.
- Hire slowly; fire quickly.

We pick up the rest of this story on managing people in Chapter 21. But for now, remember that managing people is not just about management: It's about leadership. Your job as the founder, until you hire a CEO, is to lead the organization strategically, culturally, operationally, and emotionally. Cooperation and communication solve most problems. It's your job to take the lead in modeling both.

QUESTIONS

- How will you balance the need for people to do the work and the overhead they will cost you? How will you make those decisions?
- How will you manage people as you bring them on? If you don't have the management experience, where will it come from?
- What growth rates are appropriate? Who will help you make those choices?

NOTES

1. Sir Walter Raleigh (1552?–1618) was an English aristocrat, an adventurer and explorer, writer, poet, spy, and entrepreneur. In 1584 he planned the Colony and Dominion of Virginia, which ended with the failure of the Roanoke Island Colony (1586–1587), the first English colony in the New World.
2. Bagley, Constance E., and Craig E. Dauchy, *The Entrepreneur's Guide to Business Law* (Mason, OH: Thomson/West, 2008): 267–271.
3. Tuckman, Bruce, "Developmental Sequence in Small Groups," *Psychological Bulletin* 63, no.6 (1965): 384–399.
4. Shepherd, Jean, *In God We Trust: All Others Pay Cash* (New York: Doubleday, 1966).
5. See http://www.gonnerman.com/book.htm (accessed September 30, 2010).
6. Chapter 13 covers the most common employee contract documents, including ownership of invented intellectual property, confidentiality, and noncompetition.

Chapter 11

The Competition

Competition brings out the best in products and the worst in men.

—David Sarnoff[1]

One of the first questions people ask about a new idea or venture is: Who is the competition? Who else is doing this? The worst rookie mistake in the world is to answer: *No one.* There is *always* a competitor. Even if you can't find anybody else who is doing what you're doing, someone probably is thinking about it. And even if nobody is thinking about it, you'll always have indirect competitors, including the status quo and your customers' thrift.

WHO IS YOUR COMPETITION?

In 2007 four engineering students at Dartmouth's Thayer School of Engineering developed a belt-mounted light for runners to use at night. Using light-emitting diodes (LEDs) and new battery technology, they created a very effective product they called Night Runner. Market research and field testing established a strong potential for customer interest at an attractive price. They looked carefully for competing patents or other prior art and found nothing conflicting. They filed a provisional patent and planned to use the year until they had to decide whether to file a non-provisional patent to fund a start-up or license the technology to an established company. After graduation they started to put together a company and had angel investors seriously interested, but in early September they found an almost identical product already on the market. Two people with experience in sports and retail had launched a company, GoMotion, about a month before and had a patent pending on their own version, which they called the Litebelt. It turned out that GoMotion's patent was in the confidential phase when the Thayer team did its prior art search. Our students eventually concluded that even if the GoMotion patent did not preclude their design, a start-up without an experienced team or a manufacturing-level design could never compete successfully with an experienced team and a product already on the market.

In 2006 Aaron Teitelbaum, another engineering student at the Thayer School, developed a crutch with a spring-loaded length adjustment that made it easy to go up and down stairs. He searched prior art diligently, and although he found several alternative designs that proved unworkable in practice, he found nothing like his own. Customers seemed to like his prototype. When he began an independent study to launch the invention as a commercial product, one of his first assignments was to look even more carefully for prior art, and he found again nothing. Only when Aaron engaged a patent attorney to help him with a provisional patent did a patent identical to his own turn up. Some of the drawings and claims language so closely mirrored his provisional patent that Aaron felt the inventors must have seen his work—except that the patent had been filed in 1990.

In short, you'll always have competition. If someone isn't already thinking about your idea, someone else will imitate you and compete with you for customers and market share as soon as you show any signs of success.

Think about competition in three ways:

1. *Barriers to entry.* Competition often means that there is a barrier to entry: someone or something that stands between you and your customers. Facing a barrier to entry doesn't necessarily mean that another person or company is doing exactly what you are or that it has a specific barrier such as a patent that impedes your entry. If a customer's needs are being met, there is a barrier. Always ask: What barriers to entry will I have to surmount? How is the customer's need being met right now?
2. *Differentiation.* Failing to differentiate and set up barriers to competitors and imitators inevitably leads to profit erosion. In this race to the bottom, the most efficient producers and the least profitable competitors drive down margins to push out their competition:

   The larger theme … is the ordeal of what could be called "commodity hell," the place where executives find themselves when they cannot convince customers that their widgets or services are better than those of their ever-burgeoning competitors. All they can say is: "Yep, we got 'em too." [2]

   Failing to differentiate will eventually land you in commodity hell.
3. *Resources.* Competitors are not just a problem; they are a great source of information and ideas.

HOW DO YOU GET INTO THE MARKET?

You must think relentlessly and incessantly about your competition: past, present, and future. A competitive landscape analysis starts with a thorough assay of the market: Who are your direct and indirect competitors? You should know everything about direct competitors, including how you measure up: your relative competitive advantages and disadvantages. There's lots of information out there on public companies in the press, reports to shareholders, analysts' reports, and filings with the Securities and Exchange Commission (SEC). Information on private companies is less accessible, but you'll often find press coverage in addition to their own public relations and Web sites. Conferences, trade shows, distributors, retailers, and customers also can be good sources of information. You should always keep up with your competitors' products. Buy and study them carefully.

Once you've gathered the information, it's imperative that you be able to talk about it and show how you are different in a concise and compelling way. A features table is a particularly helpful device, especially in presentations. In 2000, we built a features table for a company working on a business-to-government Internet platform, a portion of which is shown in Table 11-1. For the row headings, we listed all the market-relevant products and features we could identify, and then we added our company and all our competitors as the column headings.

Table 11-1 Features Table for a Business-to-Government Internet Platform

	Parbuckle	AMS Buysense	Fedmarket/Bidengine	Fedcenter (Digital Commerce)
Services to Government				
End user–focused; not dependent on government-buying bureaucracy	Yes	No	Focused more on vendors; only resource to buyers is a vendor directory	Yes Focused primarily on credit-card purchases
A full-service resource to end users and purchasing agents alike	Yes	No	No	Yes. Focused primarily on credit-card purchases
Accessible to all with no training or software acquisition required	Yes	Partially	Yes	Yes
Query-based decision tree to analyze and define purchase and assess compliance	Yes	No	No	No
Database of pending purchases (for comparison and bundling), GWACs and indefinite delivery/indefinite quantities so that purchaser can search for existing resources	Yes	No	Government-wide Acquisition Contracts (GWACs)	No
Analyzes and certifies regulatory compliance; provides full documentation of compliance actions and status, including warrant of compliance	Yes	No	No	Links to arnet and numerous Federal Acquisition Requirement (FAR) sites
Capability to query FPR database and provide data on recent comparable purchases	Yes	No	No	No

168   From Idea to Success

Table 11-1 is only an excerpt, adapted from the original table, which was much larger. See Figure 11-1 to get an idea of how large the full table is, far too large to be legible here.

If you can put together a table with all the backup research in an appendix on competitors, no one will question your understanding of the competition. Of course, the table is only as exhaustive as your research, so make sure your research is thorough. You don't want to end up like the Night Runner or, worse, have an investor call your attention to a direct competitor you haven't considered. You also want to think carefully about any future competition that may develop. Once

Figure 11-1 Original full version of Table 11-1.

you've done this analysis, you can make a realistic assessment of the barriers to your entry and start forming a plan to overcome them.

Harvard's Michael Porter has been writing on competition and competitive strategy since 1979, when he created the Five Forces framework[3] to help companies think about competition. Like all frameworks, it has its advocates and its detractors, and it covers every aspect of the competitive universe, not only start-ups. However, it's a constructive way to think about the marketplace:

- *Competitive rivalry.* How many direct competitors do you have? How closely do they overlap? How effective are they? Is the industry fragmented[4] or consolidated[5]? How attractive are growth rates and profit margins? Low growth and intense competition make for thin margins but sometimes offer unexploited opportunities for service or niche strategies.
- *Potential for new entrants.* Is innovation opening new opportunities? How easily might new players enter? Are there high fixed-investment costs, cost advantages to existing players, issues with access to resources or distribution channels, existing relationships, or regulatory barriers? If entry is easy, it's good for you now and bad later unless you can make entry by others more difficult by creating new barriers.
- *Threat of substitution.* What is the indirect competition? Are there alternative solutions or products in the market that fill the same need you fill? Are there factors that hinder substitution that can work for you or against you, such as brand and customer loyalty, switching costs, and pricing?
- *Buyer power.* How much pricing power do you have over your customers? How concentrated is the market?[6] It's risky to have only a few big customers; this generally means they have the pricing power and you can lose significant market share if one suddenly decides to leave you. What are the buying capacity and willingness of customers to buy? How differentiated are you? How high are the costs for customers to switch to competitors?
- *Supplier power.* How much pricing power do they have? How many options for alternative suppliers or substitutes do you have? How high are your switching costs?

Beyond the Five Forces, which generally address directly competing products and services, there are also alternative products. Sometimes your biggest competitors are not the products that look just like yours, say, a Mac instead of a PC. Instead, sometimes you'll have indirect competition that fills the same need but in a completely different way. Michael Clarkin, our HP executive friend from Chapter 4, often illustrates the idea of indirect competition with a conversation he had with a friend who was a marketing manager for the Porsche Cayenne. Clarkin's friend explained that he often found that the Cayenne's big competitors were not just other high-end SUVs such as the Range Rover, but a Bang & Olufsen sound system for the living room. Said the friend, "When a guy comes onto one of our lots, often he's looking to spend $100,000 to show off how much money he has." Seen through that lens, Porsche is selling a car, but it's also selling status, self-esteem, and reputation. Looking at it this way opens up a host of competing alternatives from boats to artwork, jewelry, and real estate. Cadillac marketers used to say that diamonds were their biggest competitors.

Sometimes the alternatives are not something else customers can purchase to satisfy their need but an established habit or way of doing things that is entrenched in the customer base. This is the so-called "better-than" problem: Your product or solution must be sufficiently better than the current way of doing things to over-come old habits and customer inertia. Look again to Michael Clarkin's experience at Hewlett-Packard with LEDs in Chapter 4.

Investors often worry most about large established companies. Unless you're lucky enough to be looking at a market that has no dominant big companies, you'll be asked how you plan to secure a beachhead against those big companies. Fortunately, bigness, like most things, can have disadvantages as well as advantages. Convention and size favor incumbents but also leave holes for creative and nimble small companies to exploit. Always question convention and old assumptions. The fact that something is done or structured a certain way doesn't mean that's the best way it can be done. Be willing to be different. Speed, agility, flexibility, and will-ingness to change are tremendous assets in environments marked by innovation or rapid and fundamental change. Big companies aren't known for any of those traits, but you can be. Use your speed and ability to adapt quickly when entering and growing in an established market.

It's hard to make a noticeable impact on a big revenue base with a small cus-tomer or market, and so big companies focus on big sales accounts that will affect the bottom line. Those neglected smaller customers and opportunities offer start-ups and small, low-overhead companies an opportunity even in a crowded market. Once inside, those companies can work their way up the food chain as they become effective and established.

HOW DO YOU KEEP COMPETITION OUT?

A differentiated product that you can defend against imitation is fundamental to maintaining your competitive advantage. *Differentiated* is the key word here—remember commodity hell? If you have a product that is no more than a commod-ity, that indeed is hell because you cannot differentiate it; consumers focus only on its utility. Price becomes the primary differentiator, pressuring margins and costs. Differentiation moves you from utility to value. Utility is about usefulness; value is the "monetary worth of something."[7] For example, think about some products that are all related to wheat: a bushel of wheat, a bag of branded flour, a loaf of branded organic whole-wheat bread, and the bread and pastries in a full-service, high-end specialty bakery. Is the utility of each of these products the same as the value customers perceive in them? Which is more like an undifferentiated commodity? Which would you rather be selling, wheat by the bushel at the farm gate or full-service specialty bakery breads in a fast-casual dining chain? Which adds the most value to the wheat and thus offers the most opportunities for margin and profits? More to the point, which offers the best opportunity for proprietary differentiation?

You also could compare the share of retail price attributable to utility versus value in a $2 branded high-end beverage such as SoBe Green Tea versus a 50-cent generic soft drink. The SoBe brand is a clear triumph of value over utility. The same is true of a leather winter jacket that retails in a discount store for $50, whereas almost the same jacket sells online with a New England Patriots logo on the back for $350. They have a similar cost of goods sold but very different prices. What value are people paying for over and above the utility? This is an important question as you think about defining, positioning, differentiating, and pricing a product.

In 1943, the psychologist Abraham Maslow created a framework called the hierarchy of needs[8, 9] to analyze human motivation. See Figure 11-2. Maslow said that people generally fill their needs in a certain order, and at any given moment they are motivated to fill some classes of needs in a certain order. According to the hierarchy, people start at the bottom and fill those needs before moving up the pyramid to fill others. Maslow believed that once we fill the needs in one layer, we have little motivation to seek more: How much can you eat? How much shelter do you need? Instead, once a layer's needs are filled, most of the motivational energy and resources (aka money) that people allocate will move up and focus on filling the next layer's needs until that layer too is filled.

Maslow's hierarchy predicts that people will spend their money on physical needs such as food and clothing first. In the developed world today, those physical needs are mostly or completely met for a large number of people in the marketplace. If Maslow is correct, once they have enough to eat and stay clothed, consumers will focus more attention up the hierarchy and allocate their next dollars on shelter, safety, and security and then on social activities. In the developed world today it's probably fair to say that the majority of consumers have basic shelter and their choice of social activities, and so the need at the margin becomes ego, and that is where the marginal dollar of consumer spending will be most motivated.

Ego is about identity, signaling who we are, our preferences, and who we want to be like. Perhaps this explains why people place such a high value in the marketplace on trademarks, logos, and other forms of identity signaling. Start-ups should think carefully about the hierarchy framework and their product strategy. Where can you maximize your value-to-utility spread and use it as a competitive advantage? SoBe carved out a nice market share in an incredibly tough and glutted market dominated by big companies with great execution and smart branding. SoBe

Figure 11-2 Maslow's hierarchy of needs.

succeeded because the team understood what really drives consumer behavior in today's market. They marketed *identity*, creating a value over and above being just another commodity beverage. Sobe means health, vitality, and cool. The New England Patriots are our team; they're winners.

Today you can find ego-based products all over the marketplace. In that case, are consumers moving up to the next category of needs: self-actualization? Maslow predicts that they will do that. What kinds of products might fill the self-actualization needs at a high value-to-utility ratio? What are the opportunities in this space? Maslow predicts that this will be an attractive, high-margin place to be in the market.

In Chapter 4 we discussed the different components of your value proposition. These are your building blocks in differentiating yourself from the competition and defending your competitive advantage. You probably can think of companies that have built great businesses by differentiating themselves on one or another of the different elements. If your competitors cannot replicate something about your product—a product element, a service strategy, or the experience of using the product—they won't as readily be able to send you into commodity hell by matching your prices and reducing your value to utility alone. Table 11-2 lists ways you might successfully differentiate.

Table 11-2 Options for Achieving Competitive Differentiation

Product Elements	Service	Price	Access	Experience
Features	Access to service	Financing	Channels	Expectations
Aesthetics	Replacement	Comparative	Web presence	Consistency
Performance	Quality	Perception	Transportability	Follow-up/ support
Ease of use utility	Customer care	Relation to need	Cost	Function
Availability and access	Warranty	Switching cost	Delivery	Emotion
Quality	Maintenance contract	Margin	Regulation	Fun
Durability, reparability	Cost of service	Total cost of ownership	Limited access	Social proof
Safety	Automated	Residual value	Location	
Flexibility	Customer relationship	Visible	Easy to find	
Selection	As a product development tactic	Consistent	Convenience	
Useful life	Self-help	Reasonable	Timeliness	
Guarantee policy	Ordering	Stable		
Follow on products	Delivery	Comparable		
Emotional connection	Returns			
Brand	Use and repairs			

Beyond differentiation, you can defend yourself from competition with the following:

- *Intellectual property.* This was discussed in Chapter 5.
- *Legal and regulatory.* You can position yourself to take advantage of legal restraints, government regulations, and leases on key assets. If you choose to rely on the law to defend your competitive advantage, you should plan to retain the necessary legal resources and allocate effort and overhead to keep current and vigilant.

- *Access to resources, suppliers/distributors, or capacity.* If your product requires an essential component or resource to function properly, you can try to lock up its producers with an exclusive agreement. For a while at least, this can block competitors and imitators from following you. In some businesses, distribution is state-controlled—think alcohol—or there is a de facto monopoly or oligopoly of specialized distribution. This limited access to distribution is a powerful barrier to competition.
- *Technical expertise.* A specialized competency that is difficult to replicate or access can provide an enduring competitive barrier. Unfortunately, this barrier is more a fundamental component of your idea than a tactic you invent as a barrier to entry.

Beyond these basic strategies, companies have used a variety of other value proposition components to increase their market competitiveness. Table 11-3 gives some examples.

Table 11-3 Value Propositions That Create Competitive Advantages

Competitive Advantage(s)	Example(s)
Efficiency, low costs, economies of scale	Walmart, Alcoa
Product innovation	Apple, Intel, Medtronic
Quality, reliability	Mercedes
Customer responsiveness	Dell
Manufacturing innovation	Toyota
Customer service	Starbucks, Amazon
Sales effectiveness	Pfizer
Expertise in design and functionality	Apple, OXO

Many first-time entrepreneurs want to generate a sustained advantage by developing a *brand.* Although branding is an important strategy and you should deliberately create your brand from the start, a recognized brand is a result of success, not a cause. You can't rely on brand identity until you have captured a market position and delivered consistent value to customers. Brand strategy is a good barrier to competitors, but only once you're in the market. It seldom works for market entry.

One last barrier to competition that is mentioned frequently is the *first mover advantage:* the supposedly insurmountable competitive barrier that the first company into a market can erect behind itself to make it difficult or impossible for others to enter and compete. Some argue that this competitive advantage comes from the first company's access to and control over resources. Others say that first movers have an advantage because identity and brand recognition prevent switching. Whatever the reason, start-ups believe that because they are first, they will take a commanding lead and thus erect a competitive barrier.

We're not so sure. For example, have you ever heard of Eiger Labs' MPMan F10, Diamond Multimedia's Rio PMP300, or the Rio Riot? Maybe you've heard of Compaq's Personal Jukebox? Probably not, but we're pretty sure you would recognize an Apple iPod; you may own one. Apple released the iPod in 2001, a full four years after Eiger Labs introduced its MPMan F10 and two years after Compaq's Personal Jukebox. This is hardly atypical. There is a problem with the so-called first mover advantage: It seldom exists. Actually, most of the products people think were first movers, such as the iPod, were actually fast followers. How many of these first movers did you know? Mostly, you think of the fast followers (below in italics) as the first mover!

- The "mouse," Doug Engelbart and Bill English (Xerox PARC) (1951, 1963): *Apple, Microsoft*
- Sketchpad, WIMP (Xerox PARC) (1968): *Apple, Microsoft*
- U-matic, Betamax (Sony, 1969): *JVC and VHS*
- CP/M (Gary Kildall, 1974): *MS/DOS*
- Visicalc (1978): *Microsoft*
- Wordstar (1979): *Microsoft*
- Prodigy (1988): *AOL*
- Mosaic (1993): *Microsoft*
- Bot-fed search engines (1993): JumpStation, the World Wide Web Worm, and the Repository-Based Software Engineering (RBSE) spider: *Yahoo!, Google*
- Friendster (2002): *MySpace, Facebook*
- 84 Lumber, Handy Dan, Builders Square: *Home Depot, Lowe's*
- California Cooler wine cooler: *Gallo, Seagram's*
- Royal Crown Diet Cola: *Diet Pepsi, Diet Coke*
- Wisk liquid detergent: *Liquid Tide*
- Circuit City: *Best Buy*
- DHL: *Federal Express*
- Chux disposable diapers: *Proctor & Gamble*
- Ampex video recorder: *Sony, JVC, Matsushita*

- Rheingold Brewery's Gablinger, Meister Brau light beers: *Miller Lite*
- Book Stacks Unlimited (1992): *Amazon* (1994)

The idea of a first-to-enter advantage found support in business research in the early 1980s in the so-called PIMS and ASSESSOR studies: "[M]arket pioneers have enduring advantages in distribution, product-line breadth, product quality, and market share."[10] Unfortunately, those studies looked only at long-term survivors and lumped all early entrants together, first movers and early followers alike. Later studies have shown that for pioneers—defined as the first to sell in a category—the failure rate is 47 percent, whereas the failure rate for fast followers is "minimal."[11] Indeed, pioneers are current leaders in only 11 percent of the categories, and their mean market share is 10 percent, whereas the fast followers' mean market share is 30 percent.[12]

In reality, moving first has strong disadvantages. For one thing, the first mover assumes all the risk of proving a market demand and converting customers to a new product or concept. The company that moves first proves the market not only for itself but also for everyone else. Worse, first movers must learn all the subtleties and land mines in an unknown market, and learning curves cost. Early product versions often are clunky, costly, and crude. Fast followers can poach the best ideas, imitating and improving on what they see. At the outset, no one knows enough to build only the absolute minimum infrastructure for internal production, sales, and support needed to meet a market most efficiently, and so first movers are often slow to streamline and reduce underutilized overhead. Imitators never need to deal with these cost burdens. Often these disadvantages more than outweigh the advantage of early proprietary knowledge. Further, pioneers are frequently small companies or start-ups whereas later entrants are strong, established companies that bring significant financial and execution strength to the opportunity defined by the pioneers.

We think there is a first mover advantage, but not where most people think it is—first to enter. Remember Everett Rogers' and Geoffrey Moore's crossing the chasm chart (Figure 4-1). Notice where the first mover starts: at the far left with the innovators and early adopters. Moore said that the biggest challenge for first movers is the leap from those early markets to big-market, majority adoption. The goal is not to be first to the market but first across the chasm. Remember one of Moore's fundamental points: First movers who have to introduce fundamentally new products have to make their appeal to innovators and early adopters, and what appeals to those groups often fails to appeal to the majority on the other side of the chasm. Fast followers don't carry the baggage of that first strategy and can learn from the first mover to tailor an appeal specifically to the majority across the chasm, essentially starting on the other side and never having to leap it at all. Thus, if you have to be first to market, plan your entry strategy as not just an entry but a race to cross the chasm (Figure 11-3). That is the only first-mover advantage that counts.

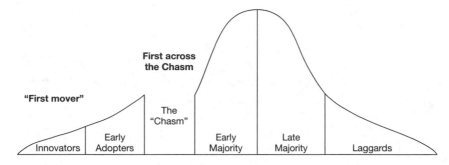

Figure 11-3 First-mover advertiser: the race to cross the chasm.

Source: Geoffrey Moore, *Crossing the Chasm: Marketing and Selling High-Tech Products to Mainstream Customers* (New York: HarperCollins: 1991): 17.

WHAT CAN YOU LEARN FROM YOUR COMPETITION?

A lot! For one thing, you may find that you're not the first mover after all. Many first-time entrepreneurs are crestfallen when they discover that someone else is working on the same idea or market they're targeting. Sometimes this knowledge freezes them out—like the Night Runner students at the beginning of this chapter—and they quit. More often being a fast follower is a better position than first mover so long as you diligently and conscientiously consider how to overcome barriers to entry. Your competitors are one of your most valuable sources of information. You just have to get the information and then think creatively about how to profit from it.

Sadly, many start-ups do only a cursory job of studying the competition and don't sufficiently incorporate competitive strategy into their plans. This is just as silly as failing to conduct a thorough market validation. Competitive research and strategizing don't require a monetary investment, just time and focus. Unaddressed competition can kill your profits, put pressure on your market share, and even bar your entry into a market. The more you research the competition, differentiate, and develop barriers to competitors, the more you lower one of the biggest risks in starting a business, and that makes your idea more valuable.

WHAT I KNOW NOW THAT I WISH I HAD KNOWN THEN

Abe Clayman

While an engineering student at Dartmouth, Abe Clayman was a cofounder of the Night Runner company mentioned at the beginning of this chapter. Abe is now vice principal at KIPP DC: LEAP Academy, a public charter school in Washington, D.C., where he has worked since graduating in 2007. He offers these lessons learned from the Night Runner experience:

In my senior year at Dartmouth, a group of students and I designed a lightweight belt that runners could use for illumination while running at night, first as academic work and then as a business. Based on interviews with runners and customer research, we were convinced there was a market.

Being blindsided by the discovery of a daunting competitor in GoMotion, we learned the hard way about the importance of researching competitors. While I can't point to a specific action that would definitely have prevented our outcome, now I encourage future entrepreneurs to check daily on known competitors and research potential ones. Multiple advisors (including Professor Fairbrothers) said to us, "If your idea is a good one, then you have to think about why someone else hasn't done it yet." It probably is true more often than not. So you have to keep looking. And competition is not the end of the world—unless, that is, you are not fit as a company to compete.

On the project I learned the difference between working on an engaging project and putting a concerted effort behind a potential business. During our time working on the Night Runner, we always talked about ways to continue the project, but we never stopped planning for the careers we already had in mind. If we had decided to seriously pursue the Night Runner as a business, we would have needed to invest significant personal time and money, put other plans or jobs on hold, and live in a new or unfamiliar place. While the emergence of GoMotion made it clear we should stop, we would never have succeeded anyway without fully committing to the project.

Our team frequently struggled to define a road map for taking our product from a few prototypes to a viable business. We never defined clear roles, responsibilities, and decision-making power. We lacked the right structure for discussing how to move our project forward. Had we been more focused as a team, we might well have known sooner about a competitor like GoMotion and been better prepared to be willing to compete with it. In retrospect, we should have more rigorously researched potential competitors, committed fully to the project as a *business,* and clearly defined roles and responsibilities for the team.

QUESTIONS

- What barriers will you be facing when you try to enter the market? What do you plan to do about them so that you don't fail before you establish a position?
- What do you anticipate your competitors will do? How far ahead can you think in this chess game?
- How creative can you be in developing barriers to competition? What will it take to make them a reality? Can you justify the cost against the rewards?

NOTES

1. David Sarnoff (1891–1971), the first president of RCA, was a pioneer in consumer television.
2. Buchholz, Todd G., "Drowning in Red Ink," *Wall Street Journal* (May 30, 2007): D8.
3. Porter, Michael E., *Competitive Strategy* (New York: Free Press, 1980).
4. Fragmented industries are not dominated by one or a few major players. There may be room for new entrants or consolidation strategies such as roll-ups.
5. Consolidated industries typically have large established players, making entry difficult for a start-up.
6. Market concentration is a measure of how many customers there are per dollar of sales.
7. *Webster's Collegiate Dictionary,* 11th ed. (Springfield, MA: G&C Merriam & Co., 2003).
8. Maslow, Abraham H., "A Theory of Human Motivation," *Psychological Review* 50, no. 4 (1943): 370–396.
9. Maslow, Abraham, *Motivation and Personality* (New York: Harper, 1954): 236.
10. Tellis, Gerard J., and Peter N. Golder, "First to Market, First to Fail? Real Causes of Enduring Market Leadership," *Sloan Management Review* 37, no. 2 (Winter 1996): 65–75.
11. Ibid.
12. Ibid.

Chapter 12

Financing

What's nice about investing is you don't have to swing at pitches. You can watch pitches come in one inch above or one inch below your navel, and you don't have to swing. No umpire is going to call you out.

—Warren Buffett

Some founders can launch their enterprises and achieve financial stability solely with their own and/or their families' and friends' money. Others start and grow their companies with revenue from customers who pay in advance for products or services before they exist. These are the lucky founders, and this is not as easy as it sounds. In fact it's often incredibly hard. For everyone else there is the even harder challenge of raising outside financing—often raising it and raising it and raising it.

Too many people fall into the trap of declaring victory when they raise money. Raising money is just a means of selling your company with the right to buy it back (also known as *borrowing,* and you should be so lucky as to be able to borrow) or selling the company in big blocks at a time with no buy-back option, otherwise known as *selling equity.* It's important to remember that raising funds is not a measure of success; it's only a tool to achieve it. Money comes with a cost. Count that cost.

Many entrepreneurs say that getting investment in a company is a mixed blessing, and too much of it is often not a blessing at all. Anecdotally, it seems that bootstrapped companies often have a better chance of succeeding than companies that start out with all the money they need and more. Experience certainly says that money alone does not solve most problems or make companies grow. Too often, throwing money at a problem or opportunity ends up creating a lot of structure and process, wasteful spending on nonessentials, and precious little progress on the problem or opportunity. Money doesn't solve problems; people solve problems with or without a lot of money. Money can make people complacent, even lazy. When it suddenly dries up, old habits are hard to unlearn, and time is short. The most important advice many entrepreneurs feel they can give is never to waste a dollar even if you can afford to. A business that has grown up living lean knows how to live when hard times come. It isn't carrying a lot of extra baggage such as overbuilt overhead and impatient, panicky investors or, worse, dependent on continuing investment that often is shut off abruptly when times turn hard.

Occasionally there is an enterprise that can be started and built without infusions of cash from somewhere, but it doesn't happen often. Starting up takes a lot of time and effort, but it especially takes resources. The start-up needs money for things such as prototyping, entering the market, building out capacity and inventory, and fueling expansion. Cash is the key focus in an early-stage enterprise, not profits. Businesses don't fail when they are not profitable; they fail when they run out of cash.

There is a mountain of information in print and online on how to finance early-stage enterprises. Here we will only try to set out a useful framework, provide some guidance on resources so that you can learn more, and offer some advice on how to finance your enterprise in a way that best protects you and maximizes your chances of getting what you need. Financing is never an easy chore or one lightly taken on by anyone but the uninformed.

HOW MUCH SHOULD YOU RAISE?

What do you need? Actually, you should always ask the question differently: "What do you *really* need"—as contrasted with "What would be ideal?" Financing is expensive, and the earlier the stage, the more expensive it is. What would you think if you went to a bank for a home loan and they wanted 20 percent interest? *Interest* is another way of talking about the *rate of return (ROR)* on money raised. Another term investors use is *internal rate of return (IRR)*.

A target IRR of 20 percent can be *low* for seed and angel stage investing. Investors need those kinds of returns if their companies are successful because the risk that they will never get anything back is so high. The bank can foreclose and take your house if the loan sours. If a start-up fails, usually there is little or nothing to take back. The point? Early-stage investment is really, really expensive when you can get it at all, and finding money is almost always terribly time-consuming, in fact often all-consuming. In addition, early-stage money often comes with all sorts of strings, such as involvement by investors, which may be very valuable but can be counterproductive and frustrating. It's not uncommon for investors to take control of a company from its founders and put it in other hands.

In light of the cost of early money, always try to take your venture as far as you can on as little as you can before you raise money. Remember risk versus valuation: The more risks you can take out of the venture by getting things done before you seek outside financing, the higher your chances of raising the money you need and the lower its cost. Staging investments as you reduce risk helps keep the cost of capital down. As you prove up a phase or eliminate a major risk, you can (one hopes) raise additional money on more attractive terms.

However, balanced against this is the fact that not only is early-stage money expensive and hard to get, it may not be available at all when you need it. Many investors and entrepreneurs say you should raise all you can when you can. Investment opportunities sometimes come in waves; suddenly a sector is all the fashion and money is flowing. You may find yourself with an opportunity to raise money when you may not feel you need it. Investor psychology can have a herd mentality to it. Enthusiasm and pessimism come in cycles, so learn to recognize when investors are hungry to invest in early-stage deals. Times like this, rare as they are, often mean raising money is easier (relatively), and valuations are often better as well. What to do? Raise money when you might not need it? Take more than you absolutely need? An angel investor friend of ours in the financial community often reminds entrepreneurs, "When cookies are passed, take a cookie." Another friend describes the waves of enthusiasm in financing as water sloshing back and forth in a bathtub. "When it comes your way," he says, "take all you can."

In the end, this is another of those moments for judgment : Take more or less? Sooner or later? Circumstances determine, and *you* need to make the call, not the investors or common wisdom. There are few things less sensible than deciding to do something because everyone else is doing it. Have a solid work plan and budget tied to exactly what you need to hit the milestones you have defined. cost-effectiveness is always vital. Nothing can set up a company for failure faster than building a culture of wasting money, of spending more on anything than you really need to. Ravi Kalakota, author of *E-Business: Roadmap for Success* and founder of the failed online marketplace Hsupply.com, wishes he hadn't burned through his venture capital investment so fast. He launched the company in March 1999, and when he closed down Hsupply.com in December 2000, the company had 90 employees and had spent $5 million. "We hired like crazy," he said. "Don't hire marketing people. The race is not to an IPO; it's to build a sustainable business model."[1] Gail Goodman, founding CEO of Constant Contact, says the biggest thing she learned in building the company through some really tough times is, "No matter how much money you have, never waste a dollar."[2]

WHERE DO YOU FIND INVESTMENT?

You will always be worrying about where available cash will come from, or at least you should be. There is a progression of sources of cash that can be available at different stages of growth. Some sources are available at the beginning; some, such as venture capital and banks, only when you are more developed. What are your funding choices?

1. *You.* This is sometimes called *bootstrap* financing, pulling yourself up by your own bootstraps. The National Federation of Independent Businesses found in one survey that 70 percent of small business owners started with less than $20,000.[3]

   a. Some people max out as many credit cards as they can. Remember, though, that you have to pay back that money, and credit card interest is expensive. You may have savings or assets you can use to secure bank loans, but take care not to expose more than you are prepared to lose.

Some founders work part- or full-time to pay their living costs and get money for a business. If this seems to be an option, be sure to take into account that there are only so many hours in the day; at some point making money to start a company can become a full-time demand and crowd out your ability to build the company.

b. Some companies, particularly in technology and IT, get consulting engagements to bring in dollars they can use to build the company. In this mode, strategies that generate cash quickly are a must. Pay attention to receivables and collections; slow-paying customers are a problem for any company but especially for a hand-to-mouth bootstrap. Some companies raise cash by borrowing against their accounts receivable (factoring), though this can be expensive. Some companies lease equipment and any other capital assets they can, until there is enough free cash that the economics of purchasing are better. Often they have an office at home or share offices with other companies.

c. Investors generally want to see that you are invested in your company, that you have "skin in the game." Some want to see you put in everything you have first so that they know you are committed to making it work for you and them. We emphatically give other advice. You may need to invest some of your money in the early days—that's almost inevitable—but don't invest it all. Obviously, you should never put at risk more than you can stand to lose. But there's another reason to hold back a significant portion of your powder. Almost invariably somewhere along the line to sustainability there will come a moment (or more than one) when you are down to the last dollars and there is nowhere to turn on short notice to bridge the gap. At that moment you may or may not want to go all in with the last of the dollars you allocated to the project, but if you have held some money back, you will be glad to have that option. We have seen more than one company make it past a tight spot that might have been fatal because it had held something in reserve for when it really needed it.

2. *Customers* are the single best source of cash. Sales are revenue; they don't cost you equity or interest. Sometimes you can get customers to pay in advance for products or services you will develop and deliver later. For a long time this was a standard model in the software industry, though it's not as common as it once was. Always test the chances that a customer will buy in advance. It's the best cash and the best market validation all at the same time.

3. *Family and friends* are the most common source of first outside investment. This mixes relationship and money, always a dangerous proposition. The risk of losing an investment is highest at this stage. Valuations are often

impossible to guess. Frequently, friends and family are inexperienced and trust you more than they should. Valuations often are way too high, causing problems in later financings. Fortunately, there is a mechanism to help with this; see the section below on convertible notes. A good rule: Never take an investment that you're not prepared to face at the Thanksgiving dinner table when it's gone sour. Friends and family should assume they will never see their investments again, and if that's okay, maybe it's safe to proceed … *maybe*!

4. *Foundations and grants* support research, especially in biomedical applications, and often bridge the funding gap between the end of basic science funding from organizations such as the National Institutes of Health and the National Science Foundation and money from venture capital or industry. If you are launching a social enterprise, foundations and grants are your main target. Chapter 14 covers social enterprises in detail.

5. *Government programs* often are a great source funding for early-stage companies. The Small Business Innovation Research (SBIR) Program is the best-known and one of the most important subsidies to small businesses in the country. It has invested over $16 billion in small businesses through 11 government agencies, including the Department of Defense, the National Institutes of Health, the National Science Foundation, the Department of Energy, and NASA. You can learn more at http://grants.nih.gov/grants/funding/sbirsttr_programs.htm.

   a. There are a number of other federal programs, including Small Business Technology Transfer (STTR) grants; the Advanced Technology Program (ATP) at the National Institute of Standards and Technology; the guaranteed loan programs of the Small Business Administration; numerous contracts and grants from places such the departments of defense, agriculture, and energy; and new programs at the National Institutes of Health supporting translational research. Most states also have a variety of loan, grant, and investment programs to foster company formation and growth in their states. Occasionally there are state and federal tax credit programs that are attractive.

   b. On the plus side, government funding is usually nondilutive, consisting of grants or contract work. However, most of those grants are competitive, meaning you must invest a lot of time in chasing them and have to take a chance that you'll get the funding. There are often lots of restrictions on the use of funds, and there are almost always heavy reporting requirements.

6. *Strategic partners* are generally large companies that enter into financing and joint venture arrangements with start-ups to align a new opportunity with their current strategies, explore new opportunities, or complement

current business lines or sometimes just for the financial returns in a business they understand. Several major technology companies have corporate venture capital groups charged with making early-stage investments. Some have mandates to stay within strategic connections to existing business lines of the company; some focus on financial returns. Usually there is at least a goal of leveraging the assets and resources of the company. Examples include funds at Intel, Cisco, Microsoft, Google, Amazon, and Johnson & Johnson. An online search will turn up directories and other listings of potential partners.

On the plus side, the start-up gains credibility and access to technical and market resources. On the minus side, big company processes can be time-consuming and frustrating. More important, a close association with a big company has significant implications for the future, when you may want to sell your company. At that time being so closely tied to a major player can be an impediment to getting other competitors interested in buying the company. Worse, strategic joint ventures or investments often carry preemptive rights in the event of a sale, and that can suppress your cash value. Still, sometimes partnering is the best way to launch a company at the beginning. It's a judgment call between pay me now and pay me later.

7. *Banks* lend money at lower interest rates than other forms of early-stage investment; that would be good news except for the fact that banks don't lend money to start companies. The reason banks lend at lower rates is that they take less risk of not getting paid back. Generally, they lend only to the extent that they can get pledges of assets whose value more than covers the amount owed. Start-ups generally have few or no securable assets.

Banks will lend against your personal assets, however, and many start-up entrepreneurs guarantee loans to their companies or borrow on home equity lines to raise money. The Small Business Administration has programs of loans to small businesses that are placed through banks, but in almost all cases the borrower has to pledge assets against the borrowing and put in cash from another source as well. Even if you are not getting bank funding, you should always establish a good working relationship with a bank right from the start. Get an operating line of credit open as soon as you can and use it. At first it probably will have to be secured, but over time you may be able to get the security released or at least expand the line over the amount you have pledged as security. Lines of credit don't solve all your financing needs, but they can be valuable cash management tools.

Perhaps the best-known sources of start-up funding are angels and venture capitalists.

WHAT ABOUT ANGELS AND VENTURE CAPITAL INVESTORS?

Some people loosely use the term *private equity* synonymously with venture capital. Venture capitalists are a subset of the larger world of private equity, a tiny one at that. In terms of dollars under management, private equity is dominated by later-stage investment and buyout funds. Types of private equity include:

- Leveraged buyout
- Venture capital
- Growth capital
- Distressed and special situations
- Mezzanine capital

- Secondaries
- Search funds
- Real estate
- Other strategies

In 2008 private equity as a whole had over $2.5 trillion under management. Venture capitalists in total represented about 0.8 percent of the industry. They raise capital in the high twenties to low thirties of billions of dollars per year, though they have been under significant stress since 2009. They invest in the twenties to thirties of billions annually in 3,000 to 4,000 transactions. None of the largest private equity firms, as measured in dollars under management, is a venture capital firm. Venture capitalists focus on early-growth to midgrowth stages, but some do invest seed capital. Table 12-1 shows venture capitalist investments by sector.[4]

Table 12-1 Venture Capital Investment by Sector in 2009[5]

Sector	$ Millions	% Share	No. Transactions
Biotechnology	3,611	20.0	423
Business products and services	248	1.4	81
Computers and peripherals	307	1.7	53
Consumer products and services	370	2.0	83
Electronics/instrumentation	300	1.7	60
Financial services	366	2.0	54
Healthcare services	102	0.6	38
IT services	1,102	6.1	215
Industrial/energy	2,362	13.1	230
Media and entertainment	1,227	6.8	258
Medical devices and equipment	2,511	13.9	315
Networking and equipment	736	4.1	99
Retailing/distribution	186	1.0	34
Semiconductors	851	4.7	126
Software	3,224	17.8	663
Telecommunications	550	3.0	144
Undisclosed/other	14	0.1	17
TOTAL	18,068	100.0	2,893

Apart from venture capitalists, private equity includes another major group of investors in start-up companies: wealthy individuals or groups of individuals known as *angels*. In an average year angels invest about the same amount of money as venture capital industry and participate in many more deals. Table 12-2 summarizes angel investments over a sample three-year period.

Table 12-2 Angel Investments for a Sample Three-Year Period

Year	$ Millions	Number of Transactions
2007	26,000	57,137
2008	19,200	55,480
2009	17,600	57,225

Source: http://www.wsbe.unh.edu/files2008_Analysis_Report_Final.pdf; and
        http://www.unh.edu/news/docs/2009angelanalysis.pdf.

Many kinds of people are angels, including entrepreneurs, successful managers, and professionals in medicine, law, or finance. Often angels' experience and networks can be as valuable as their money. Their level of expertise and experience varies widely, as does the time they will devote to being involved. As with anything involving people, get comfortable with your angels before taking their investments to avoid unhappy surprises. Because angel investments often involve substantial ownership positions and sometimes significant control rights, you want to see good compatibility and no potential for destructive micromanagement or worse.

Angels generally look for returns of 15 to 25 percent over five to seven years. No one wants to be paid back with interest and/or collect dividends; they expect a return of capital and profit through a sale, a merger for liquid stock, or an initial public offering (IPO). Historically, about 35 percent of angel investments end in acquisition, 27 percent in IPO, and 5 percent in a buyback; 32 percent are written off.[6]

There is substantial regulation around raising money privately from individuals under the Securities and Exchange Commission (SEC), as well as securities laws in all states in which securities are offered or sold. For example, under the Securities Act of 1933 the SEC's Rule 501 requires that your angel investors be *accredited*. Accredited investors are defined as individuals who have a net worth of at least $1 million[7] or an annual income of at least $200,000 in the most recent two years (or $300,000 combined income, including a spouse). There are extensive regulations and requirements for registering securities offered for sale to investors, but Section 4(2) of the Act provides an exemption for private offerings that meet certain requirements, including the amounts offered (up to $1 million, Rule 504; up to $5 million, Rule 505) and the number of accredited and sophisticated investors (Rule 506). In addition, SEC Rule 10b–5 prohibits any act or omission resulting in fraud or deceit in connection with the purchase or sale of any security.[8] If you plan to solicit angels for investment—or anyone else for that matter, including friends and family—you must do your homework and be sure you have oversight from a knowledgeable attorney. Compliance failures can be lingering liabilities in the company and often are caught by investors' attorneys during the due diligence associated with investment rounds, sales, or IPOs.

Some angels invest alone, and others cooperatively in groups. There are many ways to find them. Organized groups actively source deal flow. There are a number of resources to search for angels, including the Angel Capital Association and Inc.com's Web site. Use your networks. Many professionals, including attorneys, accountants, finance professionals, and venture capitalists, know of angels and are often angels themselves.

Angels' investment processes vary widely. Groups tend to be structured, with scheduled meetings and formal presentations. In these cases, if an investment is going to happen, generally at least one of the angels will step up to lead the investment and act as the primary interface with the company. Outside groups and solitary individuals may take a presentation from you or just want to have a conversation. As with any investors, the people factor dominates: the way they assess you and the team will dominate the investment decision.

Angels usually look to buy equity ownership in the company in return for their investment. Documenting an equity investment in a company is not a trivial undertaking and has to be done by attorneys. Since there are two parties involved, there will be at least two attorneys: one for the investor group and one for the company. Sometimes the individuals in the company also want personal legal advice and need a lawyer separate from the one advising the company. Conventionally, the company bears all the costs of legal work on the transaction for both the investors and the company. So legal bills can mount quickly, especially if you let the negotiation process run away with itself. When you are raising smaller amounts of money, the legal costs alone can eat up a significant fraction of the investment you just raised with your precious equity.

The Convertible Note

An alternative form of investment for early stages—friends and family and angels alike—is the convertible debt instrument, which helps with both the legal costs of closing and the difficulty of valuing the company. This is a simple document of no more than a few pages that often can be done from an attorney's boilerplate. Essentially, the investors lend money to the company (not the founders personally), with the provision that at the next round of funding they will get the same kind of equity shares as the next-round investors but will pay a discount on the share price—or, what amounts to the same thing, get more shares for the same price—to compensate for the added risk they took by investing early. A sample term sheet for such a note might look something like Figure 12-1:

Summary of Terms for Convertible Note Financing

_____ , Inc.
_____ , 20__7

ISSUER:	_____ , Inc., a _____ Corporation.
AMOUNT OF FINANCING:	Up to $_____ (the "Principal").
INVESTORS:	A select group of "accredited investors" (the "Noteholders").
FORM OF FINANCING:	Convertible Term Note (copy attached).
TERM:	30 months
INTEREST:	Wall Street Journal published prime interest rate plus 2%.
PREPAYMENT:	Company can prepay outstanding principal and interest, but only with written consent of the Noteholders.
CONVERSION:	Upon a "Qualifying Financing" of at least $_____ , principal and interest then due will convert to shares of the same class and series, and under the same terms, as the equity security as issued by the Company in the Qualified Financing (the "Qualified Financing Stock").
PRICING AT CONVERSION:	The number of shares issued to the Noteholders will be determined by dividing the Principal by the same per-share price paid by Qualifying investors for their shares.
PREMIUM ON CONVERSION:	To recognize the earlier investment, and additional risk assumed by the Noteholders in this Convertible Term Note Financing, the number of shares issued to each Noteholder, as calculated in the Conversion, will be increased by a factor of 1.30.
BOARD REPRESENTATION:	The Noteholders, as a group, will be entitled to designate ____ director(s) to _____'s board of directors.
OPTION TO PARTICIPATE IN FUTURE FINANCINGS:	Each holder of the Notes shall have a pre-emptive right to participate pro rata (based on its deemed ownership interest in the Company) in any equity financings up to and including a Qualified Financing, and to participate pro rata (based on its proportionate ownership interest in the Notes) in any non-equity finance offerings made by the issuer.
NON-BINDING:	This Summary of Terms is not intended as a legally binding commitment by the Company or the Investors; it is intended only as a summary of the terms and conditions provided in the Convertible Term Note.

Figure 12-1 Sample convertible note term sheet.

The advantages of using a convertible note instead of equity include the following:

- A simple note means much lower legal costs.
- Since the debt amount is fixed, valuation of the company is deferred to a later time when the company has progressed, there is more information, and (presumably) professional investors are involved in the valuation.
- Convertible notes permit repeated closings. Equity offerings generally have to be closed at one time or in no more than a small number of stages. Convertible notes can be written as often as you like over an extended period, letting you raise more money as you go.
- Note holders are not shareholders and don't automatically have legal rights to participate in shareholder decision making until the notes convert.
- Doing notes reduces the number of classes of stock.
- Notes offer early investors some protection from later investors. Holders of the notes will convert to the same class of stock issue as the next-round investors. Otherwise, investors in later rounds often insist on classes of stock that assert privileges not conferred on stock issues from earlier rounds.

Not all angels like convertible notes. They don't like feeling that the step-up in value between their round and the next is capped at the share price discount. However, they avoid the risk of a *down round,* in which the valuation actually drops, or of seeing less than the fixed step-up in the next round. You can alleviate the "capping" objection by sweetening the offer with *warrants,* which give the investor the right for a period of time to buy a certain number of shares at a pre-determined (low) price. A new model caps the funding amount in the next round so that even if the round raises more than the cap, the conversion is capped at the defined amount, meaning that the upside gets better the higher the valuation of the company above the cap. Still, some angels want the equity and the rights to participate in decision making in the company that go with owning shares. At the friends and family stage, convertible notes are definitely preferable, especially because they defer the dicey issue of pricing the company to a later round when it's done more at arm's length and presumably by experienced investors.

Often the involvement of angels, which comes along with their investment, can be one of the biggest advantages you get. Many angels invest for more reasons than just the money. They often say they remember people who helped them be successful along the way and look at investing as a way of giving back. Some invest to stay active and get involved in interesting things. Good angels can provide a wealth of experience, advice, networking, encouragement, and accountability that is often what a team needs to make the leap to effective and consistent execution.

WHAT I KNOW NOW THAT I WISH I HAD KNOWN THEN

Bob Molinari, Retrotope, Inc.

Bob Molinari specializes in biotechnology reagents, genomics, proteomics, and biopharmaceutical research. He is currently the founding CEO of Retrotope, Inc., focusing on isotopic control of diseases related to oxidative stress. He was the founding CEO of Coda Genomics/Verdezyne, a computational proteomics company, and the cofounding CEO and president of Protogene Laboratories, Inc., where he led the company to become the world's largest supplier of custom DNA before it was acquired by Life Technologies, Inc. An active angel investor and start-up board member, Bob is on the biotech screening committee of the Bay Area Life Science Angels. He has this advice for raising angel investments:

- Court potential investors who have built or managed companies in your industry or by using similar technology. Even if they don't invest, if you impress them, they will lead you to the right knowledgeable investors.
- Not even highly expert industry investors or organized angel groups respond to cold calling. Network aggressively for referrals to mentors and "smart money" investors. Go to industry events and work the room. If you can't afford the events, meet people outside the conference rooms and chat them up. Get introductions. Generously reward people who help you with stock options; it's the best way to incentivize them without using precious cash.
- Don't solicit all your friends and family for money under the terms you want. For one thing, this will fundamentally change the nature of your relationships whether you succeed or fail. Take this sort of investment only if the investors/friends honestly say they don't believe your relationship will change if they lose everything they invest.
- Angels often expect you to invest your own cash. Invest only what you can afford to lose. If you are investing your time, skill, and reputation and are forgoing a salary for sweat equity, you need at least some offsetting balance in your personal risk profile.
- Finally, never, ever take "dumb money" simply because you can get people unfamiliar with your industry to invest at high prices. These investors will be the first to become disillusioned and will be no end of trouble if their expectations are not met.

In contrast to the unstructured world of angel investing, *venture capitalists* are experienced investment professionals who work in formal partnerships. These limited partnerships are organized to raise money from limited partner investors—generally foundations, endowments, pension funds, and wealthy individuals—and invest in early-stage companies. They make equity investments in young companies with the potential for rapid growth and exits at high multiples of their investment over a time horizon of 3 to 10 years. They raise money in discrete funds and then make 10 to 25 investments out of each fund over a period of a few years, assist in the development of the companies, and often facilitate the eventual sale, merger, or public offering of the companies. The investment model was created in the late 1950s mostly on the West Coast by a pioneering group of technology-focused investors, including Tom Perkins, Don Valentine, Arthur Rock, and Dick Kramlich, among others. A documentary film produced by the venture capitalist Paul Holland of Foundation Capital[9] tells the story of the creation of this investment industry that went on to become one of the great engines of innovation in the last century, growing companies such as Intel, Apple, Cisco, Atari, Genentech, and Tandem.

Tuck's Center for Private Equity and Entrepreneurship compares angels and venture capitalists in Table 12–3[10]:

Table 12-3 Angels and Venture Capitalists Compared

Characteristics	Angels	Venture Capitalists
Funding amounts	$25,000 to $1.5 million	$500,000 and above
Motivation to invest	Not just return-driven, strong emotional component ("bragging rights," psychological benefits of coaching, rush from being involved in fast-paced start-ups)	Mostly return-driven with adjustments for relationships with other venture capitalists and reputation among entrepreneurs
Accessibility	Prefer anonymity, reachable via referrals or through angel groups	Highly visible, usually will only look at business plans referred by their network of contacts (attorneys, etc.)
Geographical focus	Regional, within 4 hours' drive time	Regional, national, or international, depending on the firm
Key reasons to invest	Personal chemistry with entrepreneur, detailed market analysis, sustainable competitive advantages	Nearly developed product, operating history, strong and experienced team, sustainable competitive advantages

(Continued)

Table 12-3 Angels and Venture Capitalists Compared (*Continued*)

Characteristics	Angels	Venture Capitalists
Number of investments	Less than VC firms because they have the luxury of being selective	More than angels because they need to make a minimum number of investments in a given year
Term sheet issuance	Relatively fast (one day to three weeks); terms are somewhat negotiable (more than with VCs)	Can be fast, but usually is at a moderate pace (several weeks); terms are fairly standard and not very negotiable
Investment vehicle	Common or preferred stock, occasionally convertible debt (debt convertible to equity shares)	Preferred stock (convertible to common shares)
Equity percentage	10%–30%	20% or more
Typical post-money valuation of start-ups	$250,000 to $10 million	$5 million and above
Due diligence	Relatively fast and light	Relatively slow and methodical
Funding process	Lump sum or milestone	Lump sum or milestone
Long-term value added	Operational experience, common sense advice, specific industry expertise	Experience in managing growth, deep pockets, networks of additional sources of capital, Rolodex, experience in managing IPOs and sale exits
Reaction to bad news	Roll up the sleeves and help solve the problem; open up Rolodex	Intense communication and coaching; open up Rolodex; help structure joint ventures, new financing rounds or mergers; fire management
Target exit time	5 to 7 years	3 to 5 years
Target IRR returns	15% to 25%	20% to 40%

A new sector has emerged within the venture community in recent years: the so-called *social venture funds,* which explicitly focus on a *dual bottom line:* doing well and doing good. For examples, check out the Silicon Valley Social Venture Fund (http://www.sv2.0rg/) and Grey Ghost Ventures (http://www.grayghostventures.com/), which invested in one of our Dartmouth start-ups, Pharmasecure. If you can make the argument that you are solving a social problem with your start-up and can do it in a way that harnesses the power of the for-profit motive, this can be an interesting alternative. To learn more, a good resource is the Social Enterprise Alliance (http://www.se-alliance.org/). A quick Web search will turn up many other resources.

Venture investors are highly selective. A typical venture firm's deal "funnel" is depicted in Figure 12-2.

There are two key points in this figure:

1. To put it mildly, your odds of being funded by a venture capital firm are not high. As Warren Buffett says, no umpire will call a venture investor out on strikes. Investors can stand at the plate all day long looking for the perfect pitch before they swing.
2. Note the headings toward the top of the chart that show where venture firms source their deals. There is one important source missing: unsolicited submissions. A venture investor hardly ever evaluates an investment that comes in unsolicited. Investors want to come and find you or have you come by referral from someone they know and trust. Many have young associates who do nothing but source potential investments. The conclusion: If you want to be considered by a venture firm, get the best referrals you can from people it considers credible. Beware of finders: people who say they can get you funded for a fee, usually a few percentage points of the funds raised. Most venture capitalists don't like having finders involved and don't feel their fees represent a good use of invested funds.

In seeking venture funding, presenting to venture capitalists, and negotiating with them (should you be so fortunate), it helps to understand their investment strategy and psychology. First, think of the odds of success any early-stage investor faces. For an example, look at Table 12-4, in which the chances of success are almost laughably high.

Note: This was only an illustration. In reality, only six risk factors that are risky is a low number, and a 75 percent chance of success is completely unrealistic. At a 50 percent chance of success, the same six factors turn into a 1.6 percent overall chance of success! Of course, venture investors think they can do better than these odds by doing smart screening, seeing lots of deals, choosing carefully, and adding value afterward. Even so, they need a few big wins to get the 3:1 return on capital

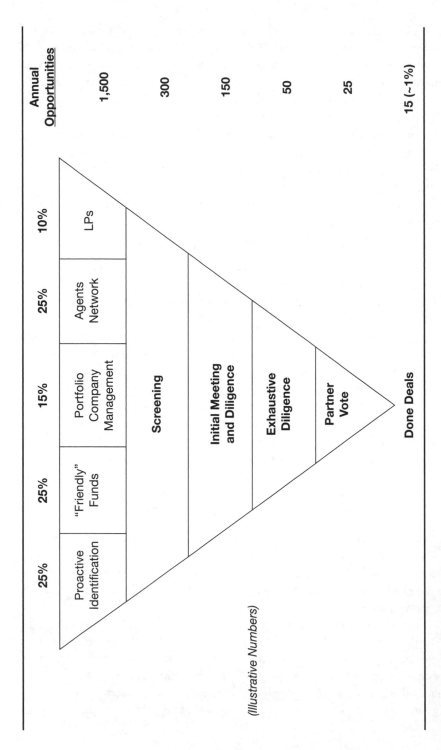

(Illustrative Numbers)

Figure 12-2 A venture firm's funnel

Table 12-4 Odds of Success for an Early-Stage Investor

Type of Risk Factor	Chance of Succeeding (%)
Team (Can they execute?)	75
Technology (Will it work?)	75
Regulatory (If regulated, will it be approved?)	75
Market (Will customers buy enough of it?)	75
Competition (Can they sustain margins and market share?)	75
Finances (Will they run out of money?)	75
Combined probability of success	18!

that produces the 25 percent internal rate of return (IRR) investors want. In a portfolio of 10 investments, for example, one may return 10 times the investment, a couple others return 5 times, maybe two return 2 or 3 times, and the rest break even or lose money. Basically, it's those two or three big wins that make or break a fund.

What does this mean to you? First, the same old point: Early-stage money is expensive. Note that venture investors look for a return three times their money to be a 25 percent IRR, but that is a portfolio average, not what happens to the individual companies. A company that achieves a "modest win" has a 15 to 25 percent IRR, which is expensive enough, but the wins that carry the fund have a much higher IRR. That's expensive money indeed. Imagine borrowing your capital at 40 or 50 percent interest.

Second, venture investors are not at the plate looking for a bunt or a single. They are looking to hit a home run on every investment. Because the risk is so high, they have to swing for the fences. That means they are looking for companies that will stretch and go for the home run, even if that means loading up on risk. The venture investors can stand the risk; they have 10 to 25 other deals to cover their risk, and only a few have to hit it big. For you, swinging for the fences means a chance of a high return but certainly high risk, and high risk means substantially higher risks of nothing—failure. If you think your chances are a lot better if you don't aim so high, you may want to think twice about doing venture financing, assuming you have a strategy to get the funding needed to chase the more modest opportunity.

A last key point: Despite all the visibility and press they get, most businesses don't raise money from venture capitalists. Not even angels are a dominant source of money to launch businesses. That honor falls to the entrepreneurs themselves and their friends and families.[11]

The list following gives more details about investments in early-stage businesses:

0–2 years (3 million ventures)

- Founders: $200 billion
- Family and friends: $70 billion

0–4 years (50,000 ventures)

- Angels: $30 billion

0.5–4 years (799 ventures)

- Venture capital: $4.4 billion

8 years (84 ventures)

- IPOs: $8.4 billion

WHAT'S INVOLVED IN RAISING MONEY FROM VENTURE CAPITALISTS AND ANGELS?

Some companies find closing early-stage investments a layup, but those are usually the teams that have done it before and made money for investors. For the rest it's generally a long and frustrating process. An important first step is to do your homework about whom to approach. Whether angels or venture firms, the best investors know your space and are comfortable with it (but are not invested in a competitor), are good to work with, and can add value intangibly with their experience and contacts.

Once you have your targets, find the referral to them—no cold calling. In a presentation, play to their investment objectives (see above). For the investor, the exercise is always a matter of tension between greed and fear. Investors fear risk but need profits, and so your job is to allay fears of the risks with your proofs of concept, market validation, and competitive advantages and the quality of your team. Feed the hopes that they will make big profits.

Phil Ferneau, a founding partner of the venture firm Borealis Ventures and a professor of private equity at the Tuck School, offers this advice about presenting for investment:

- Prepare the pitch; make it clear, concise, and compelling.
- Pick your targets: not just the firm but the person.
- Find the back door; get a referral.
- Use time effectively; be prompt and flexible.
- Get to the point; answer "So what?" up front.

- Pique interest; get a next meeting.
- Feed the dream; provide analogies.
- Be honest; if you don't know, say so and fix it.
- Be poised and personable but persistent.

Often venture firms need multiple meetings to make a decision. Even if you have a partner who buys in early and sponsors you inside the firm, generally all the partners have to agree before they commit to an investment. Often venture investors send you back to the drawing board more than once to eliminate risk factors or develop some aspect of the company and then come back. At some point they may get serious enough to do extensive due diligence on you, which will be an exercise in close scrutiny of everything from technology or science to execution capabilities, customer opinions, rights to intellectual property, and other assets. If all goes well and they are still interested, they will offer you terms in a nonbinding term sheet. Once you agree, more due diligence will be done, including finances, legal agreements, site visits, and even a look at your corporate book.

How to value the company for the investment is almost always a big issue. This is the great *valuation question:* How much is the company worth now? The answer is: It depends. There are a number of ways to look at valuation, none of them much more than a pretext to disagree. Basically, it comes down to a tension between the golden rule (of capitalism, that is—"He who has the gold makes the rule") and the fear of losing out on a great opportunity, especially to a competing firm. Unfortunately, the golden rule usually wins. Remember, investors don't have to swing. No one will call them out on strikes.

The fundamental formula underlying equity investment is simple:

$$\text{Pre-money valuation} + \text{new investment} = \text{post-money valuation}$$

For example, a venture firm offers to invest $2 million in your company for equity at a pre-money valuation of $3 million. Once the investment is closed, the company has $2 million more in cash on its balance sheet and so is worth a post-money of $5 million, and the $2 million investment represents ownership of 40 percent of the company.

A number of factors figure into a valuation. You read about them in previous chapters:

- Leadership/operating team/board.
- Technology, IP, and know-how.
- Growth potential and attractiveness of the market.
- Sales growth (profitability comes later; venture investors want to see revenue growth with a later jump in net profits shortly before selling the company or taking it public).
- Stage of development of products and sales revenue.

- Financials—cash flow, profit and loss, balance sheet (often proprietorships and closely held companies will have accounting practices that are either less than ideal—see Chapter 19—or are skewing earnings downward for tax purposes, requiring add-backs to the profit and loss statement. These need to be cleaned up before due diligence).
- Likely prospects going forward without investment (how badly do you need money now?).
- Ability to attract future financing or otherwise cover cash needs.
- Location. Some investors want companies close by, where the logistics of staying in touch are easy. Others are less concerned about this.

Note one thing that is not on the list: previous investment. Money raised in prior rounds and the valuations used in them are irrelevant. Investors have no reservations about pressing for a lower valuation than in a previous round—a *down round*—if the company has stumbled or the investment climate has changed. This means founders and employees may be taking a significant hit to their percentage ownership of the company. The same fate awaits previous investors, especially if they don't participate in the new round. Worse, if you have agreed to nondilutive provisions with previous-round investors, a down round can be punishing.

When there is any financial information to work with, a number of valuation methods can be used:

- *Multiple of earnings or cash flow.* Varies from sector to sector.
- *Multiple of revenue.* Also varies by sector.
- *Discounted present value of future earnings.* Can be run even on forecasts from companies that have no revenue yet, but it's all fiction.
- *Comparables.* Sometimes mergers and acquisitions transactions on comparable companies indicate what you might sell for in the future, which can be discounted back to the present.
- *Assets.* Book value, replacement value, liquidation value.

Of course for companies with no revenue yet or those just getting into the market, none of these methods are worth the electrons it takes to calculate them. For the earliest-stage companies there are other guesses taken out of thin air:

- *Rule of thirds.* One-third for founders, one-third for seed investors, one-third for employees. Normally investors insist that at closing the company reserve a pool for future employees—15 percent is the norm, with the rest of the third going to current employees, founders, and others.
- *Rule of one-half.* Pre-money valuation = amount to be raised.
- *Point system:*

- $1 million for idea/opportunity
- $1 million for working prototype
- $1 million to $2 million for capable team/quality advisors
- $1 million to $2 million for market validation

The most reliable method, when the information can be had, is the 'look around you" method: What are investors paying to invest in comparable deals? In the end there is no right answer. The best driver for valuations is competition. If you are negotiating with only one investor or investor group, you're not negotiating, you're begging. Conclusion: The minute you think you have interest from one group, try to get another group interested too.

Perhaps the most important point on valuation: It's not the most important point. Getting the best investor is more important than getting the highest valuation. Early-stage valuation is all a fiction anyway. Remember, in the end the value you take out of the company is a product of three factors: How much the company might end up being worth is one and your share in the company is another, but there is an all-important third: What's the chance the company will ever amount to anything? This is called *expected value:*

Expected value = future value × your ownership share × chance of success

People chronically overlook the importance of the probabilities of success. Anything times zero is zero, and realistically, there is a significant probability that the chance of success is zero. You and your investors, with hard work, good judgment, and cooperation, can have the biggest effect on the chance of success. Actually, there are any number of scenarios for the future value of the company, each with its own probability. This is why focusing on who your investment partners are is more important than getting the best valuation now. An early-stage valuation is quickly mooted by what happens afterward, but the choice of investors lasts a long time, and helful investors can change the probabilities of success significantly.

An offer to invest typically comes in the form of a nonbinding term sheet. There are dozens of basic forms, and there is a veritable library of information in print and online describing term sheets: the terms they contain, what they mean, what you should seek and avoid. Term sheets are not binding, but they contain most of the major points in a transaction. Deal terms generally are negotiated and agreed on by using a term sheet before both sides invest major effort in due diligence and bring in the lawyers. It's generally accepted that unless major adverse information is found during due diligence, the terms agreed stay agreed on once the lawyering starts. Good partners—meaning you and the investors—agree to reasonable terms that are fair to both sides and then stick to them. Speed bumps in this department are a good signal that you should consider other partners even if that means more working and waiting.

Most term sheets include most or all of the following:

- Size of raise and price
- Percent equity given for the investment; type of security (usually convertible preferred with a liquidation preference)
- Dividend preference
- Conversion rights
- Antidilution and price protection
- Voting rights
- Participation rights (preemptive rights, or rights of first refusal, and rights to participate in a cosale with a founder or other holder)
- Timing of money invested
- Milestones for the company to achieve
- Board, voting, and control issues, sometimes including the right to replace founders
- Vesting schedules for management
- Information and reporting rights
- Registration rights (right to force the company to register with the SEC so that shares can be sold in the public markets) and drag-along or cosale rights
- Rights to trigger a liquidity event and/or redemption rights (right to force the company to repurchase its stock at a future date)
- Vesting, option pool for employees (15 percent is the norm)
- No-shop/exclusivity provisions
- Closing conditions and costs

Here are some last thoughts about looking for angel and venture capital money:

- Remember, different investors want different things. Understand your investors, do your homework, and work with investors who can add value rather than just dollars. Implication: Getting a good deal means more than getting the best price.
- Be persistent: Tempt greed, allay fears. Understand the terms and pick your fights. Implication: Value is not what you think it is; it's what the market pays.
- Pick the right investors for more than their money. Rely on character, not contracts. Implication: Good people will save you from bad contracts, but good contracts can't save you from bad people.
- "When people are free to do as they please, they usually imitate each other"[12] Trends count. Investors generally run with the herd, because it's easier to explain why you did what you did if most others were doing the same thing no matter how it comes out. Most investors feel they're the contrarians finding the hidden value, but most of the time they're being contrarians together. Know the trends and where you fit in relation to them.

- Don't look over the fence whether the grass there is greener or not. Some other company is always getting funding at a level that will mystify you. Life isn't fair. Some people win lotteries; most don't. Raising money is not synonymous with business success, and often the two do not correlate. Focus on building a solid business opportunity, remove risks to increase your value, work diligently for the investment you need, and let events take their course.

- Investors respect entrepreneurs who understand that execution is what creates value. Get work done, build as much business as you can first, and then raise money. The farther advanced you are for the stage of funding you're seeking, the better your chances of getting funded and the higher the valuation.

- There's an old saying: "Ask for money and you'll get advice; ask for advice and you'll get money." Build your relationships and access to investors early, before you really want funding. Investors live on deal flow and like to build relationships with companies that show promise that they will be attractive opportunities to invest in for the future.

- Like the Wizard of Oz sending Dorothy for just "one more little thing"— the Wicked Witch's broomstick—investors often send you away for one more difficult thing after another. It's only natural: Each risk they can get you to eliminate without risking their money, the better the deal looks to them. The best way to drive this process to an offer is always a tough question. You often have to force a deal to happen. Competition and wanting to get a deal moving faster are the most common drivers to a term sheet.

- The investors are always right even when they aren't. Jonathan Swift reportedly once said, "It's useless to reason a man out of something he was never reasoned into." That's certainly true when it comes to talking with investors. Investing is more an emotional and experience-based process than a coldly analytical one. Often prejudices, rumors, and the sum of past experiences leave investors with a negative mind-set that seems completely incomprehensible. It doesn't matter. Often they haven't based their opinions on the facts, certainly not the facts you have presented. It's useless to reason a man out of something he was never reasoned into, so don't try.

It's not called capitalism for nothing. Launching a company without investment is just about impossible in our economy. If you're lucky, it won't take a lot, and if you're very lucky, you have the funds yourself or have them among your friends and family. If you do not, raising money is a critical part of the job of the start-up entrepreneur, one of the hardest, and often it never ends. Still, the discipline of the investment marketplace is one of the great producers of fitness, and in reality it's a great resource for you. Investors may not always be right, but because they are responsible for lots of other people's money, they always try very hard to be right. You do that too, presumably, so take full advantage of this powerful asset of our economy as you figure out what it will take to make you successful.

WHAT I KNOW NOW THAT I WISH I HAD KNOWN THEN

Paul Holland, Foundation Capital

Paul Holland is a general partner at Foundation Capital, a leading venture capital partnership operating in Menlo Park, California, since 1995. As a venture investor and board member, Paul helps early-stage start-ups go from zero to $100 million in revenue. A former entrepreneur and sales executive, he helped two venture-funded software start-ups grow and go public: Kana Communications (KANA) and Pure Software (RATL).

As an entrepreneur and venture investor over 20 years, I always try to see things from both sides of the table. Entrepreneurs should want a good price for their equity but also the most concrete help from their investors. Investors should want to pay a fair price and get the most competent and passionate entrepreneurs.

As an Entrepreneur

I became senior vice president of worldwide sales for Kana Communications in December 1997. A year later Kana raised a Series C round from a later-stage investor, Amerindo. The existing investors included Benchmark Capital (David Beirne) and Draper, Fisher, Jurvetson (Steve Jurvetson). The financing was very competitive, but Amerindo offered a valuation roughly 20 percent higher than the competitors.

Unfortunately, just as the financing closed, we hit hit 20 percent of our sales goal for the quarter. When I went to tell the board the bad news and our commitment to get back on plan, I wondered if I would get fired by an angry and disappointed board. I was stunned at the reaction of our new investor: "Don't worry about it; all of our public and private companies had big misses last quarter." Our existing investors were equally supportive: "We believe in you and your team. What can we do to help? More stock for your star performers? Visits to the field?"

As an investor myself now, I know their reaction was exactly the right one. They could have chosen to scold, but instead they encouraged me and my team. That next quarter we had a dramatic turnaround, achieved six times the sales of the previous quarter, and made our annual plan by 1 percent. The next year, 1999, we grew our sales tenfold, and in September had one of the top 10 IPOs of 1999.

The lesson: No one really knows what early-stage companies are really worth, but the right investors can be worth a lot. Focus on getting the right investors more than the top valuation.

As an Investor

I've had dozens of good negotiations with entrepreneurs. Recently, one of my former sales executives from Kana introduced me to the smart phone management company MobileIron, and I ended up leading a Series C investment in a competitive financing. Later we learned that MobileIron chose us because they believed that we could help them with sales and marketing. A couple weeks later, I had the chance to introduce the company to the top executive for smart phones at General Electric, prompting a copy of this message from the VP of Sales at MobileIron:

From: John Donnelly
To: miall
Date: Friday, July 23, 2010, 2:22 PM
Subject: FW: A favor

Team, On Wednesday we told Paul Holland (Foundation Capital) our newest investor we needed some help at GE. Today Paul drove a call with Greg Simpson the GE CIO. In my years as a sales leader I can count on my hand how many times this has happened. Incredible. Everyone is dedicated to making MI a great company.

The Lesson

Being an investor who can add value is a competitive advantage, not to mention smart investing.

QUESTIONS

- How much can you get done on your own money or other noninvestment sources?
- When do you think you must have investment? What kind? From whom?
- What forms of investment might be acceptable to you? How realistic are you being about that?
- How long can you go before you run out of the money you plan to raise?

NOTES

1. Gilbert, Alorie, "Lessons Learned from Failure," *Information Week* 817 (December 18–25, 2000): 111.
2. Gail Goodman, in a DEN-Boston event, "The Constant Contact 'Adventure' from Startup to IPO—A Candid Conversation about Entrepreneurs, Venture Capitalists, and Boards of Directors." November 28, 2007
3. Dennis, William J., "Business Starts and Stops," Wells Fargo-NFIB Education Foundation Series, November 1999.
4. Venture capitalists like markets with a lot of change or growth and prefer technology to consumer goods and manufacturing sectors.
5. Source: Center for Study of Income and Productivity, Federal Reserve Bank of San Francisco, "Venture Capital, VC Investments," Data and Charting, http://www.frbsf.org/csip/data/php.
6. Bygrave, William D., and Andrew Zacharakas, *The Portable MBA in Entrepreneurship* (Hoboken, NJ: Wiley, 2010): 194.
7. The Dodd-Frank Wall Street Reform and Consumer Protection Act was signed into law on July 21, 2010. It contained a provision in which the net worth test remained $1 million but required the SEC to issue a regulation excluding the value of the investor's primary residence in the calculation of net worth. In addition, the act requires the SEC to review the accredited investor definition not earlier than four years after enactment and at least once every four years thereafter.
8. Codified at 17 C.F.R. § 240.10b–5, accessible at http://ecfr.gpoaccess.gov/cgi/t/text/text-idx?c=ecfr&sid=958fa2ab168a6d7b5dd6044510616ca0&rgn=div8&view=text&node=17:3.0.1.1.1.1.57.71&idno=17.
9. *More Than Money: The Untold Tale of Risk, Reward and the Original Venture Capitalists,* www.morethanmoneymovie.com Directed by Dan Geller and Dayna Goldfine, produced by Paul Holland of Foundation Capital and Molly Davis of Rainmaker Communications. (Paul Holland was one of the early investors in EnerNOC, Inc., featured in Chapters 8 and 22.)
10. Wainwright, Fred, and Angela Groeninger, "Note on Angel Investing," Tuck Center for Private Equity and Entrepreneurship, Case #5–0001, January 10, 2005.
11. Bygrave and Zacharakas, 2010: 185.
12. Hoffer, Eric. *The Passionate State of Mind.* (New York: HarperCollins, 1954).

Chapter 13

The Law

When men are pure, laws are useless; when men are corrupt, laws are broken.

—Benjamin Disraeli

From the moment someone first contemplates starting an enterprise around an idea, issues immediately arise involving law, liability, and eventually taxation. In the current environment, getting legal things wrong can be very damaging; only a collapse of your market can harm your enterprise as badly as stumbling into legal trouble. Few companies fail because of legal troubles alone, but if you are sloppy or lazy on legal issues, sooner or later you will pay a price. If you are starting a company, you have to be conversant enough in all the diverse elements of business law that you do things right the first time and make good decisions from the standpoint of legal issues. You don't have to know everything in this area. You can't; that's what lawyers and specialists are for. Lawyering is not a place to waste money, but neither is it a place to scrimp unwisely.

There are three high-level things you need to learn and manage on your own. Professionals can help you with these things, but no one can or should do them for you:

1. *Define the key issues.* Basically, you have to decide which factors you should worry about. This means defining issues that can lead to major problems in the future and knowing how to prevent them—which means basically knowing when and how to ask for help.
2. *Find the resources.* You should know where to go for more information and effective professional resources.
3. *Choose wisely.* Which legal issues are most important for your company is not just a question of technical issues. In the end it is about philosophy and judgment. Some lawyers will help you think through these decisions, whereas others want to stay safely with the mechanics and leave strategy to someone else. Never abrogate to your lawyers your responsibility to define key issues and make good decisions. Your attorneys can advise you, but in the end you must make the decisions. After all, the lawyers work for you. You don't work for them.

There is no end to the resources covering the issues of business law that will affect you as you start an enterprise. This chapter is no place to try to reproduce them. One handbook every start-up entrepreneur should have handy and consult often is Constance Bagley and Craig Dauchy's *Entrepreneur's Guide to Business*

Law.[1] It has 17 detailed chapters on all the key areas of law affecting entrepreneurs. Whenever you deal with attorneys and legal matters, you save time and money in the long run and get a better result if you educate yourself on the fundamentals of the area of business law that is at issue. The best reference we know for learning the basics of a legal area is *Business Law Today* by Roger Miller and Gaylord Jentz.[2] Below are some of the major subject law areas of concern to start-up entrepreneurs. Think of it as a worry list: a checklist of sorts for the different kinds of things you will have to cover adequately sooner or later. Each area needs proscriptive thinking to head off difficulties, and each regularly will require judgment calls and often tough decisions on your part. If you don't find yourself affected in all these areas as you launch and start operating, you should worry.

FINDING AND MANAGING ATTORNEYS

You need to have a good corporate attorney when starting a business. This is not a place to cut costs and handle everything yourself. There is no reason it should cost a lot for what you will need in the early days. What will the lawyers do? Everything from advice to incorporation mechanics, to drafting and closing agreements, to getting you out of trouble. Most of all, a good attorney will focus on keeping you out of trouble in the first place and protecting you from risks. Good attorneys think an ounce of prevention is worth a pound of cure.

1. *Where do you find them?* Referrals are by far the best: directors/advisors, people you know, investors. There are directories, but you can spend a lot of needless time screening candidates from directories instead of checking out referrals from people whose judgment you trust. Always interview more than one candidate, preferably at least a handful. First encounters— *consultations*—should be at no charge, usually lasting at least an hour. They have the form of a getting-to-know-each-other interview, but they also should be opportunities to ask questions about substance and technical issues. You can learn a lot about your issues in these meetings as well as about the attorney. If you don't learn much, keep looking.
2. *What are you looking for?*
    a. *Competency*. Can you work with them?
    b. *Personality*. Are they compatible with you and your operating style? Are they practical and entrepreneurial?
    c. *Prompt, responsive, and timely*. Do they get things done before the last minute? (Many don't.)
    d. *Reputation*. Check references, especially with other clients. What is their street reputation?
    e. *Experience/expertise*. Do they have technical knowledge of your field? Do they understand start-ups?

f. *Litigation experience.* Attorneys who have prosecuted or defended clients in court are more sensitive to how things will play out and include this in their strategies and drafting of documents.

g. *Size of firm.* You often get more personal attention from a small firm, but the resources will be thinner. Large firms have an incredible depth of resources, but they can be impersonal and unresponsive to small clients who don't affect their bottom lines, and they can be risk-averse. Also, their rates are often higher. Be sure you know who will do the work within the firm: how much by associates and with what review by more senior partners.

h. *Contacts.* Do they know potential investors and advisors well enough to introduce you, and will they do that?

i. *Rates* (you get what you pay for) and terms.

3. *How do you engage one?* Any attorneys you seek to engage will first check to see if they have a conflict because of past or current relationships with other clients who might have conflicting confidentiality needs or end up opposing you in the future. Define expectations on both sides explicitly up front. Get agreement on roles and how you will work together. Negotiate. (You don't get what you don't ask for.) Will they offer special terms such as lower rates and/or deferrals of all or part of their billings until you raise money? Will they take part of their bills in equity? Will they work with you as you go, helping you contain costs through things such as budgets or not-to-exceed arrangements and having you do some of the preparation and drafting? Will they offer flat fees for routine matters? Always get engagement letters, which are essentially service contracts setting out the terms of the work and payment, and review budgets with them frequently. You're poor and starving—resist retainers.

4. *How do you manage them?* Manage time carefully. Don't give open-ended projects or mandates. Negotiations and contracting can be budget busters; tightly control negotiations with other parties that involve your lawyer. There are some ways to keep lawyers from turning negotiations into major make-work projects for themselves. Not-to-exceed arrangements are valuable when you can get them, though often when the cost is capped, the scope of work shrinks and you can end up getting less work than is needed to do the job properly.

Prenegotiating the business points with a counterparty before going to the lawyers and memorializing the points in a nonbinding term sheet[3] is usually a good practice. Give the term sheet to the attorneys with defined limits on how they will turn them into agreements and close them. Sometimes attorneys have template documents or checklists for conventional transactions. Get them early and use them. Offer to assist in the preparation and drafting. Limit the number of back-and-forth reviews. Nothing says that you can't create documents or negotiate deals for yourself to save money, but you should always have final products reviewed and blessed by your attorney.

Always remember that you manage your attorneys, they don't manage you. Keep straight the distinction between business issues and legal issues. Always consider both. If you have good attorneys, they generally will assign themselves the role of your personal worrywarts. This is a good thing. It leaves you free to focus on trade-offs and judgment, confident the attorney will call important issues to your attention. However, you can have too much of any good thing if you haven't defined roles properly at the beginning or have not chosen your attorney wisely. A common problem: Some attorneys can fall into a habit of bringing up risks beyond all sense of materiality and then offer to spend your money to protect you from them. Where prudence ends and overkill on lawyering begins is impossible to define; it's one of those things you have to recognize when you see it. The best way to handle this is to confer and consult, and jointly arrive at reasonable balances of risk and cost/caution. In the end you should decide, not the attorney.

INCORPORATION

Why Incorporate?

Whether you are planning a for-profit or nonprofit, there are several reasons why incorporating your enterprise is almost always a good idea:

1. Getting sued is an ever-present risk, and the ingenuity of enterprising tort lawyers in inventing new classes of liability claims shows no signs of running low. When you operate as a sole proprietorship—that is, as an individual operating in your own name—you are fully liable for all obligations and risks involved in the business, both financial and legal. This means that at any time you could find all your family's personal assets fully in jeopardy. The same is true of unincorporated partnerships. All state laws provide several options for incorporation to let individuals form a business and reasonably isolate themselves from these legal risks. One or more people can own a corporation, but in most states more than one person is required to incorporate (the *incorporators*). This can be anyone, an owner or otherwise.

   a. In essence, the law considers a corporation a legal person separate from its owner or owners. So long as you honor certain structures and practices, the courts look to a corporation only to fulfill debts and bear legal responsibility for its actions. Caution: In certain circumstances courts will reach through the legal isolation of the corporation to you as shareholders—this is called *piercing the corporate veil*—and put your personal assets at risk. There are a number of practices you should honor to prevent this. For example, maintain records of board and shareholder meetings and actions, keep accurate capitalization records, and keep your corporate assets and finances separate from your personal ones.

b. Corporate structure also offers protections from liability to directors and officers so long as they honor their basic obligations to the corporation.[4] However, under certain circumstances these protections also can be breached by the courts and the individuals can be held responsible. These situations are complicated and beyond the scope of this chapter. Get a good tutorial from your lawyer on this important area when you incorporate.

2. The incorporation process organizes founders and owners, defines ownership stakes, and clarifies boundaries that indicate who among the early-stage participants are in the company and who are not. At the formation stage, there are often people who think they should be owners when they shouldn't, and sometimes vice versa. Almost always, interpretations will vary as to who is going to get what ownership in the company at some future stage. Incorporating can't eliminate potential future claims, but generally incorporation codifies ownership. Although not necessarily making everyone happy, the process of incorporating brings most founders' claims to the surface and makes their resolution clear to all.

3. The corporate structure is a principal means of defining governance: how the corporation will make decisions and function effectively. Some forms (corporations) have statutory requirements to provide for a minimum of governance structure, such as shareholder meetings, boards, and officers. Others are more flexible and allow owners to create their own governance and management structures (limited partnerships and limited liability companies [LLCs]). In corporations, boards make almost all decisions. (An important exception is the sale of shares in an acquisition.[5]) In LLCs you can specify how decisions are made. You may want to require specifically in the corporate bylaws a supermajority vote of directors or even shareholders for certain important decisions, such as funding events, mergers or sales, changes in the bylaws, and the taking on of new partners. In all cases, the structure of the corporate entity clarifies how decisions are made, how roles are defined, and how the entity operates.

4. Most often, start-ups will need significant funding sooner or later. Investors generally want to invest only in companies, not persons or partnerships, and they generally have strong preferences for a particular form (see below).

5. Incorporating limits lender claims, keeping your personal assets free of burdens.

6. There are certain tax considerations in forming a corporate entity, some favorable and some not (more below).

When to Incorporate?

There is a trade-off on the timing of when to incorporate a start-up enterprise. Waiting too long can lead to all sorts of loose ends that need cleaning up and often many misunderstandings and conflicting expectations on the part of founders (see point 2 in the list above). However, incorporating too soon, while the founding dynamics are still fluid and evolving, means you'll probably have to make major changes later. That can get expensive and time-consuming, and can create potential tax complications.

When people put effort and resources into an enterprise over a sustained period, what they expect to get back escalates. At some point, those expectations can grow to the point where it is difficult to meet them all. When you are approaching that point is not always obvious, but even when things pass that point, often people don't notice because they aren't paying attention. Incorporating gets all this out in the open and deals with it. Usually there is some external trigger, such as the need to enter a business arrangement or close a financing, that creates a need for a corporate entity.

Which Form Is Right?

The choice of a form of entity is fundamental and important, but there are some options that leave you with the flexibility to choose provisionally now and change to another form later without a lot of cost or hassle. There are two dimensions to the question of choice of entity, and it's important not to confuse them.

One is how to think about the choice: What are the important questions that should drive the decision? The other is: What options do you have for an entity? Too many people jump immediately to thinking about the options for form of entity, neglecting to consider the important drivers or questions that should inform their choice, the factors that should be important to them. Here are some examples:

- Are you planning a for-profit company or a nonprofit?
- Reporting and administrative obligations vary. How much structure do you need taking into account the burdens that go with it? Burdens can be expensive.
- What are your personal tax considerations? Do you want to have income and losses from the company consolidate to your personal return (*flow-through entities*) or be isolated in the corporation and subject to double taxation?
- What might be important to your investors? Generally, all but the earliest-stage investors don't like flow-through entities such as Subchapter S corporations and LLCs.

The options among forms of entity are thoroughly treated in many resources, and most attorneys have a briefing brochure on incorporation options. Selected features of corporate forms are summarized in Table 13-1.

Note: If you are thinking about creating a nonprofit corporation, remember that the 501(c)(3) designation is a tax status, not a form of corporation. Nonprofits will be treated in detail in the next chapter.

What Are the Steps

First, unless you are considering a sole proprietorship, don't attempt to do this by yourself. Even a sole-owner corporation or LLC has filing, state law, and tax requirements that can trip you up. Attorneys will have a checklist of decisions needed once you jointly agree on the right entity and the state in which to incorporate. You will need a name that passes a "confusingly similar" conflict test; check with the secretary of state in the state where you are filing. In addition, you will look carefully to see that there are not company names on which you might be infringing in other states, as trademarks are often an issue. Among the documents you and your attorney will create are the following:

- Initial incorporating documents (articles or certificate of incorporation); certificate of formation (LLC). The attorney creates these.
- Corporate bylaws (corporation); operating agreement (LLC). These will require many decisions on the terms in the bylaws, including composition of the board, creation of officer positions, and any decisions for which you want approval to require more than a simple majority vote of directors or shareholders (such as major financing decisions, sale of major assets or the company, major transactions such as mergers and partnerships, and changes in the bylaws).
- Stock subscription or purchase agreements. Decisions include the price of shares, vesting, restrictions on selling shares, and provisions on potential sales (right of first refusal, right to participate in a sale, or drag other parties along in a sale).
- Initial corporate actions, including issuance of shares and price, and authorization of officers to conduct different business and finance functions.
- Election of officers and directors.
- Employment or "key-person" agreements, including any confidentiality and noncompete provisions needed.
- Subchapter S election forms (IRS 2553) if you decide to do a Subchapter S flowthrough.
- Employer identification number application (IRS Form SS–4). You will need this to open a bank account.

Table 13-1 Selected Features of Corporate Forms*, †, ‡

	Sole Proprietorship	Partnership		Corporation		Limited Liability Company
		General	Limited	C-Corporation	S-Corporation	
Limited liability?	No. Liability is unlimited	No. Liability is unlimited, joint and several	General partner —no. Liability is unlimited, joint and several; limited partners, yes	Yes	Yes	Yes
Flow-through of gains and losses	Yes—not a separate entity.	Yes—not a separate entity	Yes—not a separate entity	No. Separate entity with double taxation.	Yes—with limitations on disproportionate distributions of income and losses	Yes—no limitations on disproportionate distributions of income and losses
Ability to change structure without tax	Yes	Yes	Yes	No	No	Yes
Simple to set up?	Yes	Yes	Yes	No	No	No
Cost to set up and maintain	Low	Moderate	Moderate	High	High	High to very high (management agreements can get complicated)
Number of owners allowed	1	Unlimited	Unlimited	Unlimited	Up to 75	Unlimited

	Sole Proprietorship	Partnership		Corporation		Limited Liability Company
		General	Limited	C-Corporation	S-Corporation	
Management control	Sole proprietor has total control	Equal among partners unless otherwise specified	General partners share control	Board of directors, as elected by shareholders	Board of directors, as elected by shareholders	Members share control or appoint a manager by management agreement
Limits on eligibility	Yes	No	No	No	Yes	No
Limits on capital structure	Yes	No	No	No	Yes	No
Ease of equity grants	N/A	N/A	N/A	Yes	Yes	No
Continuity of business	Ends with death of owner	Ends with death or withdrawal as a partner unless otherwise specified	Death or withdrawal of general partner	Perpetual	Perpetual	Normally limited
Flexible profit/loss allocations	N/A	N/A	N/A	No	No	Yes
Charter documents are flexible?	Yes	Yes	Yes	No	No	Yes

*Bagley, Constance, and Craig E. Dauchy. The Entrepreneur's Guide to Business Law. (Mason, OH: Thompson/South-Western/West, 2008), pp 67–68.

†Barringer, Bruce R., and R. Duane Ireland. Entrepreneurship: Successfully Launching New Ventures. (Upper Saddle River, NJ: Pearson Prentice Hall, 2006), p. 185.

‡Bygrave, William D., and Andrew Zacharakis. The Portable MBA. (Hoboken, NJ: Wiley, 2010), p. 271.

LETTERS OF INTENT

Letters of intent (sometimes called term sheets, memoranda of understanding, or heads-of-agreement) are a mechanism to force clarity and resolution of vague issues, memorialize verbal intentions, and protect against changes in conditions— or changes in someone's mind. Properly done, a letter of intent is not a binding legal agreement. Letters of intent clarify and memorialize in writing key terms in a transaction or negotiation. They play an invaluable role in negotiations by forcing parties to be methodical and systematic about covering key issues. Positions are clarified by putting them in writing. This is one of the more important things you as leaders in an organization can do, both for your companies and for your attorneys. Attorneys can create binding documents much more efficiently when working from a letter of intent that has the business issues worked out. Usually you will draft them without active involvement of your lawyers. Trying to have attorneys get involved from the start and negotiate all the business and legal issues at the same time not only complicates things but generally ends up taking longer to reach agreement on the business issues and sometimes makes it impossible. Also, both parties are paying for all that extra legal time to do things they probably can do more effectively on their own. Use letters of intent to get things done efficiently and use your attorneys for what they do best: craft good agreements.

Letters of intent should not be binding agreements, only outlines of important deal provisions resolved in principle between the parties. In fact, they should lack the form of legal agreements. When done correctly, they are drafted specifically and explicitly to be nonbinding. Failing to make this clear in the document leaves a risk that in the event of a breakdown, one party may try to enforce a carelessly drafted letter of intent. Drafted poorly, such letters can have some of the elements of a binding agreement even though they are not complete and specific enough that parties' interests are fairly covered. This is the worst of both worlds: a vague agreement that courts feel is binding but in which many of the terms are unclear. The best advice: Open the document with a clear statement that what follows is a "nonbinding recital of terms and understandings discussed with respect to the subject transaction." Never use the word *agree* or *agreement* in the document. We prefer to write letters of intent as "memorializing what the parties discussed," containing "understandings that will later be negotiated as part of binding agreements."

In light of the care taken to avoid appearing to bind the parties, it's fair to ask what value there can be in a letter of intent. In most cases, parties understand there is a moral commitment to honor terms resolved at this stage. It's a bad sign when someone fails to honor terms previously memorialized in a term sheet without a reasonable change in conditions. You may want to reconsider proceeding with a party too quickly to try to change terms previously resolved. Here are some of the important issues that normally turn up in a letter of intent:

1. Form of transaction (terms): a list of alternatives if there are more than one
2. Important transaction elements: what each party will give and get
3. Expectations management
   a. Responsibilities of all parties
   b. Timeline
4. Key considerations
   a. Confidentiality?
   b. Exclusivity?
5. Process going forward
   a. How will decisions be made?
   b. What kind of agreements will be needed?
   c. Who will be involved?
   d. Authority lines of the parties?
6. Next steps

KEY CONTRACTS AND AGREEMENTS

A contract is a legally enforceable agreement or commitment. A contract need not be in writing: In certain circumstances courts will recognize oral and even implied agreements. Courts can hold that promises made in some circumstances are implied contracts that are legally enforceable, especially in areas involving employment. This is why it is so important to memorialize negotiations in good notes and nonbinding letters of intent and to follow that with properly drawn contracts. For a contract to be enforceable there must be four elements:[6]

1. There must be an agreement between the parties involving an offer and an acceptance.
2. There must be *consideration:* Something of value must be exchanged between the parties.
3. The parties must have the capacity to enter into a contract (mentally competent and of legal age).
4. There must be a legal purpose.

Many agreements are written in the form of contracts:

- Employment agreements and noncompetition/nonsolicitation agreements
- Stock-purchase agreements
- Consulting or independent contractor agreements
- Sales contracts or licenses
- Distributor agreements
- Purchase and sale agreements on real property
- Lease or rental agreements

- Loan agreements
- Confidentiality agreements

For an early-stage enterprise, an important agreement is the confidentiality agreement, also called a confidential disclosure agreement (CDA) or nondisclosure agreement (NDA). These are contracts between at least two parties that define confidential information the parties will disclose but wish to hold confidential from other parties. Usually employee, consulting, and independent contractor agreements will contain confidentiality language. Confidentiality agreements must do the following:

- Have the statutory elements of a binding contract to be enforceable.
- Contain a promise by the receiver of information to do the following:
  - Avoid unauthorized use or disclosure—use only as intended.
  - Limit use and disclosure to parties identified in the agreement or obtain written permission to disclose.
  - Exercise appropriate care in preventing disclosure by others.
- Describe what information is protected. It's a good practice to create a schedule or exhibit, mark all documents as confidential, and number and label them.
- Include preservation of intellectual property rights, current and future.
- Include a reasonable term and expiration.
- Avoid ambiguity (e.g., verbal representations).

If you are going to be the recipient of a disclosure and are being asked to sign a confidentiality agreement, remember that you are binding yourself to protect confidentiality and exposing yourself to claims of damage if you breach the provisions. Parties have been sued for damages even when they didn't feel they breached an agreement. Be aware that you are incurring a potential future liability whenever you commit to protecting confidentiality under such an agreement.

Be sure the agreement is limited to a reasonable time; anything beyond two to three years is unreasonable in most normal circumstances. Look for areas of knowledge or technologies that are defined too broadly or vaguely. Also, watch for non-competition, nonsolicitation, or assignment of ownership of inventions language. These can slip into confidentiality agreements. They may be appropriate to the circumstances, but that should be for you to decide. Especially when lawyers draft agreements for their clients, the practice is to ask for everything conceivable and then negotiate on the assumption that the other side is going to do the same thing.

There is ample further reading on the details of all these contracts in several good books, such as *The Entrepreneur's Guide to Business Law*,[7] among many others. When you see a transaction or situation arising that probably will end in such a contract, do your homework in advance. Look them up, and if necessary talk with your lawyer so that you understand the main factors and potential pitfalls in advance. Otherwise you may find you have to do cleanup work when it comes time to draft a contract.

DISPUTES AND LITIGATION

In the end contracts are not a substitute for consensus, good intentions, continued alignment of interests and benefits; a guarantee there won't be disputes in the future; or magic. Contracts can't fix things you negotiated poorly and can't turn bad behavior in your counterparty into good behavior. You want the best, most enforceable contracts your lawyer dollars can buy, but you can never rely exclusively on the existence of a contract to make everything go right. Unfortunately, at the core, a contract is only a license to sue. Good agreements can keep you out of a lot of trouble but can't save you from poor intentions or people gone bad. The first line of defense is always the character of the people you deal with. Choose wisely.

The second line of defense is being realistic and diligent in the negotiation and contracting phases, thinking ahead about what might go wrong in the future. Look for areas where problems could develop and deal with them early. Wishful thinking and willful disregard of problem signs have been the cause of much subsequent misery. Never rely on future litigation as your defense against potential problems you foresee. Litigation is sometimes a resort of necessity, but it's never wise to think of it as a resort of choice. Get things right the first time, document them thoroughly in agreements, and don't leave items lingering that can cause problems later ("no skeletons in the closet").

Yogi Berra supposedly said, "It's hard to make predictions, especially about the future." (The physicist Niels Bohr and others also may have said it.) Since things don't always happen in the future the way we anticipate, agreements sometimes don't work out as hoped even when it's no one's fault. Of course, sad to say, sometimes we misjudge counterparties and sometimes people change their minds and don't live up to terms of agreements. When this happens, there are only so many options: live with it, dispute it, or see if amendments can leave parties reasonably satisfied. Who can change the terms of a signed agreement? The parties to an agreement can make changes at any time by mutual written consent. Sometimes this is the best way to avoid having things spiral out of control.

Then there is the ever-present possibility that litigation will come to you unbidden, not related to contract disputes. Sometimes you may have created this opportunity for an enterprising member of the tort bar. Unfortunately, today sometimes it's a result of creative claiming. In any case, if you operate in business long enough, in today's climate you probably will have to confront disputes or claims that have the potential to land you in court. Count the costs before initiating litigation, but of course you have to be prepared to defend your interests if someone initiates a claim against you that you think is without merit. Don't reach that decision casually or without coldly calculating the costs going forward, taking care to ignore sunk costs you can never get back. Usually, people drastically underestimate litigation costs in time as well as fees. Unless you're the litigating attorney, litigation is saldom a good way to make money even if you think you're pursuing a valuable entitlement. Judgments are hard to collect. However, if you decide you have to litigate, do it with thoroughness and intensity.

There are a number of increasingly popular alternatives for dispute resolution, including negotiation, mediation, and arbitration. Often in contracts parties will commit in advance to submit contract disputes to arbitration and designate one of the major arbitration bodies for referral. Even without such a clause, it's always wise to see if both parties can agree to go to arbitration with a dispute. Sadly, in the absence of a prior commitment, often there is an advantage to one party in using the threat of costly and time-consuming litigation as a lever in settlement negotiations. Consider including an alternative dispute commitment in contracts.

EMPLOYMENT LAW

Hiring people immediately puts you into the world of employment law, one of the most complex areas of business law. There is a bewildering array of legislation and regulation—state and federal—regulating the conduct of business with respect to employing people. For example, there are the antidiscrimination laws: the Civil Rights Act of 1866 (Section 1981), the Equal Pay Act of 1963, Title VII of the 1964 Civil Rights Act, the 1967 Age Discrimination in Employment Act, the Vietnam Era Readjustment Assistance Acts (1972, 1974), the Vocational Rehabilitation Act (1973), the Veterans Reemployment Act (974), the Immigration Reform and Control Act (1986), the Americans with Disabilities Act (1990), and the Civil Rights Act of 1991, along with tort cases on discrimination and harassment. There are the Family and Medical Leave Act of 1993, the Fair Labor Standards Act (1938) that regulates minimum wages and overtime pay, the Occupational Safety and Health Act's regulations and inspections, the Employee Retirement Income Security Act, and the National Labor Relations Act. And that is only at the federal level!.

Then there are all the things employees are entitled to receive by statute and regulation: FICA and Medicare contributions, worker's compensation insurance, unemployment compensation, severance (in some states), vacation pay, medical plan coverage, and so on. Most of these elements can be avoided by contracting with people as independent contractors. This is an alternative for a company at any stage, though the larger the company, the greater some of the practical disadvantages, including high turnover and loss of control. For early-stage companies, hiring people as independent contractors is a common practice. Often this is how all the first people are hired. Flexibility and the absence of legal burdens are both important.

There is a critical downside to be aware of: Courts and the Internal Revenue Service (IRS) can retrospectively deem someone to be an employee even if you and the contractor agree the arrangement is independent. For example, by IRS regulations and various employment statutes, to claim independent status, there must be agreement on the work product, but the contractor must control the means and manner of achieving the outcome, and the contractor's services must be on offer to the public at large, not just to one business.[8] In addition, there are numerous factors and criteria the courts have used to deem a relationship an employment rather than an independent contract. Written contracts are always useful but provide no guarantee that you will sustain an independent classification. Before embarking on your first arrangements, do your reading[9] and get a tutorial from your attorney. If you plan to do enough work with independent contractors, get from your attorney a template and checklist of documentation and administrative practices. Getting this wrong can be costly and time-consuming.

There are any number of specialties not just in employment law but in narrower areas within it. You cannot possibly have all the knowledge needed to cover everything, but someone in your company should be responsible for understanding enough to institute good practices, policies, and procedures. This is something you will have to grow into—one reason why starting up is usually more fun than building out. In the early days, once you confront your first hiring decisions, you should at least get from your attorney a good checklist of the most important employment law issues to cover and get right the first time. Soon you will find that good office administrators more than pay for themselves with the experience and knowledge they bring. Unless you are one of those administrators, your time and skills are better spent building the business.

LIABILITY AND INSURANCE

You have seen how there are risks in contracts that go bad and in mistakes about employment law. With those, your company's exposure to liability is just beginning. You face product liability claims, investor claims, torts for negligence related to your business, citations for pollution and environmental damage, employee claims for discrimination or harassment, violations related to recruiting employees from companies at which you or others in your company may have worked, violations of noncompetition or confidentiality agreements, anticompetitive behavior, interfering business practices, domestic and foreign corrupt practices, and fraudulent conduct. That's only a partial list, but it's more than enough to highlight the importance of thinking about preventive medicine.

The first line of defense against liability, of course, is good policies and practices designed to prevent problems from being created in the first place. In the event of litigation, an important factor that courts consider is the degree to which you have good policies and practices in place to prevent problems. In theory at least, they also help prevent problems. This is one more area for at least an overview education and a prioritized checklist from your attorney. You can't focus on your business and worry about everything at the same time, but everything can be a worry. That's why it takes judgment, not just procedures.

The second line of defense is good insurance. Today you can insure against almost anything except fraud and intentional misconduct. Insurance is one of those things you can easily overbuy, but once you have assets and a business to protect, going without is a nearly certain disaster sooner or later. Your resource for dealing with all this is a good business insurance agent. To get an agent, you can find a good broker who shops among companies and assembles packages for you or you can deal directly with an insurance company representative. There is no right answer, but generally if you are not experienced, brokers can be more valuable because of the experience and breadth of company products they bring. How do you choose one? It's about the same as finding a good lawyer: referrals and comparative shopping.

At a minimum, in the early days you probably will have to bind at least minimum directors' and officers' liability coverage, worker's compensation insurance, general liability, and product liability. If you are doing anything that could damage or pollute the environment, such as biotech, chemical work, or manufacturing, you will need environmental coverage, which is expensive. Your broker can go through a checklist of potential products and coverages. In addition to policy costs, pay attention to deductibles, caps, and coverage exclusions.

RAISING MONEY

To protect investors, the Securities Act of 1933 established the Securities and Exchange Commission (SEC). The act requires people raising money from the public to register their offerings with the SEC and provide investors with a prospectus containing specified information about the offering and the issuer.[10] Such registered offerings are expensive and time-consuming. Fortunately for start-ups and small companies, there are exemptions to the SEC rules for certain kinds of private offerings under Section 3(a)(11) (intrastate offering exemption) and Section 4(2) (transactions by an issuer not involving a public offering). Less fortunately, the conditions to qualify for the SEC exemptions can be complicated, and there are numerous state laws that are relevant as well.

Regulation D[11] of the SEC defines the requirements to claim a safe harbor[12] exemption from registration. The regulation exempts offerings to accredited investors and provides a detailed definition in Section 501. If you plan to raise money, be familiar with this definition and document that your prospective investors meet the criteria. Most attorneys provide a short questionnaire for your investors to complete and sign. Keep them on file. There are three exemption categories of concern: Rules 504 (offerings up to $1 million), 505 (up to $5 million), and 506 (any amount offered to no more than 35 accredited investors). There are requirements for what information must be provided, certain procedures, and filing with the SEC on the first sale of securities.

There is an exemption for sales of securities through employee benefit plans. Rule 701 states that sales of up to $1 million of securities made to compensate employees of companies do not need to be subject to Securities Exchange Act reporting requirements. Regulation A allows for a simplified registration for U.S. and Canadian companies wanting to go public with offerings of $5,000,000 or less, $1,500,000 in certain circumstances. The SEC has a good resource section on small companies and securities regulation at http://www.sec.gov/info/smallbus/qasbsec.htm.

Section 3(a)(11) provides certain exemptions for intrastate financings. All the U.S. states, the District of Columbia, and Puerto Rico have securities laws that regulate the offer and sale of securities by companies headquartered there or those offering securities to investors in their jurisdiction. Many of the states, Washington, D.C., and Puerto Rico have adopted a common code, the Uniform Securities Act, but some others, including California, still have their own statutes. The California Limited Offering Exemption—Rule 1001 provides an exemption for offers and sales of securities, in amounts of up to $5 million, that satisfy the conditions of §25102(n) of the California Corporations Code. This exempts offerings made by California companies to qualified purchasers whose characteristics are similar to those of accredited investors under Regulation D and allows some methods of general solicitation before sales. The Uniform Securities Act emphasizes disclosure for protecting investors, but some state securities administrators have the authority to deny permits unless there is a finding in a merit review that the plan of business and the proposed issuance of securities are fair, just, and equitable.[13] Certain of these provisions are overridden by the Capital Markets Efficiency Act of 1996 in the case of offerings exempt under Rule 506 of the SEC's Regulation D. Sounds complicated? Call your lawyer!

BANKRUPTCY AND CREDIT LAW

No one starts out expecting a company to take on financial obligations and debts and then go broke, but it happens. In that event, the first stage consists of attempts to arrange suitable workouts that, if not pleasant (an understatement), at least let a company continue to operate and often emerge from the problems successfully. If that does not happen, foreclosures and bankruptcy follow.

If you have started your business as a corporation or LLC and have maintained accepted practices of separating your personal business from the corporation, you are not financially at risk for the company's obligations beyond any investments, guarantees, or other pledges you previously committed to the company. If you are operating as a sole proprietorship or partnership, your personal assets can be at risk.

Starting up is not the time to invest a lot of effort in understanding the nuances and strategies in workouts, foreclosure, and bankruptcy. Still, you will be entering into all sorts of financial obligations going both ways: what you will owe others and what others will owe you. There are a number of places where you can slip up and regret it in the future if you don't have a working knowledge of some of the important factors in insolvency management. For example, priority of claims in bankruptcy should be a factor when you accept obligations from others: Where will you stand in terms of recovery if the company that owes you goes under? What kind of terms do you want to receive or offer in security agreements? How will you be able to juggle the claims various lenders and vendors will want to place on you when you are arranging financing and borrowing terms? How will you protect the security interests you hold in other companies or assets? What kinds of guarantees (especially personal guarantees) are wise to make and which kinds are not? Bagley and Dauchy's *Entrepreneur's Guide to Business Law* has an excellent chapter on creditors' rights and bankruptcy.

TAXATION

Whether you know it or not, from the first actions you take to incorporate and begin doing business you are making decisions that will have serious financial consequences. If you don't realize it then, you will when it comes time to pay taxes. Few things can be more painful than finding out too late that there were ways to save a lot of money on taxes. Tax evasion is illegal; tax avoidance is your right. Think about it early.

Like almost everything else discussed in this chapter, taxation is a thicket of specialties and subspecialties, and there are federal, state, and even local levels to deal with. If you make money through net income or sale of your business, taxes will be one of the larger financial issues, and the amounts can be substantial. Prior planning—and anticipation of future opportunities and problems—can go a long way toward making those amounts as painless as possible. Think about the following:

- Choice of entity and flow-through on taxation:
  - LLC and Subchapter S corporations flow earnings and losses through to the owners. Streaming of early losses can be valuable to some owners or investors. Note that there are restrictions on the deductibility of losses under passive loss rules.
  - Some owners may want to deduct losses and don't need current income, and vice versa. Note that Subchapter S limits the ability to stream losses and income disproportionately. LCCs have this flexibility.
  - Make sure that you don't set yourself up for *phantom income* from flow-throughs. Early-stage companies often generate net income but choose to retain the cash in the company to fund future growth. This can

create timing issues that result in income flowing through to owners that is recognized for tax purposes and not realized in cash. In other words, the owners have to report income and find cash from somewhere else to pay the taxes on the reported income.

- C corporations pay their own income taxes, and any distributions of earnings (dividends) or proceeds of sales are taxed again at the individual level. This seems punitive, but most small companies have low net incomes; they reinvest revenues for growth, and so there aren't meaningful cash dividends anyway. In addition, within limits, some earnings can be streamed to certain owners as compensation without being taxed at the corporate level. Therefore, as a practical matter, most small companies actually pay lower tax rates on their earnings than they would if the earnings were streamed back to individual owners.

- Note that if you plan to sell assets of a corporation early, before raising significant money, flow-through entities avoid having proceeds of the sale taxed twice.

- How will you set up for capital gains tax treatment on sale of assets or the company? Pay attention to basis and holding periods.
- How will you issue shares and options to founders and employees?
  - Watch for valuation issues. There are extensive IRS rules on this practice. Issuing shares at prices that reflect less than current valuations can result in a tax liability to the recipient; this is another instance of recognizing income without realizing the cash to pay the taxes. See in particular the rules around Section 409A, which governs deferrals and distributions of nonqualified deferred compensation paid by a service recipient to a service provider. Compliance is complicated; there are many gray areas, especially involving valuation questions, and penalties are stiff. Deferred amounts for the current year and all previous years can become immediately taxable, plus a 20 percent penalty. This is a job for outside expertise.[14]

  - For tax purposes, restricted shares (vesting) can be treated as owned on grant rather than when vested. This has important tax implications, particularly in terms of setting up to receive capital gains treatment on an eventual sale. To be eligible for this treatment, you must file an 83b election with the IRS within 30 days of the grant of shares, and there are no grace periods on the filing. This one bites many a founder and occasionally even the lawyers.

- Options plans have a number of taxation elements that require special attention. You should never draft one on your own, and the attorney doing it for you should be knowledgeable about tax considerations. Options granted at prices below current valuation also can trigger the "recognized and not realized" problem.

- You must set up to process and pay payroll taxes correctly. The IRS is vigilant about payroll tax accounting and prompt payment. Shortchanging the IRS on payroll taxes can be expensive and painful.
- Income tax planning. There is no greater tragedy than having a start-up find early sales success, only to discover that no one has planned ahead on matching expenses and income, leaving the company to pay precious growth capital to the IRS in income taxes. Pay attention in advance to what's deductible and the timing of expenses. Don't pay taxes earlier than you should.
- Set up for sales tax accounting early.

There are often numerous franchise taxes in your state of registration as well as state income taxes and any number of miscellaneous state and local taxes. Your accountant and attorney are your first lines of defense to be sure you pay everything you are required to pay, but realistically, there's no guarantee any one person is going to know them all.

WHAT I KNOW NOW THAT I WISH I HAD KNOWN THEN

Paul Sweeney, Foley Hoag LLP

Paul Sweeney, Esq., is a partner and deputy chair of the business department at the law firm Foley Hoag LLP, focusing on venture capital financings, mergers and acquisitions, strategic alliances, and related business transactions. Paul provides legal advice to entrepreneurs regarding corporate formation issues, contract negotiations, equity distribution and compensation matters, venture capital and debt financings, mergers and acquisitions, reorganizations, strategic investments, and joint ventures and other partnering transactions. Paul also represents venture capital investors such as Polaris Venture Partners and Highland Capital Partners in connection with their portfolio investments.

I work with entrepreneurs and their investors every day. Legal mistakes I see early entrepreneurs commonly make fall into three categories: mistakes in forming the company, issuing equity, and protecting intellectual property.

Mistakes in Forming the Company

- You can wait too long to form a company. It is sometimes unclear exactly when to incorporate, and some entrepreneurs push this off given the perceived costs involved. Before you have something of value or are dealing with third parties such as cofounders, investors, customers, suppliers, and employees, you should have your company incorporated and do all your transactions in it.

- Problems often arise when an entrepreneur chooses an unnecessarily complex legal structure. Often this means creating a limited liability company when a simple C or S corporation will do. LLCs are sometimes appropriate, but often their advantages ("pass-through" taxation treatment) are never exploited, and their disadvantages (greater complexity, higher cost to create and maintain) hamper the company in its critical early stages.

Mistakes in Allocating Equity

- Allocating equity is always a challenge, as is dividing the pie without being divisive. Often failing to face hard choices early leads to big troubles later.
- Legal troubles arise when companies are too casual in the early days about tracking who owns what. Keep accurate and updated records of equity ownership and other rights. Unresolved questions on capital structure can scare away investors and potential acquirers and result in unintended dilution to the founders.
- Promising cofounders or other recruits a percentage of the company rather than a specified number of shares can create confusion or animosity; worse, it can imply that the percentage of equity is immune from subsequent dilution.

Mistakes in Protecting Valuable Intellectual Property

- Failing to establish strong intellectual property rights and aggressively protect them can extinguish big value in a company overnight.
- Sharing confidential information without protection cannot be rectified once it happens. Disclose your ideas and inventions cautiously and gradually and be aware that even unintentional disclosure might preclude patentability or limit trade secret protection. Anyone handling confidential information should be covered by a nondisclosure agreement: employees, contractors, and outsiders alike.
- Everyone who creates intellectual property on behalf of your company should be bound by an assignment of inventions agreement with the company.

We hope we have covered most of the major worries that will appear on your worry list, though as we often tell our companies, *hope is not a plan.* In light of all the ways legal issues can affect your business and trip you up, there's no sure way to know that you have everything covered or even that your specialists will. In the end, your best defense against troubles is a broad understanding of the important issues, a good team, constant vigilance for issues of concern, and lots of ounces of prevention so that you won't have to worry about cures later.

QUESTIONS

- How will you decide on the balance between spending precious cash on legal matters and spending on other start-up needs, especially in the early days?
- How will you educate yourself about what matters are important enough to worry about? If your lawyer is like many, he or she will feel most matters are important because they are all potential risks.
- How might you minimize the effort and cost of dealing with legal risks in the early days, anticipating that you will do more as you grow and have more assets at risk?

NOTES

1. Bagley, Constance, and Craig Dauchy, *The Entrepreneur's Guide to Business Law* (Mason, OH: West, 2008).
2. Miller, Roger Leroy, and Gaylord A. Jentz. *Business Law Today: The Essential.* (Mason, OH: South-Western-CENGAGE Learning, 2011).
3. See the section on term sheets and memoranda of understanding below for details on how to do these things correctly. It's important that their form be nonbinding.
4. These obligations are listed in Chapter 9.
5. See Chapter 22.
6. Bagley and Dauchy, 2008: 182–187.
7. Ibid.
8. Ibid.: 268.
9. See, for example, ibid.: 267–271.
10. Ibid.: 157.
11. For an explanation of Regulation D, see http://www.sec.gov/answers/regd .htm (accessed October 10, 2010).
12. A safe harbor provision in a statute or regulations limits liability to penalties if certain conditions are met or defined actions or policies are in good faith.
13. Bagley and Dauchy, 2008: 165–169.
14. See http://www.irs.gov/irb/2007–19_IRB/ar07.html and http://www.irs.gov/ newsroom/article/0,,id=172883,00.html (accessed October 10, 2010).

Chapter 14

Nonprofits and Social Entrepreneurship

In charity there is no excess.

—Francis Bacon, *Of Goodness and Goodness of Nature* (1625)

If your idea is a for-profit opportunity, you can skip this chapter. If you think your idea probably should be launched as a nonprofit, you can skip Chapter 22. The rest of the book applies to launching a nonprofit as well as a for-profit, but this chapter looks at some factors unique to social entrepreneurship and starting nonprofits.

WHAT IS SOCIAL ENTREPRENEURSHIP?

There is no clean divide between entrepreneurship that seeks profits and entrepreneurship focused on the nonprofit world. In fact, there is an almost seamless continuum between enterprises whose goal is strictly commerce and profit and enterprises that engage only in charity. In between is everything from doing well by doing good to social enterprise.

There are those who say that the ideal business is a "post office box people send money to." Most entrepreneurs like to think that they are doing more than creating ways to transfer wealth, that they are doing something meaningful for others, not just taking their money. Many—if not most—profit-making businesses sell products and services that make life better in some way for their customers. Anyone who has taken a lifesaving medication or been the beneficiary of a medical device, for example, has left behind a profit for the maker and is thankful for his or her cure. It's not true of all businesses, of course, but most that make a profit also create at least some social value.

At the other extreme from the post office box, there are any number of nonprofit service organizations that help those with no means to pay for products and services—often essential products and services that the prosperous majority takes for granted. These organizations do their work by using contributed funds to help the less advantaged who live at the mercy of the next contribution cycle.

Over the last 20 to 30 years there has evolved a vibrant middle ground, blending the for-profit sector's focus on business execution and revenue generation with the nonprofit world's altruistic focus on making the world a better place. Defined and manifested in a bewildering diversity of ways, this is social entrepreneurship, or social enterprise.

Social enterprise uses market-driven business models to create social value and address critical social and environmental issues.[1] Barely a concept even 20 years ago, this is becoming an increasingly active space. A Lexis-Nexis search for *social entrepreneur* turned up 6 stories for 1991, 573 for 2001, and 1,682 for 2006.[2] There is no common definition, and there are many alternative terms, including social venture, nonprofit enterprise, social purpose business, and venture development. Organizations span the range from for-profit to a new legal form—limited-profit organizations formed to simultaneously advance community benefit and earn a return for investors—to nonprofits that derive money from activities that look like those of a for-profit (think Girl Scout cookies). Even many traditional nonprofits living on grants, government contracts, and donations are pushing to improve the effectiveness of their operations by adopting the execution and strategy practices of for-profit businesses.

In the world of social enterprise people clearly distinguish between advocacy organizations and service/product organizations. The former focus on research, opinion leading, driving change, legislation, and policy. The latter get things done, delivering services and benefits directly.

Conceptually, the question of what enforces discipline and effectiveness is a complicated issue in social entrepreneurship. In the commercial, for-profit world, winners are rewarded and the inefficient and ineffective are culled by market forces that judge on the basis of wealth creation (aka, financial profitability). These criteria provide a clear and useful means to assess not only success retrospectively but also opportunity prospectively. Jim Collins wrote a nonprofit monograph to his mega-bestseller *Good to Great* in which he noted that in contrast to the for-profit world, "the social sectors do not have rational capital markets that channel resources to those who deliver the best results.... The whole purpose of the social sectors is to meet social objectives, human needs and national priorities that *cannot* be priced at a profit."[3]

Gregory J. Dees teaches social entrepreneurship and nonprofit management at the Fuqua School of Business at Duke. He has this take on the effectiveness of the social entrepreneur:[4]

> *Any definition of social entrepreneurship should reflect the need for a substitute for the market discipline that works for business entrepreneurs.... Social entrepreneurs play the role of change agents in the social sector, by:*
>
> - *Adopting a mission to create and sustain social value (not just private value),*
> - *Recognizing and relentlessly pursuing new opportunities to serve that mission,*
> - *Engaging in a process of continuous innovation, adaptation, and learning,*

- *Acting boldly without being limited by resources currently in hand, and,*
- *Exhibiting a heightened sense of accountability to the constituencies served and for the outcomes created.*

Sound familiar? This is essentially the same definition as that of a for-profit entrepreneur. This shouldn't be surprising. Execution in pursuit of value creation should look the same no matter what the form. So what's different? For social enterprises that have the twin goals of social outcomes and earning free cash flow from revenue, mission-related impact is the central criterion, but wealth creation isn't ignored. "On the surface, many social enterprises look, feel, and even operate like traditional businesses. But looking more deeply, one discovers the defining characteristics of the social enterprise: mission is at the center of business, with income generation playing an important supporting role."[5]

The concept of social entrepreneurship is centered not just on mission but on entrepreneurship, making a social benefit–focused organization become more like a business. The idea is that nonprofits can benefit from the focus of for-profit businesses: customer focus, sound strategy, effective planning, efficient operations, and financial discipline. A social entrepreneur should focus as intently on excellence in all of these as does any back-to-the-wall for-profit entrepreneur.

ALTERNATIVE STRUCTURES

The first impulse of most social enterprise entrepreneurs is to organize as a nonprofit corporation. Odds are good that this is an appropriate choice, but there is an increasingly diverse array of alternatives.

Nonprofit Corporations

There are over a million nonprofit corporations in the United States.[6] Since the 1960s, the number of nonprofits has been growing at a higher rate than that of for-profits.[7] A nonprofit (or not-for-profit) corporation is chartered under state laws to operate for educational, charitable, social, religious, civic, or humanitarian purposes. Nonprofits have no owners. In essence, the law considers them to be created on behalf of the public. Nonprofit corporations are formed by individual incorporators who can be almost anyone. They are governed and operated by boards of directors or trustees for the benefit of the public. Nonprofits may own for-profit or nonprofit subsidiaries.

Because they are granted special tax status by the state for the benefit of the public, nonprofit corporations may not distribute surplus funds to parties with a controlling interest. Surpluses must be used to further the approved mission of the organization, and on dissolution any proceeds must be distributed to another nonprofit. Tax returns must be filed annually with the Internal Revenue Service (IRS) and certain state bodies to report financial activity and certify compliance with a number of restrictions on self-dealing and conflict of interest. In recent years many states have increased their vigilance on compliance and issued additional regulations preventing self-dealing and abuse of tax-exempt status.

Incorporation as a nonprofit can confer exemption from many state and local taxes, including sales, property, and income tax at the state level. Under the Internal Revenue Code's Section 501(c), in certain conditions nonprofits can be exempt from U.S. income taxes. This exemption is not conferred automatically by incorporation at the state level, but it can be granted by application to the IRS. In addition, organizations approved by the IRS under Section 501(c)(3) are eligible to receive contributions that can be deducted from the donor's income taxes if the central mission of the organization is in one of the following categories:

- Educational organizations and private schools
- Organizations providing insurance
- Charitable organizations
- Religious organizations
- Scientific organizations
- Literary organizations
- Amateur athletic organizations
- Organizations for the prevention of cruelty to children or animals
- Private foundations and public charities
- Lobbying expenditures

Sections 501(c)(4)–(27) provide for a wide variety of additional nonprofit classifications that are tax-exempt but, with a few exceptions, cannot accept tax-deductible contributions.[8] IRS Publication 526 (2009), *Charitable Contributions*, provides information on the treatment of tax-deductible contributions.[9]

Tax-exempt does not mean that nonprofits never pay taxes. Nonprofits are obligated for all payroll taxes on employees, the same as for-profits. Under certain circumstances unrelated business income over $1,000 will be taxed if the profits are generated by activities that are unrelated to the exempt purpose of the organization, that are considered a trade or business, and that are regularly carried on by the organization. If unrelated business activity accounts for a significant enough portion of a nonprofit's activity, its nonprofit status may be jeopardized entirely.

Low-Profit Limited Liability Companies

The low-profit limited liability company (L3C) has been created in some states as a new, hybrid form of pass-through entity with characteristics of both a nonprofit and a for-profit corporation. Like LLCs, L3Cs have the liability protection of a corporation, the flexibility of a partnership, and the ability to be sold in pieces. An L3C operates as a for-profit business but is designed for enterprises with social missions. Their charters explicitly provide that the corporation is formed to further a socially beneficial mission.

Seed investment is hard enough for any start-up to get, but it is especially difficult for enterprises that focus primarily on a social mission. Foundations like to support the launch of new social mission enterprises, but frequently they want other sources, such as private investors or revenue-generating activities, to fund sustainability. Since sustainability often implies the need to engage in the kinds of revenue-generating activities that for-profit businesses pursue, foundations can get into tax trouble if they are deemed to be investing in certain kinds of for-profit activities. The L3C provides a structure that facilitates remaining in compliance with certain IRS rules governing program-related investments.

Program-related investments are defined by the IRS as investments in which the primary purpose is to accomplish one or more of the foundation's exempt purposes. Production of income or appreciation of property is not a significant purpose, and influencing legislation and taking part in political campaigns on behalf of candidates are not purposes. In determining whether an investment is primarily program-related or primarily for the production of income or the appreciation of property, the IRS looks to whether other investors who engage in investments only for profit would be likely to make an investment on the same terms as a private foundation.[10] Failure to meet the standards of a program-related investment exposes foundations to certain penalty taxes, including excise taxes under Section 4944 of the Internal Revenue Code. In theory, the L3C structure enables attractive investment opportunities for foundations as seed investors by qualifying their investments as program-related and at the same time qualifying them for profitable, revenue-generating activities and follow-on private sector investment, generating returns to all investors while fulfilling the social mission.

The IRS cannot provide a blanket determination of qualification of the L3C structure. It has publicly stated that foundations may not rely solely on L3C status in determining whether an investment qualifies as a program-related investment, but it will issue private letter rulings on a case by case basis.[11]

As of 2010, Vermont, Illinois, Maine, Michigan, North Carolina, Utah, and Wyoming had created L3C options.

B Corporations

A B corporation is a type of corporation that writes into its corporate governing documents mandates to serve the interests of employees, the community, and the environment in addition to the standard focus on return to shareholders. The intent is to harness the power of business to solve social and environmental problems.

To become a B corporation, businesses are certified under a rating system by B Lab, an independent 501(c)(3). "B Corporations' transparent and comprehensive performance standards enable consumers to support businesses that align with their values, investors to drive capital to higher impact investments, and governments and multinational corporations to implement sustainable procurement policies."[12] State laws are evolving with respect to B corporations. There may be certain tax benefits. Procedures on sales and mergers have not been defined, particularly concerning who has standing to approve or object.

Cooperatives

Cooperatives are legal entities owned and democratically controlled by their members. Often they are organized as corporations without capital stock under state cooperative laws. They can be for-profits or nonprofits. For-profits can distribute profits, subject in some cases to threshold limitations. Sectors in which cooperatives operate include consumer cooperatives, producer cooperatives, agriculture, housing, utilities, health insurance, and jobs/employment. They generally have open membership, economic participation, and a social or community focus.[13]

WHAT IS THE MISSION?

A mission is what an organization does. It describes the organization's purpose. In his book *How to Change the World—Social Entrepreneurs and the Power of New Ideas*, David Bornstein writes:

> An important social change frequently begins with a single entrepreneurial author: one obsessive individual who sees a problem and envisions a new solution, and builds organizations to protect and market that vision, who provides the energy and sustained focus to overcome the inevitable resistance, and who—decade after decade—keeps improving, strengthening, and broadening that vision until what was once a marginal idea has become a new norm.[14]

Everything that can be said about the imperative of for-profit entrepreneurs to find a need and identify customers with that need fully applies to the social entrepreneur, maybe more so. Recall that the beneficiary and the customer need not be the same person. The customer is the one who pays you money for your product or service. Every time someone uses Google, that person is a beneficiary, but Google's customer is the advertiser who pays Google for access to users. The beneficiary-customer map for nonprofits is important and often is overlooked.

Revenue-generating products and services of social enterprises have customers just as for-profits do, but often the beneficiaries of products or services may not be the ones paying money for them, or at least not paying their full cost.

These beneficiaries of social enterprises should be treated like customers, because that is good manners and effective operations, but frequently they are not really customers because someone else is paying the cost. That someone is the customer: a foundation, an individual donor, a government agency. The one who makes the funding decision is a customer, and that customer has its own needs, as well as a basis for making funding decisions. In conceiving and launching an enterprise, it is imperative that a social entrepreneur go through the same thought process as any for-profit entrepreneur in defining the needs of those customers. Their needs are often very different from the needs of the beneficiaries, and if social entrepreneurs want their money, they must figure out how to meet their needs, recognizing fundraising is a terribly competitive environment.

Do you have a clear idea of what the funder is looking for? Is there a match of mission? Is your articulation of mission clear, and is there a good connection between it and your plan? What research and validation have you done to support your idea? What operating and infrastructure criteria are they expecting you to have? Who will do the work? Is the team adequate and qualified? What is your funding plan for launch and later sustainability? What is the competition; is this need being filled elsewhere already? What metrics of effectiveness do they want to see? Often funders don't want to assume a long-term obligation to sustain you. How will you cover longer-term costs? Resources are more than just money. Where will you get them?

METRICS: HOW WILL YOU MEASURE SUCCESS?

Increasingly, social enterprises are being pressed to demonstrate efficacy quantitatively. Measuring the creation of social value is much more complicated than it is in the for-profit world, in which one looks to profitability and growth. Social enterprises don't provide products and services out of nothing. They consume resources: dollars, people's time, and possibly contributed goods. Do they create more social value than they consume? If you are a social entrepreneur, sooner or later you will need to make the case that you do, especially if you're dependent on donations and volunteer labor for support. How will you do that?

Of course, the point of departure is an accounting of what you have done. The cost input side is easy to quantify. But what units of success will you use to show performance relative to the mission? Do you have consensus among the various stakeholders that these are the right measures? Have you agreed on realistic targets for achievement? What reporting systems will you use, and who will maintain them? Who will receive the data, and what will they receive? (This is an important one.) How will you solicit and receive feedback?

SUSTAINABILITY

Total charitable giving in the United States exceeds $300 billion in a year, but few givers are excited about paying for overhead. People want to target the cause, not pay for bureaucracy. You want to be an effective social entrepreneur and everyone wants to be efficient, but there is a point at which you can't be effective or even efficient if you don't have enough funding to pay for basic infrastructure and resources that anyone needs to be effective and efficient. Alongside a clear mission and a commitment to it, having a plan for financial sustainability is paramount in social entrepreneurship. It forces the creation of an operating plan that ensures success and survival in the long term. A credible plan for sustainability is one of the most important things foundations, government agencies, and individual donors consider when deciding whether to seed the launch of a new social enterprise.

It's a common misperception that nonprofits rely mainly on donations and grants. The variability of funding sources is enormous,[15] but as in the for-profit world, no options are easy ones. Competition for funding is as intense in the nonprofit world as it is in the for-profit, probably more so. Grant makers and foundations are overwhelmed with proposals for "free money." Most funding applicants successfully document a compelling need. They fail to get funding when they lack a credible operating plan and a path to sustainability. Remember, donors are your customers—treat them that way. That doesn't mean giving them nice treatment; it means finding out what they really want and giving it to them. Almost always they want you to show how you will operate as effectively as any for-profit business and how you will quickly become sustainable. They want to take credit for catalyzing another successful enterprise and move on to help the next one launch.

Nonprofits have some options to cut costs that are not usually available to for-profits. Volunteers can substitute for the cost of hired help, but of course managing volunteers is a huge challenge that often limits effectiveness. A nonprofit can solicit contributions of in-kind materials and products, but often there are inherent inefficiencies in working with in-kind contributions. Generally, it's about the same as comparing a primitive barter economy and a modern market economy.

One of the main reasons people start social enterprises is that the beneficiaries can't pay the full cost of the services or products they receive. But before you reflexively go out looking for donations to cover their costs, it makes sense to convince yourself that this is true. Are there financing alternatives (e.g., student loans) or demand aggregation (health insurance) that would make the service or product affordable for the beneficiaries, in which case you could turn them into paying customers? Is there someone else who would pay on their behalf (employers, government)?

Some social enterprises try to generate profits from a side business to produce revenue for their mission. Making profits in social enterprises by selling things is no easier than it is in for-profits even when you don't have to pay taxes, have lots of volunteer labor (with all the challenges that presents), and pay your people less than your for-profit competitors do (and those are significant advantages).

Jerr Boschee, director of the for-profit Institute for Social Entrepreneurs, says, "Unless a nonprofit organization is generating earned revenue from its activities, it is not acting in an entrepreneurial manner … only earned income will ever allow a nonprofit to become sustainable or self sufficient."[16] This may be true, but acting in an entrepreneurial manner is not an end goal, only a means to an end goal. For a social entrepreneur, the end goal is the mission. Sustainability makes fulfilling the mission possible. Some organizations achieve sustainability through fund-raising, grants, and donations, hard as that is. Others make it through revenue-generating, for-profit activities. If you try for-profit activities, you're into everything written in the rest of this book, and you will need to do all those things as well as any for-profit competitors—and there will almost always be competitors if there is a profit to be made. Many social enterprises have great success stories about doing just this, and of course many others struggle or fail, just like in the rest of the for-profit world. If you choose to pursue one of these "double bottom line" strategies for sustainability, just hope you don't end up so consumed with the challenges of making a profit that you lose sight of your mission. Most people find one bottom line hard enough. But don't lose hope. The amazing thing is how many social entrepreneurs are succeeding every day. It can be done.[17]

PEOPLE: SPECIAL CHALLENGES

We started to title this section "Special People Challenges" but decided readers might misinterpret it. Thought about in the right way, it often takes special people to start and work in social enterprises. The tension between bottom line profit and creating social value for others is not just a burden on enterprises; it weighs on people too. A social enterprise has to recognize that there are special challenges in being effective and efficient with people who often are not choosing the work because of the financial rewards.

Nonprofits can pay market wages, but they tend to struggle to do so and most don't or can't: refer back to the previous sections on funders' reluctance to pay overhead. Profit-based incentives and pay-for-performance are largely or completely excluded by both common practice and the law (the so-called bar on distribution). Thus, freedom to recruit and motivate with compensation is limited. The answer is generally to look for great people with a heart for the mission and the willingness to accept below-market compensation, but it's a hard thing to do successfully and consistently. Many social enterprises compensate by using lots of volunteer time, but volunteers have to be recruited, trained, and managed and are often difficult to manage and hold accountable. You can "fire" volunteers if you have to, but you can't do it too often, and the threat of firing doesn't have the same motivating effect it has with employees taking home market-competitive salaries.

As a result, there is a career stigma, or stereotype, in regard to nonprofit people in the eyes of the for-profit world. It's sort of a vicious circle: People assume the nonprofit world tends to attract less-qualified people, making career transitions from a nonprofit to a for-profit career difficult, which leads to self-selection against careers in the nonprofit sector.[18]

Perhaps even more significant to you as someone considering launching a social enterprise, what might launching a nonprofit mean to you personally in terms of compensation and career? A for-profit entrepreneur delays gratification with the expectation of a big payoff in the future. As a social entrepreneur, unless you come up with a fabulously successful dual bottom line for-profit company, you will be operating as a nonprofit. In nonprofits there is no liquidity event, no payoff for you at the end.

The same is true for the key team members you will recruit to help you build the organization. In nonprofits, often intangible job characteristics such as freedom to pursue professional interests (especially in fields such as health care, research, and education) and the personal satisfaction of association with the mission are the main incentives that interest many people. However, this often brings personnel management challenges significantly more complicated and demanding than those in the for-profit sector. Look at yourself and be sure you have the personality and management skills to take on this added challenge.[19]

GOVERNANCE

All corporations are accountable to their boards of directors or trustees. There are some special factors involved in governing social enterprises, especially if they are nonprofits. For one thing, metrics and measuring performance are complicated. In addition to the accountabilities common to all corporations that we discussed in Chapter 9, you will have to combine accountability on efficient operations with performance relative to the mission. Boards are often tough on costs of overhead and support operations. They tend to press management to put all possible resources directly into the mission. Good communication with boards goes a long way toward smoothing governance and preserving consensus on operations and mission.

Generally, there is less autonomy for leadership in a nonprofit than in a for-profit. Traditional nonprofits usually use boards as fund-raising vehicles, which leads to large boards heavily weighted with people who give money.[20] This can create unwieldy boards that don't focus much on operations or your management challenges or, worse, have little operational or business experience and focus on them too much. Both are situations you don't need, and they are avoidable in the beginning as you build the board if you balance the tension between fund-raising and board recruiting.

Your board has a statutory responsibility to look after the public interest. This means that the board members have to ensure that you are executing effectively in fulfilling your mission. They're obligated to be vigilant against self-dealing, conflicts of interest, and abuse of tax-exempt status. Most states require extensive provisions in the corporate bylaws and policies on these points and look to the boards to enact and enforce them. Although more a matter of degree than of difference, this is an added responsibility for board members of nonprofits, though lately the burdens on public company for-profit boards have increased also.

WHAT I KNOW NOW THAT I WISH I HAD KNOWN THEN

Leslie Fall, MD, iInTIME

Drs. Leslie Fall and Norman Berman are cofounders of a nonprofit educational enterprise, the Institute for Innovative Technology in Medical Education (iInTIME—http://www.i-intime.org), which supports the clinical education of medical students with online virtual patient cases.[21] A majority of U.S. and Canadian medical schools pay for subscriptions to iInTIME's cases series, with over 10,000 registered student users per year and more than 500,000 case sessions completed annually. Drs. Fall and Berman have received numerous national medical education awards for their work. This was their first start-up, and they offer these lessons learned:

1. Ask yourself this question every day: What would I attempt to do if I knew I couldn't fail?—then do it.
2. A passionate vision, regardless of how original the idea may seem, is not sufficient for success. If you don't begin with a clear and unmet need and a deep understanding of what your stakeholders value, you are sunk from the beginning.
3. Listen to your stakeholders. Trust them to tell you what they need and what to do next.
4. Maintaining a commitment to excellence in innovation is hard work, especially when there is no profit motive. Your vision and passion will have to get you through. Surround yourself with others who support you and your vision. You will need them in the darker days—and there will be darker days.
5. It takes at least seven years to make a sustainable change.

6. In a nonprofit, many people will help you because they think it is a good thing to do. Express your gratitude often.
7. Estimate your costs—then do it for half as much.
8. Take the time to celebrate intermediate successes—but never assume that you've reached the summit.

Regardless of the form, launching an enterprise to drive change and create social value demands excellent execution in all the things covered in this book: understanding and serving customers, market validation, innovation, strategy, planning, funding and sustainability, operations, managing risk, financial management, metrics, accounting, finance, law and governance, and team building—all in a context of low financial rewards and no big payoff at the end. It sounds daunting. What's amazing is how many social entrepreneurs and volunteers remain undaunted. Remember the main reason you're thinking about social entrepreneurship: the mission. Social entrepreneurship is about some form of helping the disadvantaged, making life better for someone, creating social value. If it was easy, everybody would be doing it. Of course, in reality everybody ought to be doing it, so good for you if you are.

QUESTIONS

- What form of business is best for your idea: for-profit or nonprofit? Why?
- Can you make a clear connection between your idea and who you identify as the customers and the beneficiaries?
- Do you have a credible plan for sustainability?
- How will you measure your success? Who will care about your success? How will you communicate with them?

NOTES

1. Dees, J. Gregory, Jed Emerson, and Peter Economy, *Enterprising Nonprofits—A Toolkit for Social Entrepreneurs* (New York: Wiley, 2001): 4–5.
2. Bornstein, David, *How to Change the World—Social Entrepreneurs and the Power of New Ideas* (New York: Oxford University Press, 2007): 307.
3. Collins, Jim, *Good to Great and the Social Sectors*, a monograph to accompany *Good to Great* (Boulder, CO: Jim Collins, 2005): 19.
4. Dees, Gregory J., "The Meaning of Social Entrepreneurship," http://www.caseatduke.org/documents/dees_sedef.pdf, 2001 (accessed September 15, 2010).

5. Dees, 2001.
6. The National Center for Urban Statistics, http://nccsdataweb.urban.org/ PubApps/profile1.php (accessed September 15, 2010).
7. Weisbrod, Burton A., *The Nonprofit Economy* (Cambridge, MA, Harvard University Press, 1988): 62.
8. IRS Publication 557, *Tax-Exempt Status for Your Organization*, June 2008, http://www.irs.gov/publications/p557/index.html (accessed September 15, 2010).
9. IRS Publication 526, *Charitable Contributions*, http://www.irs.gov/publications/p526/index.html (accessed September 15, 2010).
10. http://www.irs.gov/charities/foundations/article/0,,id=137793,00.html (accessed September 15, 2010).
11. Dinning, B. Ray, "Structuring Social Ventures: The L3C as a Non-Traditional Business Entity," December 7, 2009, http://lawpartners.wordpress.com/ 2009/12/07/using-the-13c-to-structure-social-ventures-by-ray-dinning-jd-llm/ (accessed September 15, 2010).
12. B Lab, http://www.bcorporation.net/about (accessed September 29, 2010).
13. Dawans, Vincent, Kim Alter, and Lindsay Miller, "Social Enterprise Topology," http://www.41enses.org/setypology#_blank (accessed September 15, 2010).
14. Bornstein, 2007: 3.
15. Weisbrod, 1988: 3.
16. Boschee, Jerr, and Jim McClurg, "Toward a Better Understanding of Social Entrepreneurship: Some Important Distinctions," http://www.se-alliance.org/ better_understanding.pdf (accessed September 15, 2010).
17. Tishler, Carla, "Enterprising Nonprofits: A Toolkit for Social Entrepreneurs— Why Running a Nonprofit is the Hardest Job in Business," May 29, 2001, http://hbswk.hbs.edu/archive/2265.html (accessed September 15, 2010).
18. Oberfield, Alice, and J. Gregory Dees, "Starting a Nonprofit Venture," Harvard Business School Case 391–096 (1992).
19. Leete, Laura, "Executive Leadership in Nonprofit Organizations," in *The Nonprofit Sector: A Research Handbook*, ed. Walter W. Powell (New Haven, CT, Yale University Press, 2006): 159–179.
20. Middleton, Melissa, "Nonprofit Boards of Directors: Beyond the Governance Function," in *The Nonprofit Sector: A Research Handbook*, ed. Walter W. Powell (New Haven, CT, Yale University Press, 2006): 141–153.
21. See Chapter 20 for more on iInTIME.

Part Three

Managing the Company

Chapter 15

Everything Is Negotiable

In business, you don't get what you deserve, you get what you negotiate.

—Chester L. Karrass

If you've read books about entrepreneurship, have you ever seen a chapter on negotiating? We haven't. In one sense, this is reasonable. Negotiation is everywhere. Most things in life seem to involve some form of negotiation. Just ask your children. If it's universal, why cover it in a book on starting a company? We cover it here because too many of the first time entrepreneurs we meet are surprised to hear that they will need to negotiate effectively for virtually everything they seek and because people on the other side are going to be negotiating relentlessly with them. Apparently, no one has ever told them.

Whether you know it or not, people negotiate with you every day, and if you don't know it, the odds are that someone is taking advantage of you. Unfamiliarity and inexperience with the negotiation that is always present in business encounters is one of the great obstacles to success facing first-time entrepreneurs.

Many people new to the business world find the thought of negotiating distasteful. Many feel it is both demeaning and unnecessary, like haggling with a rug merchant. They feel that people ought to agree on what's fair, not argue about it. Agreeing on what is fair might be nice, but what is fair is never more objective than an opinion in the eye of the beholder. Sad to say, at least some of the people you encounter in business won't be worried about fair, only about getting all they can. Thus, you should develop a good negotiating sense and have a working familiarity with some effective negotiating tactics to protect yourself and your company. Ideally, you will find it an enjoyable part of the process. Negotiating can be fun, but fun or not, accept the fact that you will have to negotiate all kinds of things every day and prepare yourself to do it well.

As with law and accounting, there are ample resources to teach you about negotiation. It's a big subject and is well treated, so here we will provide only a framework and some key basics. With this introduction you should be able to go deeper into all the information that's available and no longer be the unwitting victim that so many of your fellow first-time entrepreneurs are.

WHEN ARE YOU IN A NEGOTIATION?

"Negotiation is the means by which people deal with their differences."[1] One hopes they deal with their differences through trade-offs that leave everyone reasonably satisfied. Seen this way, you probably are negotiating something most of the time, at least whenever you want something that is controlled by someone else. The question isn't whether you're in a negotiation—business or otherwise—but whether you know it and are deliberately working to maximize value or behaving more like a roasted turkey served up on a plate. Whether negotiating to bring people into your team, with vendors, with customers, or with investors, every day you will have to interact and transact with counterparties, many of whom are practiced negotiators. Negotiations can be zero sum (there is a fixed pie; one party wins, one loses) or positive sum (the pie is enlarged, offering the possibility that all parties can be better off). Zero sum usually is no fun unless you win and the other party loses. Positive sum can be good for everybody if handled well. The way it comes out depends largely on you.

WHY NEGOTIATE?

To many people, negotiation seems a protracted exercise in posturing, a colossal waste of time. In an ideal world in which all facts were known and fair was fair, divergent interests could be resolved quickly, leading to a solution ideal for all parties. However, since this is not an ideal world, facts are not openly known and interests often collide. There are really only two alternatives to the frequently protracted and challenging exercise of a negotiation: capitulation and conquest. Fortunately, negotiations act as a means of selectively sharing information and testing alternatives. In them, parties can explore transactions of mutual benefit and try to resolve differences. If done constructively and with some degree of skill, negotiation is the process by which parties can figure out ways to work together or transact in a way that leaves both significantly better off than they would have been without negotiating.

HOW TO NEGOTIATE EFFECTIVELY

First, prepare well. Experienced negotiators will tell you that thorough preparation is the single biggest determinant of who succeeds in a negotiation. Script the encounter and objectives. Below are descriptions of some important dimensions in negotiations.

Preparation

Generally, the party who has prepared better does better and the party committed to being more diligent, thorough, and successful usually will be. There is an important discipline in preparing for meetings that we try to drill into all our students and start-ups, and it's even more valuable in preparing for negotiations. Preparation starts with gathering information, defining your objectives and parameters, guessing the other sides' positions, and strategizing the negotiating style and tactics.

At the beginning, say out loud what you visualize as a successful outcome for you. Working backward from that, project what you think will happen in the encounter: where the negotiation will take place, who will be there, how long it will take, the roles everyone will play, and the course it is likely to follow. This seems self-evident, yet you would be surprised how frequently people don't prepare like this for important negotiations and end up letting events carry them where they will.

Do your homework on the counterparties. List what you know. Guess what they want, what they need, and what their alternatives are. Do the same thing for yourself; make a shopping list of what you want to get from them and prioritize it. Mentally drill potential arguments and counterarguments. If more than one person from your side will be involved, script roles. Plan ahead to logistics and process, things such as how to communicate with each other, when you will take breaks in the negotiation to advantage, how long to stay with the negotiation, and when to stop.

Information

People are different. Many psychological studies have shown that we have a persistent habit of assuming that other people are more like ourselves than they actually are. When you sit down to negotiate, this is a particularly dangerous assumption. Don't rely on assumptions; you want good information.

Information is one of the most valuable commodities in any negotiation. If there are 10 important lessons in life, this is surely one of them. In your research and in every conversation in the negotiation, seek as much information as you can get about the counterparty's interests, circumstances, background, strengths and weaknesses, and, most of all if you can get it, positions and ranges of aspirations. Also, you want the counterparty to have only information about you that helps you in a clearly defined way.

Information in a negotiation is valuable because it is a significant source of power. Some people look on power as dangerous or even evil. Power is dangerous only when you don't know how to use it (or it's used against you) and evil only when you use it to bad ends. In a negotiation, you never want to end up with the people in the other party having power over you because they have lots of information about you—your circumstances, motivations, objectives, bottom lines—and you having little or none about them. This is called *information asymmetry*, and if it is going to exist, you want it to be in your favor. Nothing will give you more of an advantage in a negotiation than knowing all you can about a counterparty and having counterparties know only what you want them to know about you.

How do you get information? Not to belabor the obvious, but the most effective means is to ask. You will be amazed at how much people will tell you if you just ask them questions. Obviously, there are effective, polite ways to ask and intrusive, rude ways. Open-ended questions are especially effective. You never know what you might hear. It's surprising how few people, even skilled negotiators, can answer open-ended questions and succeed in telling you nothing.

Generally, there is no glory in appearing smart. In addition to helping you get the information you need, appearing less smart reduces the motivation for counterparties to be on their guard.

Take every opportunity to observe. For example, we always like to meet with counterparties in their offices if possible. When we do, we spend every second acting like detectives, observing everything we can about how the offices are set out, how people are acting, and what is there (and isn't). We're curious with everyone we meet and ask all the questions we can think of. We think meeting face to face is usually better than communicating over the phone or by e-mail. Social or casual time can be incredibly valuable for the same reason. A nice bottle of wine over lunch or dinner can do wonders for information acquisition.

For negotiations that are important enough, you can learn a wealth of information about a counterparty by negotiating for a parallel item or transaction you don't care about and fully intend not to do. For example, good negotiators will go to a car lot and bargain for a car they don't want, taking the salesperson to his or her bottom line without buying. Then they return, having a good idea of the lot's markup and tactics, and bargain for the car they really want. Circumstances don't always permit running a scrimmage negotiation first, but when you can, you can learn a lot. An easy pretext is to negotiate over the location of a negotiation: who will come to whom.

One other point that might seem silly at first: There are times when it pays to repeat the same question in a variety of ways, over and over. Why? Think about this example. We had an engineer who used to drive us crazy in data rooms for companies we were bidding to buy. He was a bit slower-moving and more methodical than most and had a habit of going on and on, repeating questions in one form or another. One time, about when the rest of us were ready to kill him for asking the same question for the ninth time in a two-hour stretch, he got a different answer. We all found that odd. A little more digging turned up a major problem the company had been trying to hide, and it was clear that the acquisition was unattractive on account of it. Asking variations on the same question nine times may be excessive, but often you get more information each time you ask, and there's always the chance of uncovering something bad if the answers don't agree.

In the end, of course, the goal is not just extraneous information but the kind of information that will deepen your understanding of the counterparty's constraints and objectives. That means careful analysis and synthesis of information.

Communication

A little conversation at the beginning to set out expectations and keep them in line goes a long way toward structuring a successful negotiation and focusing on the meaningful issues. You want to strike a balance between communicating *positions* and communicating *interests*. Telling too much about interests can cross the line into giving away too much information, but telling too little precludes discovering opportunities to broaden the dimensions of a negotiation and be creative in looking for win-win opportunities.

Carefully navigate between sending signals that are just posturing and ones that identify key areas in which you are not flexible. We like to get our own "must-have" factors on the table early and repeat them often. This is not to say that the other side will take them seriously, but by stating them at the beginning you are in a stronger position to hold firmly to them later. It's good expectations management.

Time

In a negotiation, time is usually more to the advantage of one party than the other. The more time pressure there is on a party, the more leverage the other party has to let the pressure of deadlines work in its favor. Common wisdom says to let a deadline pass, if only to see what the other party does. There's a rule of thumb that 80 percent of concessions happen in the last 20 percent of the time. Although that may not be a precise number, the principle holds. Patience is key if you are the party with more time, and planning is key if you're not. How do you know which party you are? That was the subject of the second section: information asymmetry.

Win-Win versus Zero-Sum Negotiation

Common synonyms you may have heard for *zero sum* include *constant sum, distributive negotiation*, and *win-lose*. You are in a zero-sum negotiation when the values at issue are fixed and cannot be expanded by the transaction either because of circumstances beyond anyone's control or by choice of one or more of the parties. Think of these as tragic negotiations. There is a pie of fixed size, and the only contest is over how it will be split. A negotiation strictly over price is an example. The parties can transact or not, but if they do, what one party gains, the other loses.

By contrast, in a win-win negotiation the parties find ways to expand the pie; by transacting they add more value than either party could achieve alone. This often means getting creative about how to add value by working together and figuring out how to share the extra benefit equitably. The fastest way to convert a zero-sum negotiation to a win-win discussion is to add more dimensions to the negotiation. For example, in addition to arguing over price, think of ways both parties could cut costs by working together.

If you are good at holding lots of factors in your head at one time, you can learn a lot and potentially find creative solutions with a "buffet menu" approach: offering a mix-and-match variety of options and exploring different combinations of choices with the other side. This has the benefit of learning a great deal in a short time about the other party's value sets, even if most of the options eventually are discarded. In win-win, the parties seldom get everything they want, but if it is done well, both come out ahead.

Best Alternative to a Negotiated Agreement and Zone of Possible Agreement

Good negotiators always mentally define in advance the boundaries within which they are willing to deal. They set some clear boundaries for when they will be better off walking out than agreeing. Many successful entrepreneurs say that you have to be willing to "show your back" in a negotiation. You walk out when there is not enough on offer to leave you better off than your best alternative to a negotiated agreement. This floor is the so-called *reservation price*, based on what you know about your alternatives to a negotiated agreement. Define your best alternative to a negotiated agreement (BATNA) and reservation price before the fact and let them hold you back like Ulysses lashed to the mast as he sailed past the sirens' island. Otherwise you will find yourself chasing a deal downward past the point where it makes no sense to you. This happens more often than you would guess, and it's almost always due to laziness about setting a BATNA and honoring it.

It sounds simple, but defining exactly where your BATNA lies is often complicated. Many factors can affect the value of your alternatives. Worse, the factors can shift quickly as information changes. Even what transpires in real time in a negotiation can affect your alternatives. Still, this is an important focus. You need to have the discipline to keep your eye on your BATNA throughout a negotiation, keep it current, and use it if you need it.

One of the best BATNAs is to develop competing opportunities with other parties. There is no more powerful position in a negotiation than having acceptable alternatives and no weaker one than having none. It's said that if you're negotiating with only one party, you're not negotiating, you're begging. Think carefully about strategy options you might employ to minimize your weakness if you have no competing offers or alternatives.

The zone of possible agreement (ZOPA) is the overlap that lies inside both your reservation price and your counterparty's. Normally you can only speculate on the boundaries of a zone of possible agreement, because you can't be sure you know the other party's lowest (or highest) possible number and certainly don't want the counterparty knowing yours. The zone is one of the most important elements in the negotiation. When it turns out the zone is nonexistent—that is, there is no room for both parties to deal—everyone is wasting time. This is a compelling reason to get negotiations onto multiple elements—out of fixed sum and into win-win—as early as possible, which widens the zone of possible agreement.

Beware of sunk costs and don't let them blind you. They are not part of your BATNA. It can be emotionally hard to do sometimes, but you have to ignore past costs that can't be recovered. Always look at opportunities purely on the basis of their going-forward economics.

Negotiating Styles

There are probably as many styles of negotiating as there are people, but most fit a few profiles. There are the tough, demanding, competitive negotiators and the nice, accommodating, easy types. Some negotiators focus on numbers, some on intangibles. There is the haggler who focuses only on price. Some work from the premise "what's ours is ours, what's yours is negotiable." There are smooth talkers and blusterers, pragmatists and strategists. More experienced negotiators are adept at many styles and switch between them as circumstances dictate. Less experienced ones have a limited repertoire. Try to develop as broad a range of styles as you can. Think of them as tools, each appropriate to a particular circumstance. But don't overreach your competence. Nothing rings more hollow or outright comical than a patently fake style.

Power

Everyone pays attention to the power calculus in a negotiation, probably to excess. Power can be drawn from circumstances, relative assets and resources, factors in the people themselves, and a number of alternatives. Competing offers are especially powerful. Authority, reputation, experience and expertise, resources and financial strength, and personality all bring a power calculus to the table. Some power elements are more in your control than others. Remember, information asymmetry is a major source of power. That's one that is well within your control. The power dynamic obviously influences the course of a negotiation, but you should take care not to be overawed by or overreliant on power dynamics. There are plenty of tactics to weaken or neutralize the advantages of power in the hands of the counterparty. Periodically take an inventory of your power levers as a negotiation progresses and strategize how to maximize their value in the negotiation.

Tactics

In the end, tactics are the language of negotiation. Here are a few examples:

- *Limited authority*. A familiar tactic is the *reservation*: "I have to check with my manager" or "I need approval by my board." It calls to mind the image of a car salesperson going in the back to check with the manager when in fact there's no manager there. Sometimes he or she even *is* the manager. Often negotiators will surprise you late in a negotiation with a claim they have to check with higher authority and use the tactic to chisel off one more round of concessions demanded by the higher authority.

Some negotiators say you should never represent that you have authority in a negotiation; always reference a higher authority you need to check with. This may be overkill. There are times when it's better to have the higher authorities at the table and just get a deal done. But never go into a negotiation saying you have full authority when the other side has limited authority.

- *Good cop, bad cop.* Everyone is familiar with this tactic: the tough, irrational, garrulous partner and his or her nice partner. Use it if you like but don't fall for it.

- *Jostling over who makes the first offer.* Most practitioners work on the maxim "The party who offers first always gives up too much." Many remember when a first offer from the other side surprised them in their own favor, an opportunity that would have been missed by going first. Many professionals who study negotiations say science proves that going first produces a better result. They argue that offering first *anchors* the negotiation around your number. This may be more applicable in zero-sum situations.[2,3] Circumstances vary so widely in negotiations that there is no one answer, because there is no one underlying dynamic and so few facts can be known. Studies often are done in controlled or artificially constructed environments that fail to take this into account. All things equal, we like the other side to show its cards first (see "Information," above). Also, there is one cardinal rule on which everyone ought to agree: For reasons that should be self-evident, never *take* the first offer!

- *Timing and magnitude of concessions.* There is a rule: Never make a concession without getting one in return even if it's not a concession you feel is worth little to give up. It's a good rule. Conceding without compensation creates a bad incentive for the other side to keep seeking more concessions. When to concede and how far to move are key drivers of the dynamic in a negotiation. Learn all you can about the nuances of this from reading resources, experienced negotiators, and your own experience.

- *Bidding against yourself.* Never do it. Always get a concession for making one. But never miss the chance to try to get counterparties to improve their offers before starting to negotiate. Often this works, at least in the early stages, in which your first concession could be merely being willing to engage seriously in the discussion. Tell them, "You'll have to be at least realistic or this isn't worth continuing." It works more often than you'd think.

- *Splitting the difference.* This is commonly the path to closing a successful negotiation, but how it's done is important. Offering to split first often sets up the counterparties to treat your suggestion of the middle as your new number. They then offer to split the remaining range, effectively leaving you splitting the difference twice.

- *Flinching.* Theatrics are a natural part of negotiations. They can range from subtle to histrionic, even comic. Flinching spans the range. Still, it's wise always to telegraph at least mild dislike of a proposal, especially in the early going. Remember, negotiations are not rigidly structured but dynamic, and every signal you send is factored into the calculus of the other side as it tries to figure out what it's possible to extract from you.

- *Silence.* People hate silence. Good negotiators use this to devastating effect. After making a proposal, especially a tough one, many negotiators just sit silently and wait. There is an old saying about this: "The one who talks next loses." It can help to recite this to yourself as you wait, because waiting silently in a stare-down is hard.

- *Withdrawing an offer or walking out.* Some negotiators believe withdrawing an offer forces concessions and conclusions. There is a saying, "A successful negotiation doesn't end until someone has walked out at least once." This has an element of truth, but walking out can be risky. If you walk out, there's always the chance the other side will let you stay out. After that, if you come back, you are in a weakened position, if you can get back in at all. Telegraphing that you may have to walk away is far smarter than doing it.

- *Red herrings.* In that list of objectives you made in preparing to negotiate, always include some things you believe the other side won't want to concede. Ask for them anyway and hold them as concessions you can make in exchange for things you do want. Negotiators call these points red herrings: diversions whose purpose is to distract from a main issue. It can sound manipulative, but rest assured, an experienced negotiator will be doing it to you. Information asymmetry can help you a lot here. If you know enough about the other side, you can often intuit which of its items may be red herrings and strategize your concessions accordingly.

- *Nibbling.* When an agreement is reached and headed to closing, it's a common tactic for a party to throw in one more concession, relying on the momentum and emotional investment in the deal to get compliance. This is the so-called "tie with the suit" strategy. When buying an expensive suit, negotiators will say to the sales clerk, "You *are* going to throw in a tie with this, aren't you?" Some people think it's playing hardball, but frequently it works. Plan ahead if you think it's going to happen to you and you want to resist.

Pay attention to personality types. Different types of people respond better to different approaches. For example, how fast people think or act, how they respond to stress or contention, how amiable or abrasive they are, how stubborn or flexible, rigid or creative—these can all have a powerful influence on the tenor and progress of a negotiation. Ignore personality types only at peril, and of course be aware of the range of personality types you can project. The more you can train yourself to adjust to different people and circumstances, the more effective you will be.

Also, train yourself to pay attention to body language, things such as blinking and signs of impatience, nervousness, anxiety, and glee. Of course paying attention and actually understanding what body language means at any particular time are two different things. Many people think they have a fine understanding of body language: what different behaviors and postures mean. There are many books on the subject that claim they have certain knowledge. Maybe they do, but it's hard to see how they can all know, since there's an awful lot of disagreement on the details. That said, there's no question that our behaviors send volumes of signals about what we are thinking and feeling. You will do well to be aware of and alert to this information and do your best to sense the meanings. A good standby resource is *The Definitive Book of Body Language* by Allan and Barbara Pease.[4] Even a cursory search will turn up quite a number of others. Interpreting body language can get as idiosyncratic as tarot card reading or astrology, so take care not to think you can find too much authority or that you know more than you really do about what body language is saying.

Impasses are part of negotiation. In an impasse, setting aside a tough issue to deal with easier ones can lessen the sense there are too many obstacles to continue. But this can be no more than a waste of time if the tough issue really is a deal breaker. Good expectations management at the beginning can reveal such potentially tough issues early. Mediators sometimes can help, though they are generally more applicable in dispute resolution than in transactional negotiations.

Eventually you have to move a negotiation to closure. Sometimes this is the hardest part. Walking out at a difficult point to signal that there will be no more concessions is one tactic. Withdrawing an offer is another. Some people set deadlines, but like all ultimatums, deadlines can be dangerous if they are only bluffs. Reducing the magnitude of concessions as time goes on sends a signal that the end is getting near without resorting to brinksmanship. Clearly you should avoid the reverse—making bigger concessions as time goes on; that's a powerful incentive to the other side to keep coming back for more. Sometimes a final, important concession can be tied to agreeing you are at closure. In all cases, having those competing alternatives working with other parties is always your best leverage.

HOW CAN YOU BE A BETTER NEGOTIATOR?

As a start-up entrepreneur, you don't have infinite time to learn effective negotiating. When an enterprise is starting up, the opportunities for important negotiations come fast and furious. Whether acquiring assets, landing people, contracting, buying, or, most of all, securing financing, you are either negotiating or capitulating. The middle of an important negotiation is no time to learn the elements of successful negotiating. From the very first moment you decide to start an enterprise, get comfortable with negotiating and develop an effective regimen for preparing and executing negotiations. As a start-up entrepreneur, you have a lot of demands on your time, but you have to carve out time to build effective negotiation skills. This will more than pay off in the long run. Anyone on your team involved in transacting should be part of a deliberate learning effort.

How do you learn? This chapter has been no more than an overview of negotiating. At most we hoped to give you a checklist of things to focus on and some background for context and relevance. There is a wealth of resources you can access in training yourself to be a better negotiator. Larger organizations often have effective training programs.[5]

There are countless books on negotiations, ranging from popular to rigorously academic and plenty in between. There are also a number of good audio resources, some of which we have found to be effective. Learning a practical skill such as negotiating from books can be hard, but at the least you should read one or two to have a solid grounding and learn the buzzwords. Remember, learning is 5 percent hearing (reading), seeing is 10 percent, and doing is 85 percent.

Advisors and directors are often a gold mine for learning as well as hands-on help with negotiations. We frequently go along with our start-ups and pitch in on early negotiations or send an experienced advisor from our network. The advisor is simultaneously a bodyguard and a role model (10 percent seeing).

In the end, how do you become a better negotiator? There is no substitute for experience (85 percent doing). The good news is that you don't have to wait for an important negotiation to come up for your company to start getting experience. Most negotiations instructors encourage people to start negotiating everything. It can get obsessive, but there's real value in practicing on things that don't count and making your mistakes when they don't handicap your enterprise in its earliest, most vulnerable days. It will also toughen you up about asking for things and testing limits. Often even fixed prices in stores are negotiable. The same applies within the company. Inexperienced people should be exposed to negotiation situations before the stakes are serious. Negotiation apprenticeships pay big dividends in the future.

Every actual negotiation in which you participate is a valuable learning opportunity. Never throw one away. Real deals call for real commitment of focus in the moment, but keep track of what happens, even to the point of taking good notes in a journal. Afterward take the time to gather feedback, do assessments, and memorialize important lessons learned. When this is done as a team, it is a compelling learning opportunity and will pay dividends for a long time.

WHAT I KNOW NOW THAT I WISH I HAD KNOWN THEN

Robert Baum, Attorney

Bob Baum (www.bobbaumlaw.com) is an attorney and mediator specializing in negotiations and dispute resolution. For over 25 years he has been assisting and advising clients in effective negotiating. Bob has participated in negotiations involving hundreds of millions of dollars, down to small start-up companies with a great idea and no tangible assets. He offers this top 10 list of considerations before negotiating:

1. Knowledge is power. Do your research first. Know the strengths and weaknesses of the other side: what they hope and need to accomplish. Check shareholder reports, SEC filings, trade papers, investors' analyses, anything you can find.
2. Keep expectations realistic. Start-ups often make wild promises and crazy demands. This dooms a negotiation from the start.
3. Know your interests and theirs. Be able to distinguish positions from interests. A position is one party's proposed solution to an issue. An interest is a concern, need, or desire—the *why* behind a proposed solution. Prioritize your interests before the negotiations and be prepared to change priorities during the negotiations as you get more information.
4. Know the BATNA and WATNA—worse alternative to a negotiated settlement—for your side and theirs. Promote your BATNA and downplay theirs. WATNA is what keeps parties at the table.
5. Know your options before entering the negotiations. Can you be flexible on timing? Can you accept more risk or change your priorities? Can you create incentives for future performance or accept contingencies?
6. Confidence-building measures are important. Build up credibility during the negotiation. Don't lie or make commitments you can't keep. Once damaged, trust is difficult to repair.
7. Know what type of negotiator you are: Understand your strengths and weaknesses.
8. If the other side has skilled negotiators, bring someone with negotiation experience with you. Don't be a rookie facing an all-star.
9. Decide whether you want to make the first offer. Offering first sets the mark, but you will never know if the other side might have offered more. Waiting to respond to the other side's offer may make it harder to get into your range.

> 10. Separate the person from the issue; don't let the fact that you cannot
>   stand the negotiator on the other side prevent you from coming to
>   agreement.

Remember, few things are fixed. Almost anything is negotiable. In the press of all the things coming at you as you start an enterprise, it's all too easy to leave negotiations to fate and just wing it. Sometimes you're in such time triage that there's no alternative. But make no mistake about the cost. Failing to prepare yourself—first with the skills you need, and second for the actual negotiation—will have a cost. It may not be a fatal cost, but botched and suboptimal negotiations will be a perennial headwind against your progress unless you focus on getting it right the first time. Fortunately, it's not a hard skill to learn, and the yield over time is both substantial and cumulative. Always get your fair share and then a little more.

QUESTIONS

- Can you make a list of the major things you should negotiate during your launch?
- Can you take that list and note who will be responsible to prepare thoroughly, define with the team what is a must-have and what is a nice-to-have, and manage the negotiations?
- How well prepared are these people (or you) to negotiate effectively? How do you know? Who can you call on to help you learn or actually participate in the negotiation with you?

NOTES

1. Watkins, Michael, *Harvard Business Essentials: Negotiation—Your Mentor and Guide to Doing Business Effectively* (Boston: Harvard Business School Press, 2003): i.
2. Galinsky, A. D., and T. Mussweiler, "First Offers as Anchors: The Role of Perspective-Taking and Negotiator Factors," *Journal Personality and Social Psychology* 81 (2001): 657–669.
3. Bazeerman, Max H., and Margaret A. Neale, *Negotiating Rationally* (New York: Free Press, 1992): 23.
4. Pease, Allan, and Barbara Pease, *The Definitive Book of Body Language* (New York: Bantam Dell—Random House, 2006).

5.   Ertel, Danny, "Turning Negotiation into a Corporate Capability," *Harvard Business Review* 77, no. 3 (May–June 1999): 55–70.

Chapter 16

On Sales and Selling

If a man can write a better book, preach a better sermon, or make a better mousetrap than his neighbor, though he build his house in the woods, the world will make a beaten path to his door.

—Ralph Waldo Emerson

Sarah B. Yule in her anthology *Borrowings* (1889) attributed this quote to a lecture Ralph Waldo Emerson delivered in San Francisco or Oakland in 1871.[1] There is no other indication that Emerson actually said this. The first spring-loaded mousetrap was invented by William C. Hooker of Abingdon, Illinois, who received a U.S. patent for his design 23 years later in 1894. A similar, better-documented quote appears in Emerson's journal in 1855: "I trust a good deal to common fame, as we all must. If a man has good corn, or wood, or boards, or pigs, to sell, or can make better chairs or knives, crucibles, or church organs, than anybody else, you will find a broad, hard-beaten road to his house, though it be in the woods."[2]

Apocryphal or not, about half the books on sales and salesmanship open by emphatically disagreeing with Emerson's mousetrap quote to make one important point, and it stands regardless of the accuracy of the citation: Products, even great products, don't sell themselves. Only salespeople sell products. Of course, today some products can be sold over the Internet and there is never a human-to-human interaction. Nonetheless, most sales still require a salesperson and a sales encounter. Even Internet commerce companies need a sales plan, not just a marketing plan. What's the difference between sales and marketing? For some reason, many entrepreneurs apparently think the two are synonymous, and when they talk about selling, they refer to the four P's of marketing: product, price, place, and promotion. Selling means getting people to purchase a product or service: to write a sales order and give you money. It's a rare business plan that includes so much as a sentence about how the company will set up to actually *sell* the product. Often the company hasn't even thought about it.

A sales plan is critically important. A good operations plan focuses not just on product promotion but especially on selling. Who? How? How often? What are reasonable numbers? Although you don't usually start hiring salespeople until you have a proof of market, a product, and a scalable production system in place, you can't start sales planning too early. The easiest gotcha an investor normally finds in a start-up presentation is the absence of a sales plan and realistic projections based on what the salespeople will be able to do. Sales planning should be one of your top priorities in allocating overhead and raising capital because *sales produce revenue*. From the first moment you start thinking about a product or service, think about why people will buy it and how you will sell it to them.

Sales is a discrete discipline backed by a mountain of information and educational material. You, as the founder, should know enough about selling to understand how sales works, know good salespeople from bad, and manage the sales process in your start-up. Like negotiations or legal matters, this is a huge discipline. The U.S. Department of Labor counts over 9.5 million full-time sales professionals working in the United States today.[3] There is more to learn about sales and selling than you could ever know, unless you are one of those sales professionals. You don't have to know it all. You need to know just enough to be your first, best salesperson; then you will hire good professional salespeople when you can afford it.

WHEN?

Market validation comes first. If you do a good validation in the beginning, not only will you will have the right product and value proposition, you will have people lined up to contact for your first sales. These first sales dramatically increase the value of your enterprise because they answer the most important question: Will your customers buy your product for a good price? A footnote: In the past, founders often could fund a company's launch by preselling their product to their customers, especially in the software industry. It's far less easy to do that today, but you should always try. It takes persistence, determination, and good sales skills, but there is no better or cheaper form of financing.

Never stop selling. Keep in touch with interested parties from the market validation phase, and once you have product ready to go to market, ramp up sales by starting with them as soon as possible. The best barrier to entry is capturing a strong market share and keeping it. Remember, it's not the first mover who has the advantage; it's the first to get across the chasm between early adopters and the majority.

Getting into the market quickly means having not only an infrastructure of people to perform and manage sales but also an inventory management and distribution system. You need to get products to where the customers want them, when they want them. Building a sales and sales support force costs serious money. You either raise expensive capital to pay for it or grow your sales effort organically from operating cash flow. This strategy decision can make or break a successful launch.

One last point regarding sales that's often overlooked until too late: Pay attention to your *customer acquisition costs*. This is the total cost of promoting and selling, divided by the number of customers who actually buy. It is easy to overlook the costs of marketing and sales and find you are spending way too much money to capture a sale. Your per-unit revenue and margins have to cover not only the direct costs of making or delivering the product or service but also the unit sales and marketing costs and still have enough left over to pay for general overhead and make an attractive profit. Google AdWords, for example, generally produce click-throughs to a company's Web site at a low cost per click, but since only a small fraction of click-throughs convert to serious interest and even fewer to a sale, the fully loaded cost of acquiring a buying customer can add up quickly. It's often hard to justify promotion methods such as AdWords for low-cost products because the margins are eaten up by customer acquisition costs.

HOW?

Author and sales trainer Jeffrey Gitomer makes a key point at the beginning of one of his several books on sales training, *The Little Red Book of Selling*: The most important question you should want answered is not how to sell to your customers. The question is why your customers buy from you.

Preparation

Gitomer points out that there's a simple way to find out: Ask them. Included in his list of what he hears when he talks to customer focus groups are the following:

- I like my sales rep.
- I understand what I'm buying.
- I perceive a difference in the person and the company I am buying from.
- I perceive that my salesperson is trying to help me build my business in order to earn his commission. My salesperson is a valuable resource to me.
- I perceive a value in the product I am purchasing.
- I feel there is a fit of my needs and his or her product or service.
- The price seems fair, but it's not necessarily the lowest.[4]

Note that the first four points are focused on you and the sales team. Remember Chapters 8 through 10: It's always about the people. This is especially true in selling. Sales is about relationships, reputation, and how much your salespersons' help is valued. Value and relationship count more than tactics, product, price, or even promotion.

Sales professionals all agree that effective sales starts with effective prior preparation. Do your marketing homework. Understand the environment, the overall industry, and the addressable market. Break out and analyze market segments. You can segment by product type but also in many other ways: by utility, by customer type, by geography, by means of distribution, and so on. Do your competitor analysis (Chapter 11). Understand the customers' contexts: needs, requirements, strategy, internal situation (decision making), competitive advantages, and challenges. What risks in purchasing are potential customers worried about? How can you reduce those risks? Relate your understanding of your product and/or service to their worries and develop a value proposition.

With this in hand, you can define your promotion and distribution strategies. Note: This is not the sales plan, only the preparation. Promotion equals advertising, publicity, product promotions, and personal selling. How will you get out the word and make people aware? Who will do this marketing plan and execute it? You? Is there someone in the team with this ability? If not, do you know someone you can hire temporarily to put a promotion plan together and do the work to carry it out? There are countless marketing consultants and consulting firms that specialize in this and charge rates ranging from reasonable to ridiculous. As with almost everything, personal referrals are the best source of candidates.

How will you make the first sales calls? Who will do them? Is there a template script tied to your background investigation? Word of mouth is one of the best forms of promotion and sales. Try to collect some third-party testimonials. Can you develop reference customers whose patronage will give you credentials? Will they take calls and provide endorsements to other prospective customers?

Come up with questions to ask potential buyers, preferably ones that are concrete and make people think. Gitomer has a good example: Don't ask, "Do you have a pager?" Ask, "If your most important customer called right now, how would you get the message?"[5] In the pitch, relate your understanding of customer needs and preferences to your value proposition.

Remember, you're selling solutions, not products. The best sales approach is not so-called hard-selling—manipulative, overly persistent badgering. It's acting almost as a consultant, understanding the needs and problems of the customer and helping solve them, at the same time helping the buyer make a purchase decision.[6]

Sourcing

Salespeople call the process of identifying potential future customers *prospecting*. The lifeblood of a start-up's sales process is a pipeline filled with qualified potential customers. In an established organization there is a customer base and sales history. A start-up usually has to disrupt existing customer-competitor relationships to get revenue. Where do experienced salespeople identify new qualified customers and get information about them? Here are some of the places:

- Referrals from relationships, vendors of sister products, and existing customers.
- Databases and publications:
  - Internet searches and industry databases online such as ABI/Inform Global, Hoovers, Mergent Online, LexisNexis, and Reference for Business (http://www.referenceforbusiness.com/index.html).
  - Business references, usually available in most larger libraries, such as Standard & Poor's *Corporation Services; Register of Corporations; Directory of Corporate Affiliations*; Dun & Bradstreet's *Reference Book of Corporate Management*; Moody's *Industrial Manual*; H.W. Wilson Company's *Business Periodicals Index* and *Applied Science and Technology Index; Funk & Scott's Index of Corporations* and *Index of International Industries; Encyclopedia of American Industries; International Directory of Company Histories.*

- Government data; for listings, see the *Monthly Catalogue of United States Government Publications* and the *Monthly Checklist of State Publications*. There are numerous surveys and census reports.[7]
- Trade associations; see the *Encyclopedia of Associations* and the *National Trade and Professional Associations of the United States and Labor Unions*.
- The phone book.
- Civic groups (Rotary, service organizations, country clubs, professional groups).
- Chambers of commerce.
- Contests.
- Mailing lists, many of which can be purchased.
- Trade shows, conventions, and professional meetings.
- Canvassing; spot new potential clients and call on them.
- Advertising.
- Direct mail.

Once they have been identified, study your prospects. Do your homework on them, both the people and the company. Are they qualified? That is, do they actually have the need, the willingness, and the means to buy? Who are the gatekeepers? A gatekeeper's job is to screen out unwanted calls and meetings. Who are the people with influence, those who use and know about the product or service but don't have buying authority? Who actually makes decisions to buy? Often this is more than one person. Discover their authority levels and decision processes. Getting a meeting with the right people in the company is the first sales job. How can you get that meeting? Work it hard.

Contacting, Presenting, and Closing

Cold calls to get a meeting are part of selling, but they have the lowest success rate. External referrals and internal advocates increase success dramatically and often at least get you a hearing. Deliberately plan your call, including the following:

- A list of who to try to contact or involve in a meeting.
- The objective of the call: What is success?
- What questions to ask to understand needs and circumstances.
- Something to show: Do you have a prototype? Specs? A demonstration?
- A list of benefits and points of differentiation from competitors.
- Potential concerns or objections that could come up and persuasive answers.
- Possible closing strategies.[8]

In meetings, remember that sales and negotiation have this in common: Information is the highest value. For all the homework you may have done off-site, getting inside a customer's offices exposes you to orders of magnitude more information. Absorb and pry out as much as you politely can and integrate it into your plan of attack on the spot.

The presentation is the core of a meeting. Most good books on sales devote much of their content to the mechanics and tactics of sales presentations. Chapter 9 of B. Robert Anderson's *Professional Selling* is a good place to look. Many books tell you to make the link between customer needs and product features. Look for ways to create and exchange value. Do demonstrations that spark interest. Be prepared to answer objections and rejection. Foster commitment and look for the close.

Objections and rejection may or may not be bad news. Potential customers may be blowing you off, or their objections may indicate that they're thinking about the product. No may mean no, or it may mean press on. If you can tell which is which, you may have an opportunity to explain more and move from concerns to commitment. Here are two favorite sayings of effective salespeople: "Sales begins with the first no" and "The salesperson who gets the most nos also gets the most yeses."

Novices often find asking a customer to close a sale the hardest part of selling. Maybe it's fear of being refused. The close is the whole point of the exercise. Buyers expect to be asked. Anderson devotes one chapter to the presentation and two to the close. A good salesperson tests openness to closing throughout an encounter with *trial closes,* which have the added benefit of revealing concerns and objections. Two examples are, "How do you feel about our product? And, "What do we still need to resolve to help you decide to purchase?" Some salespeople advise creating "yes" momentum with a string of questions that are likely to be answered in the affirmative. Sometimes buyer and seller reach a point cooperatively from which to move to a purchase order, often by way of removing stumbling blocks. Buyers sometimes start talking as if they are presuming a sale: "When can you have it here?" Sometimes the seller has to ask, "What do I need to do to close this sale?" Common sales wisdom: Always be closing.

Remember that the easiest sale is a repeat sale to a satisfied customer. Earn a reputation for good customer service. Support and follow-through after a sale are critical. Get all the follow-on feedback you can. It reveals information that helps with troubleshooting potential problems that may lead to dissatisfaction or loss of an account. Making follow-up calls to your customers communicates that you care. Follow-through is also a great source of feedback for your design and manufacturing people, and it positions you to seek referrals and endorsements for other potential customers.

WHO?

Generally, as you launch, the first selling falls to one or more of the founding team members. For one thing, generally there isn't anyone else to do it. For another, early high-touch involvement with customers is rich in information. If the same people did the market validation exercise earlier in the process, they should have kept those relationships warm so that they can be activated for first sales. Later, when you bring in salespeople, you will have established a baseline of customer adoption that sets the tone for future expectations and also helps you break in new salespeople quickly.

It's rare today for a start-up to have plentiful investment before establishing sales and sustainable revenue growth. Sales professionals are paid fairly healthy salaries, and the good ones earn even more. Thus, in building a sales and revenue base, there is a cash flow shadow during which sales expenses run well ahead of sales revenue. That funding gap has to be filled from somewhere, but often at this early stage those funds are nowhere to be found. Accordingly, all but the most amply funded start-ups must find a way to bridge the gap from first trial customers to growing sales volumes without spending a lot of money on a sales force.

Although not ideal, there are some sales resources that can help mount a sales effort on more of a pay-as-you go basis, sparing you from having to spend significant cash up front:

- *Option 1.* Use independent sales reps. These salespeople often market an assortment of related products and work mostly or entirely on a percentage of sales. Advantages: They require less training. There are no recruiting and hiring costs. They are geographically dispersed. Generally, they already have an established base of customers. Disadvantages: They generally sell for a number of firms, sometimes including your competitors. They often focus most of their efforts on the few products in their mix that generate the most revenue. They can be difficult to control and manage. They leave you distanced from your customers and not in control of those relationships. Also, they may not have a good understanding of your product.

- *Option 2.* Use commission-only salespeople. These people work for you exclusively but are paid no or low salaries. Essentially you're leaving them to eat what they kill. In some situations this is an effective solution, but more often than not you will be getting only what you pay for, if not less. The fact is that skilled salespeople are valuable enough that they usually command healthy compensation packages. Your best chances of doing well on commission-only arrangements come through working with younger people looking for experience in sales, and even then a few will shine and many will get discouraged quickly and drop out.

- *Option 3.* Use a channel sales strategy. Companies selling related products often take on a supplement to their product lines from an outside company and use their own sales and marketing staff to sell it alongside their own products. In return for this, they take a significant share of gross revenue. For some types of products or services, channel sales can be a good option not only in the beginning but indefinitely. Cost is the biggest downside; channel sales easily can squeeze margins to little or nothing.

By contrast, conventional sales employees generally receive a salary plus commission. Ideally, they know your products well, are 100 percent focused on you, are intimately involved in the marketing and sales plans, and develop relationships with the customer base that consistently yield benefits over time. At some point you will grow revenue to the point where you can build a sales force on cash flow or you will have established enough sales validation that you can raise the additional investment needed to scale up a major sales effort. These are the two common outcomes of early sales success, and which one you choose is one of the more fundamental and important strategy calls you will make.

It is also one of the more important execution efforts you will make. Getting sales right is a huge competitive asset. It may not happen all at once; more likely, it will come in stages. But eventually you will have to define your selling needs, organize a structure, recruit talent, set goals and quotas, forecast, measure, and motivate. *Professional Selling and Sales Management* by Ralph W. Jackson, Robert D. Hisrich, and Stephen J. Newell[9] is an excellent source for learning to build a sales force and manage it.

The effectiveness of a sales effort is one of the easiest things to measure. This is not to say that measurement is immune to the law of unintended consequences. For example, if you care about current-quarter sales growth, will salespeople shift effort to the current quarter at the expense of ultimate long-term success? Which might be more important to you, maintaining a loyal customer base or letting the base churn because sales efforts are all focused on obtaining new customers? Any sales metric has the potential to unbalance a sales effort as people chase the aspects you measure and reward. Still, at least sales can be reduced to a number, and a number can become a quota. Salespeople need quotas. Set quotas wisely. Too high a quota and you lose motivation; too low and your sales force probably won't perform to potential. Once quotas are set, however, they should be met. Change salespeople as needed until you find ones who perform.

WHAT I KNOW NOW THAT I WISH I HAD KNOWN THEN
Kevin McClamroch, Adams-Burch

Kevin McClamroch is the vice president of sales at Adams-Burch in Landover, Maryland, the nation's largest independent distributor of restaurant supplies. He has a long career of sales and sales management at the Mead Corporation and International Paper Co., where he was president of the Crown Supply Co., CDA Div. For the past 18 years Kevin has been with Adams-Burch, where he manages a large sales force and conducts extensive training of new hires. Kevin says the following:

1. Don't focus on the product. This risks comparisons to competing products. Focus on the solution the product provides.
2. Show customers they have a need. This is the heart of selling. It's almost impossible to sell customers products for which they have no use.
3. Marketing is not sales! Elements of a successful sale include:
    a. Do your homework. Discover customers' goals, define the solutions you can offer, differentiate yourself.
    b. Interrupt customers' preoccupations and get the kind of attention that can start a sales discussion.
    c. Maintain customers' interest and don't waste their time. Become a "Master Questioner."
    d. Present solutions with conviction. Avoid just talking about features; shape conversation to customers' specific needs. Don't be shy about showmanship.
    e. Buying decisions are not always logical. There are always objections; be sure you understand the true ones and answer them.
    f. Get commitment—ask for the sale! Never make compromises on price without changing a corresponding value of the product or solution.
    g. Follow up and follow through. Never justify errors. Fix them. Keep customers' long-term interests in mind and develop relationships.
4. Sales is a process. It can be learned.
5. Hire people with good sales characteristics—organized, good attitude, people and communication skills, drive, and teamwork. Train them well, set quotas, track results, and reward success.

In presentations to investors or even in our classrooms, it can rise almost to the level of comical how blind entrepreneurs can be to the importance of a granular, operational focus on the way products actually will be sold. What is the sales plan, and who will do it? How, when, and for how much? There eventually will be a host of people involved, but founders and early employees will be the first. One hopes they will still be responsible for all the others as the company grows and new people come onboard. Always, there is a lot to learn.

How to learn? Some people may have more aptitude for selling than others, but like entrepreneurial effectiveness, selling can be learned by almost anyone who wants to learn. Learning behavioral skills from books is never easy, but there are a number of resources that can provide a good start. There are numbers of training programs and sales coaches. Even better is imitation: Follow a couple of great salespeople around. Of course, there is no substitute for getting in the pool to learn how to swim—experience. It's that kindergarten poster: Learning is 5 percent hearing, 10 percent seeing, and 85 percent doing. There are so many aspects to building and running an enterprise. That's entrepreneurship, after all—looking after everything. Whatever the aspect of the business, it's always the same: Knowledge reduces risk. Learning adds value.

QUESTIONS

- Do you have a sales plan? Does it start with your market validation? Can you write it down in a page or less?
- What do you calculate to be your costs of customer acquisition? Can your margins support them? How well do you expect them to scale as you grow?
- What trade-off do you anticipate between focusing on growth in sales at the cost of profitability and achieving profitability at the cost of growth in sales?

NOTES

1. Shapiro, Fred R., *The Yale Book of Quotations* (New Haven, CT: Yale University Press, 2006): 245.
2. Emerson, Ralph Waldo, *Complete Works*, vol. VIII, *Journal* (1855, rev. ed. 1912): 528.
3. Jackson, Ralph W., Robert D. Hisrich, and Stephen J. Newell, *Professional Selling and Sales Management* (Garland Heights, OH: NorthCoast Publishers, 2007): 3.
4. Gitomer, Jeffrey, *The Little Red Book of Selling* (Austin, TX: Bard Press, 2005): 7.
5. Ibid.: 113
6. Bygrave, William D., and Andrew Zacharakis, *The Portable MBA* (Hoboken, NJ: Wiley, 2010): 331–334.
7. Jackson, Hisrich, and Newell, 2007: 88–89.
8. Bygrave and Zacharakis, 2010: 343.
9. Jackson, Hisrich, and Newell, 2007.

Chapter 17

Communication

You can have brilliant ideas, but if you can't get them across, your ideas won't get you anywhere.

—Lee Iacocca

Communication takes place in the mind of the listener, not of the speaker.

—Peter Drucker

Alex Pentland, author of the 2008 book *Honest Signals*,[1] wanted to study communication in business, so he asked two groups of investors to evaluate the same set of businesses and independently choose the ones they liked best. The catch? He asked one group to read the businesses' execution plans and the other group to watch their live presentations. Pentland found that there was little similarity between the choices of the two groups. How is this possible? When investors read a business plan, all they have is the content, but when they watch a presentation, they have another source of information—the presenter. Pentland discovered that you, your body language, and the way you communicate are more important in getting a good result than your content is. How you say it can be more important than what you say.

Not all ideas are equal, but most of the time ideas have some kind of merit worth thinking about—call it a 90 percent success rate. Maybe 70 to 80 percent of execution plans have some kind of plausibility. However, when it comes to getting your idea and plan across to other people so that they understand it and can repeat it (never mind be persuaded by it), we find that the success rate drops to somewhere between 10 and 20 percent! One of the most difficult things you will face in launching and building your enterprise is effectively and persuasively communicating your vision, your idea's essential elements, and your enthusiasm to listeners so that they understand it, can repeat the essentials accurately, and, one hopes, want in. There is no value in an idea or plan if no one understands and remembers it.

We assign only one book for our students to read each year in our advanced entrepreneurship course at Tuck: Chip and Dan Heath's book on communication *Made to Stick*. If you haven't read it, we suggest that you read it too. The Heaths write about "how ideas are constructed—what makes some ideas stick and others disappear."[2] They say, "A sticky idea is one that is understood, remembered, and creates some kind of change—in opinion, behavior, or values."[3] In another useful book, *Words That Work*, Frank Luntz added a subtitle that says it all in terms of how you should think about communication: *It's Not What You Say, It's What People Hear*.[4]

Good public speaking skills don't necessarily mean effective communication. An experiment at Stanford found that the people rated as the best speakers did no better than anyone else at making their ideas stick. Foreign students who were rated poorly for their speaking skills in English did just as well as native English speakers.[5]

"Managerial communication is different from other kinds of communication. Why? Because in a business or management setting, the most brilliant message in the world will do you no good unless you achieve your desired outcome."[6]

In this chapter we will talk about effective communication, focusing on the ultimate goal: getting the desired outcomes. We will talk about how you can help your readers and listeners do the following:

- Pay attention
- Learn—understand and remember
- Agree and believe
- Care
- Be motivated to act

WILL THEY REMEMBER IT?

Chip and Dan Heath opened *Made to Stick* with this:

A friend of ours is a frequent business traveler. Let's call him Dave. Dave was recently in Atlantic City for an important meeting with clients. Afterward, he had some time to kill before his flight, so he went to a local bar for a drink.

He'd just finished one drink when an attractive woman approached and asked if she could buy him another. He was surprised but flattered. Sure, he said. The woman walked to the bar and brought back two more drinks—one for her and one for him. He thanked her and took a sip. And that was the last thing he remembered.

Rather that was the last thing he remembered until he woke up, disoriented, lying in a hotel bathtub, his body submerged in ice.

He looked around frantically, trying to figure out where he was and how he got there. Then he spotted the note:

DON'T MOVE. CALL 911.

A cell phone rested on a small table beside the bathtub. He picked it up and called 911, his fingers numb and clumsy from the ice. The operator seemed oddly familiar with his situation. She said, "Sir, I want you to reach behind you, slowly and carefully. Is there a tube protruding from your back?"

Anxious, he felt around behind him. Sure enough, there was a tube.

The operator said, "Sir, don't panic, but one of your kidneys has been harvested. There's a ring of organ thieves operating in this city, and they got you. Paramedics are on their way. Don't move until they arrive."

The Heaths continue: "You have just read one of the most successful urban legends of the past fifteen years."[7] Having read this account just now, only once, in all likelihood a year from now you will have no trouble giving an account of this tale that's accurate in most of the details you just read. Like most urban legends, this anecdote has all the elements that make for a communication that is easily understood and remembered for a long time.[8]

Contrast it with this communication, which the Heaths present next:

> *Comprehensive community building naturally lends itself to a return-on-investment rationale that can be modeled, drawing on existing practice ... a factor constraining the flow of resources to CCIs is that funders must often resort to targeting or categorical requirements in grant making to ensure accountability.*

Without going back to study this passage carefully, close your eyes, count to 10, and try to repeat the key points of what you just read. You probably will fail. What might be the odds you could remember a communication like this long enough to go into a business meeting next week and argue persuasively for the points you just read?

Certain ways of relating information are intrinsically memorable. Other ways make remembering almost impossible. Two important things can help you avoid useless and ineffective communications: avoiding the curse of knowledge and using some simple tactics anyone can master to turn information into effective communication.

THE CURSE OF KNOWLEDGE

If you know much of anything about your idea and your plans for the enterprise, you are already fatally and incurably infected with what the Heaths call "the curse of knowledge." The curse of knowledge is arguably one of the greatest obstacles anyone faces in communication in business or anywhere else. Probably, the authors of the short passage about comprehensive community building in the previous section were having this problem.

Here is the problem: Once you know something, it is impossible to know what it's like for someone else not to know it. The curse leaves you unwittingly assuming that your audience somehow knows far more background information than in fact it does. It frequently leaves you telling them nothing because what you say demands that they have supporting knowledge that they just don't have.

In a 2006 *Harvard Business Review* article, "The Curse of Knowledge,"[9] the Heaths reference an insightful Stanford psychology thesis about research into this all to a common communication problem. In that research, Dr. Elizabeth Newton, now a social and business psychologist at the University of British Columbia, showed how drastically people underestimate the curse of knowledge when they communicate with others. In her basic experiment she told subjects that they would be asked to have another person guess the name of well-known songs such as "Yankee Doodle," but the only hint they could give that person was to tap out the song on a table. Newton asked the subjects to guess in advance what proportion of the songs their partners would guess correctly. The average guess was 50 percent. When the pairs actually tried the exercise, the average success rate was 2.5 percent. Some tappers couldn't believe that the answers weren't more obvious to their partners.[10]

This is the perceptual gap of the curse of knowledge. Once you know something, it's impossible to imagine what it's like not to know it. Once you have that knowledge, you make all sorts of wrong assumptions about what you need to say to communicate effectively to people who don't have it. The curse hangs over every entrepreneur who has ever tried to pitch an idea to a listener who was not already well informed about the business and the opportunity. What to do?

HOW CAN YOU MAKE IT STICK?

Creating a meaningful context for your information in the minds of your listeners is the biggest problem you face. You want to help them catch up with all the knowledge you have accumulated about your idea. Learning research shows that context provides a framework to absorb information, understand it, and remember it. Mary Munter teaches business communication at the Tuck School of Business at Dartmouth. Mary has written a short, effective book, *Guide to Managerial Communication*.[11] One of the important foundations of the book is simple: Think about who your audience is, what they know and expect, what they feel, and what might persuade them. That is, where are they starting from as they listen to you, and what will make your message stick?

SUCCESs

There is no simpler framework to get people to pay attention, understand, remember, and act than the SUCCESs framework Chip and Dan Heath created in *Made to Stick:*

Simple

- Blaise Pascal said, "I didn't have time to write a short letter, so I wrote a long one instead." (So, apparently, did Mark Twain.)
- Long, complicated sentences and paragraphs bury meaning in camouflage.
- "If you say three things, you don't say anything" (James Carville, 1992).

- Relentlessly exclude; prioritize.
- Sound bites are not ideal; proverbs are more memorable. ("Sew slowly because the wrong stitch costs" versus "A stitch in time saves nine.")
- Make it simple *and* profound:
  - "Are you better off than you were four years ago?" (Ronald Reagan, 1980).
  - "It's the economy, stupid" (James Carville, 1992).
- Analogies create memorable frameworks. Example: Disney park employees are "cast members." They don't "interview" for a job; they "audition." "Uniforms" are "costumes."
- You may be tempted to write something like: "Utilizing the 2048-bit Diffie-Hellman key exchange and 168-bit triple-DES, we provide intrusion protection for digital voice, fax, and wireless communications." Cut the geek-speak. Say what you mean: "We safeguard your communications with state-of-the-art encryption technologies."
- Same with MBA-speak. This doesn't work: "We provide the leading business-to-business solution for clinical data capture and management for the pharmaceutical and biotech industry." This does: "We streamline information processes that speed new drug therapies to market."

Unexpected

- You can't get through if you don't get attention and interest.
- Use surprise: break a pattern:
  - The brain suppresses consistent patterns; it watches for changes.
  - Mental schemas help us make predictions. Violating them opens the brain to absorb new information.
- Be counterintuitive; violate people's expectations. (Remember the "kidney heist.")
  - Surprise increases alertness and attention.
  - Make the connection to the message.
- Avoid "empty surprise": Exploit riddles and mysteries:
  - Make listeners work, not just listen.
  - Open gaps in knowledge and fill them.

Concrete

- Something is concrete if it can be examined by the senses.
  - Research shows that the brain remembers object nouns better than concept nouns.
  - An example would be "high-performance" versus "450 hp V–8 engine."

- Avoid overuse of vague adjectives like *unique* and *improved.* Guy Kawasaki gives some good examples in *The Art of the Start:*
  - "Intuitive" versus "You can set it up in one day without training."
  - "Fast" versus "Five times increase in throughput on tests"[12]
- Corollary: Emphasize benefits, not features.
- Communicate concepts with examples:
  - Use mental images; they are more easily grasped than concepts: "A bag of movie popcorn has 37 grams of fat" versus "more saturated fat than a bacon-and-eggs breakfast, a Big Mac and fries at lunch, and a steak dinner with trimmings—*combined.*"
  - Use unifying concepts. Example: Boeing told its engineers to design the new 727 to have 131 seats, be able to fly nonstop from New York to Miami, and land on LaGuardia Runway 4–22.
  - President John Kennedy didn't say, "Our mission is to become the international leader in the space industry through maximum team-centered innovation and strategically targeted aerospace initiatives." He said, "I believe that this nation should commit itself to achieving the goal, before this decade is out, of landing a man on the moon and returning him safely to the earth."[13]

Credible

- External authorities make people believe an idea.
- Honesty and trustworthiness enhance credibility.
- Details and examples are effective in a framework.

Emotional

- Emotional engagement enhances attention and retention.
- We're wired to feel more readily than to absorb abstractions. Abstract thinking inhibits emotion-driven reactions.
- "If you want people to care, tap into things they care about."

Stories

- Our brains are wired to remember stories better than numbers, concepts, and statistics.
- Stories invite simulation and identification.
- "Mental simulation is not as good as doing something, but it's the next best thing."

Kawasaki adds two important points that we always pass on to entrepreneurs: Relevance is key. Facts are not. When talking, imagine there is a little man on your shoulder. Every time you say something, the little man says, "So what?" Here's an example:

You: "Our hearing aids use digital signal processing."

Little Man: "So what?"

You: "Our product increases the clarity of sounds."

Little Man: "So what?"

You: "If you're at a cocktail party with many conversations going on around you, you'll be able to hear what people are saying to you."[14]

Impersonal doesn't arrest attention or stick. Make it personal:

"Reduce the size of the global ozone hole."

Compared to:

"Prevent you from getting melanoma."

"Increasing the mean test scores for children in your school district."

Compared to:

"Ensuring that Johnny can read."[15]

ENHANCE RECALL: USE PICTURES

In 1936, if you wanted to convey the desperate plight of many people in the country, you might have published an account of your journey around the country as you photographed people. You probably haven't read this account before:

> *I saw and approached the hungry and desperate mother, as if drawn by a magnet. I do not remember how I explained my presence or my camera to her, but I do remember she asked me no questions. ... I did not ask her name or her history. She told me her age, that she was thirty-two. She said they had been living on vegetables from the surrounding fields, and birds the children killed. She had just sold the tires from her car to buy food. There she sat in that tent with her children huddled around her, and seemed to know that my pictures might help her, and so she helped me. There was a sort of equality about it. ...*[16]

It's not particularly memorable, and that is probably why no one would have remembered it even if it *was* published in 1936 (which it wasn't). Countless similar accounts were published then, and no one remembers any of them today either. However, if you saw any of the photographs in Figure 17-1, you probably would get the point. In fact, you might think you actually do remember seeing them, even though it's highly improbable that you have.

Figure 17-1

In contrast, the photograph by Dorothea Lange in Figure 17-2 is instantly recognized. (See page 277.)

This is arguably the most famous photograph from the Great Depression. Lange's account above, first published in 1960, is all the more vivid when you have her pictures alongside, and it only takes one. Your brain is wired to absorb and remember information that the eye sees.

It is almost inconceivable how many images the brain can encode and remember. Think about a study published by the psychologist Lionel Standing in 1973.[17] Standing showed subjects a long series of unrelated words or pictures for only a few seconds each and then, two days later, tested them for recall by showing them pairs: one the previous sample and the other a distracter. The question was how many discrete items people could remember they had seen. In a sample set of *a thousand* pictures from a single session, how many do you think the subjects remembered correctly? 99.6 percent! For single words, the comparable number was 61.5 percent. Imagine how much harder it would be to remember phrases and sentences. Pictures stick. Use them.

Figure 17-2 Dorothea Lange's *Migrant Mother.*

EMOTIONS DECIDE; REASON EXPLAINS

As Pentland found in his MIT experiments comparing decisions based on presentations and decisions based on plans, the dynamics of presentation and people chemistry count a lot in how reviewers judge presenters. The amazing part is that it doesn't take long.

In the early 1990s, Nalini Ambady and Robert Rosenthal studied how people form impressions of strangers: how accurate early impressions are and how long it takes to form them. They were stunned to see how accurately people were able to form valid impressions of other people and, even more significantly, how quickly it happened. They had students passively review video clips of professors and then fill out ratings of the professors as if they had taken their courses. They found that students who had never seen the professors before could match ratings by students who had taken the professors' courses by viewing only what Ambady and Rosenthal called "thin slices" of the professors' behavior. What was even more impressive was how short a video slice it took for the students to reach this level of accuracy: as little as 6 to 15 seconds.[18] These findings have held up in numerous studies since.

When you present, people form impressions of you even before you start talking. We've seen this happen numerous times in investor presentations. Pentland didn't measure how long it took his business plan reviewers to form lasting impressions, but the Ambady and Rosenthal findings suggest that it wasn't long. Other studies suggest that it's the emotional brain at work, matching patterns to past experience. Since emotions tend to run in the background, most people don't recognize that their impressions of others are being driven by their fast-thinking emotional brains. Think about how to make the best impression first and fast. It may be the only chance you get.

Emotions decide; reason explains. There is abundant psychology research literature arguing that emotions are not only important but essential in decision making. Chapter 18 will look more closely at the role of emotions in decision making. Emotions are the real drivers in getting your ideas across in a way that persuades a person to take action. If you want to engage people, talk to their emotions. If you wonder what touches emotions, start by looking in the mirror. The emotions you show will be mirrored in others—literally.

Arguably, one of the more profound findings from the exploding field of cognitive neuroscience is knowledge about what have come to be called *mirror neurons*. Mirror neurons allow us to read another person's emotions by literally experiencing them through the firing of parallel neurons in our own brains. These specialized circuits read signals from another person and trigger the same emotion or motor centers in our brains. Whether kicking a soccer ball, picking up a teacup, or punching someone out, our brains not only mirror the action without actually doing it but intuit the motivation or emotion behind the action. It's through mirror neurons that we're moved by images, movies, or the characters in a book.[19] "Vicarious is not a strong enough word to describe the effect of these mirror neurons. When we see people suffering or in pain, mirror neurons help us read their facial expressions and actually make us feel the suffering or the pain of the other person."[20] A German brain-scanning team even documented their role in the voyeuristic thrill of pornography.[21]

This has implications across the range of human experience. More concretely, for you as a presenter, understanding mirror neurons can help you be a more effective communicator and persuader. Giving new meaning to the expression "I feel your pain," it's literally true that people will mirror you. They can't help it; it's how their brains are wired (the same way as yours). Show people what you want them to mirror: confidence, enthusiasm, seriousness, resolve, how easy you are to work with. This is where those first impressions come from. Before people have even begun to size each other up systematically, their brains know how others make them feel.

APPLYING IT: SUMMARIES AND PITCHES

First impressions apply to the first encounter people have with an idea. Therefore, it's important to focus on the two ways (other than a referral) those encounters usually happen: the summary, or *pitch sheet,* and the so-called *elevator pitch,* the short, high-level persuasive summary you give verbally when someone asks you to describe your idea. Both of these have only one important goal: to get the response "I'd like to know more." Pitches and summaries are valuable distillations. Don't dilute them:

- Don't ramble.
- Don't repeat.
- Get to the point.

The young founders of one of our companies, Sportspage, Inc., were visiting an advisor in Washington, D.C., shortly after they launched the company and started raising money. As they walked to the elevator, their advisor happened to mention that the building was owned by Ted Leonsis, one of the founders and the vice chairman of AOL, not to mention an owner of the Washington Capitals, the chair of SnagFilms, and an owner in Clearspring Technologies and Revolution Money. As they got in the elevator, the advisor said, "Well, speak of the devil, here's Ted! Ted, meet my friends, David and Kase. They're working on a sports-related Internet start-up."

"Pleased to meet you, David and Kase," Ted said as he shook hands. "Tell me about your company."

It was a six-story building.

There are two takeaway lessons: Be ready any time, and be sure it's short and memorable. Ted didn't invest in the company, but according to the advisor, he liked it and summarized it faithfully a few days later in a meeting.

People are always asking about your deal. Sometimes they are even interested. Either way, you have only two goals: get the key information into their heads in a way that makes it stick and can come back out accurately later and get them to say, "I'd like to know more." Pitches should be:

- *From memory.* Never work from notes.
- *Conversational.* Don't recite a script.
- *Passionate.* Remember first impressions and the role of emotions.
- *Relevant.* Remember Guy Kawasaki's little man: "So what?"
- *High-altitude.* Stay at 30,000 feet. Details come later.
- *Seductive.* Remember, the only words that matter are "I'd like to know more."

Arguably, the most important document you will write—and write and write—is a one- or two-page summary. This is the written equivalent of the spoken pitch for the elevator. Sometimes it's called the pitch sheet.

Summaries don't sell deals. They invite interest. They frame the opportunity and quickly get across what you are trying to accomplish now. As with an elevator pitch, the goal is to get your chance to meet and tell more. This is a document you want anyone to get. It should never be more than two pages; most are one page. It's not the same as an executive summary in a business plan; think of it as more like a brochure about your business.

This is not the place for confidential or proprietary information. The world is a tough place, and people sometimes inappropriately use (aka steal) ideas. But the fact is that investors generally won't sign confidentiality agreements to look at an opportunity, nor should they. *Later* is the time for secret information; a first meeting is not the place for secrets. Every founder needs to learn what he or she can safely say and what to hold back. It's a good idea to mark your materials "Copyright 20##" and "Proprietary and Confidential" and leave it at that. Remember that your goal is to spark interest in knowing more, to tell enough to get that reaction, not to tell everything someone might want to know.

One last point: Include contact information. This should seem so obvious that it doesn't bear mentioning. Unfortunately, it's amazing how commonly contact information is overlooked in summaries. In one of our Tuck classes in 2009, we had two student groups start food companies they planned to launch locally when they graduated. One, Red's, planned to sell all-natural frozen burritos. The other, FONS, planned to sell a healthy and tasty breakfast food: Fruit-Oats-Nuts-Squares. All our students have to prepare pitch sheets for investors as part of their class assignment, which both did. And yes, we did remind them in class to include contact information. Both companies were getting good market validation with customer testing and local trial sales.

After the course ended, the local paper asked if it could have copies of the summaries on the businesses in the course. The editor planned to choose one and feature it in a series of articles over the coming year on the life of a start-up. When we checked back to see what had come if it, the writer told us that at first he thought the frozen burritos company sounded more interesting.

Unfortunately, he couldn't find contact information on the company, and so he called the Fruit-Oats-Nuts-Squares guys instead. Their summary did have contact information and got the great press visibility for the next year. The founder of Red's missed a great opportunity. Ironically, the founders of FONS eventually decided not to pursue the opportunity, whereas Red's got off to a solid start and two years later was being sold in over 4,000 stores all over the country.

As often and emphatically as we reminded students about including contact information, before we told this story in class, we were lucky to see 50 percent of summaries turned in with contact information on them. Since then, we have yet to see one without. Stories are indeed made to stick.

As with business plans, pitch sheets should succinctly address the main questions that come to mind as people absorb your information. Pitch sheets represent your chance to create a good first impression, so they are about more than content. There is no single perfect format, and so we don't give our students a cookbook of procedures and principles for writing effective summaries. Other than a reminder of a few main points, we find it's more effective when we make available a collection of samples and suggest they find a few they like and imitate them. Usually the results are much better than they would be if we tried to explain a long list of abstract rules and practices, and it's easier on everybody.

Appearance and readability count. Information should be easy to grasp. Readers should be able to see the structure and the key points at a glance and easily find what they are looking for. Strip it down to the minimum—no extra words. The goal is always the same: to get them to

- Pay attention.
- Learn—understand and remember.
- Agree and believe.
- Care.
- Be motivated to act.

The pitch sheets Dartmouth and Tuck companies have created over the last few years adhere to a basic template, and so should yours. Think about the appearance and readability. Plain text may say it, but will readers find it? Will it stick? Headings help, and so do bullets and short phrases. Readers can scan to find what they want. Formatting helps readability. Diagrams can get across key points, and pictures are memorable, especially if they emphasize the points. Combinations of the two are even better, though. For examples of Dartmouth and Tuck companies' pitch sheets, please see the resources section online at www.greggfairbrothers.com.

Remember, very few deals ever sell themselves. The best opportunity in the world is nearly worthless if people don't understand it. The way they come to understand it is up to you. You can't just give people information, no matter how good: It's not what you say, it's what they hear and understand and, most of all, are motivated to act on. You can never pay communication too much attention, and you can never practice too much. The more you pitch and (especially) the more you hear what people actually understood and remembered, the better your story will become and the more success you will have. Your company will never be better than you can make it, but if you can't explain yourself clearly and compellingly, it can easily be far less.

WHAT I KNOW NOW THAT I WISH I HAD KNOWN THEN

Robert O. Wetzel, Investor

Bob Wetzel joined the management consulting division of Arthur Andersen and Co. in 1982. Over a 20-year leadership career at Anderson and Accenture, Bob was a founding partner of their Change Management Practice. He led the Insurance Industry Consulting Practice in Europe; the design, build, and marketing of software for insurance investment operations; and the Enterprise Management Practice to financial services companies. He is currently a gentleman farmer, private investor, and consultant to nonprofits and recently created a consulting practice to develop public speaking skills for managers and entrepreneurs. In 35 years as a consultant, executive, and private investor, through hundreds of presentations, Bob has one bottom line: The presenter is the project. If presenters are not passionate, articulate, confident, and engaging, their presentations will not be as compelling as their ideas. In his presentation teaching Bob focuses on five things:

Vocal and Personal Engagement

You have many tools at your disposal to take on the role of a successful entrepreneur. Use them all to engage your audience:

- *Voice:* pitch, tempo, tonal variety, volume, and expression
- *Body:* gesture, movement, eye contact, and personal engagement
- *Language:* diction, enunciation, language choice and usage, and accent
- *Dress:* matching your audience, but always slightly better

Structure

A presentation tells a *story.* Follow a clear and logical structure:

- A beginning that tells the audience what you are going to tell them and why they should pay attention.
- A clear exposition of the *relevant* facts, compiled in groups of three. A person generally can hold only three things in mind at one time.
- A compelling conclusion that focuses on benefits, actions, and passionate belief in what is presented.

Audience

A presentation must fit the audience. If you are making the same presentation to every audience, you will fail. Audience analysis includes the following:

- Know the cultural, generational, demographic, socioeconomic, psychographic, and other characteristics of the group.
- Identify and understand the *influencers* in any room.
- Evaluate and use the physical environment of the presentation.

Simplicity and Visual Interest

A presentation is an introduction to an idea, concept, or project. Engage your audience but never overwhelm them:

- Keep the content of any single slide to no more than two minutes.
- Incorporate visual aids in a clear and compelling way.
- Limit any slide to no more than three topics.
- Avoid jargon, techno-speak, or insider language.

Passion and Confidence

Audiences will believe you only if you believe yourself. Presenters who do not believe passionately in their subject and who are not supremely confident in their presentation will fail.

- Be passionate about your subject matter.
- Engage skeptics and questioners without malice.
- You may be wrong, but never be in doubt!

QUESTIONS

- What is your central message? Why is what you do valuable and important? Can you compress it to one or two sentences?
- Can you write down what you want to happen before you communicate your message or present it in an important context? If you can, how will you evaluate whether you think your message and presentation will get you there?
- Who in your team should do the presenting? How do you know this is the right choice?

NOTES

1. Pentland, Alex, *Honest Signals: How They Shape Our World* (Cambridge, MA: MIT Press, 2008).
2. Heath, Chip, and Dan Heath, *Made to Stick: Why Some Ideas Survive and Others Die* (New York: Random House, 2007): 13.
3. Heath, Chip, and Dan Heath, *Teacher's Guide to Made to Stick* (New York: Random House, 2007): 2.
4. Luntz, Frank I., *Words That Work: It's Not What You Say, It's What People Hear* (New York: Hyperion, 2007).
5. Heath and Heath, *Teacher's Guide,* 2007: 23.
6. Munter, Mary, *Guide to Managerial Communication* (Upper Saddle River, NJ: Prentice Hall, 2009): 3.
7. Heath and Heath, *Made to Stick*, 2007: 3–4.
8. Heath, Chip, "Loud and Clear: Crafting Messages That Stick—What Nonprofits Can Learn from Urban Legends," *Stanford Social Innovation Review* 1, issue 3 (Winter 2003): 18–27.
9. Heath, Chip, and Dan Heath, "The Curse of Knowledge," *Harvard Business Review* 84, issue 12 (December 2006): 20–22.
10. Newton, Elizabeth, "Overconfidence in the Communication of Intent: Heard and Unheard Melodies," unpublished doctoral dissertation, Stanford, CA: Stanford University, 1990: 33–46.
11. Munter, 2009.
12. Kawasaki, Guy, *The Art of the Start* (New York: Portfolio, 2004): 40.
13. President John F. Kennedy, "Special Message to the Congress on Urgent National Needs," May 25, 1961, before a joint session of Congress.
14. Kawasaki, 2004: 47.
15. Ibid.: 38.
16. Lange, Dorothea, "The Assignment I'll Never Forget: Migrant Mother," *Popular Photography* 126 (February 1960): 42–43.
17. Standing, Lionel, "Learning 10,000 Pictures," *Quarterly Journal of Experimental Psychology* 25, no. 2 (May 1, 1973): 207–222.
18. Ambady, Nalini, and Robert Rosenthal, "Half a Minute Predicting Teacher Evaluations from Thin Slices of Nonverbal Behavior and Physical Attractiveness," *Journal of Personality and Social Psychology* 64, no. 3 (March 1993): 431–441.
19. Iacoboni, Marco, *Mirroring People: The New Science of How We Connect with Others* (New York: Farrar, Straus and Giroux, 2008).
20. Iacoboni, Marco, "Mirroring People: The New Science of How We Connect with Others," *Wall Street Journal Online*, May 30, 2008, http://online.wsj.com/article/SB121191836113423647.html (accessed September 17, 2010).
21. Hotz, Robert Lee, "How Your Brain Allows You to Walk in Another's Shoes," *Wall Street Journal*, August 17, 2007: B1.

Chapter 18

Leaders Decide

An executive is a person who always decides; sometimes he decides correctly, but he always decides.

—John H. Patterson

The entrepreneur's world is an uncertain one full of risks and messy, incomplete, and incoherent data. That's a tough environment for making decisions, but indecision is fatal. John H. Patterson (1844–1922) was the founder of the National Cash Register Company, which he took public in 1925 in what was the largest public offering of its time. As a CEO he pioneered the notion of creating humane working conditions and established the world's first sales training school and the first "daylight factory" buildings in 1893. (He was also Dartmouth class of 1867.) He both hired and fired Thomas Watson, Sr., who later built the Computing Tabulating Recording Corporation into one of the most effective selling companies in history; in 1924 it was renamed IBM. Patterson was fond of saying, "An executive is a person who always decides; sometimes he decides correctly, but he always decides." This should be taped to the bathroom mirror of every start-up founder and leader. Decision making is one of the most important attributes of a leader in any organization, especially one that is starting up, because the decisions come every day, and they have to be made or they will make themselves.

In June 2007 Yahoo cofounder Jerry Yang assumed the role of CEO of the company he founded, hoping to pull it together in tough times. Employees were excited, but the mood quickly turned as Yang began "punting tough decisions." At the time one of Yahoo's former executives said, "The thing that Yahoo needs most is someone who can make decisions and who is comfortable with the risk of making fast decisions." It had become clear that "Mr. Yang's inability to make tough decisions on matters ranging from new products to strategic alliances stymied his effectiveness and failed to get Yahoo out of its hole." In November 2008, Yang stepped down as CEO. He didn't get fired for turning down a purchase offer of $33 a share from Microsoft in April 2008 and running the stock price down to $9; he got fired for being indecisive. The stock went up 9 percent when the board announced his resignation.[1]

A 2005 *Wall Street Journal* article titled "Non-Deciders Make Everyone Else Suffer" said it perfectly: "A non-decider possesses a hypnotic ability to redirect everyone's attention. … Indecisive managers may not accomplish much. But on the long list of things they don't do is this: get fired."[2]

This is the challenge entrepreneur founders and leaders face every day: decision or indecision? There's a fully developed field of decision science, complete with models, texts, a research canon, and a curriculum in most business schools. However, no entrepreneurship book we know has a chapter about what it's like and what it takes to make decisions in an entrepreneurial setting. Perhaps the assumption is that entrepreneurs already know how to decide effectively, however doubtful that seems.

Decisions—big decisions, often with long-lasting and profound consequences—come fast and furious in the entrepreneurial setting, and they seldom allow much time to make them. In fact, often it's not clear which decisions are called for and when. Defining decision-level issues and their timing is in fact part of the art—and make no mistake, decision making is at least as much art as science, if not more. Rational decision making has long been studied. Recently, investigators have begun examining the role of experience and intuition in decision making. Good decisions are hard to come by, but they're worth a lot. Hard work and good execution are keys to success, but they can't make up for bad decisions.

It's hardly possible, of course, to cover the rich field of decision making in a short chapter in a book on start-up entrepreneurship. As with most of the chapter topics in this book, there is ample literature if you want go deeper. Some of it is quite good and relevant to instinctive decision making in entrepreneurial settings. There analytical methods based on reams of data are almost useless, and creativity and framing are essential. We do, however, want to sensitize you to a few key points. We particularly want to help frame for you what really goes on in the brain when humans make decisions. We hope this can help you get into a mind-set in which you are comfortable making complex, difficult decisions when you don't have all the information you need (you seldom will) and there isn't the luxury of time to deliberate and ponder (there hardly ever is). Nondeciders make everyone suffer, but in an early-stage entrepreneurial setting it's the enterprise that suffers most of all, sometimes terminally.

SCIENCE OR ART?

Much of decision science focuses on the notion of rational decision making. Here is a popular definition: the "systematic, step-by-step method in which 'hard' (quantitative) data obtained through observation or mathematical (statistical) analysis or modeling is used for making long-term decisions."[3] A quick search of the literature turns up a rich sampling of various rational decision-making models:

Two-stage model

- Get the idea.
- Evaluate the idea.

Three-stage model

- Find the problem.
- Devise alternatives.
- Choose.

Four-stage model

- Understand the problem.
- Devise a plan.
- Carry out the plan.
- Evaluate the results.

Five-stage model

- Identify the problem.
- Define the problem.
- Evaluate possible solutions.
- Act.
- Evaluate successes.

Six-stage model

- Identify the problem.
- Obtain information to diagnose causes.
- Generate possible solutions.
- Evaluate the various solutions.
- Select a strategy for performance.
- Perform and revise the solution.

Seven-stage model

- Sense the problem.
- Define the problem.
- Generate alternatives.
- Evaluate alternatives.
- Choose.
- Plan action.
- Implement.

Eight-stage model

- You get the idea.

Unfortunately, much rational decision theory is drawn from algorithm-based models or has been developed through experimental work, which mainly uses artificial tasks. These are based on comparisons of multiple options defined by the experimenter that don't require problem definition or domain experience. Rational decision making often is taught by people who haven't had careers infused with the trial and error of real-world problem solving.[4] The roles of experience, intuition, intangible insight, and emotion are deemphasized or unclear.[5]

How useful are models like these? Mechanistic, rational problem solving teaches rules, facts, and procedures. It may make sense for simple procedural tasks, but it is not clear that it's useful at higher levels of expertise or for making complicated judgment calls that take into account what is going to happen in the future. Input consist primarily of information about the past and present. The future is largely ignored as unknowable. It's like trying to drive a car by looking in the rearview mirror.[6] Trends are often the least reliable indicator of the future. Yogi Berra had it right: "It's tough to make predictions, especially about the future."

"Decision Theory is frequently inapplicable because too often its information requirements cannot be satisfied. The theory is irrelevant because real-world decisions are frequently made by matching or assessment."[7]

In a seminal paper in 1955, Herbert Simon suggested that because people cannot possibly take into account all the factors involved in economic decisions or make all the necessary computations, they put boundaries on the decision process and settle for options that are "good enough"—what he called "satisficing." This is the concept of *bounded rationality* in decision making.[8]

Never mind the data or the algorithms; in the entrepreneurial world, even the problems often are ill-defined. You have to continue clarifying the goal even as you try to achieve it, and often the goal does not remain constant because changes of information are so frequent. "The first dreary conclusion is that unknowable situations are widespread and inevitable. ... The second dreary conclusion is that most investors—whose training fits a world where states and probabilities are known— have little idea of how to deal with the unknowable."[9]

Thus, rational decision-making models work mostly with lots of data from the past and present. However, they fail to take into account the idea that past trends often are poor predictors of the future, and they are unwieldy in an entrepreneurial world of messy, incomplete, and incoherent data. Even more important, it's not clear that the models take into account how our minds really think about decisions—especially in circumstances of data overload and massive uncertainty—or show how to use that information to make more effective decisions. That said, researchers looking at decisions made under constraints of time and uncertain information find that fast decision makers in such environments tend to use more information than slow decision makers, develop more alternatives, and make better decisions.[10]

Decision research published by Lowell Busenitz of Oklahoma University and Jay Barney of Ohio State University compared decision making by entrepreneurs and managers in large organizations and found that entrepreneurs and innovators are more likely to use nonrational decision processes and more frequently employ biases and heuristics: rules- or intuition-based methods for making decisions. Two in particular stand out: overconfidence (overestimating the probability of being right) and representativeness (overgeneralizing from a few characteristics or observations).[11] Many entrepreneurial contexts involve complex problems and multiple hurdles that render rational decision analysis overwhelming or impossible. In contrast to large, long-standing organizations in which there is history, performance, and other information, in the start-up environment entrepreneurs have no past history, only a bewildering complex of information from all directions in the environment. In such circumstances, decisions are nearly impossible without the simplifying power of a number of biases and heuristics that different people use at different times.[12,13] Also, overconfidence helps inspire and motivate a team and investors. Busenitz and Barney note, however, that the tendency to rely on biases and heuristics may be a handicap for entrepreneurs who want to make the transition to being managers of their growing organizations.

Other researchers have looked beyond compartmentalized behaviors such as biases and heuristics. Writing about his best-selling book *Blink*, Malcolm Gladwell posted this online at *Slate*:

> *One of the key arguments in my book is that human beings think in two very different ways. Sometimes we consciously and carefully gather all facts, traditionally sort through them, and draw what we take to be a rational conclusion (the Standard Model). And sometimes we reach conclusions unconsciously—our mind quickly and silently sorts through the available information and draws an immediate judgment, which may be done so quickly and so far below the level of awareness that we may have no understanding of where our conclusions came from.*[14]

Blink popularized a growing field of decision research that is focused not on models and systematics but on observing what goes on when people actually make decisions in real time and real circumstances. Gladwell talks about what he calls thin-slicing—finding significant patterns in narrow slices of experience, for example, marriage counselors accurately judging the likelihood of future divorces by recognizing "contempt" signals such as eye rolls and tone.[15] Gladwell summarizes research showing that thin-slicing doesn't pay attention to everything head on; it removes the "fog of too much data"[16] and the distractions of the stereotype,[17] instead coming at an issue "sideways."[18] We can change the way we thin-slice by changing the experiences that constitute our impressions.[19]

One of Gladwell's main sources is the work of the research psychologist Gary Klein, who began studying what he now calls naturalistic decision making in the early 1970s. His work with firefighters, medical professionals, and the military led him to conclude that laboratory-based decision-making models aren't representative of what happens when decisions are made in contexts of uncertainty. His book

Sources of Power summarizes his work and the model he calls Recognition Primed Decision Making.[20]

Here is an example of what Klein and Gladwell are talking about:

The Sixth Sense

It is a simple house fire in a one-story house in a residential neighborhood. The fire is in the back, in the kitchen area. The lieutenant leads his hose crew into the building, to the back, to spray water on the fire, but the fire just roars back at them.

"Odd," he thinks. The water should have more of an impact. They try dousing it again and get the same results. They retreat a few steps to regroup.

Then the lieutenant starts to feel as if something is not right. He doesn't have any clues; he just doesn't feel right about being in that house, so he orders his men out of the building – a perfectly standard building with nothing out of the ordinary.

As soon as his men leave the building, the floor where they had been standing collapses. Had they still been inside, they would have plunged into the fire below.[21]

What does Klein want us to see in these circumstances? Experience sees a situation as a prototype of things seen and experienced before. It identifies a reasonable reaction without having to see all the facts and without having to generate and compare options. These deciders don't *refuse* to compare options; they don't *have to*. Klein quotes a fire ground commander: "I don't make decisions. I don't remember when I've ever made a decision."[22] These deciders don't generate options one at a time; they look for the first workable solution, not the best. They evaluate by imagining how it will play out, not by analysis and comparison to others. Imagining suggests improvements, not just choices.

There is an impulse to act rather than waiting to evaluate all choices. Often they use analogues and metaphors to direct thinking, framing situation awareness, identifying appropriate goals, and flagging relevant pieces of information. This provides a structure for making predictions when there are many unknown factors, linking familiar sets of causes to past outcomes. Klein believes that most of this happens without a deliberate thought process. Like the firefighter, these people hear emotion talking to them in their heads, not calculation. Granted, the context of the example is one of crisis, with no time for contemplation or calculation, but Klein's research shows that the same thought processes seem to be at work in less pressed and stressful situations too.

There are some surprising empirical studies supporting this less-than-rational model for how people make decisions. In a psychology study done at the University of Amsterdam, Ap Dijksterhuis and colleagues looked at how consumers made a number of purchase decisions and what they thought later about how good those decisions were. The researchers concluded:

> *Contrary to conventional wisdom, it is not always advantageous to engage in thorough conscious deliberation before choosing. On the basis of recent insights into the characteristics of conscious and unconscious thought, we tested the hypothesis that simple choices (such as between different towels or different sets of oven mitts) indeed produce better results after conscious thought, but that choices in complex matters (such as between different houses or different cars) should be left to unconscious thought. Named the "deliberation-without-attention" hypothesis, it was confirmed in four studies on consumer choice, both in the laboratory as well as among actual shoppers, that purchases of complex products were viewed more favorably when decisions had been made in the absence of attentive deliberation.*[23]

Admittedly, in their study Dijksterhuis and his colleagues couldn't fully equate "post choice satisfaction" and objective "advantageous choices." Their focus was not on that but on the mechanics of how decisions are made. They talk about "thought or deliberation in the absence of conscious attention directed at the problem." Unconscious choosers made better choices than did conscious thinkers or immediate choosers. In fact, the authors concluded that whereas conscious thought is precise, "conscious thought has a low capacity." What's going on? Is there another channel that has more capacity? Klein thinks so. He thinks he sees people making complex decisions by analogy, pattern match, and emotion. The key question is how deciders' brains communicate the analogies and pattern matches they find.

Science writer Gretchen Vogel says, "Psychologists have long known that when people make decisions, whether it's choosing whom to marry or which breakfast cereal to buy, they draw on more than just rational thought."[24] As cited by Vogel in her article, the psychologist Stephen Kosslyn of Harvard University says, "Emotion apparently is not something that necessarily clouds reasoning, but rather seems to provide an essential foundation for at least some kinds of reasoning."[25] Vogel reported on an important study done at the University of Iowa by a group of psychologists studying patients with damage to specific centers of the brain and how those patients fared in decision-focused experiments. Quoting the Harvard psychologist and author Howard Gardner, she further noted that "the new work 'fits in with an impressive heap of individual studies showing that people rely on a variety of emotional cues—ranging from a general sense of déjà vu to specific feelings like fear—when making decisions."[26]

Listening to emotions is critical in making decisions, "recognition-primed" or otherwise. If you really pay attention to how you make decisions, we think you eventually will concede that usually it's an experience of emotion, often several, and that the reasons for the decision often follow rather than precede the moment of choice.

Here's the study Vogel was writing about. The details are fascinating and help illustrate the complex process going on in our heads when we are making decisions.

A group of neuroscientists at the University of Iowa College of Medicine led by Antoine Bechara have a registry of over 2,000 brain-damaged patients, among whom is a valuable group of people with lesions in the ventromedial prefrontal cortex, an area of the brain above the eyes that has been linked with emotion. Patients with damage to this area display little to no emotion. They score well on IQ and memory tests but are terrible decision makers. Notes Vogel: "Some drift in and out of marriages; others squander money or often offend co-workers inadvertently … when faced with real-life decisions, they at first waffle, then make unwise choices."[27]

Bechara and Hanna Damasio state in the 1997 paper that Vogel referenced, "Deciding advantageously in a complex situation is thought to require overt reasoning on declarative knowledge, namely, on facts pertaining to premises, options for action, and outcomes of actions that embody the pertinent previous experience." Sound familiar? "An alternative possibility was investigated: that *overt reasoning is preceded by a nonconscious biasing step* that uses neural systems other than those that support declarative knowledge" (emphasis added).[28]

Bechara and Damasio tested this idea by comparing 10 "normal" control subjects and 6 patients with bilateral damage to the ventromedial sector of the prefrontal cortex. They were given a gambling task with rewards and penalties designed to simulate real-life decision making under uncertainty. They played for money, choosing to turn over cards from four decks. Turning each card carried an immediate reward ($100 in two decks, A and B, and $50 in the other two decks, C and D). Unpredictably, turning over some cards also carried a penalty, large in A and B and small in C and D. Playing mostly from the disadvantageous decks A and B led to an overall loss. Playing from the advantageous decks C and D led to an overall gain. The players had no way of predicting when a penalty would arise in a deck, no way to calculate with precision the net gain or loss from each deck, and no knowledge of how many cards they had to turn to end the game. All subjects were wired to measure skin conductive responses (SCRs), a rapid, direct physiological indicator of emotional arousal.

After experiencing a few losses, normal participants began to generate SCRs before selecting a card from the bad decks, indicating an emotional response even though they were not consciously aware of it. They also began avoiding the decks with large losses. Patients with bilateral damage to the ventromedial prefrontal cortex did neither. At the twentieth card, none of the subjects—normal subjects and patients—indicated that they had a clue about what was going on. By about card 50, all 10 of the normal participants began to express a "hunch" that decks A and B were riskier and all generated anticipatory SCRs whenever they pondered a choice from those decks. None of the patients generated anticipatory SCRs or expressed a "hunch."

By card 80, 7 of the 10 normal participants expressed accurate knowledge about why, in the long run, decks A and B were bad and decks C and D were good. Even the three normal participants who did not reach the conceptual period still made advantageous choices. Three of the six patients eventually could describe which were the bad and good decks correctly, *but they still chose disadvantageously.* None of the six patients ever generated anticipatory SCRs; they never activated emotions. Write Bechara and Damasio:

> *Thus, despite an accurate account of the task and of the correct strategy, these patients failed to generate autonomic responses and continued to select cards from the bad decks. The patients failed to act according to their correct conceptual knowledge. ... We suspect that the autonomic responses we detected are evidence for a complex process of nonconscious signaling, which reflects access to records of previous individual experience—specifically, of records shaped by reward, punishment, and the emotional state that attends them.*[29]

In a subsequent 1999 paper the Bechara group went further, reporting on the results of a study comparing decision making in patients with damage to either of two major centers of emotion in the brain: the amygdala and the ventromedial prefrontal cortex. They found that damage to each of the centers critically impairs decision making and, even more interesting, does so in different ways.[30]

What is the takeaway? Emotions play a critical role in decision making, something rational decision-making strategies ignore at their peril. It's your peril too if you follow them. Consideration, deliberation, and doing lots of homework and analysis are valuable in framing a decision—within the time allowed, of course. But in the end your emotions will decide, and the only task your rational brain will fulfill is to rationalize to yourself why you decided what you did. Emotions decide; reason explains. Therefore, the more tuned you can be to your emotions, the more effective you will be at getting all the centers of your brain working together. Remember, even though the patients with impaired emotions figured out the right strategy to play the gambling game, it didn't affect their decisions.

Gladwell says that quick, intuition-guided decisions can be good ones, sometimes better ones. The acuity of emotions in analogizing from relevant factors among complex patterns appears to be a major asset in deciding effectively. This may explain why seasoning and experience seem to be so highly valued in decision makers. Gladwell offers some important lessons in decision making:

- Successful decision making relies on a balance between deliberate and instinctive thinking.[31]
- Try to screen out sources of first impressions not relevant to the question.[32]
- Frugality matters—reduce a problem to its simplest elements. Information overload can paralyze decision making.[33]

- Sometimes you have to consciously resist a particular kind of snap judgment: In some circumstances, it's better to slow things down to get more information. At other times this can only cloud the issue.[34]
- Analytic and intuitive decision making can both be effective, but only if used in the appropriate circumstances.[35]

How do you know when intuitive decisions are appropriate? You don't. That's just one more intuitive decision, at best an educated guess based on a library of learned experiences.[36]

FRAMING TO DECIDE

It isn't that they can't see the solution. It's that they can't see the problem.

—G. K. Chesterton

What do you really know? Most knowing is not disinterested knowing. Perhaps your greatest enemy as a decision maker, after ignoring the central role of emotions, is failing to take into account the biases and preferences that shape your sense of what you think you know. The best thinking sorts through this maze of subjectivity and self-interest.

In almost any setting involving responsibility, the quality of decisions is no better than the knowledge and judgment that support those decisions. Critical to good decision making is honest discipline in determining what "knowledge" is valid and relevant. What is the context? What issue needs deciding? This is another way of saying that before you let your emotions loose on a question, you need to be sure you are thinking about the right question. This is epistemology in decision making: How do you know what you know? How much do you really know? What is the degree of validity or the level of confidence that your facts are complete and accurate? For this, you need to steel yourself to be a bit of a skeptic about knowledge. Pause, and before you think about deciding, think through some careful epistemology.

In philosophy, epistemology means being deliberate and disciplined in determining what we think we know. This is not to say that entrepreneurs need to become philosophers about the nature of knowledge or beat a question to death. But deciding on the basis of poor or incorrect knowledge is bad business. Defining the right question and getting the facts right the first time—as well as you can, anyway—is the beginning of good business. In our entrepreneurial world of messy, incomplete, and incoherent information, this is not always as easy or obvious as it seems. More often than we might like, it turns out that many things we think we know are either unknowable or just not so.

ERRORS

It ain't so much the things we don't know that get us into trouble. It's the things we know that just ain't so.

—Artemus Ward

There are some consistent glitches in our thought processes that seem to be hard-wired in all of us, and they lead to predictable epistemology errors. Decision psychologists talk about things such as the following:

- *Priming or anchoring effect.* Being influenced by recently absorbed information, especially in a guess or estimate. For example, studies show that when people are asked to make estimates, they are predictably influenced by a recently heard number even if that number has no relation to the issue at hand.
- *Selective perception bias.* Internalizing or screening out information because of prior experience, attitudes, beliefs, preferences, or habits. Selective perception bias makes pure objectivity almost impossible. We confuse the reliability of a source of information with its predictive ability, for example, using trade statistics to forecast the stock market because they are hard numbers, not because we know that they have a connection to stock prices.
- *Confirmation bias.* Giving disproportionate weight to what supports our prevailing views and ignoring information we don't want to hear.
- *Representation bias.* Assessing the likelihood of an event on the basis of how closely it resembles a known event or events. Web site founders who pitch their marketing plans on the basis of the success of Facebook's launch are falling for a representation bias.
- *Framing bias.* Letting definitions or the framing of a problem affect what we attend to and what we filter out.
- *Availability bias.* Remembering and attending to information that is most recent, vivid, or frequently heard. We put too much confidence in memory; we remember events better than statistics. For example, after the 9/11 terrorist attacks, many people avoided airplanes and drove instead, even though the odds of dying in a traffic accident (1 in 6,000) are astronomically higher than those of dying in a terrorist attack on an airliner (estimated at 1 in 135,000).[37] A Dutch decisions researcher estimated that over 1,500 people died as a result of this increase in driving, more than died on all the 9/11 airliners put together.[38] Related is the *Von Restorff effect*: selectively remembering the striking or unusual.
- *Affect heuristic.* Biasing perceptions of risk based on perceived benefits.

- *The winners' effect.* Attributing genius to winners and stupidity to losers even when the quality of their thinking about a problem is the same. Every day some people come out of Las Vegas casinos big winners, but that doesn't mean they have a system.
- *Limited search effect.* Perhaps the most tragic of all, oversimplifying a complex or challenging situation by limiting the search for more information or alternatives. We indulge in what psychologists call bounded rationality, constructing models that are based on essential features and ignoring subtleties or richness of information. An example would be a college graduate who takes the first job to come along instead of planning a long-term career path.

Thomas Gilovich, a professor of psychology at Cornell University, has spent a career studying these kinds of things, many of which he summarizes in a book every entrepreneur ought to read: *How We Know What Isn't So.*[39] Among the more annoying of these practices are the following:

- Seeing regularity and order where only the vagaries of chance are operating. He calls this a "Clustering Illusion," and it consists of failing to appreciate the nature of randomness or misunderstanding statistical regression to the mean. For example, people talk about the so-called hot hand in sports. Random strings of data are not uniform—clusters are normal. If you flip a coin 100 times, you will get close to 50 heads and 50 tails, but clusters of all heads or all tails will be common.
- Failing to detect and correct for biases that result from incomplete or unrepresentative data.
- Interpreting ambiguous and inconsistent data in light of preferences, pet theories, or a priori expectations.
- Believing things because of wishful thinking and self-serving distortions of reality.
- Relying on secondhand information and distortions introduced by communicators such as the media and celebrities.
- Thinking that others believe what we believe and are more like us than they really are.
- Failing to balance the import of outcomes: "the tendency to be more impressed by what *has* happened than by what has *failed* to happen, and the temptation to draw conclusions from what has occurred under present circumstances without comparing it to what would have occurred under alternate circumstances."[40]
- Failing to distinguish correlation from cause and effect. The fact that two events correlate does not mean that one causes the other. For something to be said to cause an effect, it has to be both necessary and sufficient. When

human behavior is involved, cause and effect can be almost impossible to establish. Attributing an event to cause and effect anyway is little more than wishful thinking or prejudice.

Sloppy thinking about cause and effect is one of the great decision bloopers. Incorrectly learning from hindsight is another. Every decision maker should read the article "The Silly Certainty of Hindsight" by the psychologist Baruch Fischoff.[41] That silly certainty dooms us to learning the wrong lessons from our past. Fischoff found that hindsight gives a false sense of inevitability. When we know an outcome, we tend to believe that others, with foresight, should have recognized things we know only from hindsight. He cites an example: In 1974 in Eugene, Oregon, Cletus Bowles, a convicted murderer and bank robber, left the Oregon penitentiary on a four-hour pass. While out, he fled, kidnapped, and murdered two people. There was an outcry over incompetence and failure to foresee the danger. The prison warden was pressured to resign. "Bowles' record, in the prison and out, shows he could not be trusted," ran one newspaper editorial. However, it turns out that Bowles was a model prisoner before he left the penitentiary.

Hindsight affects the way people judge results. We rationalize results, retrospectively manipulating information or selectively attending to data. This is so pervasive that we tend to have difficulty remembering accurately how we viewed a situation before knowing the outcome. In experiments people interpret the same facts differently, depending on the reported outcome. In one of Fischoff's experiments, groups of subjects were given the background of a colonial struggle in Nepal and asked to judge the probabilities of four possible outcomes. Some of the groups were told in advance that one of the four outcomes actually happened. Those given the outcome judged it as twice as likely as did those who were given no outcome, even when the outcome was fictitious and wrong.

Fischoff says that a human tendency to see events in retrospect as foreseeable gives people a false sense of inevitability, denying the element of surprise in the way things work out: "*Without a sense of surprise, we feel little need to reevaluate the implicit assumptions and rules we use to interpret what goes on in the world, and we repeat our mistakes. A surprise-free past is prologue to a surprise-full future*" (emphasis added).

It seems almost daunting—messy, incomplete, and incoherent data sloshing around in a sea of emotions and psychological biases, haunted by the certainty of hindsight that is almost certainly wrong. What to do? Here are some suggestions:

- Start by reminding yourself constantly about the uncertainty in people's judgment of the past.
- Hunt down objective records of the past as it was originally experienced. Keep written records. Take notes and date them, especially in regard to predictions and the considerations that guided them.

- For past events with a known outcome, try to imagine alternative futures for them. Think about what could have gone wrong.
- Disguise an actual event and present the circumstances to other experts for their opinions.
- Ask yourself whether a hypothesis of random outcomes is equally likely or even more likely. By giving up illusory control and concentrating on the nonrandom aspects of a situation, you can often exercise greater control.
- Start by asking yourself, What are the key uncertainties? and To what level of detail does the question have to be answered?
- Have at least a working familiarity with the basic principles of statistics and probability. Exposure to the "probabilistic" sciences may be more effective than experience with the "deterministic" sciences in evaluating the messy statistical phenomena of everyday life.
- Never confuse correlation with cause and effect. Be sure you see necessity and sufficiency before assuming cause and effect. Accept the fact that there are many things we can't know even when compelling correlations make us think we do.
- Groups trump individuals. Find ways to access the power of groups. Assemble them from your team. Use your boards and advisor networks.

Don't underestimate the value of mistakes. Oscar Wilde said, "Experience is the name everyone gives to their mistakes." Mistakes are often the best teachers. In fact, most businesspeople will tell you they learned far more from their mistakes than from their successes. However, you can benefit only if you realize you made a mistake and examine it carefully to learn from it, all the while recognizing the distortions of the silly certainty of hindsight.

WHEN TO DECIDE?

There is one last point about decision making that is often underemphasized: *When* do you need to decide? It's not always obvious that because a decision has presented for choosing, it has to be decided then. Indecision can be paralyzing, but deciding peremptorily can be damaging too. Sometimes deferring a decision for lack of information or conviction can be a good idea—if there's no time pressure and more data will improve the decision rather than complicate or impair it. This happens more often than we think. Decide or delay—it's a tension. Deferring a decision can be wise or tantamount to choosing one alternative by default; no decision can end up being a "no" decision.

You can balance between deciding too quickly and deciding too late—when there is the luxury of time—by developing multiple options to choose from. Having more than one option for the way things can work out can be valuable. All things equal, develop as many options as you can effectively (and cost-effectively) manage and hold them open as long as circumstances don't force you to choose. In this way, you will be taking advantage of the possibility that additional information will surface that may favor one or more of the options. Think about it this way: Deciding, in the end, is more about eliminating poorer options and keeping the best one than about choosing one alternative. As options demand a take-it-or-leave-it decision, look one more time at all the remaining alternatives; is the one calling for a take-or-drop choice more attractive than the potential of all the remaining options taken together? If so, take it. If not, drop it. Keep working the options until only the one you like the best is left standing. It's sort of a natural selection evolution of opportunities—the fittest survive. Just as in nature, on the surface the process can seem wasteful, generating more options than you will use. But the cost of too quickly choosing a suboptimal alternative because you didn't get information that was available or didn't properly conceive alternatives can be expensive too. More often than not, what really happens is that multiple options suggest combinations and creative solutions that single-channel thinking might not have revealed.

WHAT I KNOW NOW THAT I WISH I HAD KNOWN THEN

Paul Holland, Foundation Capital

Paul Holland is a general partner at Foundation Capital, a leading venture capital partnership operating in Menlo Park, California, since 1995. As a venture investor and board member, Paul helps early-stage start-ups go from zero to $100 million in revenue. A former entrepreneur and sales executive, he helped two venture-funded software start-ups grow and go public: Kana Communications (KANA) and Pure Software (RATL).

As a venture investor at Foundation Capital and former entrepreneur, many times I have seen a crisp decision make the difference between billions of dollars of success and filing for bankruptcy.

When I think about the complex decision making that goes on in a fast-moving start-up, I remember my days at Pure Software and its CEO, Reed Hastings. Several times Reed would address the company and talk about "bet the company" decisions. In one such case, at a time when the company was profitable but growth was slowing, Reed came to believe Pure's survival meant changing our licensing scheme to improve our profit margins and expand our market reach. He knew that this probably would antagonize our existing customer base but that we could never grow without a new model. It was a wrenching choice. In addition to all his analytical skills, in the end

Reed drew on an incredible sense of intuition to frame the decision and make it.

Once he made the difficult choice, Reed and our key product managers locked themselves away for a long weekend and emerged with a new model and a plan to implement it. Over the next several weeks Reed worked tirelessly to help the sales and marketing teams with the very difficult task of convincing existing and prospective customers to accept the new scheme and its higher prices.

In part because of the successful transition, Pure's sales skyrocketed. The company went public in 1995 and ultimately achieved a market capitalization of over $1 billion. Reed Hastings went on to found Netflix, one of Foundation's portfolio companies, and he's still the CEO.

The lesson: Always pause to listen to your instincts. Rational analysis of all the facts and details is important, but so is "gut instinct"—the sum of experience and intuition. No decision is better than the question it addresses. Intuition and experience are essential in knowing when to decide and important in seeing through the blizzard of facts and figures to the best decisions.

All things considered, in decision making you can't always consider everything, but you always need to decide eventually. You can get lost in a fog of precision and granularity or just as easily get lost in a fit of intuition and limited search effect. You can hip shoot a decision that quickly appears cavalier and stupid. There are no right answers when it comes to decision making, only opportunities and pitfalls. Most entrepreneurs find it exhilarating to have the challenge of making decisions that matter, day after day, decisions that they have to make or no one will. Thrilling or not, decisions have to be made. When your head, your heart, your experience, and your homework line up, that's the best you can hope for. Concentrate, be disciplined, and make that happen whenever you can.

QUESTIONS

- Can you describe clearly to someone you know how you approach making decisions?
- Ask half a dozen people who work with you or know you well how willing they think you are to make decisions when they're needed. Do you avoid making decisions? Do you make them too quickly or casually?
- What do you think is the proper balance between getting more facts to work the details and making a decision and getting it carried out? (There is no single right answer.)

- What do you think is the proper balance between intuition and deliberate, calculated decisions?

NOTES

1. Vascellaro, Jessica E., and Joann S. Lublin, "Yang's Exit Doesn't Fix Yahoo," *Wall Street Journal*, November 19, 2008: B2.
2. Sandberg, Jared, "Non-Deciders Make Everyone Else Suffer," *Wall Street Journal*, November 8, 2005: B1.
3. http://www.businessdictionary.com/definition/rational-decision-making-approach.html (accessed September 11, 2010).
4. Lipschitz, Raanan, and Orna Strauss, "Coping with Uncertainty: A Naturalistic Decision-Making Analysis," *Organizational Behavior and Human Decision Processes* 69, no. 2 (February 1997): 149–163.
5. Klein, Gary, *Sources of Power* (Cambridge, MA: MIT Press, 1998): 28–30, 286–292.
6. Ibid.: 155.
7. Lipschitz, Ranaan, "Decision Making in Three Modes," *Journal for the Theory of Social Behavior* 24, no. 1 (1994): 47–65.
8. Simon, Herbert A., "A Behavioral Model of Rational Choice," *Quarterly Journal of Economics*, 69, issue 1 (February 1955): 99–118.
9. Zeckhauser, Richard, "Investing in the Unknown and Unknowable," *Capitalism and Society* 1, issue 2, article 5.
10. Eisenhardt, Kathleen M., "Making Fast Strategic Decisions in High-Velocity Environments," *Academy of Management Journal* 32, no. 3: 543–576.
11. Busenitz, Lowell W., and Jay B. Barney, "Differences between Entrepreneurs and Managers in Large Organizations: Biases and Heuristics in Strategic Decision-Making," *Journal of Business Venturing* 12, issue 1 (1997): 9–30.
12. Pitz, Gordon F., and Natalie J. Sachs, "Judgment and Decision: Theory and Application," *Annual Review of Psychology* 35 (1984): 139–163.
13. Haley, Usha C. V., and Stephen A. Stumpf, "Cognitive Trails in Strategic Decision-Making: Linking Theories of Personalities and Cognitions," *Journal of Management Studies* 26, no. 5 (September 1989): 477–497.
14. Gladwell, Malcolm, Web posting, "Challenging the Standard Model of Decision-Making, a Reply to James Surowiecki," *Slate*, January 10, 2005, http://slate.msn.com/id/2111894/entry/2112064/ (accessed Sept 11, 2010).
15. Gottman, John M., James Coan, Sybil Carerre, and Catherine Swanson, "Predicting Marital Happiness and Stability from Newlywed Interactions," *Journal of Marriage and Family* 60, no. 1 (February 1998): 5–22.
16. Gladwell, Malcolm, *Blink* (New York: Little, Brown, 2005): 32, 34.
17. Ibid.: 37–38, 245–254.

18. Ibid.: 39.
19. Ibid.: 71.
20. Klein, 1998.
21. Ibid: 32.
22. Ibid.: 11.
23. Dijksterhuis, Ap, Maarten W. Bos, Loran F. Nordgren, and Rick B. van Baaren, "On Making the Right Choice: The Deliberation-without-Attention Effect," *Science* 311, no. 5763 (February 17, 2006): 1005–1007.
24. Vogel, Gretchen, "Scientists Probe Feelings behind Decision Making," *Science* 275, no. 5304 (February 28, 1997): 1269.
25. Ibid.
26. Ibid.
27. Ibid.
28. Bechara, Antoine, and Hanna Damasio, "Deciding Advantageously before Knowing the Advantageous Strategy," *Science* 275, no. 5304 (February 28, 1997): 1293.
29. Bechara and Damasio, 1997.
30. Bechara, Antoine, Hanna Damasio, Antonio R. Damasio, and Gregory P. Lee, "Different Contributions of the Human Amygdala and Ventromedial Prefrontal Cortex to Decision-Making," *Journal of Neuroscience* 19, no. 13 (July 1, 1999): 5473–5481.
31. Gladwell, 2005: 141.
32. Ibid.: 154–155, 173, 179–183.
33. Ibid.: 141–142.
34. Ibid.: 183.
35. Ibid.: 70–71.
36. Hogarth, Robin M., University of Chicago Graduate School of Business, "Judgment and Choice," in *Educating Intuition* (Chicago: University of Chicago Press, 2001).
37. Gardner, Daniel, *The Science of Fear* (New York: Dutton, 2008): 3.
38. Gigerenzer, Gerd, "Out of the Frying Pan into the Fire: Behavioral Reactions to Terrorist Attacks," *Risk Analysis* 26, no. 2 (2006): 347–351.
39. Gilovich, Thomas, *How We Know What Isn't So: The Fallibility of Human Reason In Everyday Life* (New York: Free Press, 1991).
40. Ibid.: 186.
41. Fischhoff, Baruch, "The Silly Certainty of Hindsight," *Psychology Today* 8, no. 11 (August 1975): 71–76.

Chapter 19

Accounting and Money Management

I don't know technology and engineering. I don't know accounting.
—Bernie Ebbers[1]

Upon arrival at business school, many students ask, "What subject is most important to my success in business?" Most experienced businesspeople answer, "Accounting." Anyone in an enterprise that involves activity and money needs to know three important things: How well has he or she done in a particular period in the past? Where do things stand today? Where do things appear to be headed? Bookkeeping and accounting address these questions. Once you grow beyond managing your profit by checking the cash in your wallet, the only way you can manage a business effectively is with good accounting systems and reports. Don't put off creating them.

The good news is that accounting is a subject like law, in which there are professionals who will do most of the work so that you don't have to do it yourself. Really, you can't. There is too much to learn and not enough hours in the day to manage accounting and treasury functions and still run a business. To learn enough to get started and manage effectively, there are lots of tools for early-stage companies, and later on you'll use professionals. It is important, though, that you know enough about accounting to set your company up for each stage of growth, effectively manage the accounting, and clearly understand what the numbers are telling you.

Cash doesn't manage itself. In the earliest days, cash management is usually a survival issue. Later, it's an important optimization issue. The treasury functions of cash management are important.

Founding teams often think of taxes as a problem they would like to have someday but don't have today, and so they put off focusing on taxes. What you do at the start with respect to tax structuring often has serious future implications, including mistakes such as having to pay taxes on early revenue when a little careful planning could have avoided them. Tax issues can arise as early as the first incorporation and eventually have a tremendous financial impact. Some problems can be fixed later; others are not so easy to deal with.

In this chapter we won't try to teach you financial and managerial accounting, taxation, corporate treasury, or finance. There are whole branches of knowledge and practice on all of these functions and literally millions of full-time professionals who handle them. We just want to set a utility framework that describes all these functions, what they do, and why they are important, along with some suggestions on how you can prepare to build out each of them as you grow.

START EARLY: BOOKKEEPING

Often the founding team in a start-up will have someone with the title chief financial officer (CFO). This is overkill, generally a sign of inexperience. Start-ups don't
need CFOs. Until they have revenue and recurring costs, they may not even need
a part-time bookkeeper. However, they will need to keep track of financial activity.
Many a start-up has found to its regret that it's never too early to get on top of
tracking finances.

WHAT I KNOW NOW THAT I WISH I HAD KNOWN THEN

Leslie Fall, MD, iInTIME

*Drs. Leslie Fall and Norman Berman are cofounders of a nonprofit educational
enterprise, the Institute for Innovative Technology in Medical Education
(iInTIME, http://www.i-intime.org), which supports clinical education of medical students with online virtual patient cases. A majority of U.S. and Canadian
medical schools pay for subscriptions to iInTIME's cases series, with over 10,000
registered student users per year and more than 500,000 case sessions completed
annually. Drs. Fall and Berman have received numerous national medical education awards for their work. If you ask Dr. Fall today what was the single
biggest thing she would say she knows now that she wishes she had known then,
it would be to get on top of accounting systems and financial reporting sooner.*

As physician educators with no formal business background, working through
an incubator was critical to our success. In addition to space, the incubator's
network connected us with an information technology attorney, entrepreneurs experienced in marketing and business strategy, an insurance agent, and
many potential board members. We had everything we thought we needed,
but we now realize a critical component was missing: guidance on managing
finance and accounting. As a nonprofit with solid initial cash flow and no
need to present to investors or pay taxes, we didn't focus on those at the time.

We knew we would need to use good accounting practices to meet federal standards, but everyone assured us that hiring a bookkeeper was unnecessary because Quickbooks is "so easy to set up." This assumes, however that
most start-up teams have founders who are experienced in business—not
two busy physicians!

Our first meeting with an accountant was a disaster. Our lack of experience and understanding of what to expect, combined with the lack of a common language, left all of us frustrated. We ultimately established a functional
system that generated an accurate balance sheet that satisfied our exasperated

CPA. However, we failed to understand that systems are more than bookkeeping—they also support or limit the ability to produce useful management reports. As our business and revenues grew, we increasingly relied on board members with business expertise to rework clunky reports we used to inform our important business decisions. It wasn't until we hired an experienced entrepreneur as our president that we upgraded to an effective accounting system. Only then did we realize how blind we had been flying, which had made our early decision processes so much harder than they needed to be.

Lesson learned: if you are not experienced in this area, work with a qualified professional from the beginning to set up the right systems; and if you don't know how to tell a qualified professional when you see one, that's what your advisors are for.

Accounting starts with *bookkeeping*. This means gathering data; analyzing, classifying, and entering it into systems; and maintaining standardized records for use in creating financial and managerial reports. At first you probably will keep your own records. Some people use a spreadsheet, but you should put things in good order right from the beginning. Most people use QuickBooks. Companies with $60 million in revenues can still operate comfortably with QuickBooks.

In an afternoon you can become conversant enough to choose your fiscal year and accounting basis (cash or accrual), set up a chart of accounts and a general ledger, enter data, and generate simple reports. Professionals can (i.e., should) help you set up a complete and proper chart of accounts and extract more complicated reports from QuickBooks. It will save a lot of heartache from the beginning if you create a structure of accounts, subaccounts, and departments that can accommodate complexity as you grow. In the early years companies manually create Excel reports to extend what they get out of QuickBooks, but eventually they convert the Excel reports to another forecasting system, such as Adaptive Planning. Any investor will want to see this information in good form, even if it's just your own form that you generated in QuickBooks. From the very first activity, you should classify all transactions to the right accounts correctly and consistently.

Since it's likely that you will engage an accountant and bookkeeper eventually, start early with interviewing and building relationships. This has the benefit of getting you some good guidance on setting up record keeping. That way you already have things in good order when it comes time to bring in a bookkeeper and accountants. It won't be long before you need some part-time help with bookkeeping. Many bookkeepers work for several companies simultaneously on this basis. Certified public accountants (CPAs) must have a college degree with a concentration in accounting, pass a national examination, and be licensed by their state of residence. Public accountants or registered accountants don't need to meet all the requirements of a licensed CPA and are less uniformly regulated by their states.

ACCOUNTING

There are two kinds of financial reports that any business needs:

- *Financial statements* are done according to accepted standards and are used to report historical performance in a standardized format for management and external parties: investors, banks, creditors, and government entities.
- Businesses use *managerial reports* that are based on internal operating and financial data. Some are standard reports, and some are customized to manage and plan internal activities. Managerial reports provide important measures, analyses, and projections used primarily for management and decision making.

Reports must be

- *Accurate.* You need to close quickly at the end of a month, followed by a detailed close a few days later.
- *Timely.* You want to know the cash and sales number each day of the month, not 20 days after the month has ended.
- *Readable.* Your managers and officers should be literate in reading reports. You may need to educate them on this.
- *Useful.* The reports should provide information the team uses and embraces.

FINANCIAL ACCOUNTING

The U.S. government does not set standards for accounting and financial reporting. Generally accepted accounting principles (GAAP) are standards of financial accounting established and improved by an office of an independent private foundation—the Financial Accounting Standards Board (FASB)—for use by public, private, and nonprofit entities. Today the collection of GAAP rules runs to over 25,000 pages. There is no legal requirement to use GAAP outside of publicly traded companies, for which the SEC requires that they be used.

Audits are examinations by independent certified accountants that include tests of the accounting records, internal control systems, and other procedures, culminating in an independent opinion or certificate. All public companies, many private companies, and most nonprofits obtain audits annually. Many investors and all banks want to see audited financial statements.

There are four basic statements in the financial report:

1. *Balance sheets* are a snapshot at a specific moment of a company's assets, liabilities, and shareholders' equity. In other words, they show what a company owns and what it owes on a specified date. Think about your personal financial situation: You have assets and liabilities (debts). Your net worth equals your assets minus your liabilities. On the balance sheet the assets are listed first, then liabilities, and then the residual shareholders' equity. The

sum of the liabilities and the shareholders' equity will equal the assets on the balance sheet. The format is assets equal liabilities plus shareholders' equity.

2. *Income statements* show how much revenue a company earned during a specific period, the costs and expenses associated with earning that revenue, and the resulting net earnings or losses.

3. *Cash flow statements* report a company's inflows and outflows of cash from operations, investments, and financing activities: whether the company accumulated cash or consumed more than it generated. A cash flow statement is an aggregate of the activity in the period, not an indication of what might have happened to cash balances in that period. For example, a quarterly report may show a net positive cash flow even though one month in the quarter saw a big negative number that later was offset by a bigger positive number. From an operations point of view, you must have cash or financing reserves to tide the company over periods of negative cash flow. Businesses fail when they run out of cash.

4. *Statements of shareholders' equity* show changes in the value of the shareholders' ownership interests over time.

Footnotes to financial reports are critical. They often address things such as accounting policies and practices, taxes, benefits plans and retirement programs, stock options, and significant contingent liabilities or legal issues, if any.

Ratios can indicate a lot about a company's financial health and resilience. Bankers and investors pay special attention to ratios such as the following:

- Gross profit margin = gross profit/sales
- Operating profit margin = operating profit/sales
- Net profit ratio = net income/sales revenue
- Return on equity = net income/shareholders' equity
- Current ratio = current assets/current liabilities (they like to see 2 or higher)
- Acid test ratio = cash + securities + accounts receivable/total current liabilities (they like to see 1 or higher)
- Debt to equity = total liabilities/owners' equity

The Securities and Exchange Commission (SEC) has an excellent summary description of financial statements at http://www.sec.gov/investor/pubs/begfin stmtguide.htm.

MANAGERIAL ACCOUNTING

Financial accounting produces statements that are important as a financial report card for you as well as outside parties. Managerial reports are essential to you for planning and managing, for revealing opportunities and problems, and often for assuring your survival and success. Managers pay close attention to the basic financial statements, but managers often need additional information drawn from the financial data and operations and presented in more detail or differently. Managerial accounting reports are for *you*. They place as much emphasis on the future as on the past and present. Timeliness often is more important than completeness and accuracy. Relevance and analysis are central. Managerial accounting focuses on things such as budget planning, cost discovery, cost and profit analysis, overhead, inventory, sales, and performance reporting.

There is no regimen or required collection of managerial reports. Many are derived from the details in QuickBooks or your other financial accounting system. Here are some of the more important ones that are used commonly, all of which can be drawn from QuickBooks.

Integrated Financial Reports

These reports include the standard income statement, balance sheet, and cash flow statement showing actual results to date and forecasted balances, typically by the month for the remainder of the fiscal year. The balance sheet and forecasts of required cash track increases in accounts receivable, inventory, changes and investments in capital equipment, and financing.

Cash Flow

You will find that the cash flow statement is the most important part of the financial model. You will rely on this report more than on any other. It captures in real time all your cash inflows, outflows, and cash balances. Many start-ups review it weekly, sometimes daily. Often tied to it are projections of sales in units, revenue, expenses, and capital outlays. The numbers often are broken out in great detail to allow for management of activity and early warning of potential problems. You can't start too early on a cash flow report and the discipline of updating it and using it every day. Once you update the model and the cash flow on a frequent basis, you will develop a financial dashboard that summarizes the operating and forecast highlights for the team.

Contribution Margin and Cost of Goods and/or Services Sold

Unit costs of production are critical for operations management. Often measures such as contribution margin (margin over cost of goods sold, also called gross profit) and marketing and sales costs per acquired customer are more important than traditional financial measures such as net profits.

Other Cost Categories

Variable costs and fixed costs frequently are broken out, as are direct costs to an operating segment versus indirect costs such as general office overhead. For the same concepts, some people use the terms *controllable* versus *uncontrollable* costs. Of course all costs should be controllable at some level, but often the financial activity of operating segments is reported separately for use by their managers, and so it's important to categorize and report the costs managers can control separately from the costs that are controlled by higher management and allocated to it. Often cost performance is measured as a variance against defined standard costs to help identify problems and opportunities for improvement.

Variance Analyses: Actual versus Budget

An important variance report compares actual performance against planned or projected budgets. These reports often are prepared on many of the key operating measures, such as demand, sales pipeline and sales, expenses, overhead items, and necessary resources. None, of course, is more important than projected versus actual cash flow and cash balance. Prepare a *waterfall chart* to measure your actual results against your plan and your revised forecasts. Salespeople often dislike them because they give early warning of changes in forecasts, which are downward more often than upward (see Figure 19-1).

Inventory Metrics

It's important that you track inventory levels, inventory flows, and comparisons of sales projections to inventory buildups and drawdowns. Many start-ups get in the bind of finding that their sales suddenly take off and they lack the financing and production capacity needed to build inventory ahead of demand and avoid delays, back orders, or lost sales. Also watch inventory turnover, the cost of sales divided by the average inventory balance for the period.

Working Capital

The technical definition of working capital is current assets minus current liabilities, as found on the balance sheet. A more relevant definition is cash available to keep the business running in any particular period without running out. Typically, the lag between paying expenses and collecting accounts receivables makes it difficult to fund ongoing operations without a cash cushion that originally came from somewhere: personal credit cards, delayed payments, terms from trade creditors, loans against accounts receivable (factoring), bank lines of credit, or short-term loans. The cash flow report is your early warning tool for working capital problems.

THINK ABOUT TAXES

One of the fastest ways some people try to build net worth is to not pay taxes. Of course, when done incorrectly, this is also one of the fastest ways to end up out of business and in jail. Tax *avoidance* is the correct way; it's legal. Tax *evasion* is the wrong way; it's not. Your first order of business is to understand the difference and be sure you are on the right side of it.

Tax planning for a small business is a perpetual effort. It should start before you ever make decisions on corporate structuring (see Chapter 13). It should look ahead to planning revenue, expenses, and capital commitments, and it should contemplate final liquidity events such as how the company or ownership interests in it are sold.

Taxes are a huge factor in your financial performance. The law changes constantly, of course, but as of this writing, after 2010 individual federal income tax

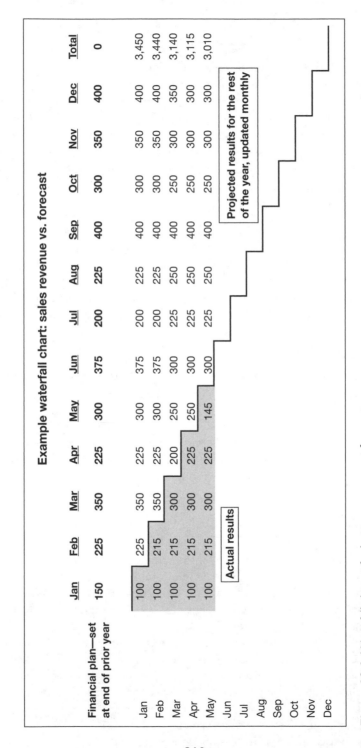

Figure 19-1 Waterfall chart of sales revenue versus forecast.

rates for ordinary income and dividends will top out at 35 percent, long-term capital gains at 20 percent, and the corporate income tax at 35 to 39 percent. Then there are state taxes: individual income rates up to 11 percent and corporate rates up to 10 percent. The good news is that thoughtful planning and diligent accounting can make a big difference in how bad it can be.

There are three main areas to think about.

Payroll Taxes

Few things can get a company in more trouble than messing up on payroll taxes—Social Security (FICA) and Medicare—both withholding from employees and company matching amounts. These have to be accounted for and deposited in a timely manner with the IRS. Separately you will deposit federal unemployment taxes and withholding of your employees' federal income taxes, as well as state unemployment taxes and state income taxes. These need to be set up correctly as employees are hired. Funds have to be accounted for properly, and the IRS must be paid on time. Penalties for missing any of these deadlines are serious. Many start-ups and smaller companies outsource the entire payroll administration function to services such as ADP or Paychex.

Income Taxes

One of the biggest income tax decisions comes at the formation of the company: whether to structure it as a flow-through entity, in which case all income and expense activities are streamed through to the owners and there is no taxable event at the corporate level. As was discussed in Chapter 13, there are pros and cons to the decision to flow through or subject oneself to double taxation. As a practical matter, most early-stage companies don't report enough income to get into the higher tax brackets and hardly ever pay out dividends that are taxed a second time as individual income.

Income tax planning can make a huge difference in the amount of precious operating cash drained out of a young and growing company in the form of taxes. For most early-stage companies, expenses far outrun income, but for some grant-supported companies or companies funding early development with prepaid purchases, poor tax planning can result in unnecessary tax bills. We know several companies that were caught like this because of failure to plan ahead. Be sure to think about the timing of income recognition and expenses, the depreciation benefits of capital expenditures, and capturing all deductible expenses and any eligible credits. Technology companies should pay special attention to the timing of research and development expenditures to take full advantage of Section 41 R&D tax credits and Section 174 R&D tax deductions. There are special rules for eligibility. Some states also have R&D-related tax incentives. Other tax strategies that can have a big effect on taxable income are moving income into capital gains wherever possible, like-kind exchanges (e.g., Sec. 1031 exchange of property), installment sales, and the formation of charitable trusts. Tax planning is definitely a place for professional help.

Sales Taxes

Many states levy a sales tax at the retail level. They look to vendors to collect, account for, and deposit taxes on all sales they make. Some states even require advance deposits. Sales to out-of-state customers are taxed according to the laws of the state in which the customer lives or takes delivery, and so if you are doing mail-order or Internet sales, you will have multiple jurisdictions to worry about.

MANAGING YOUR MONEY MATTERS

It won't take long before managing and investing your cash becomes a full-time job. Even before you are big enough to need a full-time CFO, you may need a controller or even a treasurer to manage a number of functions in which money matters overlap with accounting, operations, and finance. Controllers often have responsibility for accounting activities, but a key function of controllers is fiduciary responsibility and control of access to company funds.

Corporate finance and treasury manage the following:

- *Financial flows.* Treasury establishes and maintains banking relationships. It handles payments and collections, deposits, disbursements, the way money is moved around within the company, and the way it is invested to maintain flexibility and maximize earnings on cash held.
- *Controls.* Controls are essential in a company of any size. Who tracks money flows, who authorizes them, and who executes them need to be defined clearly in ways that maximize transparency and minimize the chances for misappropriation or lax accounting. In public companies, this is a big issue.
- *Tracking and forecasting.* Treasury monitors and forecasts the company's financial needs.
- *Working capital management.* Treasury has the final responsibility for managing cash flow and making sure cash is available when it's needed.
- *Inventory.* There is always a delicate dance between inventory management, cash, and financing. Many parties in a company need to help the people in treasury manage cash by coordinating their work with inventory management, sales, and production. The goal is always optimization of the relationship between cost of capital and effective inventory levels.
- *Capital budgeting.* Treasury participates in capital decisions. In more mature growth companies it often drives decisions about allocation among the investment opportunities available to the company, frequently balancing its understanding of internal capital resources and financing alternatives with opportunities to invest.

- *Cost of capital, financial structure, and execution.* As companies mature, treasury integrates the multiple threads of operating finances, investment earnings, capital investments, and financing alternatives and resolves a unified plan with management. Once that plan has been resolved, treasury makes sure adequate cash and financing are in place as needed.
- *Cash management, financial accounts, and marketable securities.* Treasury manages investment of the company's cash in short- and longer-term instruments as appropriate, within the financial plan.
- *Investor relations.* As companies grow, often treasury (eventually the CFO) shares with the office of the CEO responsibility for investor relations.

WHAT I KNOW NOW THAT I WISH I HAD KNOWN THEN

Mike Gonnerman, Gonnerman.com

Mike Gonnerman has 42 years' experience as a board director, advisor, financial consultant, CFO, and auditor. He has helped companies deal with issues involving corporate oversight, financial management, financial reporting, forecasting, and financing. His financial tools have been adopted by hundreds of companies, and he speaks frequently on finance and entrepreneurship.

Entrepreneurs generally seem to understand income and expense (I&E) and cash flow statements but not balance sheets. Balance sheets are important. Here's why.

All through my career, hundreds of founders and CEOs have asked questions like how long cash will last, how much money to raise, and what can they do to change the financial picture. The theme always comes down to *cash.* They are really asking about the items that drive cash balances—things such as sales and expenses, how long it takes to invoice and collect receivables, and how effectively you purchase and use inventory and fixed assets, pay vendors, and raise financing. They have all these numbers somewhere, but none of them could pull them together to answer questions about cash. The answers all derive from the balance sheet.

Over the years I developed integrated financial models linking balance sheets, I&E, and cash flow statements for each of these situations. In the models the balance sheets reign supreme. They summarize the current financial position and tie together all of those items that affect near-term cash balances that are not on the income statement. They are the basis for cash forecasts and credit-based lending decisions.

> Because businesses are dynamic, not static, financial models (read, balance sheet forecasts) must be updated monthly for actual amounts from recent activity. The models should be run and revised frequently. Companies short on cash may run them daily. If cash positions are more comfortable, updates monthly, quarterly, or even annually will do.
>
> You won't really have a handle on your financial outlook until you can explain to investors, employees, bankers, customers, and anyone else how your balance sheet will change during the next month, quarter, or year. Understand your current financial situation (balance sheet). Think carefully about your assumptions; it's always tough to predict the future.

A brief overview like this can do little more than give you an idea of the breadth and importance of managing your numbers and your money with discipline and forethought. This is an area where a little knowledge quickly becomes dangerous, and unless you want to make this your lifetime profession, you will never have enough knowledge to stop it from being dangerous. The key takeaway is to get systems in place early and use them. Be sure that at each stage of the company's development the systems, reports, and practices are adequate for your needs. The last thing you want when you are trying to profit and grow is to stumble on gaps in which your scale of operations exceeds your capacity to track and manage effectively.

QUESTIONS

- How much cash do you have on hand today? How do you know?
- What are you doing to manage your money effectively and profitably?
- What controls do you have in place for managing the flow of money properly?

NOTES

1. Bernard John "Bernie" Ebbers is a cofounder and former CEO of the telecommunications company WorldCom. In 2005, he was convicted of fraud and conspiracy for his role in WorldCom's illegally false financial reporting, which led to a $100 billion loss to investors. Until the Madoff scandal of 2008, WorldCom was the largest accounting scandal in U.S. history. Ebbers is serving a 25-year prison term at the Oakdale Federal Correctional Complex in Louisiana. Portfolio.com and CNBC named Ebbers the fifth worst CEO in American history; *Time* named him the tenth most corrupt CEO of all time.

Chapter 20

Correcting Your Course

You can learn from someone else's failure, but the only way to really get your money's worth is to fail yourself.

—Randy Komisar, partner, Kleiner Perkins Caufield & Byers

Business failure is highly underrated. Too many people keep delaying start-ups because they fear they're going to fail. I believe daring to fail is perhaps the hardest obstacle for potential entrepreneurs to overcome.[1]

—Rieva Lesonsky

Rieva Lesonsky is right. Fear of failing is not an obstacle only when one is starting up; it's debilitating at every stage. It can be handicapping, even immobilizing. We live in a culture that celebrates success and perfection and makes everything a competition. It reduces even intangibles such as learning and performing to quantitative grades; only those who get the highest grades are considered worthy. We're constantly organized "for someone else's consumption: universities and employers evaluate young candidates on their grades, numbers based on scores from tests unforgiving to mistakes."[2]

We are conditioned like this so consistently since childhood that it's no wonder everyone presses early-stage businesses for the perfect idea (no such thing), perfect planning and execution on budget (don't exist), on time (never happens), by a great team of superstars who all go the distance (in your dreams!). Entrepreneur wannabes are pressed by others, but often they're pressed by themselves most painfully of all. Even the 22 chapters of this book have tried to lay out all the important things you need to think about to improve your chances and how to go about doing them, as if the only thing required for success is that you do them all and get it right the first time. You can't do them all, and even if you do, there's still no guarantee. No wonder so many people never try.

But there's good news: You don't have to get it right the first time. This next point is perhaps the most important thing you will read in this book. There is virtually no chance you will get it right the first time; hardly anyone else does either. It's a truism in the entrepreneurial world, especially among professional investors and repeat-success entrepreneurs: Almost every start-up team that has succeeded has made at least one major course correction along the way, often more than one.

Intel was founded in 1968 by former Fairchild Semiconductor physicists Gordon Moore and Robert Noyce to make memory products. Almost at once Intel was approached to make a microprocessor chip: in 1970 by Computer Terminal

Corp., a Texas company working on what was arguably the first design for a personal computer (that chip later became the 8008),[3] and again in 1971 by Busicom, a Japanese calculator maker, to work on what became the 4004 processor.[4] People from Computer Terminal Corp. recalled meeting with Robert Noyce in 1970 to suggest "'that Intel develop the chip at its own expense and then sell it to all comers, including CTC. ... 'Noyce said it was an intriguing idea, and that Intel could do it, but it would be a dumb move. ... He said that if you have a computer chip, you can only sell one chip per computer, while with memory, you can sell hundreds of chips per computer.' Nevertheless, Noyce agreed to a $50,000 development contract."[5] For another 15 years Intel focused on memory, but by 1984, 40 percent of its revenue and 100 percent of its profits were coming from microprocessors and it was spending 80 percent of its R&D on memory.[6] It was time for a course correction. Albert Yu, a retired Intel senior vice president, recalled, "Our strategy and investments were completely out of line with reality. ... This was a very difficult option for us to swallow: admitting defeat on something that our corporation had created and was founded on."[7] "We finally overcame the emotional burden of letting go of a failing business that we had invented and focused all our energy on the business we would build our future on. It was tough. It was gut-wrenching. But it was right."[8] A year later, in 1985, Intel reluctantly left the memory business.

In 1975, Paul Allen was working in Albuquerque, New Mexico, as an engineer for Honeywell and Bill Gates was a sophomore at Harvard when they saw an opportunity to create a programming language based on BASIC (developed at Dartmouth) for MITS Computer's Altair 8800 personal computer kits. They launched a product they called "Altair BASIC" under the name "Micro-Soft."[9] They made the famous licensing deal with IBM to create PC-DOS in 1981. "By 1983 Microsoft was facing competition from the just-released VisiOn and the forthcoming TopView. Apple had already released Lisa."[10] They created Windows 1.0 (announced 1983, released 1985), Windows 2.0 (1987), and finally a market success with Windows 3.0 (1990). Microsoft's Web site says, "Many longtime PC users trace the Microsoft Windows operating system to the 1990 release of Windows 3.0, the first widely popular version of Windows and the first version of Windows many PC users ever tried."[11]

Two of the biggest entrepreneurial successes of the last half century were course corrections that turned frustration into success by staying with it and listening to the market. That is true of almost every other successful business, big or small. There is an interesting implication of this nearly universal principle: How in the world can anyone accurately predict the true potential of a start-up idea? It's almost surely not the idea that will make you successful. Some ideas are more promising than others, no doubt, but there's always the course correction that takes you from close to a big success. Intel and Microsoft did it. The good news is that you have the opportunity every day to do it. There is no such thing as the perfect deal, at least not the first time.

Quitting after the first try may be smart (fail fast), or it may be lack of perseverance. Course correction inevitably means perseverance. Of course, perseverance can be a virtue or a curse. At any specific time, how do you know which is which? You don't. That's what course corrections are for. You don't have to get it right the first time. What you do need to do is get in the neighborhood of a valuable opportunity and then know enough to recognize it when you see it. Smart entrepreneurs position themselves for the course corrections that inevitably come. They look for them and try to make them as quickly, cheaply, and wisely as possible.

IS SOMETHING WRONG?

You can't solve a problem you haven't recognized. Will you know if there is a problem? Sometimes it seems that nothing is coming together and it's clear as day that something is wrong: For example, Intel making all its money on processors and focusing most of its attention on memory. When problems are clear, you don't need a lot of clues to make you think about things. Things can get off track in all kinds of places. Maybe you have the need defined correctly and the product is wrong. Maybe it's the plan, the team, or the execution. Constantly look for obvious problems. Ask lots of questions. If there's no need or market, sometimes you can switch to others. Most execution problems can be fixed once they're identified clearly, but you have to look.

It may be the wrong product. In 2007 Dartmouth engineering doctoral student Ashifi Gogo had the idea to certify organic produce grown in Africa and marketed in Western Europe, tagging products with unique identifier bar codes that could trace products back to the farm of origin. He won lots of attention and prizes in international competitions with the idea, but within a year he realized he had missed the window of opportunity in the organic produce market and didn't know how he could make money with the system. Looking at other problems in his home country of Ghana, he recognized there was a huge public health problem in the $75 billion market for fake medication: counterfeit drugs that have few or no active ingredients, often contain dangerous chemicals, and are responsible for hundreds of thousands of deaths in the developing world each year.

Ashifi thought he could leverage the widespread use of cell phones in Africa, enabling consumers to confirm the authenticity of a drug with a simple text message. His new company, Sproxil, guarantees the authenticity of safe drugs while helping genuine pharmaceutical manufacturers reclaim market share lost to counterfeiters. Ashifi bootstrapped Sproxil with $100,000 of his own money, funds from friends, and grants, including $10,000 from the Clinton Foundation. In January 2010, Sproxil won a $100,000 award from the Washington, D.C.–based African Diaspora Marketplace, a not-for-profit organization sponsored by USAID and Western Union that provides grants to African-American entrepreneurs who create jobs in Africa. By the start of 2011 Sproxil had 12 staff members in Somerville, MA, and Lagos, Nigeria, and in March 2001 closed a $1.8 million venture funding round.

It may happen that the market fails. John Bello, Tuck School class of 1972, launched the South Beach Beverage Company, Inc., in December 1995, marketing upscale noncarbonated soft drinks with an Art Deco Miami motif. Within the year South Beach flopped. John reconceived the company around health benefits and launched again in December 1996 with SoBe Black Tea 3G, "a reference to ginseng, ginkgo, and guarana, herbal derivatives that purportedly improved concentration, endurance, and energy."[12] The product was an immediate hit. Bello quickly expanded to a line of exotic teas, fruit juices and blends, elixirs, vitamin- and antioxidant-enhanced water, and sports drinks and added a strategy focused on extreme sports and irreverent promotion. In the darkest hours of 1996 his shareholders doubled down on their investment and John invested almost everything he had, including his house. In all, he had about $9.5 million invested. In 2001 PepsiCo bought 90 percent of SoBe for $370 million.

It may be the wrong model. In 1999, Drs. Leslie Fall and Norman Berman were practicing pediatricians and codirectors of the pediatrics clerkship at Dartmouth Medical School. Frustrated with an outdated paper-based case study platform, they decided there had to be a better way to take third-year medical students through the required pediatrics curriculum. The system was fragmented, inefficient, and frustrating for instructors and students. Drs. Fall and Berman secured a two-phase $885,000 grant from the National Institutes of Health (NIH); signed up the best academic pediatricians in the country to write top-quality cases; found a small IT shop in Munich, Germany; and created CLIPP, an online system that made it possible for students around the country to work the highest-quality cases online, with follow-up tracking and instruction.

Within three years, more than half of all the medical schools in the country were using the CLIPP system to do pediatric case study work. The results improved. Schools across the country got onto a uniform system and collaborated. The only problem was that they built CLIPP with grant support. When the grant money ran out, Fall and Berman faced the real possibility that all their success would be lost for lack of resources to keep the project going. As MDs, they realized they had no idea what to do with their organization or how to do it. All they knew was that it filled a need, people loved it, and they didn't want it to die. Rather than give up, they found help at Dartmouth College and turned CLIPP into a not-for-profit corporation, iInTIME. They created a going concern, built a commercial-grade product, hired staff, persuaded accrediting boards to recommend CLIPP, persuaded medical schools to pay for the product, expanded the offerings to cover family and internal medicine, and built a fully operational start-up company with a stellar board, six full-time staff members, and editorial boards made up of 25 part-time medical educators. Today more than 80 percent of all medical students in the United States are doing casework on iInTIME systems, and the company is expanding into broader medical education, including the interfaces between cultural, legal, ethical, and practice management issues and medical practice. They are exploring ways to make the system available in the developing world to bring state-of-the-art medical education to doctors struggling to get adequate education in their home countries.

IS SOMETHING MISSING?

What about if things are not going as well as they could? Before Windows, Microsoft tried any number of other approaches: menus at the bottom of the screen, pull down menus, and dialogues.[13] Maybe your definition of the need is slightly off or you have the right need for the wrong customer. Would you know?

Getting it *almost* right happens often. Sales aren't happening and calls don't quite jell, but it's not clear why. Tally Systems Corp, a Dartmouth IT spinout, was founded in 1990 to create a complete line of IT system management tools. Tom Cecere, a former vice president of marketing and business development, recalls that when they first took their line to the market, in one sales meeting after another he and the CEO would get a quizzical look from potential customers: "They would say, 'Yeah, it's all nice ... but could we just have that one piece there?'" That one piece was a utility to tell IT managers what was running on their systems and who was running it, something no one could do at that time. It had become a serious problem with the proliferation of networked desktop machines. Cecere said, "After about the tenth time we heard that, as we were getting in the elevator to leave, the CEO said to me, 'Do you think they're trying to tell us something?'"[14] They went back and built out that component, and with it Tally launched a business that ended up a "leading supplier of full-featured asset management products" until it was sold to Novell Corp. in 2005.[15]

Many of the most valuable course corrections happen when you meaningfully interact with your market the way Tally did. As part of a research project, Saras D. Sarasvathy at the University of Virginia interviewed 30 founders of highly successful companies. She quotes one entrepreneur, who said that

> instead of asking all the questions I'd go and say ... try to make some sale. I'd make some ... just judgments about where I was going—get me and my buddies—or I would go out and start selling. I'd learn a lot you know ... which people ... what were the obstacles ... what were the questions ... which prices work better and just do it. Just try to take it out and sell it.[16]

Occasionally the lab or the shop can help correct something in your product or its development, but most of the time course corrections happen when your customers begin telling you what they really need. This is why we devoted a whole chapter to validating the market and talking to customers. That chapter talked about doing it prospectively, before you invested a lot in getting started. Chapter 16 talked about doing it as you try to make sales. The conversation never ends. Customers will always tell you valuable things, but most of the time only if you ask. The more you ask, the more they will tell you. "No" is an important answer from a customer.

"Not quite" is even more important. The most important questions you can ever ask are the ones you come up with after hearing one of those two answers. Never stop asking customers about what you're doing wrong or what you might do better.

WHAT TO DO?

Remember, an entrepreneur focuses most on opportunity, not on process or control. Control is about taming the environment and circumstances to protect oneself from risk. The environment and circumstances can be problematic, but they are not the real threat. The real threat is not finding opportunity, and it's always tragic when this happens, because opportunity is everywhere. The entrepreneur doesn't stop thinking about opportunity and looking for it once the launch is under way. Stop thinking about opportunity and you change from an entrepreneur to an administrator, someone with the trustee mentality we talked about in Chapter 1. Course correction thinking means focusing even more deliberately and relentlessly on opportunities *after* you launch and being as ready to pounce as you were before you started.

Psychology researchers studying entrepreneurs talk about entrepreneurship as an *enactment process* in which acting precedes thinking.[17,18] In Chapter 6 we talked about Saras Sarasvathy's *causal* and *effectual reasoning*. Causal reasoning begins with a predetermined goal, and a specified set of means is used to determine the optimal alternative to achieve the goal. We're taught causal reasoning all our lives, virtually everywhere, especially in business schools. Here's what Sarasvathy says about this:

> *Effectual reasoning, by contrast, does not begin with a specific goal. Instead, it begins with a given set of means and allows goals to emerge contingently over time from the varied imagination and diverse aspirations of the founders and people with whom they interact ... effectual thinkers are like explorers setting out on voyages into uncharted waters (Columbus discovering the new world).*[19]

It's interesting that Sarasvathy chose Christopher Columbus as an example of an effectual innovator. Columbus's story is all about course corrections. Remember your history? He was one of the best navigators and sailing captains of his time. He had a well-defined plan. It took him a while, but he got good financing and a great deal: the title of Admiral of the Ocean Sea, viceroy of all the lands he found, a 10 percent perpetual royalty on the revenue from all those lands, and a one-eighth buy-in option into all future ventures in those lands. It just turned out that his plan was a little off. He calculated the circumference of the earth at 19,000 miles (it's 24,901 miles) and overestimated the size of Asia, giving him a sailing distance to Asia of 2,400 miles, just about the range of a sailing vessel at that time (it's more like 12,000 miles). Only by sheer luck did he find something even more valuable where he thought Asia would be. He changed the plan to meet the opportunity and became the first governor of Hispaniola, the first colony in the New World. He was on his way to riches when he and his brother blew it with their mismanagement of the colony. Worse, he later made a disastrous fourth voyage to Central America in which he missed discovering the Pacific Ocean by mere miles, ending with mutiny and arrest. He returned to Spain in disgrace and died in poverty, forgotten for generations. Sometimes even course corrections can't save you from yourself.

In Sarasvathy's model of effectual reasoning, life becomes essentially a never-ending course correction:

> *Plans are made and unmade and revised and recast through action and inter-action with others on a daily basis. Yet at any given moment, there is always a meaningful picture that keeps the team together, a compelling story that brings in more stakeholders and a continuing journey that maps out uncharted territories. Through their actions, the effectual entrepreneurs' set of means and consequently, the set of possible effects changes and gets reconfig-ured. Eventually, certain emerging effects coalesce into clearly achievable and desirable goals—landmarks that point to a discernible path beginning to emerge in the wilderness.*[20]

Causal reasoning is not course correcting. It's analytical, rational, and conceptual. In its essence, effectual reasoning is course correcting. Sarasvathy defines three important contrasts:

- Causal reasoning focuses on expected return. Effectual reasoning emphasizes affordable loss.
- Causal reasoning depends upon competitive analyses. Effectual reasoning is built on strategic relationships.
- Causal reasoning urges the exploitation of preexisting knowledge and prediction. Effectual reasoning leverages contingencies.[21]

When you launch, even if you think you are carrying out a well-defined plan, you are in reality embarking on an exercise in turning the unexpected into the profitable.[22] It's ready-fire-aim, and fire-aim, fire-aim, fire.

The best course-correcting culture discourages overchampioning any single idea. Remember the definition of insanity: repeating the same action over and over, expecting a different result. There is always more than one solution. Don't anchor on things previously resolved. It may not be the product that's off target. It could be anything: the market, the value proposition, the business model, even the need. Course correcting works best when you have an environment that consistently encourages consideration of multiple alternatives, even alternatives to things already in execution (remember Intel!). Diversion of effort and lack of focus are always a danger, but so is the kind of myopia that misses opportunities to change direction such as the ones we've discussed in this chapter. The fact that you're always looking and considering doesn't mean you have to follow every lead and opportunity.

Instead, evaluate alternatives objectively and look for the best long-term opportunities. Never get hung up on past costs.[23] You can't recover past costs by spending more money on a failing idea. Getting good at course correcting means getting comfortable with small failures. It means having leaders who create an environment that is safe for taking risks and who share stories of their own mistakes. People may fear failure, but they fear the consequences of failure even more. Breakthrough innovation and success require that well-honed organizations do what feels unnatural: explore, experiment, foul up sometimes. Then repeat. Most people naturally seek positive outcomes and set about trying to prove that an experiment works. But in their everyday professions, designers, inventors, and scientists—all models for companies struggling to be more creative—take the opposite tack. They try to prove themselves wrong. A focus on potential flaws makes failure and the lessons that come with it happen earlier—and cheaper.[24]

WHAT I KNOW NOW THAT I WISH I HAD KNOWN THEN

Jason Freedman, FlightCaster

Jason Freedman is the cofounder of FlightCaster, which provides intelligent travel tools, including flight delay prediction, fare prediction, and day-of-travel solutions (www.flightcaster.com). Previously, Jason cofounded Openvote Inc., a Web site and Facebook application that allowed users to create polls for their community, vote, and see what everyone thought. Before Openvote, Jason was a product manager for Mocospace, a mobile phone–based social networking start-up funded by General Catalyst Partners.

In 2009, I was working on my second company, FlightCaster. We spent the first 12 months of our company's life building a product that predicts flight delays. It was an awesome product featuring advanced machine learning algorithms. We gave up our jobs, recruited employees, and raised venture money based on the vision that our technology would disrupt the way airlines communicated with passengers.

We met with everyone in the travel industry to pitch our product. We finally convinced some household names to distribute our product on a trial basis. Millions of users would be exposed to our flight delay prediction technology. If they liked it, we would sign them on for long-term, revenue-generating deals.

For months we had been working to reduce our error rate. No one could tell immediately, but our error rate was too high, and I knew people would lose trust in us over time if it didn't come down. Each month, our engineers told me that we were one month away from fixing it. I lost faith it would ever happen. If we signed those distribution deals, we would spend the next six months and the last of our money supporting a product that promised more than it delivered.

And so we killed it. We turned down the distribution deals, informed our investors, and stopped all further development. It was a very tense time. Not everyone agreed with the decision. Investors were furious. We had to let people go. I knew it was important to be decisive, but that didn't make it any less reassuring, especially since we had no plan B.

But we still had 40 percent of our money in the bank. We went to the whiteboard and brainstormed brand-new product ideas. We set up meetings with the top players in the industry and spent six weeks talking to people face-to-face in 10 different cities.

We emerged with a pivot. We found a new problem in the industry that we were uniquely qualified to solve. It was a massive problem, far bigger than flight delays. We got to work on it immediately and, in doing so, have created far more lucrative opportunities. We've rehired everyone back, and our investors want to put more money in the company. Of course, I can't yet say if we'll make it, but I know with certainty that killing our product was the best decision I could make.

Mistakes and failure are a part of the process, not just at the end when you shut down a failure. They're there all along the way, pointing you back toward opportunity. Rosabeth Moss Kanter perhaps said it best: "The middle of every successful project looks like a disaster." Take comfort: The darkest hour may mean you are on your way to success. It's the course correction that will get you there.

QUESTIONS

- How can you put in place a culture that is always actively questioning the current plan but still is committed to carrying it out effectively until decided otherwise?
- Would you know if you should change course? How?
- If you had to change course, how would you approach the decision and get buy-in from all the affected stakeholders?

NOTES

1. Lesonsky, Rieva, *Start Your Own Business* (Irvine, CA: Entrepreneur Press, 2007): 648.
2. Berkun, Scott, "How to Learn from Your Mistakes," blog no. 44, July 17, 2005, http://www.scottberkun.com/essays/44-how-to-learn-from-your-mistakes/ (accessed September 11, 2010).
3. Wood, Lamont, "Forgotten PC History: The True Origins of the Personal Computer," *Computerworld*, August 8, 2008, http://www.computerworld .com/s/article/print/9111341/Forgotten_PC_history_The_true_origins_of_t he_personal_computer (accessed September 11, 2010).

4. Anthes, Gary, "Happy Birthday, x86! An Industry Standard Turns 30," *Computerworld*, June 5, 2008, http://www.computerworld.com/s/ article/print/9090978/Happy_birthday_x86_An_industry_standard_turns_30?taxonomy Name=Hardware&taxonomyId=12 (accessed September 11, 2010).
5. Wood, 2008.
6. Yu, Albert, *Creating the Digital Future: The Secrets of Consistent Innovation at Intel* (New York: Free Press, 1998): 124.
7. Ibid.
8. Ibid.: 130.
9. Microsoft Web site, "Microsoft Fast Facts: 1975," http://www.microsoft.com/presspass/features/2000/sept00/09–0525bookff75.mspx (accessed September 11, 2010).
10. Alfred, Randy, "Gates Opens Windows a Bit Early," November 10, 1983, http://www.wired.com/science/discoveries/news/2008/11/dayintech_1110 (accessed September 11, 2010).
11. "Windows Desktop Products History," March 7, 2006, http://www.microsoft.com/windows/winhistorydesktop.mspx (accessed September 11, 2010).
12. "South Beach Beverage Company, Inc.," in *Reference for Business—Encyclopedia of Business*, 2d ed., http://www.referenceforbusiness.com/history/Sh-St/South-Beach-Beverage-Company-Inc.html (accessed September 11, 2010).
13. Alfred, 1983.
14. Dartmouth Entrepreneurial Network workshop, October 2, 2002.
15. "Tally Systems Acquires Baran of Software, Forming Messaging Management Powerhouse," *Business Wire*, October 21 1997, http://www.allbusiness.com/company-activities-management/company-structures-ownership/7016323–1.html (accessed September 11, 2010).
16. Sarasvathy, Saras D., "What Makes Entrepreneurs Entrepreneurial?" Darden Case Collection ENT–0065 (2004): 4–5.
17. Busenitz, Lowell W., and Jay B. Barney, "Differences between Entrepreneurs and Managers in Large Organizations: Biases and Heuristics in Strategic Decision-Making," *Journal of Business Venturing* 12, issue 1 (1997): 9–30.
18. Gartner, William B., Barbara Bird, and Jennifer A. Starr, "Acting as If: Differentiating Entrepreneurial from Organizational Behavior," *Entrepreneurship: Theory & Practice* 16, issue 3 (Spring 1992): 13–31.
19. Sarasvathy, 2004: 2.
20. Ibid.: 3.
21. Ibid.: 4.
22. Ibid.: 5.
23. Thurm, Scott, "Reconsidering," *Wall Street Journal*, February 6, 2006: B3.
24. McGregor, Jena, William C. Symonds, Dean Foust, Diane Brady, and Moira Herbst, "How Failure Breeds Success," *BusinessWeek*, issue 3992 (July 10, 2006): 4252.

Chapter 21

Growing

Without continual growth and progress, such words as improvement, achievement, and success have no meaning.

—Benjamin Franklin

If you think that attempting to cover business law or accounting in a single chapter is trying to do a lot with a little, imagine doing it for the management and growth of a successful business. A whole business library at a place like Dartmouth has only the smallest fraction of the existing knowledge and literature, yet if you want to make a vibrant, valuable enterprise out of your start-up, you need to learn this. There are not many alternatives: maintain a small company that provides you and your team a nice living—a so-called lifestyle company, because it supports a particular lifestyle—or sell the company early for whatever it will bring.

Managing growth differs from conceiving and launching. It involves not only new challenges but a different experience and requires a different mind-set. Starting a company is obstetrics; growth is pediatrics. In this book we've focused on conceptualizing and launching a business to the point where the business is viable and capable of growing. In one sense, once you're established, the start-up job is done. But remember that *how* you launch often has a profound effect on your chances of surviving and growing the enterprise to its full potential. Many things you do in those early stages set up or foreclose opportunities in foreseeable ways. From the start, be growth-oriented and plan for growth. The thoughts that follow may help frame your expectations about that postlaunch future, sharpen your sense of the possibilities and the challenges, help you imagine what you may see when you get there, and give you options for what you can do about it.

THE CHALLENGE

Almost 50 years ago the sociologist Arthur L. Stinchcombe compared outcomes for older, established organizations and new ones. He found significantly higher rates of failure in new organizations. He proposed the term *liability of newness* for this phenomenon. He wrote: "New organizations, especially new types of organizations, generally involve new roles, which have to be learned; … the process of inventing new roles, the determination of their mutual relations and of structuring the field of rewards and sanctions so as to get the maximum performance, have high costs in time, worry, conflict, and temporary inefficiency."[1] The new enterprise has to learn or invent new roles, processes, and tasks, all of which can be costly diversions from pressures of operations and selling. The new company lacks a track record with outside buyers and suppliers.

These are significant challenges for a new enterprise. The liability of newness has been studied extensively, and not surprisingly, a number of researchers have confirmed that failure rates roughly track the age of an organization—the older the organizations, the lower their rates of failure.[2] Looking more carefully, it turns out there is a large range in the outcomes of survival and success.[3] One of the drivers of success is leadership: leaders who "can and do influence the performance of firms, particularly young and small ones."[4]

If you launch successfully, it seems the liability you face is not being new but having to grow up. Not surprisingly, this has been studied too. When you look more carefully you see an important stage that comes after first growth. A term for this phase has been proposed: the *liability of adolescence*. Here the challenges shift from honing an idea, devising an executable strategy, securing resources to launch, and proving the viability of the idea making sales to customers, and setting up operational and managerial functions.[5]

In one sense, this sounds like the same survivability problems Stinchcombe identified, but we miss an important point by thinking that the risk of failure is highest at launch and declines steeply afterward. This leads to a sense of complacency, a feeling that if you launch successfully and prove your idea in the marketplace, it will get easier from there—the risk will go down. In fact, the liability of adolescence highlights a crucial point: The risk curve is U-shaped. Mortality risks actually peak between 1 and 15 years after a successful launch: "In an early phase, referred to as adolescence, death risks are low, because decision makers are monitoring performance, postponing judgment about success or failure. Meanwhile, organizations often live on a stock of initial resources. In a later phase, initial monitoring has ended and organizations are subject to the usual risks of failure."[6] In other words, the risk *goes up* after a successful launch:

> instead of being a time for entrepreneurial celebration and relief, a period of over 50% growth is a time for wariness and some very difficult decisions. Such firms face a fragile transition: they are beyond being intimate, cohesive entrepreneurial ventures, but they have not yet become secure, stable entities. Not only are they in flux, but these firms are often disoriented by the pace at which change is occurring.[7]

This is less appreciated by most entrepreneurs than it should be. When you assume that your risks are dropping when in fact they are increasing, you find yourself lulled into misplaced complacency. Worse, you start to focus on solving the wrong problems. The implication: If you have been worrying about launching successfully and now you've actually cheated fate and done it, this is the time to start really worrying. Not only do you have new things to worry about, there are more of them. The skills and mind-set that got you this far probably are not going to be useful for addressing what's next. The challenges are no longer about proving the market and increasing sales. They have shifted to learning how to build a viable, efficient organization—in short, not just a proving machine but a going concern. Further, the focus shifts from how to launch and whether to pursue to whether to grow and how to do it.

GROWTH

Growth alone does not necessarily guarantee rich enterprise value, but the two tend to go together. Profitability is important too, but acquirers generally pay most aggressively for growth. Static earnings bring poor multiples on cash flow. Growth actually promotes viability: "An enterprise that is self-sustaining can enter a virtuous cycle: expectations of longevity attract customers and other resources that further consolidate [a company's] position and open new opportunities."[8]

Generating consistent growth is not easy, and growing brings a raft of challenges and problems. However, not growing often brings risks of its own: losing competitiveness, failing to innovate, eventually being forgotten in the market. Always maintain the search for new opportunities and competitive advantages, but at the same time be vigilant that you and your company do not lose focus. Yes, entrepreneurship is the pursuit of opportunity without regard to the resources available and no doubt it's opportunistic skill that got you this far, but chasing too many opportunities can be just as fatal as not seeking enough. "Left untended, growth will eventually overwhelm an organization."[9]

How do you grow in a healthy way? Often entrepreneurs prioritize building sales revenue over preserving profitability. The idea is that conquering market share is more important and the company can be concerned with profitability later. Venture investors like to see their companies invest heavily in building sales volumes and revenue and shift to a few quarters of profitability just before going public. In the crazy Internet boom years, even the shift to profitability was forgotten, with mostly disastrous results for investors and companies.

When successful growth drivers are studied, it turns out that profitability is a better focus if your goal is long-term survival and ultimate enterprise value. In other words, growth for its own sake, at the expense of profitability, usually doesn't work out well. Researchers at the Queensland University of Technology in South Brisbane, Australia, studied 3,500 small businesses over time, looking at the relationship between profit or growth orientation and successful growth. They found that "for both young and old firms a focus on achieving above-average profitability and then striving for growth is a more likely path toward achieving sustained above-average performance than is first pursuing strong growth in the hope of building profitability later."[10]

Managing growth means focusing on two dimensions simultaneously: external and internal. *Externally*, the focus is on market forces, customer segments (are there more?), innovations, rivals and substitutes, resources, and suppliers. Often the markets that launch a company are too small to sustain growth. Remember

Moore's early adopters and majority markets. There are almost always more market segments to go after once an initial segment has been proved. Suppliers and vendors, especially outsourced manufacturing and services, may have to be changed to meet increased volumes. Competitors who ignored you on launch probably will take you seriously now, confronting you with new challenges, forcing you to focus on substitution, potential intellectual property infringements, switching cost issues, and stresses in the market. Brand building becomes important. Access to additional capital and resources becomes an issue at a new level of volume and, often, complexity.[11]

Internally, the people, the structures, and even the culture that got you this far often are not adequate for the next stages. What internal management processes will you need to change and build now? Most likely, you will conclude that the answer is almost everything and all at once. How can all this change be reduced to defined execution plans that can be structured and coordinated? Who will do the work? We'll discuss this further in a later section.

Dealing with accelerating growth (early) and dealing with slowing growth (later) pose different problems calling for different responses and often different people. Perhaps most challenging and alarming, who you are and what you are good at may become one of the biggest issues of all.

YOUR CHOICES: WHO ARE YOU?

If you have launched and are growing, your focuses and challenges will change dramatically, not least with respect to yourself—your sense of who you are and where you fit in the organization. No doubt you brought important entrepreneurial skills needed to launch and grow: boundless optimism and self-confidence, opportunism, flexibility and agility, a willingness to do anything and everything that had to be done at any given moment. As the enterprise grows, however, new skills and operating behaviors will be needed: delegation, cost control, efficiency in operations, people management skills. Whereas once you had to be on top of everything—perhaps to the point where nothing material could happen without you—as you grow, you'll find that you can manage less and less hands-on (see Figure 21-1):

> *In seeking higher growth entrepreneurs will need to rely on capable managers—leadership teams with entrepreneurs in more specialized roles suited to their expertise and interests (marketing, technology). ... To pursue growth they must delegate responsibilities to others, work as a member of an effective leadership team, and in some cases, step aside and let others make key decisions.*[12]

If the company is going to grow, the founders have only three options: grow with it and build their leadership skills, bring in experienced leadership and take an alternative position, or leave the company. The pace of growth affects the nature of management skills you need (Table 21-1).[13]

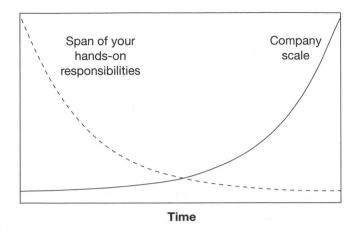

Figure 21-1 As the company grows, the founding CEO's role shifts from hands-on to managing the work of others.

Table 21-1 Growth Considerations at Three Levels

	Low Growth	Moderate Growth	High Growth
Type of Business	Local, lifestyle	Regional or focused business	Knowledge-based in high-potential industry
Organization	Basic systems emphasizing efficiency. Reporting to entrepreneur.	Delegating responsibility areas. Budgets and control systems.	Sophisticated control systems. Formal management practices. Decentralized management.
Leadership	Founder	Founder with managers	Professional management
Strategy	Anticipate and adjust to changes in external environment.	Focused on exploiting and renewing source of differentiation, recognizing new difficulties.	Portfolio of investments ranging from extending current advantage to exploring potential breakthroughs.
Resources	Retained earnings, credit cards; loans from family, friends, and local banks.	Asset-based lending, equity (angels).	Equity: angel, venture capital, investment banks, with exit strategy (sale, IPO)

The entrepreneur has vision and creates companies out of opportunities. The manager is an organizer and a planner. The entrepreneurial leader blends the two, working at a high level to ensure that culture, systems, and operations maintain an opportunity-driven corporate personality while protecting competitive advantage and maintaining profitability.[14]

The roles of entrepreneurs, managers, and leaders are detailed in the list that follows.

Entrepreneurs

- Locate new ideas.
- Establish and implement a vision.
- Build whatever organization they can to pursue the opportunity.
- Lead and inspire.

Managers

- Maintain operations.
- Plan.
- Organize.
- Staff and control.
- Enhance efficiency.
- Supervise and monitor.
- Maintain consistency and predictability.

Leaders

- Maintain core businesses while exploring new opportunities.
- Establish a vision and empower others to carry it out, ensuring accountability.
- Maintain culture, structure, and systems.
- Remove barriers.
- Develop people and groups.
- Orchestrate change.

Delegation does not come easily to many entrepreneurs even if it does free up their time and energy to focus on what is important, not merely what is urgent. Delegation means organizing people and turning them loose to carry out objectives. It does not mean controlling them closely, doing their thinking for them, or, worse, doing everything important oneself. Admittedly, delegation often starts as assigning specific tasks, but eventually it means assigning problems, not procedures, and letting people work out solutions for themselves, even if at first the solutions seem less effective than the ones you would have come up with yourself. This is part of developing people, not just developing controls and systems. It means letting people make mistakes and learn from them, something not every manager or employee can embrace.

Not every entrepreneur can make the transition through these roles. When this is the case, the question becomes whether the entrepreneur can give the company freedom to make the transition or will hold the company to the pace of growth he or she can manage personally. At a distance, the choice of prioritizing company growth or personal control seems a dispassionate one, a choice that seems should not be either-or. In the heat of the moment, though, it is not nearly so cut and dry, and that is why the heat of the moment is not the time to think about it. Many entrepreneurs fail to think about these things at the beginning: who they are, what they are capable of, and what they really want. Then, when the time comes and circumstances demand that they share control so that the company can grow, they find themselves unable or unwilling to do it.

This issue has been studied, and the findings are clear: Few founders can take a company the distance if growing to the full potential of the idea is the goal. In the late 1990s and early 2000s Noam Wasserman at the Harvard Business School studied 212 companies, looking at the question of success versus how much control the founding CEOs maintained.[15] "By the time the ventures were three years old, 50% of founders were no longer the CEO; in year four, only 40% were still in the corner office; and fewer than 25% led their companies' initial public offerings." Four out five were forced out by investors. Wasserman concluded, "The manner in which founders tackle their first leadership transition often makes or breaks young enterprises."[16]

STRUCTURE, POLICIES, AND PROCEDURES

The transition to structure, policies, and procedures is often a hard one, and not everyone on early-stage teams makes it. As an early-stage enterprise moves from the chaos of the launch to the discipline of structures and systems, it is necessary to think about some of the wide areas of activity that need structures, processes, and people to manage all the mushrooming detail. Administration and operations expand with growth in the following areas:

- Cash management
- Transaction processing
- Payroll processing
- Time and expense reports
- Benefits plans and administration
- Accounting and reporting
- Inventory planning, systems, and controls
- Fixed assets management
- Insurance

- Equity/incentive compensation plans
- Office operations
- Board and investor relations
- Tax accounting processing
- Information technology infrastructure
- Legal
- Regulatory compliance

Executive teams must recognize when it is time to put procedures and policies in place to create what Peter Drucker calls "purposeful innovation" or "entrepreneurial management."[17] However, putting structures and procedures in place requires employees to adjust, to change their habits. Adjustment almost always creates issues, but management practices can help in this area.

Michael J. Roberts of the Harvard Business School has a helpful hierarchy for thinking about this transition:[18]

1. Doing it yourself.
2. Managing the behavior of others.
3. Managing just the results (setting goals, measuring results) and letting people work out how to get there.
4. Managing *context*—the people, mission, values, culture, and direction.

The primary concerns are as follows:[19]

- Recruiting and hiring good people to build a professional team, especially managers (this was covered in Chapter 10).
- Coordinating among a growing array of independent work groups and departments.
- Balancing profit and growth.
- Creating controls and systems (especially performance assessment reporting and management; this was covered in Chapter 19).
- Defining structure, policies, and lines of reporting.
- Creating reporting systems and using them to manage larger groups of people.
- Defining operating procedures and authorities.
- Defining policies to ensure proper compliance and operations.
- Creating and perpetuating culture.
- Gathering intelligence and information: Where will input come from? Scanning the environment is critical, for example, getting ahead of changes in the environment or business cycle such as recessions and high-growth periods.
- Budgeting, controlling costs, and making efficient use of capital and human resources.

- Launching new initiatives to maintain competitive advantage.
- Managing an expanding universe of stakeholders: customers, vendors and suppliers, boards, investors, owners, employees, community.

While doing this, it is necessary to maintain the entrepreneurial culture that created your success in the first place. This is hardly easy.

CORPORATE CULTURE

Corporate culture is one of those buzzwords that can be used to mean so much that it ends up meaning little or nothing. Still, it's a critical concept. At its most basic, it refers to the way the people in a company think, act, and relate to one another. It includes values, practices, presumptions and accepted knowledge, ethical frameworks, and even basic behaviors and protocols. You probably won't be surprised to hear that emotions are a key factor in corporate culture and that culture is fundamentally influenced by founders and leaders. Daniel Goleman has written a number of books on emotional intelligence and corporate culture.[20] Corporate culture always exists, whether it is deliberately fostered or happens on its own, and it generally reflects the individual culture, values, and personality of the leaders. It can be transformed, but leadership has to do it.

Here is the issue: Making the transition from launch to growth means that the culture has to change. In the early days of the venture, company culture is a natural outgrowth of the core people: a set of assumptions and shared values, a work style and ethic. A good culture is critically important as a performance driver and, in a start-up, helps foster creativity, diligence, and a sense of ownership in the founders and employees. However, the very traits that often make the difference between success and failure—freewheeling innovation, high flexibility so that anyone can pitch in to do almost anything, fluid structure, moving fast without lots of controls and reporting—all can be fatal to more complex and high-volume operations. The transition to growth requires that you preserve the optimism, creativity, and faith in your products that made the launch successful while at the same time settling into more managing, structuring, and results-focused reporting. Developing a persistent corporate culture and, more important, preserving it and disseminating it across a larger and more diverse group of people becomes increasingly complex and difficult. But it is increasingly important as the head count and scope of operations grow, because the founders no longer can reinforce all those things in one-on-one interactions. Company performance and the ability to attract and motivate the best people depend on a vibrant and positive culture.

Many people who are attracted to the start-up world love the atmosphere, the lack of structure and rigidity, and the chance to improvise and be creative. The unrealistic ones believe it can always be that way, but you can't avoid the challenges to culture that growth brings. A smart founding team faces up to this reality from the very beginning and goes into the start-up with full acceptance of the fact that the fun, freewheeling stage eventually will end and that making a transition to more structure and less improvisation is a sign of success, not failure. When expectations on this point are more realistic, the transition can come sooner and more smoothly, and the company can remain a fulfilling—if different—place for the team members who made it possible in the first place.

REMEMBER: PEOPLE NEEDS CHANGE OVER TIME

Eventually almost every successful company grows to the point where it needs a professional management team and becomes less and less a place for people who love the early stage. Experienced start-up entrepreneur types have been through this enough times to know that it is natural and inevitable. Generally they make the cultural transition or move on gracefully when the structure gets to be too much for their taste. For others it may not be so seamless. With this in mind, from the beginning you should create a fluid system that keeps the team and the corporate structure stable while members join and leave. Among other things, this means good vesting policies and clear work or employee agreements with team members. Most of all, it means managing expectations from the very beginning so that the changes surprise no one. If you do it correctly, changes will be seen as a positive, not a tragedy in which something good and beautiful was ruined by success.

Overhead is costly. Having too many people around weakens a culture of efficiency and productivity. It's tempting to hire too quickly as growth takes off. No doubt you have to grow to meet the demands of an expanding business, but take care not to build expensive staffing levels that may be difficult and costly to shed if times change and you find you have overrun your needs. It's never easy to downsize a company for the people whose lives are disrupted and for the company that's left behind. When you can, define what you think is the *base load* need for people—the level of staffing you need to handle workloads near the low end of the range—and outsource to fill the greater needs that happen only occasionally in peak periods.

Motivating, retaining, and developing employees are critical to the success of a company. In the early days you won't have much time to think about this and not many employees to make you worry about it. When growth demands that you expand the employee pool, you should plan to shift increasing amounts of your time to recruiting and hiring good people (Chapter 10) and then think about how to get the most from them. This is often a jarring transition for founder-leaders. You must decide to what extent you want to promote from within or hire from the outside. You should invest in helping existing employees with education, training, and systematic advancement. This is a great motivator and an effective recruiting tool, but it can be costly and time-consuming. It often takes more time than you have to get the talent levels you need, and frequently people don't develop the way you would like. Hiring from the outside can bring experience in-house, but often this creates hiccups around corporate culture and fit or disruption caused by misjudgments in hiring. Bringing in unknowns from the outside always carries a measure of uncertainty that you don't have with existing employees you already know, though uncertainty means newcomers can be better than you expect or worse. There is no right answer. In any case, always plan on spending at least some HR dollars on education and training both as an employee benefit and to build more value into your people. Over time, decisions will have to move closer to the action through decentralization, but people need to be prepared for this. That's the job of a good training and education program.

Early in your growth bring in a professional experienced in both of the main areas of HR and in working in an early-stage, growing company. This person will help you with recruiting; with the policies, procedures, and structure; and with ongoing programs to incentivize and develop employees.

Motivating people is the last issue we will mention here. How you do it will change as you grow, of course, but it should be part of the corporate culture from day one. Motivation starts with what researchers and consultants call *employee engagement*. Employee engagement generally is seen as a combination of emotional commitment, attachment, and behavior that leads to a heightened effort on the company's behalf. Consultants and researchers look at how people feel connected to their jobs, how satisfied they are, how hard they choose to work, especially how far to push in going the "extra mile," and how likely they are to stay with the company (retention). Good employee engagement is linked to good outcomes. "There is clear and mounting evidence that employee engagement is correlated to a number of individual, group, and corporate performance outcomes including recruiting, retention, turnover, individual productivity, customer service, customer loyalty, growth in operating margins, increased profit margins, even revenue growth rates."[21] Engagement correlates strikingly with job performance as rated by supervisors.[22]

A 2006 metastudy of 12 major research studies on the drivers of employee engagement found eight major factors that enhance employee motivation and engagement:[23]

1. *Trust and integrity.* The degree to which employees believe managers are concerned about their well-being, tell the truth, communicate difficult messages well, listen to employees, and follow through with action demonstrates the company's goals and values through the managers' behavior.

2. *Nature of the job.* The content and routine of the job, the degree of emotional and mental stimulation it affords, autonomy, and opportunities to participate in decision making.
3. *A sense of impact.* Seeing a line of sight between individual performance and company performance, understanding company goals and performance, and knowing how the employees' efforts contribute to success.
4. *Career growth opportunities.* The degree to which employees see future opportunities for growth and promotion and have a sense of a clear career path to advancement.
5. *A sense of pride in the company.* The amount of self-esteem an employee derives from being associated with the company. This is important in motivating employees to proactive actions beyond the bare scope of a job: creativity, valuable ideas, referring customers and prospective employees.
6. *Coworkers and team members.* The tenor of relationships with other people in the company.
7. *Personal development.* The degree to which an employee feels that specific efforts are being made to develop her or his skills and knowledge.
8. *Personal relationship with managers.* How valued personal—not professional or job-related—relationships with direct managers are. Some studies show that this is the single biggest driver of engagement and motivation.

Note that pay and benefits are not on this list. That is not because they weren't investigated. It's because pay and benefits generally don't turn out to be major drivers of employee engagement and motivation.[24] This finding has persisted over many years and a number of studies. When managers are surveyed about what they believe to be drivers of employee engagement, they usually put benefits, working conditions, and pay, especially incentive pay, at the top of the list. It turns out that pay and benefits are important recruiting and retention tools and that their absence causes dissatisfaction. However, they have limited value in motivating employees, especially if one is looking for internal motivators that lead to extra effort, creativity, and initiative to go beyond the defined limits of a job and generate value for the company.

This is where the intangible motivators are critical. "An employee's sense of achievement, opportunity for advancement, and recognition by one's manager were shown to be 'motivation factors' which led to greater overall satisfaction with one's overall job experience,"[25] and they cost little or nothing. Employees often say one of the biggest drivers in motivating them is to say thank you—and mean it. Leadership ought to pay a lot of attention to this simple and effective practice. The bigger and more decentralized a company gets, the more important it becomes. Research bears out the idea that small companies have a decided advantage in terms of reported employee engagement.[26] Sadly, for many larger companies, this often gets lost altogether.

WHAT I KNOW NOW THAT I WISH I HAD KNOWN THEN

Jennifer Gabler, Rochester Point, LLC

As chief financial officer of Extraprise Group, Inc., an international leader in customer relationship management business solutions, Jennifer Gabler, along with a venture-backed management team, grew Extraprise to $44 million in revenue and 400 employees. Currently a principal at Rochester Point, LLC, Jennifer is an outsource CFO, serving a number of clients, including several Harvard Business School executive program participants. In her work with multiple companies in operations and finance, as well as auditing public and private clients, Jennifer says she has learned some key lessons:

1. Don't wait too long to institute systems and policies to report outcomes and control activity.
2. Understand pricing and cost pressures early and constantly focus on them.
3. Take the minimum office space needed. Watch for long-term space commitments that may be hard to unwind if you grow more than expected.
4. Gingerly allocate salary increases, incentive compensation, and benefits to employees. They are hard to take back if the company hits hard times.
5. Keep managerial reports to a very few key performance indicators. Foster frequent proactive discussions among the management team about the steps needed to stay on a plan.
6. Understand all the options for debt and equity financing, including banks, leasing companies, subdebt lenders, and different types of equity investors. Develop relationships with as many as possible. Request funding proposals long in advance of any need for capital. Always have alternatives to avoid being caught in a cash crisis and being left with suboptimal solutions.
7. Build a strong network of operations and finance people who can help you understand the accounting standards for your industry, advise you on operational questions, assist you in hiring, and help you locate financing when you need it.

The time to anticipate sustainability and growth is the day you first start business planning. You don't need to plan every detail, but you need to plan a business that won't just launch successfully but grow and prosper. Many of the things you put in place—from expectations, to culture, to the people you choose—will have a huge effect on the chance that you will transition successfully from proof of concept to a profitable, growing, going concern. If you get it right, you not only will have fun and make profits but will have something to sell for a great price someday, if and when you're ready.

QUESTIONS

- What is your plan for growth? How much do you want and how soon?
- How will you know when it is time to start structuring?
- What will be your philosophy on policies and procedures? Do you have one? If not, how will you go about thinking this through? Who will be involved?
- Where do you see yourself fitting in as the company grows?

NOTES

1. Stinchcombe, Arthur L., "Social Structure and Organizations," in *Handbook of Organizations*, James G. March, ed. (Chicago: Rand McNally, 1965): 148–149.
2. Brüderl, Josef, and Rudolf Schussler, "Organizational Mortality: The Liabilities of Newness and Adolescence," *Administrative Science Quarterly* 35, no. 2, (September 1990): 530–547.
3. Cafferata, Roberto, Gianpaolo Abatecola, and Sara Poggesi, "Revisiting Stinchcombe's 'Liability of Newness': A Systematic Literature Review," *International Journal of Globalisation and Small Business* 3, no. 4 (2009): 374–392.
4. Eisenhardt, Kathleen M., and Claudia Bird Schoonhoven, "Organizational Growth: Linking Founding Team, Strategy, Environment, and Growth among U.S. Semiconductor Ventures, 1978–1988," *Administrative Science Quarterly* 35, no. 3 (September 1990): 504–529.
5. Brüderl and Schussler, 1990.
6. Ibid.: 530.
7. Hambrick, Donald C., and Lynn M. Crozier, "Stumblers and Stars in the Management of Rapid Growth," *Journal of Business Venturing* 1 (1985): 31–45.
8. Bhide, Amar V., "Building the Self-Sustaining Firm," 1995. Harvard Business School Case 395–200.
9. Bygrave, William D., and Andrew Zacharakis, *The Portable MBA* (Hoboken, NJ: Wiley, 2010): 363.

10. Steffens, Paul, Per Davidson, and Jason Fitzsimmons, "Performance Configurations over Time: Implications for Growth and Profit-Oriented Strategies," *Entrepreneurship: Theory and Practice* 33, no. 1 (2009): 125.

11. Bhide, 1995.

12. Bygrave and Zacharakis, 2010: 358.

13. Ibid.: 359.

14. Ibid.: 372–373.

15. Wasserman, Noam, "The Founder's Dilemma," *Harvard Business Review* 86, no. 2 (2008): 102–109.

16. Ibid.: 102.

17. Drucker, Peter. *Innovation and Entrepreneurship.* (New York, NY: Collins Business, 1993): 28, 143, 188.

18. Roberts, Michael J., "Managing Transitions in the Growing Enterprise." Harvard Business School Case 393–407, 1997.

19. Ibid.: 389–390.

20. *Working with Emotional Intelligence* (1998); *Primal Leadership: Realizing the Power of Emotional Intelligence* (2002); *Primal Leadership: Realizing the Power of Emotional Intelligence*, with Richard E. Boyatzis and Annie McKee (2004); *The Emotionally Intelligent Workplace: How to Select for, Measure, and Improve Emotional Intelligence in Individuals, Groups, and Organizations*, with Cary Cherniss (2001); *Promoting Emotional Intelligence in Organizations*, with Cary Cherniss and Mitchel Adler (2000).

21. Gibbons, John, "Employee Engagement—Current Research and Its Implications," *Conference Board Report Series* (New York, 2006): 10.

22. Corporate Leadership Council, "Driving Performance and Retention through Employee Engagement," Corporate Executive Board, 2004.

23. Ibid.: 6–7.

24. Ibid.: 6–7.

25. Ibid.: 7.

26. Ibid.: 7–8.

Chapter 22

Liquidity Events

There are more fools among buyers than among sellers.

—French proverb

In a book about starting a business, you might think the last thing on your mind would be planning for the day when you sell it. But remember from Chapter 3 that when starting out, you should have a clear vision of an end goal that is meaningful for you. That goal may be building a profitable business that creates value and generates a comfortable income—the so-called lifestyle business—or it may be building enterprise value so that you have something to sell for a good price someday. You can aim higher than a lifestyle business without planning to sell the business, but even if you don't plan to sell by a certain time, you want to have the option.

Regardless of when you might or might not plan to sell, you should understand how businesses are valued and sold for the following reasons:

1. This is how you will know if you're actually building value in your business, and everybody ought to be building value.
2. Investors always focus on valuation.
3. Odds are, sooner or later you or your investors will want liquidity.

Liquidity usually means merging for liquid stock, selling for cash, or taking the company public. Thus, like almost everything else we've talked about in this book, you need to have a working knowledge of liquidity events when starting a company and should keep them in mind as you launch and grow. At least some liquidity is, after all, your—or your heirs'—long-term target.

WHY WOULD YOU SELL?

Have you taken outside equity investments from angels or venture investors? If so, they eventually will want their money back with a profit. Novices often ask: Can't the company just pay back the investment or buy out the investors? Actually, no. Buybacks are rare. For one thing, if the company has succeeded, it's probably fast-growing, which means it's cash-hungry, not cash-rich. All available dollars will be invested back into the business. Buybacks by a company generally happen in situations in which companies are not performing well, and the buyout is a salvage operation by the investors, meaning mediocre returns or outright losses.[1]

Although investors need to get their investments and profits out so that they can put their money to work in another deal, that doesn't mean they want you to get your money out and put yourself to work in another deal. Generally, if you've done a good job building and running the company, investors want you to stay and continue building it. Often the buyer is paying a premium price because of the team. In fact, investors often test potential entrepreneurs by asking them where they see themselves in the long run. Investors want to invest in an entrepreneur who wants to build a successful high-growth company that dominates a market, plans to be in for the long term, and at the same time understands investors' need for liquidity.

Even if you don't raise money in your company from investors who eventually want liquidity, you may want liquidity for yourself. You may find your company has grown to the point where it needs the mega-resources of a larger parent. Or you may need infrastructure it would be difficult or impossible to create yourself, things such as a national sales force, a marketing and public relations department, and distribution or supply systems on a large scale. You may need incentive plans for the current employees or for new ones you want to attract. Frequently, illiquid stock options have limited power of motivation and reward in a closely held, private company. Pricing options in such companies is often an arbitrary exercise, and eventually employees may want more objective pricing as well as more liquidity than the company can afford. Often selling a company not only delivers cash rewards from past work but gets employees who stay with the acquirer new, more liquid, more objectively priced options in the acquiring company.

Even before you launch, you should think about your expectations. That way, if and when the time comes to sell or merge the company, you have emotionally prepared yourself and the team for this possible ending. Perhaps more important, along the way you should never neglect good housekeeping practices or make decisions that foreclose options you may want to have in the event of a sale, such as structuring, positioning, good records, and a lack of festering problems. Even more relevant, along the way focus on maximizing value to a potential acquirer: things such as showing consistent, profitable growth, maintaining a strong and stable team, building a pipeline of innovation and new intellectual property, tax structuring, and avoiding liabilities and legal entanglements. In an ideal world you are doing all these things anyway, but in the press of events it's easy to lose sight of important things like these, and suddenly, when you want to go to liquidity, you're not ready. In the back of your mind every day, run through a short checklist of factors that may affect future values and liquidity.

WHAT SHOULD YOU THINK ABOUT?

The type of business you choose to enter can have a significant effect on your exit options. For example, service businesses such as professional and consulting firms are often difficult to sell for good premiums. They are highly dependent on the professional skills of their people, and the smaller the firm is, the more exposure a buyer has to loss of talent. In addition, they are inherently nonscalable; every increment of growth brings proportionate additional costs, and so there are few, if any, economies of scale as the firm grows. For this reason purchase price multiples on net cash flow are low, generally no more than four to six times cash flow before interest, taxes, and non-cash items like depreciation and amortization. Another type of business that struggles to get premiums and sometimes even buyers is the so-called product-not-a-company. Buyers for one-product companies are usually limited to strategic buyers who can integrate the product into their marketing infrastructure or competitors who want to absorb customer lists. When there is no inventory of innovations and pending new products, there is little growth potential to pay for.

Why Would Someone Buy?

The most salable businesses are going concerns with a portfolio of products and a pipeline of innovations in the works, a defensible competitive position, good margins, and a record of strong growth in a healthy, growing market. These are the things we've encouraged you to seek throughout this book. Buyers may be looking for one or more of the following:

- Revenue and the opportunity to strip out costs to improve margins.
- Customers and market share.
- Growth. A history of growth sells and commands a premium.
- Innovation and an intellectual property portfolio. Innovation pipelines command premium purchase prices.
- Talent.
- The opportunity to remove a competitor.

Who Might Be the Buyer?

Even as you are thinking through your original idea, think ahead to who might want to buy your company someday. John Bello, the founder of SoBe Beverages whom we mentioned in Chapter 20, has started several beverage companies. He knows all the logical acquirers and always grooms his companies from the first day to be attractive to them. That has paid off more than once. There are many kinds of acquirers, and they buy for different reasons:

- Larger companies and corporate buyers acquire for growth, technology, and sometimes people.
- Financial buyers such as private equity funds and search funds buy for financial returns.
- Competitors sometimes buy to get a threat to their market share off the street or sometimes simply as part of a roll-up strategy that adds value by capturing economies of scale.

- The general public can acquire a company in an initial public offering (IPO). Some companies bypass the IPO and go to the market by acquiring a shell public company in a so-called reverse merger.

The kind of business you are interested in building probably will make you more attractive to one or more of these types of buyers. Try to be sure there is a match between how you put it together and the kinds of buyers you think you will attract. For example, a technology company can be interesting to any of these buyers, but the way the company is organized, how it's financed, and how you prioritize revenue versus profitability all affect who will find you most appealing.

It should go without saying that having more than one interested party is always best. The key is knowing how to get them interested. The more advance preparation you put into that, the more likely you will have multiple parties and a successful exit.

How Will the Decision Be Made to Sell or Not Sell?

We might have titled this section more succinctly "How Will You Decide to Sell or Not Sell?" but the fact is that unless you build a sole proprietorship and have no key employees or partners, the decision will not be yours alone. Depending on how you have created a corporate culture, getting to a decision to sell can be an easy or difficult process; sometimes it's impossible to do it effectively at all. Others who are involved can influence the decision whether you like it or not. Prior planning can save you a lot of heartache. For example, certain statutory and case law dissenters' rights of approval accrue to minority shareholders. Thinking ahead, you can reduce the chance of such problems when you draft the incorporation documents as well as when you build out the team. A more extreme—and not uncommon—example: If an acquirer wants to buy the entire corporation and not just assets, the sale will require the concurrence of all shareholders, meaning that any one shareholder, no matter how small, can block a sale if the acquirer wants 100 percent of the stock. You can avoid this obstacle by including a drag-along right in the incorporation documents; this forces unwilling minority shareholders to go along if more than a certain percentage of the company ownership agrees to sell.

Some buyers will want to buy the assets of the corporation and not take ownership of the corporate shell. They want to leave behind potential liabilities they may not have found in their due diligence, and buying assets can have certain tax advantages. (More on this in the next section.) You don't need the approval of all the shareholders to do an asset sale. The board of directors (in some cases with majority support from the shareholders) can sell the assets of the corporation without approval from a minority. However, note that there are state law limitations that vary from one state to another. The limitations are particularly strict in California.[2]

Secrecy and openness in the sales process frequently clash. Many discussions must occur in an environment of secrecy, but to close successfully you need the support of shareholders, directors, and key employees. Initial public offerings require huge commitments from management and concurrence from boards and shareholders. How will you be sure your team and company are ready to deal with the questions of selling? In addition to foresight in the way you structured the company, securing buy-in from critical team members will depend on the relationships you have developed, the ways you have communicated with them over the years, and the ways you have brought others into decisions in the past. The behavior of the team in a sale will greatly affect the success or failure of a sale. Good relationships are not built or repaired overnight. It is better to tend to them consistently from the first founding. Few things can do more to make a sale successful or a nightmare than the degree of commitment of the team to a smooth and profitable sale.

What Are You Selling?

Usually the question arises, Will the acquirer buy the assets of the selling company or buy the company itself by purchasing its shares?

- In an asset sale, the buyer may be looking for certain tax advantages, particularly a step-up in basis for depreciable assets. Buyers worry about overlooking liabilities during their due diligence—financial or legal—and everyone today worries about liabilities that could come up in the future related to something in the selling company's past activities. Buying assets and leaving behind the corporate shell can shield the acquirer from being sued in the future over something the predecessor company may have done, but this is not a sure thing. For example, if the acquirer continues to sell an acquired product, many courts will assess product liability against the acquirer even if the product involved was made and sold by the selling company before the sale. In terms of getting approval to sell from minority holders and dissenters, dissenters' rights may be avoided or reduced by structuring a purchase as an asset sale rather than a sale of corporate shares unless the transaction is for all or substantially all of the seller's assets. For the seller, asset sales subject the shareholders to double taxation unless the corporate form is a flow-through entity.
- An equity sale or merger is generally an attractive transaction structure for the selling shareholders. Most liability goes to the acquirer (subject to the representations, warranties, and indemnities in the sales agreement). There is no double taxation of the sale proceeds. There are also advantages to acquirers. They know they are getting all the assets of the corporation; nothing is inadvertently overlooked and left out of the agreement. There are no approvals to be obtained from third parties such as lessors, vendors,

and large customers, which often have approval requirements in their leases and contracts. There may be tax advantages for the purchaser, such as assuming net operating loss carry-forwards that can't be accessed in an asset purchase.

- A merger is a combination of two companies in which there is only one surviving entity. It has one important advantage over a purchase of 100 percent of stock from all the holders of the selling company: A merger requires a vote of only a majority of shareholders in each company unless there are special provisions in the articles or bylaws.

What Will Happen to the Team after the Sale?

In an IPO, the continuity of a team is crucial. Usually the upsides of liquidity, new investment, and listed stock options have enough appeal to retain most employees. In a private sale or a merger, in contrast, the fate of employees in the selling company can be complicated and uncertain. From the launch of your company, decide how you stand with respect to protecting your employees in a private market liquidity event. Are you committed to preserving opportunity for the team? Is maximizing the sale price more important even if it means your team will be let go largely or entirely after the sale or merger? Sometimes this is the only logical fate of a company, and if you have structured ownership sharing with the team generously, people can come out well enough and feel fairly treated. Other times, the ending is not so benign. If you have retained sufficient control, this will be your call. If not, you may find you created the potential for a bad situation step-by-step as you built the company and discover too late that you can't write a happy ending. Don't wait to confront this; do it now, when you are starting and building.

What Do You Want to Do after the Sale?

What about you? Will you want to stay on? In an IPO, you should know the answer well before you start the process. The investment banking team and the market want to know either that you are visibly committed for the long term or that you have hired solid top management to maintain the trajectory of the company. If it's not an IPO but an acquisition or a merger into a larger company, the cultural transition is often rocky. The same is true for you: Many founders have struggled to integrate into the culture of larger, more structured acquiring companies and of course had trouble working for a boss after working for themselves. Many founders don't stay any longer than they have to. Think a lot about this long before a liquidity horizon looms and position yourself—in the company and emotionally—well in advance. Too much will be happening in the heat of the moment for you to think about it during a sale.

What's Your Price?

What are your goals for price? Is maximizing the amount of cash paid at closing paramount? Often an acquiring company will want to pay some or all of the purchase in the form of stock. In strategic acquisitions and mergers this can mean a higher total price than you would get if you were paid all in cash. Of course the market can go up or down afterward, and you could end up with less than if you took all cash, assuming cash was an option. How you telegraph your interest in cash or stock can have a significant effect on how buyers price you and even which buyers look at you.

There is a whole field of knowledge on methods to value a company or its assets in an acquisition. Usually there are comparative sales that offer benchmarks on what the market is paying. If you want to maximize your sale price, study thoroughly how companies evaluate acquisitions and learn to think like a buyer. Most bottom-up methods are based on some kind of projection of the full financial performance of the company, discounted back to the present, with adjustments for risk and possible upsides. Other methods often are used to check or calibrate the results: multiples of earnings, revenue, and cash flow—that is, earnings before interest, taxes, depreciation, and amortization (EBITDA). Tax strategies are almost always a major factor in maximizing value to the buyer and seller. For example, if they are structured correctly, there are alternative structures for tax-free (deferred) reorganizations and exchanges of shares or assets.

The main goal of a seller is usually to get the purchasers to "pay too much," which is another way of saying "get the best price." Since you always want to have multiple buyers competing for the sale, paying too much means the winning bidder pays more than the others are willing to pay. Often the other bidders will say they think the winner is paying too much, but that also means the buyer is outbidding *you*. Think about it this way: If you are selling the company, it basically means the buyer is paying you more than you yourself would pay to keep it. The final decision to sell comes down to, "Would I pay that much to own this company?" It really is about getting a buyer to pay too much.

This doesn't mean committing fraud. It means doing everything possible to show the company in the best possible light, with the most future potential and the minimum risk. Timing, financial and operating history, future potential, and reputation all play into this. Getting too much usually means you have done a good job getting buyers to pay present-day cash for future upsides you have built into the business. These are the kinds of things that can't be groomed overnight. In reality the grooming should start from the launch of the company. Understand the drivers of premium value in your market and do all you can to get them built into your company.

How Do You Monetize Upsides?

One of your biggest challenges will be figuring out exactly how you will get the buyer to pay aggressively for the future upside. You, as the seller, inevitably will feel you have created lots of future opportunity and are entitled to be paid a significant share of that value now even though its realization will happen in the future, if at all. The acquirer usually will feel that if you wanted the upside monetized, you should have done it yourself. Considering it's the buyer's future capital and work that produces it, the buyer will usually feel the acquirer should keep most or all of the value and pay little or nothing for it. Remember from Chapter 1 that value is in the execution; ideas are worth next to nothing. The fact is, acquisitions generally bring a price that includes some kind of price recognition of future upsides, but how those upsides are quantified is the difference between getting a good or a mediocre price in a sale—or, to put it another way, how good a salesperson you are. Building an impression that a company is infused with exciting upside is not something you can cobble together in the last months before a sale. It's something you build into the DNA of a company from its first founding.

You sometimes can bridge this upside value gap through contingent future payments of some kind—upside payments, or "earnouts"—that are tied to the future performance of the company. Earnouts can be worth a lot of money, but they can be fraught with risks and problems. For example, unless the accounting the buyer does in the future to calculate the earnout payments is simple and transparent, the seller has wide latitude to mess with the numbers to minimize what it has to pay. Sad to say, this happens all the time to unwary sellers, and many a lawsuit has dragged on for years in an attempt to unravel the mess.

Believe it or not, the way you choose to finance your company in the early days can have a big influence on how well you can monetize your upsides in a sale. A financing that seems right at the time can later limit your freedom to negotiate for contingent upside payments or earnouts in a sale. For example, venture investors not only need their liquidity in a time horizon that works with their partnership structures—generally five to seven years from investment to liquidity—they need it in cash. Within the structure of their partnerships they can't readily feed long-term residual payments or earnouts back to their partners.

One company we know was fabulously successful with its technology and set the stage for a major disruption in its market. It sold to a big company for a great multiple on the venture investment in it. The acquirer had the needed resources to finish the development of the technology and take it to the market in a way the seller would have struggled to do. If successful, the technology would be worth multiples of what the acquirer paid. But since the outcome was not certain, it was difficult for the acquirer to pay cash for the full value that the upside might be worth. It was a situation made for an earnout to share the risk and the reward of the future upside. However, because there was a lot of venture capital invested in the company, cash was most important, and there was not an easy way for the investors to monetize a future, contingent earnout. The cash price was strong in that case and everyone did extremely well, but it doesn't always turn out that way. Certainly it's not a foregone conclusion that it will turn out that way for you. If you anticipate coming to a sale with lots of future upside, the way you fund the company can have unintended consequences you might not like. This is one more reason to think ahead about selling a company long before it's time.

What's the Timeline for a Sale?

Do you have expectations about a timeline to a liquidity event? Do you have a definite profile in mind, or are you building for the indefinite future and are comfortable being opportunistic about a sale? From the venture investors' point of view, in addition to their own internal timing needs, there is an ideal pattern of launch and growth that usually brings the highest premium. Go past this point and buyers tend to pay smaller multiples. Timing is everything in many aspects of entrepreneurship, especially in selling. How you manage the timing of growing the company and preparing for a sale will have a major effect on your ultimate reward.

Should You Try to Go Public?

If you are aiming for an IPO, the odds are not with you. Very few start-ups ever make it to IPO status,[3] as the following timeline tracing the development of early-stage business ventures suggests:

0–2 years (3 million ventures)

- Founders: $200 billion
- Family and friends: $70 billion

0–4 years (50,000 ventures)

- Angels: $30 billion

0.5–4 years (799 ventures)

- Venture capital: $4.4 billion

8 years (84 ventures)

- IPOs: $8.4 billion

The odds aren't even as good as they look in this list because these numbers don't distinguish different types of businesses. Only certain kinds of companies will ever be candidates for a public listing no matter how successful they are. For the others, going public is never an option. This reinforces one of the first points in this chapter: The kind of business you start, and in what form, has a huge influence on your options for later liquidity.

Assuming that you build the kind of business that could go public, why would you want to do this?

- IPOs give liquidity to investors and founders.
- They bring investment into the company for growth and new opportunities.
- They enhance the prestige and visibility of the company with customers, banks, suppliers and vendors, and potential future employees.
- They offer employees incentive options that are more liquid than those in a private company, with pricing set by a disinterested third party (the public markets) rather than by insiders.
- They provide liquid shares to use alongside cash and debt for making acquisitions.

However, there are downsides:

- IPOs are expensive. A bevy of expensive professionals will be involved: investment bankers, accountants, lawyers, printers, and public relations and media consultants. There will be registration fees and increased director and officer liability insurance. Costs run into the hundreds of thousands of dollars, even up to a million, plus bank fees taken as a percentage discount on the initial offering price.
- IPOs are not a sure thing. It's certain that you will spend the money but only about 50–50 that you will make it to a financing and listing.
- Once you go public, your control is diluted or extinguished altogether and you lose lots of privacy and confidentiality. Reporting requirements are extensive, even down to your compensation.
- Compliance with regulations is terribly complex and getting worse by the day; Securities and Exchange Commission regulations, accounting rules from the Financial Accounting Standards Board, listing exchange rules, Sarbanes-Oxley provisions, and state requirements are just a few. Then there is the ever-expanding creativity of the tort lawyers and the courts, creating new uncertainties over just what liabilities you and your directors may face next.
- The public markets are highly focused on short-term results. Once public, you're subject to the tyranny of quarterly earnings forecasts and reports. People talk about long-term focus, but unfortunately, the markets seem to care most about the next quarter.

- You can become a takeover target at any time, although that can be good or bad depending on how badly you want to keep control versus take home a financial win.
- Valuation of the company often is influenced by macroeconomic factors beyond the company's control such as the time in the economic cycle, what's fashionable with investors, and the value of alternative investments.

Being public can give you much greater access to financing and liquidity, sometimes at a valuation better than you could find elsewhere, but more than one company has gone public and come to regret it. More than a few eventually bought out the public and went back to being private. If you consider an IPO and plan to be part of managing a public company afterward, talk to some entrepreneurs who have done it and be sure you know what you are getting into.

If you are thinking that someday you may want to have the option to do an IPO, here are a few factors to take into account. Some won't matter until the time comes, but some are strategy issues that need to be anticipated long in advance:

- Probably most significant for your planning, in normal times, to do an IPO you generally need a history of significant revenue and growth and have to be profitable or anticipate becoming profitable soon. Abnormal times can mean anything from a feeding frenzy (rare) to a drought; compare 1999 and 2009.
- Remember that you need to be a going concern to do an IPO. Very few "one-product wonders" successfully become IPOs.
- Transaction costs to complete an IPO are high: a percentage of the money raised plus out-of-pocket costs up to another 5 percent. Investment banks normally take 7 percent of the offering amount as their fee.
- IPOs also take an incredible amount of time. You'll do months of preparation, and then there will be a road show lasting at least several weeks. The process is all-consuming.
- After closing, you can expect to be under temporary lockups that prevent you from selling your listed shares for some period, usually at least six months, and after that there will be market-driven limits on what you can sell. If you accept enough shares of an acquiring company as part of your purchase price, you may not be locked up but could fall under insider restrictions.

HOW DOES IT HAPPEN?

Private sales or mergers can be initiated in many ways. You may develop relationships and initiate a process informally. You may be contacted unsolicited by a company, an individual, or a private equity buyer. Search funds are always look-ing for smaller businesses to buy, usually in the few millions to a few tens of mil-lions. Search funds consist of one or a small number of individuals who are backed for their costs by an investor or investor group while they try to find a good business to purchase, with the intent of financing the purchase and having the individuals run it afterward. Some selling companies hire intermediaries: business brokers or, if the company is big enough, investment bankers. Today there a number of boutique investment banks that act on behalf of clients with enterprise values as small as a million to a few million dollars.

There is usually a period of informal discussion during which only a limited amount of your information is shared. At some point you may hear enough to share more information under an agreement that protects confidentiality. In a for-mal process with multiple potential buyers, you or your intermediaries will create a full information package, an evaluation process, and maybe even a data room. Buyers often seek a period of exclusivity to get an acquisition opportunity off the market. They want to know they are not investing their overhead in evaluating a deal that will end up competitive or not sold in the end. Usually multiple buyers and a competitive bid lead to a better price, but sometimes there are factors or inducements offered by a prospective buyer that justify a period of exclusivity. Often sellers seek a nonbinding indication from potential buyers of their valuation (price) and structure to qualify buyers to receive data and participate in the sales process. This is a common practice among investment bankers, especially when there is a large field of potential buyers and a need to winnow that field.

Eventually you will reach the stage of term sheets, ideally from multiple bid-ders, and have the opportunity to negotiate and seek the best bid. Remember, the highest price is not always the best transaction. Many factors make up the best transaction. Afterward there is usually a period of additional due diligence between a term sheet and a full purchase and sale agreement and yet more due diligence between the agreement being signed and the deal closed. Steel your nerves. The process between term sheet and closing can be nerve-wracking. If the transaction is a merger, multiply the process time by 5 or 10. This is when your choices of acquirer and lawyers prove fortuitous or painful.

TWO LAST POINTS

Here are two final points to consider:

1. Don't put skeletons in your closet; that is, don't create things you don't want in your records later in a sale, or leave loose ends that could cause problems in the future. It seems self-evident, but in a busy company with

lots always going on, it's harder to do than you think and takes constant diligence. In a sale you will be turned inside out by prospective buyers, and any good acquirer will look at almost everything by the time of closing. You will be required to make representations and warranties about the state of the company, your compliance situation, and your pending and potential liabilities. The best way to be able to make those representations and warranties and get to that closing without a major surprise or hiccup is to keep things organized, clean, and compliant from day one. In the press of everyday business, unfortunately, you're often sorely tempted to put off completing something properly, leaving the last details for later (or, worse, never). Here are some things that always have to be done right and kept right:

- General corporate records, including minutes of the board of directors, charter documents, and amendments
- Key agreements and contracts, properly signed and recorded, if appropriate
- Share registries, capital stock, and other securities outstanding
- Financials and audits
- Records of assets, including an intellectual property portfolio
- Liabilities and taxes
- Compliance records and environmental issues
- Employment matters, especially any pending or potential employment claims against the company
- Past, pending, or threatened litigation

2. Interesting research has identified a seemingly irrational desire people have to value what they already possess more than what they might be able to acquire. The term *endowment effect* refers to a behavioral phenomenon originally defined in 1980 by Richard Thaler of Cornell in which the owners of an object seem to value it more than nonowners do.[4] Nobel Prize winner Daniel Kahneman of Princeton suggested that this is due to loss aversion, a tendency to value avoiding losses more than capturing equivalent gains.[5] David Gal at Stanford suggested in 2006 that the endowment effect is due more to inertia than to loss aversion.[6] In reality, it doesn't really matter why people tend to value holding on to an asset they own more than buying the same asset; it's a real and compelling factor going on inside your head when it comes to deciding if you should sell or not sell your company at a particular price. Be aware of it. The best way to avoid the emotional distortions of the endowment effect is to frame this question to yourself: If you had the cash in hand that is being offered, would you spend it all to buy this company today? If not, that's the time to sell. If you want happy endings, the time to start thinking about them is at the very beginning.

WHAT I KNOW NOW THAT I WISH I HAD KNOWN THEN

Tim Healy, CEO and Chairman of the Board, and David Brewster, President, EnerNOC, Inc.

Tim Healy and David Brewster wrote about forming their original team in Chapter 8. Here they offer their lessons learned about building a company and taking it public.

Go public for the right reason. The IPO is not an endgame or an exit. It's another financing event. We took EnerNOC public to strengthen our balance sheet, create transparency and credibility with utilities, and attract top talent. We built something more sustainable and more valuable because we never thought about building for an exit. We hired with an emphasis on the long term. We hired a direct sales team early rather than leveraging the sales teams of big companies that might one day develop an interest in our company's business. We built product development teams to focus on three-year plans for our commercial offerings. We built and still build our financial plans focused on what we need to be successful in the year ahead *and* be where we need to be in three to five years. We never tried to look pretty for an exit in the next quarter or year. We focused on making our business successful and expected the rest to work itself out over the long run.

Long before you go public, become a public company in your mind and your habits in terms of quarterly planning and reporting. It will make going public easier on the organization. Plan quarters thoughtfully. Communicate with your employees every quarter. Structure your board and advisor meetings in quarterly increments. Think about public reporting requirements and the financial impact of certain contract structures as you build the business.

Administratively, an IPO is a big distraction. If you can largely isolate your CEO, president, VP of sales, and VP of marketing from it, the IPO process can be a huge marketing opportunity to attract new employees and new customers, but the legal and finance teams need to be talented enough and experienced enough to do this.

QUESTIONS

- Do you have expectations over the long term for liquidity?
- All kinds of personal needs can arise, from college costs, to paying for a house, to medical bills, to divorces. Are you thinking now about how you might realize some of your gains without having to sell your position or the whole company under duress?
- Do you have a long-term plan for succession and getting liquidity for yourself and your heirs?
- Do you know what you think your business is worth? Are you always thinking about who might be interested in buying your business?

NOTES

1. Bygrave, William D., and Andrew Zacharakis (eds.), *The Portable MBA in Entrepreneurship*, 3d ed. (Hoboken, NJ: Wiley, 2010): 184.
2. Bagley, Constance E., and Craig E. Dauchy, *The Entrepreneur's Guide to Business Law* (Mason, OH: Thomson/South-Western/West, 2008): 604–605.
3. Bygrave and Zacharakis, 2010: 185.
4. Thaler, Richard, "Toward a Positive Theory of Consumer Choice," *Journal of Economic Behavior and Organization* 1 (1980): 39–60.
5. Kahneman, Daniel, J. Knetsch, and R. Thaler, "Experimental Test of the Endowment Effect and the Coase Theorem," *Journal of Political Economy* 98, no. 6 (1990): 1325–1348.
6. Gal, David, "A Psychological Law of Inertia and the Illusion of Loss Aversion," *Judgment and Decision Making* 1 (2006):23–32.

Conclusion

In building a great institution, there is no single defining action, no grand program, no one killer innovation, no solitary lucky break, no miracle moment. Rather, our research showed that it feels like turning a giant, heavy flywheel. Pushing with great effort—days, weeks, and months of work, with almost imperceptible progress—you finally get the flywheel to inch forward. But you don't stop. You keep pushing, and with persistent effort, you eventually get the flywheel to complete one turn. You don't stop. You keep pushing, in an intelligent and consistent direction, and the flywheel moves a bit faster. You keep pushing, and you get two turns ... then four ... then eight ... the flywheel builds momentum ... sixteen ... you keep pushing ... thirty-two ... it builds more momentum ... a hundred ... moving faster with each turn ... a thousand ... ten thousand ... a hundred thousand. Then, at some point—breakthrough! Each turn builds upon previous work, compounding your investment of effort. The flywheel flies forward with almost unstoppable momentum. This is how you build greatness.[1]

—Jim Collins

WHAT I KNOW NOW THAT I WISH I KNEW THEN

David M. Mott, NEA and MedImmune

David M. Mott is a general partner at the venture capital partnership NEA, which is focused on biopharmaceutical investments. Over 16 years with MedImmune, Inc., he served in roles of increasing responsibility, including chief operating officer, chief financial officer, president, and chief executive officer, as the company grew from a venture-backed start-up (founded in 1988) into one of the top five biotechnology companies in the world. Ultimately, he initiated and executed the sale of MedImmune to AstraZeneca in June 2007 for $15.6 billion. At the time of his departure in July 2008, MedImmune had annual revenues in excess of $1.5 billion, an annual R&D budget in excess of $650 million, and approximately 3,000 employees. David shares these lessons learned from a roller-coaster ride from $50 million market value to $900 million, back to $50 million, and ultimately an exit of over $15 billion on a total investment of only $308 million:

- Shortcuts aren't.
- The failures you survive make you stronger.

- Know the difference between the tenacity needed for success and blindly staying with a deal that can't win big.
- Doing more than a few things at a time is hard.
- Unproductive times follow success; productive times follow setbacks.
- Good deals get done from strength; bad deals are done in fear.
- Your most expensive financing will be the one you didn't do.
- Make sure your partners' interests are aligned with your own.
- Continuity of management and board matters a lot.
- Always maintain a consistent commitment to culture, shared values, and an ethic for how to treat each other; they are the foundation of a shortened decision process when you most need it.
- You always want all your people to think like owners, not employees.
- Success can make you afraid to take chances and reinvest. Never lose your taste for measured risk.
- Entrepreneurship is hard, but it offers tremendous opportunities for personal growth and learning.
- Teamwork and relationships are critical to success.
- Do something you think is very important. Otherwise, there are easier ways to make good money.
- The destination is irrelevant; even the most successful ending is disappointing and anticlimactic. It's about the journey; about building something big, valuable, and important; and about doing it with people you respect and enjoy.

If you've reached this point, we hope this book has been useful. We started this story with some careful definitions, then helped you think about objectives, worked through your primary entrepreneurship tool kit, discussed how to avoid pitfalls in your launch, and offered some thoughts about operating effectively and moving from a start-up to a going concern.

There is a world of materials out there to help founders on every step of their journey, yet many entrepreneurs we meet complain that they are starved for wisdom and guidance even as they are drowning in information and input. Our purpose in writing this book was to act as a gateway for you to the mountain of resources available to entrepreneurs. It's so much information that accessing it often requires first that you know what you need and why it's important to you, where to look, and how to ask for it.

However, you can't find the best information on starting a new venture in books or articles; you must find it in your customers and the people who already have gone out and done something like it. One of the most common ah-hah moments we see in our students happens when they realize that the best entrepreneurial education comes from picking up the phone or going to see someone and asking the right questions. We hope this book has helped you learn to ask the right questions and impressed on you how important it is to go and ask.

We know that every deal, every situation, is just a mess of incomplete and incoherent information. Entrepreneurs start to add value when they begin to frame the necessary questions, extract the right answers from the messy data, and use good judgment in applying those answers to executing in an uncertain world. We know you can do this. Just remember the following steps.

FIRST

Entrepreneurship means getting things done with resources you don't control. It's about being *entrepreneurial*: learning and developing characteristics, not just starting things or being a certain type of person.

- *The implication.* Being entrepreneurial is not all or nothing; you can learn to be entrepreneurial and apply the knowledge and skills almost anywhere. Don't focus on controlling resources. Focus on getting things done.

SECOND

Ideas create opportunities. Execution creates value. "Many innovative thinkers never get anything done"[2]

- *The implication.* Don't just stand there—do something. Eliminate risks and kill ideas early. Trust natural selection; develop multiple alternatives, turn them loose in the market, and let only the fittest survive.

The secret of success is to do the common things uncommonly well.

—John D. Rockefeller

THIRD

A learning curve trumps an earning curve. Be patient about learning versus going for the big money too early. The more you focus on learning now, the bigger your success will be later. Always remember that the probability of success is proportional to the learning.

- *The implication.* Focus on learning; earning will follow. Where can you learn? Everywhere. Remember: Failed deals are great starter kits. It's a shame to learn on a good idea. Everyone can teach you something. Experience and mistakes are the greatest teachers.

The reasonable man adapts himself to the world: the unreasonable one persists in trying to adapt the world to himself. Therefore, all progress depends on the unreasonable man.

—George Bernard Shaw

There's nothing reasonable about entrepreneurship!

WHAT I KNOW NO THAT I WISH I HAD KNOWN THEN

David Hendren, Innovative Health Ventures and True North Advisors Group

Experience in multiple entrepreneurial roles has given David Hendren perspective from virtually every side of the table: as an entrepreneur, active investor, board member, and advisor. He has advised, incubated, launched, financed, and exited from a variety of technology companies as a law partner, venture partnership founder, and business advisory consultant. Seeing profound changes in the environment for new ventures and emerging businesses, David recently launched Innovative Health Ventures and joined the investment and business advisory firm True North Advisors Group to advance innovative business models for new enterprise creation, financing, partnering, mergers and acquisitions, and commercialization of novel technologies. Years ago, David learned a poignant lesson in business and life from an unlikely teacher:

Before my freshman year at Dartmouth I decided to take a year's detour from my life of social and academic privilege. I drove out of Boston in an old Ford and hired on as a roughneck on an oil rig in South Texas.

I often think back to my first day on the rig. In order to look less boyish I grew a scruffy beard. I learned the importance of caution and not making the same mistake twice. I still remember the fear the first time I threw the spinning chain after watching one of my crewmates lose the use of his arm to it. Fear was what kept you alive on the rigs. I always knew I'd return to a world where safety and financial security are taken for granted. But the guys I worked with would always live with fear, just as they had helped me learn to do.

I often look back on those times and a wise soul named Bill. On our five-man crew Bill was the "motorman" responsible for maintaining machinery. Bill had held every position on a rig crew, from roughneck to the driller who runs the rig. He had seen the world and spoke of everything from "fighting Uncle Sam's war in Europe" to driving long-haul trucks out of the Rio Grande Valley.

At the end of a hard day's work just before I left for college, Bill and I stood relaxing beneath the derrick, exhausted and covered with drilling mud, watching cattle stroll by on the way to pasture. It's unheard of to give advance notice of quitting in the oil field, but I didn't want the crew to resent me for jumping to another rig. But it's even more unheard of to quit and go to an Ivy League college.

Bill asked what college I would attend.

I replied, "It's just a little school in New Hampshire. You never would have heard of it."

Bill persisted. "Try me, boy."

"Dartmouth."

For a moment, I didn't know whether to expect a pat on the back or a punch in the face for being an impostor, slumming as a tourist in their very different lives.

Bill smiled and said, "Why, I always knew you were smart. You just didn't want anybody to know."

Then he told me he had been offered an athletic scholarship at LSU but failed to take advantage of it. "I thought I was too smart for that," he said.

Then he listed jobs he had taken over the years. His self-criticism was caustic and unforgiving. I'll never forget his conclusion: "You're a good hand, Dave. You worked hard here and never made the same mistake twice. Don't make the mistake I made. Get your education. Be a doctor, a lawyer, a teacher, an engineer. Do something important, something that makes you happy. Don't end up an old roughneck like me."

I wish I could say that in the three decades since that moment I hadn't made any mistakes, but it wouldn't be true. I did follow Bill's advice and got lots of education. I've been lucky to know and work with many talented people on any number of entrepreneurial ventures.

I've learned that lasting personal and entrepreneurial successes come from how well we see reality, how well we actually act on what we see, and how we deal with the inevitable obstacles life offers. The most important thing may be learning from our own experiences and the wisdom of others.

Life will never be perfect. It will always have surprises. But we can make the best of it if we keep an open mind, if we are honest with ourselves, and if we have the faith and courage to admit mistakes, start new ventures, change career paths if we're unhappy, or even shut down a venture that's not working and move on to start another. It's sobering and humbling to remember how many people we can learn from—some, like my friend Bill, who could have been where we are, or even be our boss if perhaps they had chosen differently. Listen to them! And especially listen to your own inner voice that often really knows best where you need to go.

AFTERWORD

Truth be told, it was never in my mind to write a book about entrepreneurship. The Tuck public relations director, Kiki Keating, is a remarkable person, and somehow in the winter of 2010 she convinced a *Fortune* magazine writer to come to Tuck and write about our entrepreneurship classes. An equally remarkable and entrepreneurial literary agent, Lorin Rees, saw the article, cold-called me, and persuaded me over my objections to write a book about our classes and the Dartmouth Entrepreneurial

Network. I didn't feel I had had anything meaningful to say, I didn't have the time, and I definitely didn't feel I was a writer. Had a coincidence not made Tessa Winter available for the spring and summer to cowrite this book before she started medical school, I would never have said yes. This book would never have happened without those coincidences and the engagement of those people.

For me the late spring at Dartmouth is a hard time each year. I watch as another class of bright young people comes to the end of their education, in a way their childhood and youth, and goes out to start the rest of their lives. In those waning months many of them come to me looking for advice or emotional support as they try to sort out what they're going to do and where they're going to be. Often the only thing on which they focus is where to start: what job to get, what career to choose.

The input I offer is always the same: Don't think about where to start; first think about where you want to end up. Where do you want to be in 20 or 30 years? What does that picture look like? Not just the picture of your job or your career (which is almost always the first answer). What are your passions? What gets you excited? What will make you feel you have added value?

Do you just want to make a lot of money and then kick back? That works for some people, though I couldn't count the number of such people in their forties and fifties I've had in my office too, successful in that goal but restless and unhappy. They come looking for something to do with their lives now that they have the financial freedom and are not at all sure what will make them feel their lives are worthwhile. A feeling of being "worthwhile" seems to come from doing something that feels like it is adding value, helping other people, or somehow making the world a better place. That, at least, seems to be the common thread among the people I meet who are on fire at any age—up, happy, motivated to do more, on a mission. The mission can be almost anything, but in every case it is *something*.

Viktor Frankl was an Austrian neurologist and psychiatrist who studied under Sigmund Freud and Alfred Adler, but he learned his most important lessons in three Nazi death camps. In 1946, after the war's end, Frankl wrote that man's "main concern is not to gain pleasure or to avoid pain but rather to see a meaning in his life. That is why man is even ready to suffer, on the condition, to be sure, that his suffering has a meaning."[3] When asked in a survey what they considered "very important" to them, only 16 percent of 8,000 students at 48 colleges checked "making a lot of money"; 78 percent said "finding a purpose and meaning to my life."[4]

This is what these Dartmouth students are really asking when they come in. They think they are asking career questions, but really they are struggling to prepare to leave the shelter of schooling, with all the freedom that offers, and begin writing the history of the rest of their lives. At some point in the future many of them probably will be like David Hendren and me, looking back and thinking about all the things they didn't think about then and wished they had, all the things they know now that they wish they knew then, and, perhaps most important, the things they want now in life they wish they had wanted then.

David recently told me in my office that he wished in the worst way that he had thought about these things more when he was finishing school. I felt exactly the same! We told each other how we sort of drifted into a career and a life path with no real idea where we were going or why we were doing it. At the time it didn't seem so improvised and shortsighted. Only the passage of time and events showed that.

Despite the lack of perspective and forethought, for David and me things turned out far better than they might have. But now, looking back, we are quite sad that we didn't do a much better job of making something of our lives and all the great investments others made in us. Speaking for myself, I never took the time to figure out what my passion was, what I could do with myself that would add value and make something of my life, things that I might feel rose to the level of *worth*. It was a long time before I even realized that these were the important questions, and that these are the kinds of questions everyone should ask as early as possible.

Many of these students at least understand that you should be diligent and systematic about figuring out what you want to do. Even if you don't know what to do or what to ask, you should do *something* and ask *someone*. Ready, fire, aim. Sadly, we can't envision how we will feel about the future and what will be best for us, because we are making decisions for someone we have never met—the person we will be tomorrow.[5] The only way to decide wisely is to benefit from the insights of people who have done what we want to do, people who can tell us about the lessons they learned the hard way. These are lessons that we will have to learn too unless we learn from them. I have so much respect for these students, because the wise ones somehow understand this and are looking for answers when they realize they don't even know the right questions. That is why it's a hard time for me: because I never did that. I never asked the questions and I only realized how important this is too late to do anything practical about it.

As we wrote this book, I asked accomplished entrepreneur and investor friends to do me a favor and write a few paragraphs loosely related to each of our chapter subjects. The idea was to imagine that someone they know well, someone who has never done something entrepreneurial, came to them and said, "I have this idea I really believe in, and I think I am going to go and do it." I asked these friends to think about what they would say to those people. What had they learned in their own entrepreneurial careers the hard way that they now wish someone had told them when they were starting out? Their answers are in the feature boxes that appear in the chapters of this book.

There are certain things you can learn only the hard way—that is, unless someone has done it before you and tells you about it. That is what David Hendren's friend Bill, who never went to college, tried to tell him on that rig floor in south Texas in the summer of 1978. That is what all of these friends of mine have tried to do for you. And this book has been my own attempt to do that for you, to tell you all the things I wish someone had told me in a way that might be useful to you. I had the hindsight. Tessa took a crash course in *entrepreneurial* over three months, extracted it, filtered the curse of knowledge, and put it in words people could follow.

Entrepreneurship, in the end, is about getting something done, one way or another, something that adds value and, most of all, adds a sense of meaning to the lives of the people who do it. It can be a trying and miserable existence when it isn't working out. But it can be fulfilling, as well as rewarding, when it is. Which way it goes for any individual person depends a great deal on two things: how much value the idea adds and how effectively it is carried out. What makes for success depends mostly on the second point: The value is in the execution.

Remember, we think success is not an end goal. We hope you feel the same way. Success is a "second thing," one of those we mentioned in Chapter 3: "You can't get second things by putting them first. You can only get second things by putting first things first." Most successful entrepreneurs we have met aimed to do something they felt was worthwhile. Sure, they wanted financial success, because financial success meant they had achieved what they had set out to do and something has to pay the bills. But financial success was only a second thing. There was always this higher thing, a first thing. It always boils down to this: What do you want to achieve, and how will you achieve it? Of course we can't help you much with the first step—defining what's important to you—because that is something that has to come from inside you. But we hope we've given you a head start on the second. Good luck with everything you try!

Don't aim at success—the more you aim at it and make it a target, the more you are going to miss it. For success, like happiness, cannot be pursued; it must ensue, and it only does so as the unintended side-effect of one's personal dedication to a cause greater than oneself or as the by-product of one's surrender to a person other than oneself. Happiness must happen, and the same holds for success: you have to let it happen by not caring about it. I want you to listen to what your conscience commands you to do and go on to carry it out to the best of your knowledge. Then you will live to see that in the long run—in the long run, I say!—success will follow you precisely because you had forgotten to think of it.

—Viktor Frankl, 1946[6]

NOTES

1. Collins, Jim, *Good to Great and the Social Sectors*, a monograph to accompany *Good to Great* (Boulder, CO: Jim Collins, 2005): 23.
2. Stevenson, Howard H., and David E. Gumpert, "The Heart of Entrepreneurship," *Harvard Business Review* 63, no. 2 (March-April, 1985): 85–94.
3. Frankl, Viktor E., *Man's Search for Meaning* (New York: Washington Square Press, 1946, 1962, 1984): 136.
4. Ibid.: 122.
5. Gilbert, Dan, *Stumbling on Happiness* (New York: Knopf, 2007): xiii–xvii.
6. Frankl, 1984: 17.

Additional Resources

Chapter 1

Baron, Robert A. "Cognitive Mechanisms in Entrepreneurship: Why and When Entrepreneurs Think Differently Than Other People." *Journal of Business Venturing* 13, no. 4 (July 1998): 275–294.

Barringer, Bruce R., and R. Duane Ireland. *Entrepreneurship: Successfully Launching New Ventures.* (Upper Saddle River, NJ: Pearson Prentice-Hall, 2008).

Busenitz, Lowell W., and Jay B. Barney. "Differences Between Entrepreneurs and Managers in Large Organizations: Biases and Heuristics in Strategic Decision-Making," *Journal of Business Venturing* 12, Issue 1 (January 1997): 9–30.

Drucker, Peter. *Innovation and Entrepreneurship.* (New York: Collins Business, 1993).

Hisrich, Robert D., Michael P. Peters, and Dean A. Shepherd. *Entrepreneurship.* (Boston: McGraw-Hill Irwin, 2008): 1–83.

Kawasaki, Guy. *The Art of the Start.* (New York: Portfolio, 2004).

Kawasaki, Guy. *Reality Check.* (New York: Portfolio, 2008).

Klein, Maury. *The Change Makers.* (New York: Times Books, 2003.).

Krass, Peter, ed. *The Book of Entrepreneur's Wisdom—Classic Writings by Legendary Entrepreneurs.* (New York: John Wiley & Sons, 1999).

Landes, David S., et al., eds. *The Invention of Enterprise.* (Princeton, NJ: Princeton University Press, 2010).

Livingston, Jessica. *Founders at Work—Stories of Startups' Early Days.* (New York: Apress, 2008).

Sarasvathy, Saras D., "What Makes Entrepreneurs Entrepreneurial?" *Darden Case Collection ENT–0065* (2004): 4–5.

Shane, Scott. *Born Entrepreneurs: How Your Genes Affect Your Work Life.* (New York: Oxford University Press, 2010).

Stevenson, Howard. *Perspective on Entrepreneurship,* Harvard Business School Case 9-384-131, Rev. April 13, 2006.

Stevenson, Howard and David E. Gumpert, "The Heart of Entrepreneurship," *Harvard Business Review* 63, no. 2 (March–April 1985): 85–94.

Zenios, Stefanos, Josh Makower, and Paul Yock. *Biodesign: The Process of Innovating Medical Technologies*. (Cambridge, UK: Cambridge University Press, 2010).

Chapter 3

Barringer, Bruce R., and R. Duane Ireland. *Entrepreneurship: Successfully Launching New Ventures*. (Upper Saddle River, NJ: Pearson Prentice-Hall, 2008): 36–67.

Bygrave, William D. (ed.) and Andrew Zacharias (ed.). *The Portable MBA in Entrepreneurship*. (Hoboken, NJ: John Wiley and Sons, 2010): 53–82.

Hisrich, Robert D., Michael P. Peters and Dean A. Shepherd. *Entrepreneurship*. (Boston: McGraw-Hill Irwin, 2008): 135–167.

Chapter 4

Barringer, Bruce R., and R. Duane Ireland. *Entrepreneurship: Successfully Launching New Ventures*. (Upper Saddle River, NJ: Pearson Prentice-Hall, 2008): 68–97.

Moore, Geoffrey. *Crossing the Chasm: Marketing and Selling High-Tech Products to Mainstream Customers* (New York: Harper-Collins, 2002).

Chapter 5

Bagley, Constance and Craig Dauchy. *The Entrepreneur's Guide to Business Law*. (Mason, OH: West, 2008): 492–560.

Barringer, Bruce R., and R. Duane Ireland. *Entrepreneurship: Successfully Launching New Ventures*. (Upper Saddle River, NJ: Pearson Prentice-Hall, 2008): 346–379.

Bouchoux, Deborah E. *Protecting Your Company's Intellectual Property : A Practical Guide to Trademarks, Copyrights, Patents and Trade Secrets*. (New York: AMACOM, 2001).

Bygrave, William D. (ed.), and Andrew Zacharias (ed.). *The Portable MBA in Entrepreneurship*. (Hoboken, NJ: John Wiley and Sons, 2010): 297–328.

Cantrell Robert L. *Outpacing the Competition: Patent-Based Business Strategy*. (Hoboken, NJ: John Wiley and Sons, 2009).

Dorf, Richard C., and Thomas H. Byers. Technology Ventures: From idea to Enterprise. (Boston: McGraw-Hill Higher Education, 2005): 218–230.

Hisrich, Robert D., Michael P. Peters, and Dean A. Shepherd. *Entrepreneurship*. (Boston: McGraw-Hill Irwin, 2008): 168–195.

Miller, Roger Leroy and Gaylord A. Jentz. *Business Law Today: The Essentials*. (Mason, OH: SouthWestern-CENGAGE Learning, 2011): 126–151.

Web Sites

http://www.uspto.gov/web/offices/pac/doc/general/

http://www.uspto.gov/patents/resources/types/index.jsp

http://www.inventorbasics.com/index.htm

http://www.wipo.int/about-ip/en/

http://www.securinginnovation.com/articles/defensive-publishing/

http://www.patents.com/patents.htm

http://www.gigalaw.com/articles/2000/pto–2000–06.html

http://www.freepatentsonline.com/

http://www.micropat.com/static/index.htm

Chapter 6

Apgar, David. *Risk Intelligence.* (Boston: Harvard Business School Press, 2006).

Dorf, Richard C., and Thomas H. Byers. *Technology Ventures: From Idea to Enterprise.* (Boston: McGraw-Hill Higher Education, 2005): 123–150.

Knight, Frank H. *Risk, Uncertaint,y and Profit.* (Boston: Houghton Mifflin Company, 1921).

Sarasvathy, Saras D. "What Makes Entrepreneurs Entrepreneurial?" *Darden Case Collection ENT–0065* (2004).

Chapter 7

Abrams, Rhonda M. *The Successful BusinessPlan : Secrets and Strategies.* (Palo Alto, CA: The Planningshop, 2003).

Berry, Tim. *Hurdle: The Book on Business Planning.* (Eugene, OR: Palo Alto Software, 2004).

Bhide, Amar, "The Questions Every Entrepreneur Should Ask," *Harvard Business Review* 74, no. 6 (Novmber–December 1996): 120–130.

Hisrich, Robert D., Michael P. Peters and Dean A. Shepherd. *Entrepreneurship.* (Boston: McGraw-Hill Irwin, 2008): 196–310.

Ronick, David. *Hit the Deck: An Upstart Bootcamp Guide.* (New York: Upstart Bootcamp, LLC, 2010).

Chapter 8

Barringer, Bruce R., and R. Duane Ireland. *Entrepreneurship: Successfully Launching New Ventures.* (Upper Saddle River, NJ: Pearson Prentice-Hall, 2008): 254–281.

Dauchy, Constance and Craig. *The Entrepreneur's Guide to Business Law.* (Mason, OH: West, 2008): 73–108.

Dorf, Richard C., and Thomas H. Byers. *Technology Ventures: From Idea to Enterprise.* (Boston: McGraw-Hill Higher Education, 2005): 259–284.

Robbins, William L. *Seed-Stage Investing.* (Boston: Apspatore, 2006): 55–60.

Thurston, Philip H., "When Partners Fall Out." *Harvard Business Review* 64, no. 6 (1986): 24–29.

Chapter 9

Bagley, Constance and Craig Dauchy. *The Entrepreneur's Guide to Business Law.* (Mason, OH: West, 2008): 109–131.

Dorf, Richard C., and Thomas H. Byers. *Technology Ventures: From idea to Enterprise.* (Boston: McGraw-Hill Higher Education, 2005): 259–284.

Robbins, William L. *Seed-Stage Investing.* (Boston: Apspatore, 2006): 179–190.

Chapter 10

Bagley, Constance E. and Craig E. Dauchy. *The Entrepreneur's Guide to Business Law.* (Mason, OH: Thomson/West, 2008): 266–342

Dorf, Richard C., and Thomas H. Byers. *Technology Ventures: From Idea to Enterprise.* (Boston: McGraw-Hill Higher Education, 2005): 259–284.

Miller, Roger Leroy, and Gaylord A. Jentz. *Business Law Today: The Essentials.* (Mason, OH: SouthWestern-CENGAGE Learning, 2011): 514–551.

Robbins, William L. *Seed-Stage Investing.* (Boston: Apspatore, 2006): 83–97.

Chapter 11

Barringer, Bruce R., and R. Duane Ireland. *Entrepreneurship: Successfully Launching New Ventures.* (Upper Saddle River, NJ: Pearson Prentice-Hall, 2008): 130–159.

Boulding, William and Markus Christen. "First Mover Disadvantage," *Harvard Business Review* 79, no. 9 (October, 2001): 20–21.

Copeland, Michael V. "Start Last, Finish First." *Business 2.0* (January–February 2006) 7, no. 1): 41–43.

Gladwell, Malcom, "How David Beats Goliath." *New Yorker* 85, no. 13 (May 11, 2009): 40.

Porter, Michael E. *On Competition.* (Boston: Harvard Business School Publishing, 2008).

Tellis, Gerard J., and Peter N. Golder. "First to Market, First to Fail? Real Causes of Enduring Market Leadership," *Sloan Management Review* 37, no. 2. (Winter, 1996): 65–75.

Yoffie, David B., and Mary Kwak. "Judo Strategy: 10 Techniques for Beating Stronger Opponents," *Business Strategy Review* 13, no. 1 (2002): 20–30.

Chapter 12

Bagley, Constance and Craig Dauchy. *The Entrepreneur's Guide to Business Law.* (Mason, OH: West, 2008): 132–179.

Barringer, Bruce R., and R. Duane Ireland. *Entrepreneurship: Successfully Launching New Ventures.* (Upper Saddle River, NJ: Pearson Prentice-Hall, 2008): 282–313.

Benjamin, Gerald and Joel Margulis. *The Angel Investor's Handbook: How to Profit from Early-Stage Investing.* (Princeton, NJ: Bloomberg, 2001).

Bhidc, Amar. "Bootstrap Finance: the Art of Startups." *Harvard Business Review* 70, no. 6 (November–December 1992): 109–117.

Bygrave, William D. (ed.) and Andrew Zacharias (ed.). *The Portable MBA in Entrepreneurship.* (Hoboken, NJ: John Wiley and Sons, 2010): 161–224.

Dorf, Richard C., and Thomas H. Byers. *Technology Ventures: From Idea to Enterprise.* (Boston: McGraw-Hill Higher Education, 2005): 387–422.

Finkel, Robert A. *The Masters of Private Equity and Venture Capital.* (New York: McGraw-Hill, 2010).

Gianforte, Greg and Marcus Gibson. *Bootstrapping Your Business.* (Avon, MA, Adams Media, 2005)

Hill, Brian E., and Dee Power. *Inside Secrets to Venture Capital.* (New York: John Wiley & Sons, 2001).

Hisrich, Robert D., Michael P. Peters, and Dean A. Shepherd. *Entrepreneurship.* (Boston: McGraw-Hill Irwin, 2008): 341–458.

Mancuso, Joseph R. *How To Get A Business Loan.* (New York: A Fireside Book, 1990).

Presser, Leon. *What It Takes to Be an Entrepreneur.* (Resserp Publishing, 2010): 96–132.

Robbins, William L. *Seed-Stage Investing.* (Boston: Apspatore, 2006): 83–97.

Sahlman, William, Howard H. Stevenson, Michael J. Roberts, and Amar Bhide. *The Entrepreneurial Venture.* (Boston: Harvard Business School Press, 1999): 272–291.

Stoller, Gregory. *Strategies in Entrepreneurial Finance* (Garfield Heights, OH: Northcoast Publishers, 2006).

Van Osnabrugge, Mark, and Robert J. Robinson. *Angel Investing—Matching Funds with Start-up Companies: The Guide for Entrepreneurs, Individual Investors, and Venture Capitalists.* (San Francisco: Jossey-Bass, 2000).

Web Sites: Angels

http://mba.tuck.dartmouth.edu/pecenter/research/pdfs/Note_on_Angel_Investing.pdf

http://www.vfinance.com/ent/ent.asp?ToolPage=angelsearch_00.asp

http://www.angelcapitalassociation.org/directory/

http://angelsoft.net/

http://angel.co/

http://www.entrepreneur.com/financing/angelinvestors/archive144004.html

http://www.fenwick.com/docstore/VCSurvey/Q1_06_VC_Survey_Trends_Report.pdf?WT.mc_id=052406

http://www.nvca.org/

http://mba.tuck.dartmouth.edu/pecenter/

http://vcexperts.com/vce/

http://allensblog.typepad.com/allens_blog/2004/11/ten_commandment.html

http://www.vfinance.com/

http://www.nvca.org/index.php?option=com_mtree&Itemid=173

http://www.business.com/directory/financial_services/venture_capital/reference/directories/

http://www.vfinance.com/ent/ent.asp?ToolPage=venca.asp

http://www.infon.com/

http://www.cooley.com/files/tbl_s5SiteRepository/FileUpload21/869/PCF%202020 06%20Q2%20final.pdf

Web Sites: Venture Capital

http://www.netpreneur.org/funding/anatomy_term_sheet.pdf

http://www.feld.com/blog/archives/term_sheet/index.html

http://www.nvca.org/index.php?option=com_content&view=article&id=108:model-legal-documents&catid=43:resources&Itemid=136

http://ycombinator.com/seriesaa.html

http://www.techstars.org/2009/02/07/techstars-model-seed-funding-documents/
http://www.wsgr.com/wsgr/display.aspx?sectionname=practice/termsheet.htm
https://docs.google.com/viewer?url=http://www.fenwick.com/docstore/publicati
ons/ip/Start-up_Legal_Resource_Guide.pdf&pli=1
http://www.allbusiness.com/management/320065–1.html
http://www.businessfinance.com/corporate-venture-capital.htm

Chapter 13

Bagley, Constance, and Craig Dauchy. *The Entrepreneur's Guide to Business Law.* (Mason, OH: West, 2008). (If there is one book every entrepreneur should have on his or her bookshelf, this is it. The authors cover all the major areas of concern to entrepreneurs, thoroughly and accessibly. There is an excellent listing of Internet resources at the back.)

Bygrave, William D. (ed.) and Andrew Zacharias (ed.). *The Portable MBA in Entrepreneurship.* (Hoboken, NJ: John Wiley and Sons, 2010): 263–296.

Miller, Roger Leroy and Gaylord A. Jentz. *Business Law Today: The Essentials.* (Mason, OH: SouthWestern-CENGAGE Learning, 2011).

Miller, Roger Leroy and Gaylord A. Jentz. *Business Law Today: Standard Edition.* (Mason, OH: Southwestern-CENGAGE Learning, 2011).

Web Site: Corporate Venture Capital, Lending
http://www.financehub.com/

Choosing and Managing Attorneys
Barringer, Bruce R., and R. Duane Ireland. *Entrepreneurship: Successfully Launching New Ventures.* (Upper Saddle River, NJ: Pearson Prentice-Hall, 2008): 190–221.

Lesonsky, Rieva. *Start Your Own Business.* (Irvine, CA: Entrepreneur Press, 2007): 149–164.

Presser, Leon. *What It Takes to be an Entrepreneur.* (Resserp Publishing, 2010): 172–179.

Chapter 14

Bornstein, David. *How to Change the World—Social Entrepreneurs and the Power of New Ideas.* (New York: Oxford University Press, 2007).

Bygrave, William D., and Andrew Zacharakis. *The Portable MBA in Entrepreneurship.* (Hoboken, NJ: John Wiley & Sons, 2010): 411–436.

Collins, Jim. *Good to Great and the Social Sectors, a Monograph to Accompany Good to Great.* (Boulder, CO: Jim Collins, 2005).

Connors, Tracy Daniel, ed. *The Nonprofit Handbook: Management.* (New York: John Wiley & Sons, 2001).

Dees, J. Gregory, Jed Emerson, Peter Economy. *Enterprising Nonprofits—A Toolkit for Social Entrepreneurs.* (New York: John Wiley & Sons, 2001).

Greenfield, James M., ed. *The Nonprofit Handbook: Fund Raising.* (New York: John Wiley & Sons, 2001).

Oberfield, Alice, and J. Gregory Dees, "Note on Starting a Nonprofit Venture," Harvard Business School Case 391–096, 1991 (rev. 1992).

Oster, Sharon M. *Strategic Management for Non-Profit Organizations.* (New York: Oxford University Press, 1995).

Powell, Walter W., and Richard Steinberg. *The Nonprofit Sector: A Research Handbook.* New Haven, CT: Yale University Press, 2006).

Weisbrod, Burton A. *The Nonprofit Economy.* (Cambridge, MA: Harvard University Press, 1988).

Web Sites

About.com—"Nonprofit Charitable Orgs" at http://nonprofit.about.com/od/becomingtaxexempt/a/nonprofittypes.htm

Ashoka: http://ashoka.org/social_entrepreneur

Board Source: www.boardsource.org

The Canadian Social Enterprise Guide at http://www.enterprisingnonprofits.ca/projects/the_guide

The Citizen Base Initiative site includes discussion of the concept, case studies, and announcements of related program activities: http://www.citizenbase.org/.

Council on Foundations at www.cof.org

Foundation Center, a national nonprofit service organization at http://foundationcenter.org/getstarted/faqs/html/howmany.html

The Free Management Library references a variety of perspectives; for example, "What is social entrepreneurship?", "Why start a business?", "What are critical success factors?", and "Where can I get money?" At http://www.mapnp.org/library/soc_entr/soc_entr.htm

Idealist.org: http://www.idealist.org/en/about/index.html

The Independent Sector (http://www.independentsector.org)

IRS Publication 557 (06/2008), "Tax-Exempt Status for Your Organization," available at http://www.irs.gov/publications/p557/index.html

"Toolkit for Developing a Social Purpose Business Plan" at http://www.seedco.org/documents/publications/nvn_toolkit.pdf

Chapter 15

For Training and Learning

Dawson, Roger Dawson. "The Secrets of Power Negotiating," (audio series available at http://www.rdawson.com/.

Ertel, Danny. "Turning Negotiation into a Corporate Capability," *Harvard Business Review,* May–June 1999): 55. A summary of education and training practices to build negotiating skills in an organization.

Books

Lewicki, Roy J., David M. Saunders, and John W. Minton. *Essentials of Negotiation.* (Boston: Irwin McGraw-Hill, 1997).

Lewicki, Roy J., David M. Saunders, and Bruce Barry. *Negotiation,* (Boston: McGraw-Hill Irwin, 2006).

Luecke, Richard. *Negotiation,* (Cambridge, MA: Harvard Business School Press, 2003). Excellent source book for fundamentals, tactics and strategy with the main focus on transactional negotiating. Accessible material, 168 pages. One of the best you can buy.

Fisher, Roger and William Ury. *Getting to Yes: Negotiating Agreement without Giving In.* (New York: Penguin Books, 1991).

Thompson, Leigh. *The Mind and Heart of the Negotiator.* (Upper Saddle River, NJ: Prentice Hall, 2009).

Thompson, Leigh. *The Truth about Negotiations.* (Upper Saddle River, NJ: Pearson Education / FT Press, 2008).

Walker, Michael A., and George L. Harris. *Negotiations: Six Steps to Success.* (Upper Saddle River, NJ: PTR/Prentice Hall, 1995).

Chapter 16

Anderson, B. Robert. *Professional Selling.* (San Jose, CA: toExcell, 2000).

Bygrave, William D. and Andrew Zacharakis. *The Portable MBA in Entre-preneurship.* (Hoboken, NJ: John Wiley & Sons, 2010): 329–354.

Jackson, Ralph W., Robert D. Hisrich, and Stephen J. Newell. *Professional Selling and Sales Management.* (Garfield Heights, OH: NorthCoast Publishers, Inc., 2007).

Jones, Eli, Carl Stevens, and Larry Chonko. *Selling ASAP.* (Mason, OH: Thomson/SouthWestern, 2005).

Cialdini, Robert B. *Influence—Science and Practice*. (Boston: Allyn & Bacon, 2001).

Gitomer, Jeffrey. *The Little Red Book of Selling*. (Austin, TX: Bard Press, 2005).

Heiman, Stephen, and Diane Sanchez. *The New Conceptual Selling*. (New York: Warner Books, 1999).

Hogan, Kevin. *The Psychology of Persuasion: How to Persuade People to Your Way of Thinking*. (Gretna, LA: Pelican Publishing, 2000).

LeBoeuf, Michael. *How To Win Customers and Keep Them For Life*. (New York: Berkley Books, 1988).

Miller, Robert B. and Stephen E. Heiman. *The New Strategic Selling: The Unique Sales System Proven Successful by the World's Best Companies*. (New York: Grand Central Publishing, 1998).

Norman, Jan. *Starting Your Own Business*. (Chicago: Dearborn Trade Publishing, 2004): pp. 135–154

Presser, Leon. *What It Takes to Be An Entrepreneur*. (Resserp Publishing, 2010): Chapter 6.

Schiffman, Stephen, *The 25 Sales Habits of Highly Successful People*. (Avon, MA: Adams Media, 2008).

Stinnett, Bill. *Selling Results!* (New York: McGraw-Hill Professional, 2007).

Chapter 17

Cialdini, Robert B. *Influence—Science and Practice*. (Boston: Allyn & Bacon, 2001).

Gilovich, Thomas. *How We Know What Isn't So—The Fallibility of Human Reason in Everyday Life*. (New York: The Free Press, 1991).

Gladwell, Malcom. *Blink*. (New York: Little, Brown, 2005).

Heath, Chip, and Dan Heath. *Made to Stick*. (New York: Random House, 2007).

Hogan, Kevin. *The Psychology of Persuasion—How to Persuade Others to Your Way of Thinking*. (Gretna, LA: Pelican Publishing Co., 2000).

Horn, Sam. *Stand Out in Any Crowd*. (New York: Perigree-Penguin Group, 2006).

Luntz, Frank I. *Words That Work: It's Not What You Say, It's What People Hear*. (New York: Hyperion, 2007).

Munter, Mary. *Guide to Managerial Communication—Effective Business Writing and Speaking*. (Upper Saddle River, NJ: Prentice-Hall, 2009).

Pentland, Alex. *Honest Signals*. (Cambridge, MA: MIT Press, 2008).

Chapter 18

Baron, Robert A. "Cognitive Mechanisms in Entrepreneurship: Why and When Entrepreneurs Think Differently Than Other People, *Journal of Business Venturing* 13, no. 4 (1998): 275–294.

Bazerman, Max H. *Judgment in Managerial Decision Making.* (New York, NY: John Wiley & Sons, 1998).

Dorner, Dietrich. *The Logic of Failure.* (New York, Basic Books, 1996).

Farson, Richard, and Ralph Keyes. *Whoever Makes the Most Mistakes Wins.* (New York: The Free Press, 2002).

Gilovich, Thomas. *How We Know What Isn't So: The Fallibility of Human Reason in Everyday Life.* (New York: Free Press, 1991).

Hogarth, Robin M. *Educating Intuition.* (Chicago: University of Chicago Press, 2001).

Klein, Gary. *Sources of Power.* (Cambridge, MA: MIT Press, 1999).

Matson, J. V. *Using Intelligent Fast Failure: The Art of Innovation.* (University Park, PA: Pennsylvania State University, n.d.).

Myers, David G. *Intuition – Its Powers and Perils.* (New Haven, CT: Yale University Press, 2002).

Plessner, Henning, Cornelia Betsch, and Tilmann Betsch. *Intuition in Judgment and Decision Making.* (New York: Lawrence Erlbaum Associates, 2008).

Robbins, Stephen P. *Decide and Conquer.* (Upper Saddle River, NJ: FT/Prentice Hall, 2004).

Russo, J. Edward, and Paul J. H. Schoemaker. *Winning Decisions.* (New York: Currency Doubleday, 2002).

Chapter 19

Droms, W. G. *Finance and Accounting for Nonfinancial Managers.* (Reading, MA: Addison-Wesley, 1990).

Garrison, Ray H., and Eric W. Noreen. *Managerial Accounting.* (Chicago: Irwin, 1997).

Raiborn, Cecily, Jesse T. Barfield, and Michael R. Kinney. *Managerial Accounting.* 3rd ed. Cincinnati, OH: South-Western, 1998.

Sahlman, William A., "The Financial Perspective: What Should Entrepreneurs Know?" Harvard Business School Case 293–045, 1992

Tracy, J. A. *How to Read a Financial Report.* (New York: John Wiley & Sons, 1994).

Web Sites

AccountingNet: http://www.accountingnet.com/

The Securities and Exchange Commission has an excellent summary description of financial statements at http://www.sec.gov/investor/pubs/begfinstmtguide.htm.

Chapter 20

Dorner, Dietrich. *The Logic of Failure*. (New York: Basic Books, 1996).

Farson, Richard, and Ralph Keyes. *Whoever Makes the Most Mistakes Wins*. (New York: The Free Press, 2002).

Matson, J. V. *Using Intelligent Fast Failure: The Art of Innovation*. University Park, PA: Pennsylvania State University, 1991).

Petroski, Henry. *Success through Failure: the Paradox of Design*. (Princeton, NJ: Princeton University Press, 2006).

Petroski, Henry. *To Engineer Is Human: The Role of Failure in Successful Design*. (New York: St. Martin's Press, 1985).

Chapter 21

Bygrave, William D., and Andrew Zacharakis. *The Portable MBA* (Hoboken, NJ: John Wiley & Sons, 2010: Chapter 13, pp. 355–383.

Gibbons, John. "Employee Engagement—Current Research and Its Implications." *The Conference Board Report Series*. (New York: Conference Board, 2006).

Hisrich, Robert D., Michael P. Peters, and Dean A. Shepherd. *Entrepreneurship*. (Boston: McGraw-Hill Irwin, 2008): 488–519.

Roberts, Michael J. "Managing Transitions in the Growing Enterprise" Harvard Business School case 393–107, 1997.

Roberts, Michael J. "The Challenge of Growth," Harvard Business School Case 393–106, 1993.

Sherman, Andrew J. *The Complete Guide to Running and Growing Your Business.*(New York: New York Times Business, 1997).

Steffens, Paul, Per Davidson, and Jason Fitzsimmons, "Performance Configurations over Time: Implications for Growth and Profit-Oriented Strategies," *Entrepreneurship: Theory and Practice* 33, no. 1 (2009): 125–148

Wasserman, Noam, "The Founder's Dilemma," *Harvard Business Review* 86, no. 2 (2008): 102–109.

Chapter 22

Bagley, Constance E., and Craig E. Dauchy. *The Entrepreneur's Guide to Business Law*. (Mason, OH: Thomson/South-Western/West, 2008): 595–728.

Bygrave, William D., and Andrew Zacharakis. *The Portable MBA*. (Hoboken, NJ: John Wiley & Sons, 2010): 184–193.

Hisrich, Robert D., Michael P. Peters and Dean A. Shepherd. *Entrepreneurship*. (Boston: McGraw-Hill Irwin, 2008): 568–627.

Kellogg, Douglas E. *Entrepreneurship in America: A Primer for Buying and Selling Small Manufacturing Companies*. (Bloomington, IN: Douglas E. Kellogg, 2002).

Kleuger, Robert F. *Buying and Selling a Business*. (New York: John Wiley & Sons, 2004).

Nottonson, Ira. *Ultimate Guide to Buying or Selling a Business*. (Irvine, CA: Entrepreneur Press, 2005).

Taulli, Tom. *The Complete M&A Guidebook*. (Roseville, CA: Prima Venture, 2002).

Index